The Technology Imperative

*To my wife, Susan, whose support and
encouragement were the lifeblood of this endeavor*

The Technology Imperative

Gregory Tassey

Senior Economist, National Institute of Standards and Technology, USA

Edward Elgar
Cheltenham, UK • Northampton, MA, USA

© Gregory Tassey 2007

Published by
Edward Elgar Publishing Limited
Glensanda House
Montpellier Parade
Cheltenham
Glos GL50 1UA
UK

Edward Elgar Publishing, Inc.
William Pratt House
9 Dewey Court
Northampton
Massachusetts 01060
USA

A catalogue record for this book
is available from the British Library

Library of Congress Cataloguing in Publication Data

Tassey, Gregory.
    The technology imperative / Gregory Tassey.
        p. cm.
    Includes bibliographical references and index.
    1. Technological innovations—Economic aspects—United States. 2. Research, Industrial—Economic aspects—United States. 3. Technology and state—United States. 4. United States—Economic conditions—21st century. 5. Competition, International. I. Title.
        HC110.T4T27 2007
        338'.064—dc22

                                                                    2007009560

ISBN 978 1 84542 912 6 (cased)

Printed and bound in Great Britain by MPG Books Ltd, Bodmin, Cornwall

Contents

Contents

Figures

Tables

Acknowledgements

I am immensely grateful to my colleagues at NIST for providing me with their insights into technology and industry trends. Numerous people in government agencies (particularly the National Science Foundation) provided or helped me obtain much of the required data for various economic and policy analyses. Many industry managers took considerable time to discuss the technologies, markets and policies that affect their corporate investment decisions. I also benefited from the assistance provided by my many colleagues in universities and the media who shared insights on the seemingly endless set of issues relevant to the topic of technology-based growth. Finally, the endless faith of my children, Wil and Liz, has been an inspiration throughout the more than two years required to complete this project.

Preface

The concept of technology-based 'creative destruction', developed by the famous Austrian economist, Joseph Schumpeter, has driven more than a half-century of research into the dynamics of technological change within the private sector. However, when he first published *Capitalism, Socialism, and Democracy* in 1942, Schumpeter did not have the advantage of observing the role of government in advancing science and technology (S&T) during World War II, let alone subsequent major contributions to the technologies currently driving global economic growth. Thus, his model and the subsequent mass of economic research that it spawned have focused largely on the private sector and its investment behavior. This focus was more than adequate for decades because (i) technology life cycles were relatively long and the role of government was remote and inefficiently linked to the marketplace and (ii) the so-called 'Pasteur's quadrant' in which invention occurs before the underlying science is understood was a dominant pattern.

Today, the world's economy is much more dependent on science as a precursor to the creation of technology. Globalization of industries and markets, the steadily growing complexity of technology, emerging organizational forms for conducting research and development (R&D), and multiple government policy institutions and economic growth strategies are major trends confronting all nations – current leaders and emerging economies alike.

That so many nations are faced with and are attempting to respond to these challenges is itself an indicator of the need for each economy to design and manage its growth strategies more efficiently. This situation demands more developed and integrated public–private economic growth models. Such models are needed because although creative destruction still drives the private sector's role as the engine of long-term growth, the growing globalization of technology-based competition raises uncertainty with respect to which economies will be the 'creative' ones in the future and thereby ascend the competitiveness ladder.

However, in the face of multiple changing dimensions of the global economy and their wrenching impacts on traditional modes of behavior, policy responses are often both timid and uninformed. During an economy's ascendancy to economic leadership, accumulated public and private assets interact synergistically with a society's culture until a high level of comfort is established. The economic growth model is then deemed perfected and signs of impending inadequacy are ignored. The accumulated skills and modes of economic behavior that have worked so well in the past create strong resistance to change. The farther off course an economy gets, the greater the required adjustments, which, in turn, increase the threat to the segments of that economy with a vested interest in the status quo.

Even the term 'industrialized nation' conveys a false sense of comfort. To most, industrialization implies an economic structure based on technology and supporting technical infrastructures. However, although leading economies like to call themselves 'high tech,' the fact is that only relatively small portions of their economic output are truly technology intensive in the globally competitive sense. As a result, most of the typical industrialized economy is today highly vulnerable to the rapid pace of global convergence in which many emerging economies are now able to imitate and even improve upon existing economic growth models, with the one common characteristic being an increasing reliance on technology.

On a positive note, globalization is raising awareness that more technology is needed to be a high-income economy in the future, and conventional wisdom in industrialized nations is slowly embracing the proposition that technology is, in fact, the dominant driver of economic growth. Moreover, to varying degrees, the concept of the 'public–private technology-based growth paradigm' in which public and private investments combine to develop, acquire, and use technology in a collaborative mode for economic gain is increasingly driving national growth policies.

Yet, for the most part, this paradigm has been only loosely stated and partially executed. In particular, US economic performance, which has been the envy of the rest of the global economy for most of the post-World War II period, is struggling with two fundamental problems that portend serious constraints on future economic growth. First, the US economy has lost its perspective on what drives growth. Excessive consumption fueled by accumulation of enormous debt precludes sufficient aggregate investment. Second, what investment is occurring suffers from serious compositional inadequacies, in particular, inadequate rates of investment in technology, especially breakthrough technologies – the ones that create new industries and thereby provide a large number of high-paying jobs.

The second problem continues to befuddle many who fall into the trap of looking backward at the dominant R&D investment profile of the US economy for most of the post-war period. However, the amount of R&D investment is only meaningful when considered relative to the size of the economy it is trying to support and when compared to similar ratios among other nations. The key metric therefore is R&D intensity. In this regard, the problem is that the US ratio of R&D to GDP is slightly below the peak reached 40 years ago in the mid-1960s. During this time, a growing number of nations have increased their R&D intensities and are progressively eating away at US leadership positions.

No single economy has to surpass the leader to cause erosion of that leader's position. Rather, the determination of multiple pursuers to catch up to the United States is collectively taking significant chunks of the US share of one technology-based market after another. This 'piranha effect,' in which each competing economy bites off a piece of the leader's domain until collective convergence has occurred, eventually leaves the leader at best as one of several competitors in markets it once dominated.

A major impetus for this process of convergence is the fact that emerging economies are only temporarily satisfied with low-valued-added output of goods and services. Increasingly, they covet the high-value-added end of markets in one supply chain after another and therefore set about acquiring innovation infrastructures that allow them to compete based on state-of-the-art technology.

The phenomena of technological and economic convergence have been repeated throughout economic history. However, every technology life cycle has some distinguishing characteristics, which defy extrapolation of successful strategies from one cycle to the next. In the current process of global convergence, the unique factor is the diminished impact of the original version of the law of comparative advantage. As conceived by English economists two centuries ago and implicitly endorsed by policy makers ever since, this 'law' is less and less valid. The reason is that the pace of technological change and evolving growth models based on technology creation enable the creation of competitive advantage, which disrupts the predicted shifting of resources among economies. In other words, the historical static model in which reallocation of existing resources is the main driver is being replaced by a dynamic one in which public–private investment strategies create technology-based assets that take market share from others, that is, new resources determine absolute and relative advantages. As a result, the path of adaptation is not always readily apparent and effective response frequently is not possible by market forces alone.

In this context, a lack of understanding of the necessary growth models leads to inadequate policies. For example, the US government is failing to invest in sufficient proof-of-concept technology research. For decades its share of national R&D has declined. Proponents of the 'black-box' model of technology-based growth find such a trend encouraging, arguing that innovation is industry's job and that government's only role is to fund basic science. But this view ignores the complexity of industrial technology and how it evolves and is used to create innovative products, processes and services.

Industry and academic groups have argued for new strategies and policies, but these proposals are based at best on limited analysis and data and at worst on anecdotes and assertions. While useful as illustrations of problems, the current state of policy analysis is neither convincing enough with respect to the nature and substance of the problem being addressed nor does it lead to solutions that match failed private investment mechanisms with the most efficient remedies. Consequently, most assessments of government economic growth strategies have had a muted impact on policy and what policies have been implemented are flawed.

This situation will continue until it is realized that the complexity of the technology-based economy demands institutionalized technology assessment and economic analysis to support growth policies. Unfortunately, current policy institutions are inadequately supported and they are organizationally structured to ensure segmentation and thereby dysfunction. The S&T policy community focuses largely on the input side, that is, on funds for investment in R&D. In contrast, conventional economic growth policy implicitly assumes that technology magically appears (the black-box model) and is then combined with the traditional inputs of capital and labor to produce desired goods and services. The main emphasis of economic policy models is on how technology is used; that is, the focus is on diffusion of technical knowledge as opposed to its development.

In today's global economy, investment must begin well in advance of the needed transitions to new technologies. The long run is not a problem until one gets there; then it becomes a crisis. By definition, a crisis is a situation with severe consequences that cannot be solved easily or quickly. Avoiding such in today's world takes much foresight, analysis, planning and the resolve to change.

This book focuses on the trends that mandate major change and then assesses the required policy responses. The three major requirements for such an analysis are to identify trends and underinvestment phenomena (Part I), then construct the economic models to understand the causes of inadequate investment (Part II), and finally to develop policy solutions that efficiently respond to specific investment barriers (Part III).

PART I

The Economics of Decline

1. Globalization of Technology

It's only when the tide goes out that you can see who is swimming naked.

Warren Buffet

The technology imperative is the following: the high-income economy must be the high-tech economy because (i) technology drives productivity growth, which, in turn, drives output and income growth, and (ii) long-term competitive advantage requires continuous renewal of technology-based assets.

THE PAST IS ONLY PARTIALLY PROLOGUE

For the first two decades after World War II, the US economy dominated the world both in terms of the size and the technology content of its products and services. However, the oil supply/price shock in 1973 marked the beginning of the end of an era in which US economic policy makers needed only to worry about domestic business cycles and their effects on employment. The obsolescence of major portions of the US capital stock, which was due to large increases in the prices of oil and other critical raw materials in the 1970s, initiated a series of changes in global competitive positions.

In the 30 years since that event, the relative productivities of physical capital stocks among the world's economies have been significantly altered. Even more important, knowledge capital has become an increasingly dominant factor in economic activity. As a result, investment in research and development (R&D) has increased and is now more widely distributed within major industrial supply chains.

This evolutionary change has been characterized by a process of 'convergence' among a growing number of economies. The implications of convergence lead to the major theme to be developed: no economy can expect to achieve and maintain high-income status in the global economy without a technology-centric economic growth strategy. As will be demonstrated along many dimensions, the US economy is squandering a substantial technological advantage by not adopting this paradigm at the level and breadth needed to respond to growing competition.

3

Even with substantial adjustments, the United States certainly cannot be expected to continue to dominate technology-based markets in the future with only 4.5 percent of the world's population. Although the US was the major initial source of information technology (IT) and consequently controlled the global marketplace for applications, including the Internet, market shares and thus sources of innovation are now spreading around the world. For example, one communication services company, China Mobile Ltd, today has 300 million subscribers, which is equal to the entire US population. Such large markets pull investment, including R&D, from all over the world, including from US-based companies. Therefore, only if current strategies and policies are drastically adjusted, can the domestic United States continue to be even one of the leaders in the decades ahead.

Such an adjustment will not be easy because of several major impediments. The single largest barrier to adaptation is refusal to admit the severity of the problem. 'Apostles of denial' will point to coincident indicators as evidence that the US economy is, in fact, quite healthy. Corporate profits and labor productivity grew at respectable rates in the first half of this decade. As *The Economist* pointed out, America is still currently among the leaders in proportion of adults with university education, produces one-third of the world's output of scientific papers, employs two-thirds of the world's Nobel prize winners, and has 17 of the 20 top-ranked universities.[1]

But, just as many Wall Street analysts and investment managers make the mistake of analyzing financial markets by extrapolating past and current trends into the future, most industry and government strategies do the same when assessing the prospects and hence requirements for economic growth, especially long-term growth. Although an increasing number of Americans are expressing concern over the competitiveness of the US economy, the conventional wisdom has considerable momentum, so change takes considerable effort and time.

The focus on indicators of current economic conditions allows defenders of the status quo to make the case that the US economy is on a sound footing now and will be so in the future. However, these coincident indicators are the result of past strategies/policies and subsequent investments. Analyzing the future competitiveness of an economy may benefit from the use of some of the same indicators, but an essential requirement is to identify the most important ones and to understand the forces changing them.

The refusal to adapt results largely from the 'installed-base' effect. The installed base of an industry or an entire economy is the accumulated public and private assets that over time have resulted in the achievement of a leading competitive position. This process includes substantial learning with respect to how to use these assets. Once so much has been invested in their accumulation and in ways of using them successfully, it is extremely difficult to recognize and then accept the fact that these assets and the associated learning are becoming obsolete. Moreover, change is both difficult and costly, which breeds considerable resistance. In addition, past success instills both a level of comfort and complacency. Such 'installed wisdom' creates additional resistance to change.

Although the US economy is still the technological leader by several metrics, the industries commonly considered to comprise the "high-tech sector" constitute only a small fraction of the total US economy – accounting for 7–10 percent of GDP (depending on the particular definition chosen[2]). To a significant extent, economic growth since World War II has resulted from technology that originates in this small group of industries and diffuses to the remaining 90 percent of US industry. Other factors, such as a skilled workforce, risk-oriented capital markets, dynamic industry structures based on new-firm formation and superior supporting infrastructures, have clearly contributed to superior rates of growth over the past century, but it has been the much greater scientific and technological capabilities of the US economy and the consequent modest technology-based global competition elsewhere that created the 'Golden Age' of US economic growth, especially in the 1948–73 period.

However, in the past two decades, this situation has changed dramatically. Although the US economy is still the single largest source of new technology, the proliferation of economies with at least a few technology-based industries has begun to 'hollow out' the high-tech supply chains that have driven the domestic economy.[3] The progressive loss of market shares, which began in earnest in the 1980s, continues unabated.

At first, market share losses were relegated largely to low-tech industries where cost differentials were the driving competitive factor. Hence, job losses were suffered mainly by low-skilled workers. In the current decade, higher-income workers (those with higher average skills) have begun to be affected by technology-based global convergence. Other economies now can not only compete at the production stage through technology absorption but are also rapidly acquiring the capability to innovate and even create the underlying science that enables more radical innovation.

Throughout history, national economies have risen to the forefront of the global economic system by the development and use of technology. To varying degrees, this technology was created and delivered through a combination of public and private investment. Even ancient societies such as the Greeks and Romans invested in specific technologies (tools, ships) and supporting infrastructure (roads, aqueducts). Organizational and institutional innovation proceeded in concert with technological change to create a superior economy that supported social and military objectives, as well as economic ones. The resulting system was honed over time to yield increasing efficiencies.

THE FUNDAMENTAL ISSUE

History also shows that resistance to adapt to changing economic conditions is built into the very factors that led to success. Thus, most former economic leaders experience sustained periods of inferior economic performance, which persist until economic conditions become bad enough to force change.

The European experience is an example of how adaptation for a former leader requires considerable time and economic pain. However, because it has experienced sub par growth rates for some time, the European Union (EU) has made more progress than the United States in the initial 'problem identification' phase of the adaptation process and is now moving on to attempt to improve its policy response mechanisms. Europe is slowly addressing acknowledged needs such as reducing employment rigidities, expanding pan-European R&D networks, expanding R&D intensities, promoting entrepreneurship and regional economic growth clusters, and increasing investment in information and communication technology-based infrastructure (Johnson, 2005). In contrast, the United States is only now approaching a threshold level of understanding of its weakness in education, R&D investment and savings strategies.

One of the most important differences of the current convergence process compared to past periods of global economic realignment is the fact that the business sector is becoming increasingly global in its reach and is thus less tied to the fortunes of individual countries. However, businesses still respond to investment and other incentives in a particular economy, so it must be realized above all else that businesses examine and respond to policy differences across economies. Thus, a critical lesson from this book is that countries, rather than private companies, are the growing factor in determining the basis for competitive advantage. Because this principle is not yet accepted in the United States, studying, understanding and formulating strategies and policies to address long-term needs of a large, technology-based economy are being short-changed.

A second important message is that an economy runs on an accumulated set of assets. Time is needed to acquire these assets and therefore movement up the global competitive ladder is a slow process. However, once attained, a leadership position has staying power for the simple reason that the asset-accumulation process is equally slow for other economies. These assets are broad in scope. Technology development and utilization capability, an educational system, financial, legal and policy infrastructures must evolve and become integrated with one another to allow an economy to excel across enough markets to achieve a high rate of growth.

But, here is the rub. Getting to the top – the result of the slow process of multiple asset accumulation – cultures the belief in immunity to challenge and thereby induces the incumbent leader to assume that its leadership position will continue indefinitely. Most difficult is the requirement to scrap the existing assets that are responsible for this leadership position. The process of Schumpeter's creative destruction must begin at the national economy level where the most influential policy institutions reside.

At the highest level, a society's progress is measured by its accumulation of wealth (commonly measured by per capita GDP). One can point to indices of 'happiness' or 'well-being' and argue that such measures are not perfectly correlated with wealth. While true, without wealth, progress toward the many social objectives that society sets for itself will not be achieved. Thus, no society shrinks from the drive to accumulate wealth and most yardsticks revolve around this metric.

Western economies in general and the US economy in particular have been rightly credited with the greatest advances in wealth accumulation in the history of the world. By virtue of being the dominant technology-based economy of the post-World War II period, US per capita income is about 30 percent higher than the average for other industrialized economies (the 15 original members of the EU). Moreover, the wealth has been distributed within all of these societies to an unprecedented degree.

However, global competition is not only lowering growth of the standard of living at the national level, but it is creating an increasingly skewed distribution of wealth. This pattern is ominous for two reasons: (i) it reflects the declining competitiveness of the majority of workers, and (ii) such distributions inevitably lead to social and political unrest. As real incomes become stagnant or even decline, anger rises, people become polarized and adopt 'us versus them' attitudes. This 'good guys and bad guys' mentality results in social and political gridlock, which, in turn, prevents consensus solutions to the main problem – sluggish economic growth.

TECHNOLOGY'S ROLE IN PERSPECTIVE

How important is technology to competitiveness and economic growth? Simply put, if the high-income economy loses technological leadership, it won't be the high-income economy for long. As a major Council on Competitiveness report (2004) on innovation policy succinctly put it, 'Innovation will be the single most important factor in determining America's success through the 21st century'.

However, as important as technology is, no single factor is sufficient to drive economic growth. Breakthrough technologies are essential to kick start long-term growth cycles, but their direct impact on productivity requires the availability of skilled labor, investment in physical capital (plant and equipment), and an infrastructure that includes such disparate elements as technology transfer mechanisms and interface standards that allow the participation of the many large and small firms required to drive fast-growing industries.

Under the right circumstances, productivity-enhancing technological change can drive economic growth for extended periods of time through capital accumulation. In fact, Jorgenson (2005) points out that investment rather than productivity gains has been the predominant source of economic growth throughout the post-World War II period. The resurgence in the rate of US economic expansion since 1995 has been led by an even greater reliance on such investment.

However, without technological change, the investment that embodies new technology and thereby drives productivity growth would quickly encounter diminishing returns and therefore have less and less impact. Without technological change to create opportunities to invest in new products and services, productivity growth slows and real incomes stagnate, and so therefore does growth in the standard of living.

This situation leads to the most important issue of all: what is the right amount and type of investment in technology? Economists would say that the right amount is the sum of all investment opportunities for which the expected rates of return exceed a minimum acceptable rate of return or 'hurdle rate'. This hurdle rate is a function of prospective returns available from alternative investments, adjusted for relative risk. The problem is that, in today's markets, calculating expected rates of return depends on a number of hard-to-quantify factors, including several types of risk and the time value of money. The complexity of investment decision making facing the private sector often leads to uncertainty with respect to what the actual level of risk really is. Moreover, the level and duration of risk varies across the several types of investment that a company must make over time.

Until recently, risk associated with investment in technology was relatively manageable. The long post-war, investment-led growth was made possible by the lack of significant competition from other economies. Large US companies with dominant market positions and hence the ability to spread risk both over a variety of investment opportunities and over time could assign relatively low discount rates to even the most risky but potentially high-payoff R&D projects.

These conditions will never be seen again. Today, companies are focusing on fewer and shorter-term R&D projects. Efforts to develop breakthrough technologies are increasingly scattered among universities, government laboratories and the remaining companies that still do such research, with the result that underinvestment and also inefficient investment predominate. Consequently, not only is such research segmented and hence uncoordinated from a portfolio management perspective, but also the various elements of the emerging technology often advance at very different rates, which leads to incomplete technology platforms and thus lower rates of innovation.

The bottom line is that larger and more efficient investment in technology and its subsequent diffusion within the domestic economy are becoming increasingly essential to maintain competitive positions in global markets.

ANALYZING THE RIGHT TRENDS

Unfortunately, while trends indicating declining competitive positions have been identified and proclaimed by an increasing number of analysts, they nevertheless continue to be rejected or minimized by an even larger number of other analysts and policy makers. The apostles of denial point to such indicators as higher rates of productivity growth in the late 1990s and the first half of this decade as proof of continued US competitiveness and therefore as a predictor of sustained economic growth.

However, if this productivity 'resurgence' were as widespread and sustaining as many analysts have claimed, one would expect to see larger positive impacts on employment and income growth. Such a trend should especially be the case coming out of a recession, when productivity growth is typically enhanced by output expansion and hence greater capacity utilization. Realization of greater efficiency should lead to superior competitive positions in global markets, which in turn should stimulate larger domestic output. Even though productivity gains often result in lower-skilled jobs being eliminated, economic history shows that the longer-term effect is to create more higher-paying and stable employment.

Today, however, the increasingly critical caveat is that these gains from domestic and global trade occur within the domestic economy only if the correct amounts and types of investment are made. That is, adjustments in competitive advantage are not automatic. Modern economies increasingly are able to create new competitive advantages through combinations of public and private investment and more such economies are appearing. As a result, recent rates of productivity growth are likely to be inadequate.

Equally important, while the profits of US-based companies have grown at double-digit rates in the first half of this decade, a major portion of this growth is attributable to increased offshore outsourcing, which provides equal-quality but lower-cost inputs. This trend increases the measured

Table 1.1 Growth Rates for Productivity, Employment and Earnings: Nonfarm Private Business Sector (average annual percent change)

	Real GDP	Labor Productivity	Multifactor Productivity	Employment	Real Hourly Compensation	Real Hourly Earnings
1948–1973	6.0	3.93	2.41	2.84	3.78	N.A.
1973–1987	3.8	1.45	0.33	2.34	0.90	-0.89
1987–1997	3.3	1.74	0.70	2.03	0.51	-0.23
1997–2005	3.4	3.48	1.90	1.01	2.97	0.91

Source: Bureau of Labor Statistics.

10

productivity of American workers. However, corporate managements know the source of the productivity gains and, as the earnings trend data in Table 1.1 clearly indicate, workers are no longer receiving pay increases that track measured labor productivity growth. Moreover, Conference Board data show that US labor productivity growth, while considerably faster than in Western Europe, is lagging significantly behind growth rates in Eastern Europe and Asia (van Ark et al., 2006). The large numbers of workers in these emerging economies predict that US global market shares will continue to decline.

From the end of World War II until the OPEC oil embargo, 1948–73, Table 1.1 indicates that productivity, employment, and real compensation all increased at their fastest rates of the post-war period. As a result, this period has been referred to as the 'Golden Age' for the American economy. The oil embargo in 1973 and the subsequent escalation of all raw material prices was a major factor in bringing a halt to this superb performance. Much of the US capital stock was in effect made obsolete by higher energy and raw material costs. These events had a more pronounced negative impact on multifactor productivity (MFP), as indicated in the table. This is because MFP shows the combined impact of labor, capital, and potentially other factors, including technology, on output. It is therefore a more accurate measure of economic efficiency than labor productivity.

By the late 1970s, a significant portion of US industry understood that globalization was a major permanent trend and increased R&D spending. In the late 1980s, US companies began to realize some initial benefits from these investments and productivity growth started to increase. However, Figure 1.1 shows that unlike past periods of accelerated productivity growth where initial negative employment effects from automation were soon offset by output expansion driven by increased efficiency, much of the past 15 years has witnessed pronounced weakness in employment growth. The culprit has been globalization.

The impact of this globalization effect is clear from these trends. Recoveries from the last two recessions, as measured by employment growth, have been dismal in absolute terms and relative to previous recessions. In the 30 months following troughs for the first seven recessions since World War II, Figure 1.1 shows that a substantial average rebound in employment occurred, beginning a few months after a recession trough. However, the recovery from the 1990–91 recession was anemic and delayed. The rebound from the most recent recession in 2001 was non-existent for the entire 30-month period. If an adequate adaptation process is underway, it is not evident. In fact, the strong implication of such trends is that the US economy has not adapted to the advent of significant global competition.

Attempts to blame this trend largely on labor-saving innovation are misplaced. For the most recent part of this 15-year period, Federal Reserve

Board data show that for the post-recession period (November 2001 through December 2005) manufacturing output has grown at only half the average rate in recoveries of the past half century. Expansion of shares of domestic

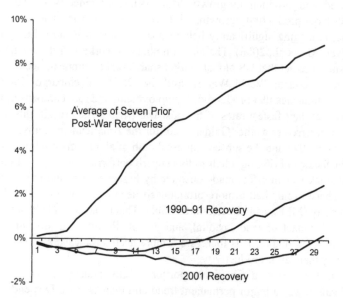

Sources: BLS for employment data; NBER for recession trough dates.

Figure 1.1 Post World War II Employment Growth: Percent Change from Recession Trough by Month

and global markets due to productivity gains and economic recovery would have increased domestic employment under pre-globalization conditions. Moreover, this trend occurred in spite of the expansion of high-tech services, some parts of which are fairly labor intensive.

However, although useful as initial indicators, aggregate data often mask a diversity of microeconomic trends that reveal differential impacts of investments such as those in technology. As a case in point, productivity growth has been skewed within manufacturing, with virtually all of this growth coming from the durable goods portion of that sector, in particular, electronic components and equipment. Figure 1.2 shows the disaggregated trends clearly. The durable goods subsector of manufacturing is the most R&D intensive. Along with an eclectic set of IT-using industries, including several service industries, this group accounted for two-thirds of the above-trend productivity growth in the late 1990s (Oliner and Sichel, 2000).

The revival in productivity growth resulted in somewhat higher real earnings growth in the last period of Table 1.1 (1997–2005). Real

compensation increased even more, but that differential was largely due to
higher payments for worker health care and retirement – both of which are
now being drastically reduced by an increasing number of companies. The

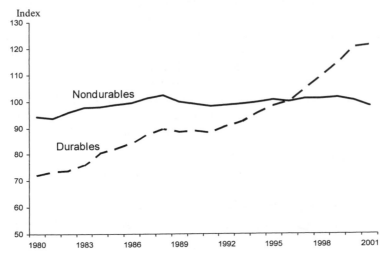

Source: Bureau of Labor Statistics.

Figure 1.2 Multifactor Productivity by Product Type, 1980–2001

modest recovery in real earnings, moreover, was largely confined to the late
1990s. Since the 2001 recession (2001–05), the average annual growth rate
has been a miniscule 0.18 percent.

Again, one must look inside the macroeconomic trends to understand the
required policy adjustments. High-tech industries are not only producing the
higher rates of productivity growth but also exhibit the highest wages and
salaries. Specifically, Bureau of Labor Statistics (BLS) analysis shows that
median earnings in all but one of the 71 BLS technology-oriented
occupations exceeded the median for all workers in 2004. In six high-tech
occupations, earnings exceeded three times the median. In 34 more, earnings
were twice the median; and, in another 17, earnings exceeded the median by
50 to 99 percent (Hecker, 2005).

In contrast, workers in low-tech industries, which constitute the majority
of the workforce and therefore significantly affect long-term national
earnings trends, are paid less and are experiencing stagnant real income
growth. These workers have the greatest risk of losing their jobs to foreign
competition as their skills are increasingly matched by emerging, low-wage
economies.

Unfortunately, it is now becoming the case that all workers' jobs, high skilled and low skilled, are at risk. The Economic Policy Institute (EPI) points out that the ratio of annual earnings of college to high-school workers rose from 57 to 93 percent in the 1975–2000 period. However, between 2000 and 2004, a large decline occurred in this ratio, driven by a 5.2 percent fall in the real earnings of college graduates compared with a modest increase in high-school graduate earnings. The EPI observed that the recent downward pressure on the earnings growth of college-educated workers could be due to the emerging trend of offshoring skilled jobs that had commanded an earnings premium earlier (Mishel and Bernstein, 2006).

The additional trend needed is income distribution. United Nations data show that the US economy has one of the most skewed income distributions among large countries. Only China has a higher Gini index (the UN measure

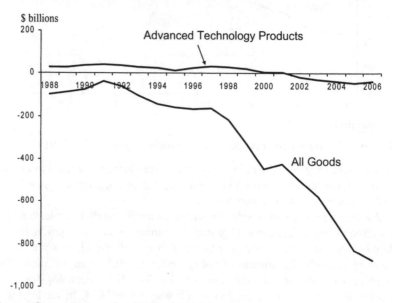

Source: Census Bureau, Foreign Trade Division.

Figure 1.3   U.S. Trade Balances, 1988-2006

of income inequality). This lack of real-income growth among the majority of the workforce is influenced by sluggish employment growth – simply a supply–demand effect. The drastic decline in the participation of workers in business-cycle upswings has been blamed in part on the decline in unions and, more recently, on the influx of illegal aliens who work for extremely low wages and are paid no benefits. At the lower end of the wage scale, these factors hold back wages to unskilled and semi-skilled workers.

However, the major determining factor with both greater reach and staying power is the globalization of labor markets whereby companies can offshore many types of work at lower cost. The offshoring of a wide range of jobs has greatly affected the US economy's trade balances. Figure 1.3 shows that the long-term trade balance for all traded products has been in deficit for decades. However, in the past decade, it has deteriorated rapidly, reaching $836 billion in 2006.

A trade balance is also calculated by the Census Bureau for a subset of these traded goods labeled as advanced technology products. This trade balance is derived from 500 product fields (out of a total of approximately 22,000) that have been designated as 'technologically advanced'. Although the balance for all traded goods has been negative for 25 years, the trade balance for advanced technology products was positive from 1988 (when the Census Bureau first began calculating it) until 2002, when it too turned negative. Still, while the high-tech balance trend is another sign of competitive decline, its relative performance is much better than that for all traded goods, and the US balance for trade in services (considerably smaller in volume than goods) remains positive.

Thus, the once dominant technology sector of the US economy has finally reached the point in its ongoing decline where a negative product technology trade balance has appeared, leaving only services with a positive balance. The percentage of services that are tradeable is increasing steadily due to their greater knowledge content and the availability of ever more powerful communications infrastructures, which implies greater competition in the future.

Perhaps the most telling aspect of the deterioration of high-tech trade is that the poster child of American technological leadership, information and communication products, now accounts for a majority of high-tech imports (57 percent in 2005, according to the National Science Foundation (NSF), with 75 percent coming from Asia). The United States is the leader in terms of overall production of IT equipment, but the fact that it imports a significant amount of such goods (components and final products) is evidence that technological convergence is well underway across the global economy.

The final major trend helping to frame the growth policy problem is the fact that multinational companies in industrialized nations are benefiting from the increasingly distributed technology-based global economy. Figure 1.4 shows that US corporate profits' share of GDP declined over much of the post-World War II period due to the relatively strong bargaining position of US labor, enabled by the dominant position of the US economy. Over the past two decades, however, unions' and, more generally, labor's bargaining power has declined drastically as US companies both increased investment in capital-intensive technology to raise multifactor productivity and

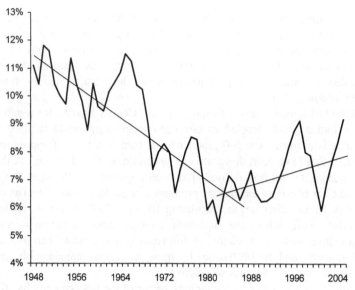

Source: Bureau of Economic Analysis.

Figure 1.4 Domestic Profits Before Taxes Relative to GDP, 1948–2005

offshored more labor-intensive work to further reduce costs. The result has
been a reversal of industry's declining share of corporate profits. In fact, in
2006, profit margins (profits as a share of output) of US nonfinancial
corporations reached the highest level in almost 40 years (Bureau of
Economic Analysis).

Such actions have not been an option for US corporations. They have been
forced to emphasize productivity as the focus of survival strategies in the
increasingly global marketplace. As explained in the following sections, this
reversal of fortunes (corporate profits gaining share of GDP and workers'
incomes share declining) is the result of the much greater mobility of
corporate resources relative to labor.

The Bottom Line

In the 25 years following World War II (the 'Golden Age'), higher rates of
productivity growth in the US economy led to higher employment and higher
income. In the next 25 years, however, productivity and income growth slowed
markedly. Most recently, investments in technology have resulted in a rebound
in productivity growth and corporate profits, but weak worker income and
employment growth have persisted.

This critical divergence in a period labeled by some as the 'New Economy'
reflects a number of underlying factors that predict mediocre or worse growth

rates in income for the majority of American workers. US-based companies are currently able to leverage past public and private R&D investments through global networks to achieve greater efficiencies for their stockholders and the domestic high-skilled workers they employ. However, these companies account for a small share of GDP, which will shrink further as larger net resource flows shift in the direction of other economies. These trends demand a policy focus on greater investment within the domestic economy.

CONVERGENCE OF COMPETITIVE POSITION

The US economy is in the process of losing its dominant technological leadership position. Defenders of the status quo argue correctly that America still conducts more R&D than any other economy. However, the US share of global R&D is steadily declining. Moreover, the *amount* of R&D is not the most important indicator of current or future competitiveness. A more critical indicator is R&D intensity. This ratio indicates the amount of current output of goods and services that an economy is committing to investment in new technology as a means of competing in the future. As stated by the Task Force on the Future of American Innovation (2005): 'We conclude that although the United States still leads the world in research and discovery, our advantage is eroding rapidly as other countries commit significant resources to enhance their own innovative capabilities'.

The Rise-and-Fall Cycle

Economists have stated for 50 years that when a high-income, capital-abundant economy trades freely with a low-income, labor-abundant economy, wages in the high-income economy will fall (Stolper and Samuelson, 1941). While this phenomenon has certainly been true for the lower-skilled, labor-intensive sector of the high-income economy, until recently the high-skilled portion of the labor force has been relatively insulated from this process of convergence. However, companies are increasingly combining global sourcing of production with globally distributed R&D, greatly leveraging the Samuelson effect (Palley, 2006a). That is, the world economy is experiencing not only job outsourcing but physical and intellectual capital migration, as well. The result is pressure on relative wages for skilled workers.

The post-war US economy emerged as the dominant economic leader by using technological innovation to power its economic engine. Relatively meager technology-based competition elsewhere in the world gave a false sense of invincibility. Today, the situation has changed drastically. While political realities mean that short-term (business-cycle) indicators of economic growth and competitiveness dominate economic policy discussions, long-term trend analysis and policy responses are essential because changes in national investment strategy and subsequent implementation of such policies can only occur over extended periods of time. It is this basic fact of economic growth that explains why it takes an economy considerable time to implement a growth strategy and also why successful economies do not deteriorate quickly when policies first begin to fail to promote adaptation to changing global economic conditions. Logically then, once an economy's competitive position has fallen, it can require a long time to recover.

These slow reversals of competitive position are due to the fact that economic growth is asset based. That is, physical, human and intellectual assets must be accumulated and organized to achieve an efficient and competitive economic system. This takes time. A growing and large investment in IT in the 1980s and 1990s showed little apparent impact on productivity until the late 1990s. This slow evolution of investment and payoff resulted in Nobel laureate economist Robert Solow's famous observation that the productivity gains from information technology are showing up everywhere but in the productivity statistics.

Similarly for economies striving to catch up to the leader, lengthy asset accumulation and implementation processes are required. For example, at the midway point in the implementation of its Lisbon Accord, Europe is still trying to close a significant gap with the United States with respect to the assimilation and effective use of IT. Its stated goal of increasing its average R&D intensity by 50 percent, from 2.0 to 3.0 percent during this decade, is lagging behind the original plan.

Japan went through several decades of intense technology assimilation before becoming a true global force in technological change. Today, in spite of its 13 percent share of global R&D, it is not a leader in 'important' patents and continues to struggle to implement a complete innovation infrastructure. Therefore, just as considerable time is required to lose technological leadership, so are long gestation periods necessary before an economy can become an innovation leader.

Thus, the leading economy finds itself in an enviable position. However, having built up an asset-based advantage over competing nations and sustained this advantage for some time, the natural tendency is to believe that its leading position will last forever. Moreover, participants in this economy acquire huge stakes in preserving the economic system and the acquired assets that have made it successful. After all, they have invested in these assets, learned how to deploy them productively, and are therefore totally dependent on the existing system for continued success. Thus, both the public and private sectors are loath to consider change. In fact, they strongly resist adaptation.

As other nations begin to imitate and, in some cases, eventually achieve parity with the leader's competitive capabilities, the convergence becomes increasingly apparent. However, the huge investment in the previously successful algorithm (the installed base) acts as an enormous barrier to adaptation, and convergence therefore progressively redistributes the gains from technology-based trade away from the innovator (Samuelson, 2004). Economies of scale and scope that originally accrued to the innovating country because of its dominant market positions are significantly reduced (Gomory and Baumol, 2000; Palley, 2006b).

The reluctance and, in fact, resistance by the leader to adapt as other economies steadily catch up and even begin to pass it initiate a period of long-term decline. The demise is typically slow enough that, coupled with the normal focus on short-term problems, reality can be ignored for some time. Even when some sound the alarm, apostles of denial appear to rationalize away the evidence presented. The European economies have required almost a century of slow growth in their average standard of living compared with the United States to reach the point of both admitting to fundamental structural problems and then beginning to take meaningful steps to redirect asset-based growth strategies.

In fact, there is much that is not unique about the life-cycle pattern of rise and fall unfolding within the US economy. History truly does repeat itself. The British economy of the 18th and early 19th centuries is a particularly relevant example because of its once unchallenged global leadership based in part on leading manufacturing technology and its subsequent long and sustained fall.

The US economy is currently in the process of having its economic model imitated. Based on current trends in innovation, technology utilization and supporting technology-based infrastructure, the next decade will finally reveal to a majority of Americans that their economy is in relative decline. As the comparative prosperity of the United States falls, many villains are being found to point fingers at.

One of the major targets is China. Because of its large size, low labor costs and zeal for pursuing economic growth – including technology-based growth – it is a more visible threat than most. For example, China is now the third-largest manufacturing economy in the world and, shockingly, it is now the leading exporter of IT products. The huge trade deficit with China ($202 billion in 2005) is seized upon as evidence of the threat posed to the US economy.

However, it also needs to be recognized that China, as a developing economy, is currently largely a re-exporter of high-tech products for the rest of Asia. In fact, China's share of exports to the United States has been rising while the share of other Asian economies has been falling (Lum and Nanto, 2006). That is, the other Asian nations send partially completed goods to China for final assembly, which are then exported to the industrialized world, particularly the United States. Thus, the rising share of high-tech products in China's and other Asian economies' exports is an unambiguous sign that convergence is occurring broadly and will not be slowed appreciably by rising wages in these nations.

In fact, India, Korea, Taiwan, Thailand, Malaysia, Indonesia and Singapore are all following the Japanese model of the 1970s and 1980s under which technology is acquired by whatever means possible (legal or otherwise), the workforce is educated rapidly and economic growth is based on exports. In all cases, the long-term goal is to become an innovation leader.

The overall result is that the US balance for the flow of payments between domestic and foreign owners for claims on all assets (products, services, financial – the so-called current account balance) reached a $668 billion deficit in 2004 and an even larger $805 deficit in 2005. These huge deficits mean that America now requires an average of approximately $3.0 billion of capital inflows each and every business day to keep its economy functioning. As a share of GDP, the current account deficit reached 6.4 percent in 2005 (Bureau of Economic Analysis).

US imports are now 51 percent larger than US exports. Closing this gap will require a huge increase in domestic production of manufactured goods and much greater restraint on imports. In fact, the Economic Policy Institute estimates that to keep the trade deficit from widening further, the growth rate of exports must exceed that of imports by 57 percent (Scott, 2006).

Part of this deficit is due to excessive US consumption and the inevitable adjustment (declining currency, lower real-income growth) will be severe. However, such a rebalancing will not address the structural problems that currently exist. Moreover, European and Japanese economies are slowly restructuring, and emerging economies are not satisfied with simply supplying the low-end technology components of each supply chain. India started with basic code writing in software, but now is moving into higher value-added software products such as video games and more sophisticated software services. China initially had a few low-end semiconductor manufacturing plants but intends to move rapidly to world-class status in both design and manufacturing in as little as five years. In 2007, China became the second-largest R&D spender (13 percent) behind the United States, edging out Japan.

The Process of Trading Places

The first step in moving up any high-tech value-added chain is to invest in an educated workforce and then to gain experience for this skilled labor by manufacturing moderately technology-intensive products. Moving up the production skill curve eventually yields enough understanding of state-of-the-art technology in a particular area to create synergies with a fledgling R&D infrastructure. From that point, the domestic industry can move toward the ultimate goal of becoming an innovator. Japan, Taiwan, Korea, and now China all started this way in semiconductors. The first three are now world-class competitors, with China driving toward this status. With increasing frequency, signs of innovation leadership, not just imitation, are appearing.

NSF data for 2003 show that US high-technology industries accounted for about 16 percent of world high-tech exports. Japan accounted for 9 percent, Germany for 8 percent and China for 7 percent (up from 1 percent in 1990). However, no matter how one views the current status, the trends and strategies being employed to affect competitive position are the critical policy variables and here the indicators are decidedly negative for the US economy.

Providing incentives to companies in innovation-oriented economies to locate production domestically greatly accelerates the process of convergence. Intel operates a $500 million plant in Shanghai, China, which produces Pentium 4 microprocessors that run the latest generation of personal computers (PCs). Hundreds of Chinese workers monitor diamond-tipped wafer saws and other automated equipment, testing and assembling chips for the world market and thereby gaining state-of-the-art engineering skills. Intel's plant is just one of more than 5,000 multinational operations now located in one of China's free-trade zones (Heim, 2004).

One step further along in the convergence process, China's leading domestic chip company, Semiconductor International (SMIC), manufactures semiconductor devices in its own plant. Currently, SMIC is several generations behind the technological leader, Intel. More generally, Chinese firms still lag the US leaders in both process and chip design technology. However, the investments being made in human and intellectual capital imply steady progress by Chinese semiconductor firms up the technology ladder.

Emerging economies such as India and China are adopting 'technology cluster' strategies, borrowed from a few long-standing US examples. The cluster concept improves R&D efficiency and is thereby helping leverage these countries' growth into world-class competitive positions. In fact, just like Intel's presence in China, SMIC has helped spawn semiconductor design houses, software start ups, and chip packaging and testing companies in China's own version of Silicon Valley. And thus, the local high-tech supply chain evolves, bringing a greater share of the global industry's value added to the domestic economy.

Highly developed clusters embody most elements of so-called 'innovation networks', which both provide and integrate complementary R&D assets.[4] Bangalore in India is often-cited as an example of the important role of clusters in emerging Asian economies. With a focus on software development supported by universities, government research subsidies and a highly skilled labor force, it has attracted the largest and most R&D-intensive multinationals, including Microsoft, Intel and Motorola. Even small specialty electronics firms, such as Rambus ($1.5 billion in annual sales) are investing in research operations in Bangalore. Such research infrastructure is springing up all over Asia. For example, Korea has an equally comprehensive cluster for photonics in Gwangju, where research institutes specializing in proof-of-concept and technical infrastructure research, industry associations, and education and training organizations all work in close proximity to one another to support private-sector investment.

The type of knowledge transferred from these organizations within a cluster is largely of the 'tacit' variety (embodied in people, as opposed to being codified in patents). The diffusion of tacit knowledge is especially critical in the early phases of a technology's life cycle when scientific and generic technical knowledge, critical to the formation of new firms and initial innovations, is being developed. Such enrichment of skilled labor pools and general technology transfer, along with the close proximity of public research and innovation facilities, generate increasing returns to R&D, which can quickly transform a pure manufacturing industry structure into one that also develops new, innovative products.[5]

THE SPEED OF CONVERGENCE

A major policy question is how fast can convergence happen? In today's global economy, the increasing deployment of IT, the ability to travel to other economies to observe, and, most important, the capacity to induce domestic investment by companies from the current leading innovative economies results in this answer: fast – although not instantly.

The distinction between instant and fast convergence is critical to national strategy development. In spite of the rapid evolution of semiconductor industries in major Asian nations over the past 20 years, the US semiconductor industry still accounts for almost half of the world market in terms of sales – more than any other country. Over three-quarters of US-owned wafer capacity is still located in the domestic economy, despite the fact that three-quarters of domestic sales are exports. An indication that US workers in this industry are still highly paid is the fact that almost 80 percent of the US domestic industry's total labor compensation is paid to US-based workers, while only 55 percent of the industry's labor force is domestic (Scalise, 2005a).

However, as consistently pointed out in succeeding chapters, ongoing and projected trends are more important than the current status of any economy. With respect to the latest generation of wafer production capacity (300mm), the US share has declined from 36 percent in 1999 to just over 20 percent in 2004. Two-thirds of new 300mm fabs and approximately 80 percent of all 300mm fabs under construction are outside the United States, primarily in Asia. Perhaps most significant is that, even though US firms still account for almost 50 percent of global sales and maintain a majority of their manufacturing capacity within the US economy, the global share of semiconductor manufacturing facilities in the United States continues to decline. US capacity dropped from 26 percent in 1994 to 20 percent in 2004 (Scalise, 2005b).

In analyzing such trends, the supply chain is a more important unit for growth policy analysis than is the single industry. For example, only examining the above trends in semiconductor manufacturing gives an incomplete picture of competitive decline in this technology. One tier back in the semiconductor supply chain, US suppliers of semiconductor manufacturing equipment maintained a 60 percent share of the global market until the last few years, when their share dropped to less than 50 percent while Japanese companies' share rose to approximately the same level (Gartner Group). In some specific categories of equipment, including the critical area of lithography, US firms are no longer even players. However, in other areas such as process control equipment, domestic firms are still market leaders. This uneven hollowing-out process is yet one more factor in enabling denial of broader trends in loss of competitive position.

Co-location synergies are an important attribute of domestic supply chains. Decline in such synergies may partially account for the overall drop in equipment market shares. While US semiconductor manufacturers still account for the largest percentage of purchases of semiconductor manufacturing equipment, that share is diminishing, having dropped from just over 43 percent in 2001 to roughly 25 percent in 2004. Of note, Chinese companies' share of equipment purchases grew from about 2.6 percent to over 8 percent in the same period (Scalise, 2005b). Obviously, as Asian manufacturing capacity expands, so must purchases of equipment. As manufacturing activity shifts to Asia, so will equipment production capacity move to that region.

Further, in the tier of this supply chain beyond semiconductor devices are manufacturers of subsystems of multiple devices. This industry provides an indicator of how fast economic activity, even in technology-based industries, can shift to other economies. A National Research Council (2005b) report found that in 2000, nearly 80,000 workers were employed in the North American printed circuit board industry; but by the beginning of 2004, the total had dropped to just over 41,000. In summary, the loss of market shares from multiple tiers collectively means a steady hollowing out of valued added from the domestic semiconductor supply chain.

The threats to established economies and the opportunities for those emerging economies bootstrapping their way up the competitiveness ladder can only be understood in the context of the cyclical nature of long-term economic growth and the public and private forces that inevitably determine this pattern. Joseph Schumpeter demonstrated how imbalances in the modern economy such as excessive capital accumulation occur and eventually cause an economic crisis, manifested in declining rates of output and real-income growth. Such a crisis opens the window of opportunity for new technologies to emerge, which diffuse widely in response to the obsolescence of the existing capital stock.

In the past, the advances in science often lay largely unused for decades until economic disarray provided both opportunity and motivation for their application. Today, however, the growing number of technology-based economies means that motivation exists continually somewhere in the world, so that the lags between scientific advance and technological applications will be increasingly short.

Leaders of US-based high-tech companies have pointed to inadequate investment in R&D as a sign of the impending decline of the American economy. The inadequate innovation infrastructure support provided to these companies in the United States is forcing them to offshore not only production but also knowledge creation by conducting R&D elsewhere. While some, including US consulting firms who profit from advising US companies on outsourcing strategies, rationalize global R&D 'partnerships' and 'networks' as necessary manifestations of the diversifying global technology-based economy, the hard fact for economic growth policy is that all offshore outsourcing removes value added from the domestic economy and thereby slows national economic growth.

The positive side of these trends is the fact that establishing a science base is only the first step in acquiring inventive and ultimately innovative capability. As described in succeeding chapters, innovative capacity consists of a number of diverse but complementary technology-based assets. Once the required multiple sets of assets are acquired, innovation rates increase. Thus, most countries with high publication rates also rank high in number of patents.

However, productivity in inventive output can only be attained slowly as a national innovative capacity is developed. Nevertheless, the trend everywhere is toward more scientific discovery and more inventive output. Discovery and invention are followed by innovation and consequent market dominance – if the correct economic growth model is followed.

The slowness of competitive asset deterioration in leading economies and the lengthy building time required of emerging challengers enables denial to dominate and hence prevent the long-term investments and other adjustments needed to adapt. Even large and determined economies such as China, while making progress in acquiring, using and now developing technologies, cannot catch up (converge) instantly because building up the entire set of innovation assets and forming efficient networks takes time. For example, China has the second highest rate of nanoscience publications but ranks 20th in nanotechnology patents. OECD (Organization for Economic Cooperation and Development) data show that while China's patenting rate is increasing sharply, its share of 'triadic' patents (filed in Japan, Europe and the United States) is growing much more slowly. In other words, China is not yet a major force in important patents with global market potential, the kind that are worth filing in multiple economic regions.

However, the long run eventually becomes the short run. Lux Research Inc., a research and consulting firm focusing on nanotechnology, estimated that worldwide nanotechnology R&D was $8.6 billion in 2004. Significantly, the company also estimated that more than half of this amount, $4.6 billion, would be funded by governments. Such a large role for government in the early phases of an emerging technology leverages the much larger investment by industry in applied R&D that follows and thereby enables the growth rates of new patents in later phases of the R&D cycle. The only uncertainty about such an evolutionary process is which national economies will receive the most support from their governments and thereby produce the most intellectual capital (patents) to leverage future innovation.

The apostles of denial can point to the still dominant US position within the global technology-based economy. With 4.5 percent of the world's population, the United States accounts for approximately 31 percent of global R&D, which was about $1 trillion in 2006 (Battelle, 2006). However, the trends tell the tale. While, the US share of OECD R&D declined only slightly from 44.9 in 1988 to 42.7 in 2002, the data show that the convergence is coming from non-OECD economies. Thus, in the context of global R&D, the US share has declined from 40 percent in 1988 to the current 31 percent (UNESCO and OECD data).[6] The US share of world article output has declined from 38 percent in 1988 to 30 percent in 2003 and its share of citations in the science and engineering (S&E) literature dropped from 52 percent in 1992 to 42 percent in 2003 (National Science Board,

2006a). Most important, these downward trends persist.

THE CONSEQUENCES

Workers in Western economies are becoming restless as they sense that, while globalization means increased profits for global companies (see Figure 1.4), higher-paying domestic employment opportunities are shrinking. For example, in the 1990s the US PC industry designed, manufactured and marketed its products within the domestic economy. Today, all assembly is offshore, as is an increasing share of the manufacturing of individual components (the next tier back in the supply chain). Design is still retained by US companies, but even at the R&D stage foreign ODMs (original design manufacturers) are now providing increasing portions of the value added, which will eventually constrain US PC firms' ability to differentiate their products.

This process of convergence repeats itself in one industry after another, as other economies pick off segments of the leading domestic industry's value added. As observed in the example of the semiconductor industry, one factor making it possible for policy makers to deny that aggregate economic decline is occurring is that individual industries and their supply chains lose competitive position segment by segment and do so at different points in time from one another. Certainly, the US economy retains leadership in a number of knowledge-intensive industries such as software because it still has the best installed base of the required complementary assets. Even though other economies are acquiring the ability to write software, their focus so far is mainly on fairly rudimentary code writing. More advanced programming is still dominated by US firms. But the same policy question applies: how long before convergence by other countries becomes significant and substantial value added in advanced software development goes offshore? Microsoft Research Group, for example, has five major installations, only two of which are located in the United States.

The key to long-term competitive position is continual domestic investment in science and breakthrough technologies based on that science, along with the infrastructure to effectively commercialize them and thereby reap both first-mover and sustained economic advantages over a technology's life cycle. As China, India and other Asian nations bootstrap themselves relentlessly toward status as technology-based economies, the primary focus has been on convergence within current technology life cycles (the cyclical pattern of R&D, production, marketing and eventual obsolescence). Convergence in the later half of an existing technology life cycle is an excellent strategy for emerging economies because success here is more dependent on factors such as cost reduction. Most cycles are long enough for substantial economic growth to be realized through such strategies and for acquisition of the assets required to enter the next life cycle at an earlier point.

Because of these shifts in market share, much attention in leading economies is focused on the threat of technological convergence within current technology life cycles. However, emerging economies are also developing scientific and innovation capabilities, which presage an ability to become innovators in future technology life cycles. A study by the US–China Economic and Security Review Commission concluded that China has made 'remarkable achievements' in a wide range of scientific fields and technologies. Within a few months in 2005, according to the Commission, China announced: a new supercomputer that operates at 11 trillion calculations per second; breakthroughs in nanotechnology; the manufacture of immunochips to detect staph infection; operation of a mini space satellite; plans to launch another 100 satellites beyond the 70 already in orbit; a new pebble-bed nuclear reactor technology; plans to build 40 nuclear reactors; a Chinese-designed Pentium-style microprocessor; a doubling of the output of robots; the design of a new space vehicle capable of launching satellites as large as 25 tons; successful cloning of a buffalo; opening of semiconductor design centers; progress by its Institute of High Energy Physics on an electron positron collider; support of a superconducting collider in Germany; partnering with the EU to deploy the Galileo positioning satellite system; and a planned state-of-the-art astronomical observation program (McCormack, 2005a, Pillsbury, 2005). These trends should not be surprising. China has had an explicit policy to rapidly increase its innovation capacity for two decades. In 2003, China had 863,000 researchers – the highest number in the world behind the United States, which had 1.3 million (OECD, 2005).

India and China get the most media attention because of their size, but an increasing number of smaller economies are collectively taking a share of global high-value-added markets. For example, Korea's Samsung was the first semiconductor firm to succeed in mass producing graphics chips for video games, it developed the first flash memory chip based on 40-nanometer processing technology, and it created the first portable digital TV technology. At the industry level, Finland in cell phones, Korea in memory semiconductor devices and photonics, and Taiwan in laptop computers are challenging for global market shares as innovators.

Singapore has one of the highest per capita incomes in the world by virtue of an excellent information and research infrastructure and a highly educated workforce. This environment makes its economy a choice location for multinationals in high-tech services and in R&D for a range of technologies, including IT and biotechnology. The only reason Singapore is not more visible is its small size, but this model is being copied by other larger Asian economies, whose economic impact potential is much greater.

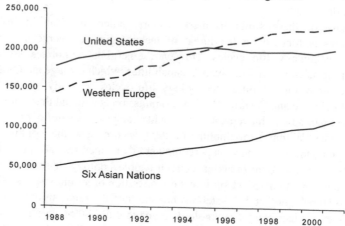

Source: NSF, *Science and Engineering Indicators 2004.* The six Asian nations are Japan, South Korea, Taiwan, India, China and Singapore.

Figure 1.5 S&E Articles Published, 1988–2001

A major manifestation of the global convergence described above is the increasing ineffectiveness of traditional rebalancing mechanisms. Economic theory teaches that a strong negative relationship exists between exchange rates and prices and a positive relationship exists between excess domestic demand and inflation. However, with the emergence of many new economies and especially the acquisition of technology-based capabilities, excess capacity is appearing in a growing number of industries. This capacity expansion, much of it embodying low-cost but highly skilled labor, is dominating global pricing.

Thus, the Schumpeterian model of creative destruction is asserting itself. It predicts that growing investment eventually creates excess capacity, which restrains pricing to the extent that the modest advances in technology typical of the later phases of a life cycle are not sufficient to maintain profit margins. Eventually, 'the crisis' arises because economic growth stagnates or even declines.

Because the life cycles of unrelated technologies are typically out of phase with each other, one might argue that a large economy can achieve a rolling adjustment. This 'portfolio' approach to growth management based on the technology life-cycle model will be discussed at length in Part Three. For now, the important point is that, in a global marketplace, an economy's entire portfolio of technologies will be under attack at all times. Although the process of creative destruction will bring new high-value-added technologies into being, they do not have to appear in the economy that dominated the previous cycle.

In this regard, established industrial economies should be most concerned about trends in emerging areas, such as biotechnology, nanotechnology and alternative energy technologies. Many in the United States seem to assume that this country will be a leader, if not the dominant leader, in these areas based on an extrapolation of past performance. However, the process of globalization will have a lot to say about such a prospective outcome. It will probably come as a shock to many Americans that Asian countries have expanded nanoscience publication output dramatically in the past decade. Analysis by Kostov et al. (2005) shows that, in 2004, China ranked second to the United States in nanoscience research publications, as indicated in the Science Citation Index. Of the six leading countries in nanoscience research (based on publications), three are Western industrialized nations (United States, Germany, France) and three are Asian (China, Japan, South Korea). The three Western countries have merely an 8 percent advantage in terms of total publications.

The stagnant investment intensity of the US economy (a national R&D intensity slightly below the peak reached over 40 years ago) is largely due to a declining government share of national R&D and is resulting in a steady erosion of the relative share of the production of global scientific knowledge. Figure 1.5 shows that Western Europe with approximately the same GDP as the United States now produces more S&E publications per year. Asia with a rapidly expanding university system is increasing its publication rate as fast as is Europe. Other areas of the world are showing signs of becoming sources of scientific and engineering knowledge, as well. NSF data show that Latin America, while starting from a low base, tripled its publication rate between 1988 and 2001. Meanwhile, the US rate of publishing has stagnated for at least a decade.

Perhaps most important for understanding the imperative to adjust national economic growth strategy is the fact that a large part of the rapidly expanding Asian R&D spending is due to investments by American companies. The chairman and CEO of IBM, Sam Palmisano, argues that to avoid a backlash against globalization, multinational companies must become truly global in all aspects of their operations, including R&D investment (Guerrera and Waters, 2006). Simultaneous with this statement by its CEO, IBM announced a $6 billion R&D investment in India.

A subtle but important distinction here is between a 'multinational' strategy, currently employed by most large companies, in which most R&D is kept in the home country and only manufacturing and marketing operations are outsourced, and the emerging concept of a truly global strategy where R&D and production assets are co-located around the world to maximize overall company productivity. This trend is evidenced by the fact that the majority-owned foreign affiliates of US companies spent $21.2 billion on R&D in 2002, almost double the amount invested in 1994.

The Bottom Line

The policy issue is where the high-value-added domestic growth will come from in the future for industrialized nations. The only recourse for the high-income (or former high-income) economies is to implement strategies that move domestic industries beyond the current technology life cycles as these technologies mature. However, many barriers exist to such transitions, including denial of the need for transition and an installed private and public asset base that must be deliberately scrapped before new technology-based industries can emerge. The transition begins with the development of a new science base, indicated by publication rates. This is followed by an increase in inventive output, indicated by patent rates. Then, and only then, can innovative output become significant, indicated by rates of new products, processes, and services. This last step in the linear innovation model requires an elaborate set of infrastructures.

RESPONSE TO THE TECHNOLOGY IMPERATIVE

The previous section discussed the convergence process that typically begins in earnest about halfway through a major technology life cycle. However, convergence does not happen automatically. It takes a combination of denial on the part of the leading economies that competition is emerging and attacking their dominant market shares and a determined desire on the part of the challengers to catch up to the leaders.

Sources of Resistance

Although such resistance sometimes appears on the surface to be cultural or political in origin, deeper down the source is most often economic. Unfortunately, economic philosophies are some of the most difficult to adjust for the fundamental reason that change always creates losers. In the US economy, the heritage of the early immigrants from Europe who were escaping religious, political and economic repression has led to a strong emphasis on individual freedom. This philosophy, in turn, led to the doctrine of the unfettered marketplace. Entrepreneurs have been expected to succeed or fail on their own merits. Failure is not viewed as socially unacceptable and thus risk taking is prevalent.

These beliefs drove the evolution of the dynamic American marketplace, which has had an enviable record of creating new, innovative firms. Other economies have envied the US growth model for decades but still struggle to emulate it. Some new firms have risen to be large and successful, replacing in the nick of time old, tired companies that had refused to adapt and thereby lost their competitive edge. Many conservatives have maintained that government's contribution to such success is simply to stay out of the way. Historically, this has hardly been the case, but lack of recognition of how a government role has contributed to economic progress is blocking adaptation now that major changes in the growth model have become imperative.

In Europe, countries such as France demonstrate just the opposite philosophy. The French used a heavy governmental hand to try to reinvent their large 'national champions' through many forms of support. Little support is provided to startup firms. The French think of themselves as being as homogeneous as the Americans view themselves as individuals. Hence, in France, one finds a dominant social welfare system, high levels of regulation, an enforced 35-hour work week, and so on.

In the German economy, large companies like Volkswagen are protected from takeovers by a 1960 law that limits a single shareholder to a maximum of 20 percent of the outstanding shares. Moreover, Germany has a 'co-determination law' that requires any company with 2,000 or more employees to give labor half the seats on its board of directors. Really large companies (more than 20,000 employees) must have 10 labor representatives on a 21-member board – seven directly from the workforce and three from the unions. In Volkswagen's case, the German state of Saxony is the largest shareholder at 18.2 percent and gets two seats on the board of directors. Thus, labor and government together have a majority of the seats. [7]

The European Commission has argued that such rules inhibit the free flow of capital across the EU but so far it has been unable to achieve much change. However, adaptation seems finally to be underway. Varying degrees of relaxation of labor laws in a number of countries, especially Germany, are actually beginning to retard offshoring.

Adaptation Takes Different Forms

After decades of resistance to change, some industrialized nations are finally responding to globalization in a positive way by attempting to increase the technology intensity of their economies. Investment in R&D is a critically important indicator of a national economy's intent to compete globally on the basis of technology. Over the past decade, Israel increased its R&D intensity from 2.7 to 4.7 percent, a ratio higher than any other OECD country. Other countries have set long-term goals for increasing R&D spending intensity, with Austria aiming for 2.5 percent of GDP by 2006,

Germany 3.0 by 2010, and the UK 2.5 percent by 2014 (OECD, 2004).

Finland is one of the best examples of adaptation. The country steadily increased government spending on R&D throughout the 1990s and by 2004 was investing 3.5 percent of GDP in R&D. The Finnish government engages in partnerships with domestic companies for strategic planning, collaborative R&D, and enhancement of technical infrastructure such as university and research institute support for clusters. The country also has an excellent educational system, which is regarded as the best in Europe.

While these attempts at adaptation and remaining competitive through transitions to new technology life cycles are in progress in industrialized nations, the emerging economies have their own designs on becoming technology leaders. The OECD notes that China doubled its R&D intensity between 1995 and 2002 from 0.6 to 1.2 percent. This rapid increase is particularly amazing given China's phenomenal rise in GDP.

However, emerging economies also have restraining legacies from their past. China insists on trying to become a technology-based market economy while continuing to rely on quantity-targeting techniques from its central planning heritage. Failure to rely on the tools of monetary, fiscal and currency policies will inhibit stabilization and hence provide a difficult environment for private investment, including R&D. More efficient financial markets will be required for long-term expansion of venture capital, the emergence of new firms, and effective use of the historically strong Chinese entrepreneurial culture.

Moreover, the challengers do not typically play fair. China has been accused of stealing intellectual property, manipulating its currency, exploiting workers, and illegally charging lower taxes on domestically designed and produced high-tech products.[8] Such practices eventually become a negative for sustained economic growth. For example, intellectual property theft discourages direct foreign investment, including research partnerships.

Some current trends in adaptation are typical of past technology life cycles, namely increased technology and market specialization. Vertical disintegration is common, as cycles mature. Large original equipment manufacturers (OEMs) divest elements of their R&D to companies in industries farther back in their supply chains in order to focus on overall system design and marketing.[9] At later phases of the cycle, distribution of R&D is not a bad thing and actually has the potential to make the overall domestic supply chain more competitive.

At later phases of the technology life cycle when competition is becoming increasingly cost based, the transfer of major shares of the value added from domestic supply chains to foreign sources occurs because of the simple fact that the foreign industries are not only cheaper but also increasingly provide quality products. That is, time breeds convergence. Unfortunately, when this happens, the remaining tiers of the domestic supply chain sometimes suffer efficiency losses due to reduced proximity to both suppliers and customers; that is, they lose location synergies from integrating R&D across tiers.

The counterpoint is that domestic industries can take advantage of opportunities in global markets while maintaining significant value added in their home countries, if they build agility and collaboration into their interactions with other tiers in their supply chain. From industry's perspective, this is essential whether the supply chain is totally domestic or more frequently partially foreign because trends toward specialization at each tier are conveying economies of scale on suppliers who often exist elsewhere in the world.

A recently evolved business model is to orchestrate the global supply chain by controlling design. For example, when Hewlett-Packard (HP) introduced ink-jet printers in the 1980s, the company established both R&D and manufacturing operations in Vancouver, Washington, to (i) better integrate design and manufacturing (especially important during early phases of commercialization), and (ii) capture economies of scale in manufacturing for the dominant US domestic market. As global demand expanded, HP offshored production and eventually concentrated it in Singapore to maintain economies of scale. As the product technology matured, HP outsourced production completely, retaining only design (Lee, 2004).

As long as the global information infrastructure is approximately equal to the domestic one, this strategy works. The fact that this is increasingly the case has induced such focused domestic strategies. As discussed in Chapter 8, agility among adjacent tiers and hence overall supply-chain efficiency depends to a significant extent on the use of advanced supply-chain management strategies based on a dynamic and efficient information infrastructure. Public investment in such infrastructure provides an essential incentive to domestic private investment; that is, an incentive to locate more of the value added in the domestic economy. The resulting co-location synergies are especially critical in the early part of a technology life cycle because of the greater importance of transfers of tacit knowledge, which is more efficiently achieved by person-to-person contact.

Factors Affecting Adaptation

Developing integrated supply chains for emerging technologies is a difficult and serious problem. The lack of codified technical knowledge early in a technology's life cycle requires considerable tacit knowledge flows not only within each industry, but vertically among tiers in the emerging supply chain. As a result, co-location is essential for rapid development and deployment of both the technology and supporting technical infrastructures. This is why the supply chain must be the focus of technology-based growth policy analysis.

When the United States was alone at the top of the global technology-based economy, the absence of coordinated and systematic policies to support breakthrough technologies and associated technical infrastructures meant that new supply chains required extended periods of time to develop. Today, the law of large numbers is relentlessly working against such *laissez-faire* strategies. As established economies in Western and Eastern Europe refurbish their innovative capacity and as emerging economies in Asia with much larger populations increasingly draw not only global manufacturing resources but also R&D investment, the disintermediation of technology-based competitiveness will accelerate.

As hinted at in the previous section, technical infrastructure is critical to modern growth strategies. The IT investment boom of the 1990s provided a much more efficient infrastructure for most industrial supply chains, thereby allowing cost reduction to accelerate. One result has been to extend current technology life cycles. Thus, although the process of convergence has been unprecedented over the past decade, US firms, in particular, have used investments in IT infrastructure to maintain competitiveness in a number of industries. However, the increasing adoption of IT by more and more economies and the explosion of technology-based production capacity, especially in Asia, have suppressed prices at least as fast as IT infrastructure has reduced costs.

As efficiency-inducing IT infrastructure has spread throughout the global economy, massive increases in global productive capacity are forcing convergence in prices independent of national economic cycles. This 'flattening' of the world's economy is underscored by IMF (International Monetary Fund) data showing that over the 1997–2004 period, global exports of goods and services expanded by 60 percent, nearly four times faster than the cumulative increase in world GDP. Global trade has increased from 17 percent of world GDP in 1986 to 31 percent in 2004.

The rapid expansion of global economic capacity is pressuring advanced economies to increase efficiency through technology, skilled labor and supporting infrastructure. In the US economy, disinflation forces have appeared in the past after surges of investment. In the period after the Civil War, rapid expansion of transportation infrastructure, particularly the railroads, led to considerable excess capacity and ultimately periods of deflation. In the 1920s, massive efficiency-enhancing investments such as mass-production technologies and electrification of manufacturing led to large productivity gains and ultimately to overcapacity. This time, the phenomenon is occurring on a global scale.

Deflation from technological change is a good thing because it provides economies with the benefits of rising productivity. The seemingly relentless drop in the cost of computing power has enabled huge gains in economic welfare. Equally important have been advances in other attributes of digital electronics, such as the miniaturization of physical features, integration of technology components, and so on that expand product functionality. Simultaneously, the markets for the technology are expanding due to its superior performance characteristics. The initial high profit margins attract competition and the resulting investment leads to capacity growth, which is the driver of disinflation. However, as the technology matures, advances in most attributes slow. Cost becomes the dominant competitive factor. Capacity expansion and cost-reduction pressures eventually lead to the Schumpeterian crisis stage.

Under such a scenario, the economies that continue to prosper are the ones that recognize the advent of the transition phase of the Schumpeterian process of creative destruction and consequently invest in the next set of technologies. Doing so allows a timely shift of labor and capital resources into these technologies ahead of competing economies. To this end, policy makers must identify and ensure the proofs of concept for a portfolio of emerging technologies and thereby enable domestic private investment in the innovation efforts necessary to effect transitions to new technology life cycles.

Many current electronics technologies, the source of most US economic growth for decades, are in the later portions of their life cycles. Recognizing this fact, the 2004 roadmap developed by the International Electronics Manufacturing Initiative (iNEMI) states that the electronics industry needs to adopt a longer-term investment vision. Compared to the early 1990s when the major issue was sufficient investment in the ability to take advantage of rapid innovation through production capacity expansion, the concern of iNEMI in the mid-2000s is that the electronics industry has become overly tactical and focused on squeezing returns out of existing technologies. iNEMI also observes that corporate labs have greatly cut back on fundamental/generic technology research and that national labs are also more focused on projects with quicker payback. Increasingly, electronics manufacturing is done offshore, so innovation is essential to add value to the domestic economy and pull additional value added in the form of future manufacturing investment.[10]

The Economic Growth Issues

This initial discussion has made two fundamental points about national economic growth in a highly competitive global economy. First, the concept of competitiveness is complex and must be addressed by a competent economic growth policy. Competitiveness is the ability to consistently sell a broad range of high-value-added goods and services into global markets to generate domestic income sufficient to raise the standard of living at acceptable rates. Managing the factors that contribute to this imperative is not a trivial challenge.

Second, old theories such as the law of comparative advantage were frequently used to rationalize free trade as the only strategy required for global economic growth. The traditional version of this law says that resources will shift to economies with relatively larger competitive (absolute) advantages. Thus, even if an economy has an absolute advantage in two goods, it will choose to produce the good in which it has the relatively greater (comparative) advantage. As a result, global economic welfare is increased.

However, when originally conceived over two hundred years ago, factors of production (mainly land, labor, and some capital) were highly stable over extended periods. That is, their endowments were largely fixed for each economy, so the static version of this law applied and economic growth policy needed only to worry about keeping trade free.

Today, the capability of a country or an economic region to significantly augment critical factors such as technology, skilled labor, and technical and economic infrastructure means that comparative advantage is no longer a stable condition. The countries that most effectively create new comparative advantages through technological innovation will have the highest growth rates because such action means resources are shifted into the higher valued added industries.

The increasingly observed economic strategy of creating new competitive (that is, absolute) advantage, which in turn causes shifts in comparative advantage, explains the rapid convergence of emerging technology-based economies with established ones. It also drives the trading of places among established economies who seek to use technology-based investment strategies to attain both first-mover advantages and then to sustain market leadership over the entire technology life cycle.

The Expanding Impact of Global Competition

As pointed out, the impact of globalization is increasingly evident in major indicators such as restrained growth in household earnings. Less obvious are effects on the dynamics of competition. Over the past 50 years, the expected length of industry leadership by any particular firm has declined dramatically. In fact, between 1980 and 1998, turnover of industry leaders (top 20 percent in terms of operating income) increased by a factor of 2.5. A company in the top 20 percent of an industry had a 1:10 probability in 1980 of falling out of that leadership position; by 1998, it had a 1:4 chance of doing so. Analysis of these trends indicates that R&D intensity is an important, if not the most important, factor in the increased volatility (Comin and Philippon, 2005).

Chapter 7 describes how technologies evolve in cycles and points out that these cycles are largely independent of each other. Thus, because unsynchronized cycles can smooth the overall pattern of growth, this same 50-year period has witnessed increased aggregate or macroeconomic stability within the US economy.

Such trends contribute to the propensity to deny the need for change. However, the growth of global markets has the potential to reintroduce volatility. The prospect of macroeconomic stability assumes that the more aggressive, R&D-intensive firms and industries that replace older, less-efficient ones are from the same economy. The major point for modern economic growth policy is that even in large and dynamic economies, the churn that characterizes loss of leadership for firms and industries dependent on existing technologies increasingly results in new leaders from different national economies.

While the phenomenon of shift in comparative advantage among nations has occurred for centuries, the pace of disruptive technological change has accelerated way beyond anything previously experienced, as many more competitors from an ever-larger number of nations have emerged to vie for leadership positions. Equally important, the public-good character of technological change with its scale and scope attributes means that national policies are increasingly important and will contribute to differences in the growth rates of competing economies.

Today, these patterns of globalization are evident as never before. Japan, Korea and Taiwan excel in various areas of electronics, Japan is the leader in robotics and related areas of automated manufacturing, China is rapidly emerging as a force in IT, India is becoming a leader in software services, and across both Western and Eastern Europe pockets of competitive high-tech industries are appearing. Developing economies are creating sophisticated pools of highly specialized and educated workers who have shown the ability and willingness to deliver high-quality, low-cost work.

Equally important for economic growth policy is the increasingly aggressive incentives provided by governments to attract domestic and foreign investment. India, for example, establishes software technology parks where companies can have 100 percent foreign equity, duty-free imports, corporate income tax exempted up to 90 percent, and dedicated data communication links. The last (communications infrastructure) is supported by additional incentives to companies providing Internet services and broadband networks, such as five- to ten-year tax holidays (Nasscom[11]). As a result of these incentives, the growth rates of high-tech sectors in emerging economies are dramatic. A Nasscom–McKinsey study estimated that India's IT industry doubled in just two years (2002–04) and now employs a million professionals. Nasscom further estimated that this industry will employ four million workers by 2008, representing 7 percent of India's GDP and 30 percent of its exports.

Thus, in today's global markets where trade is, or should be, 'free' in the market sense, the reality is that the comparative advantages that determine trade flows are increasingly 'managed' by the relative effectiveness of national economic growth strategies. In the case of the US economy, a set of investments in new technologies by both government and industry coupled with a dynamic internal market structure led to dominant global economic leadership. One can argue that part of the reason was the fact that other leading economies were recovering from the effects of World War II, but most of these economies have not yet caught up to the US economy in terms of overall productivity.

The 1970s brought the shock of rapid escalation of energy prices and the consequent obsolescence of much of the US economy's capital stock. This event was quickly followed by the first wave of significant foreign technology-based competition in the 1980s. The apostles of denial have fought reality since, but the major economic welfare indicators tell the story. BLS data show that real earnings for major segments of the workforce have declined continuously since that turning point in US economic history. Between 1979 and 2002, employer-provided health insurance coverage for recent high-school graduates in 'entry-level jobs' declined from 63 percent to roughly half that portion, pension coverage dropped from 36 percent to about 20 percent for these workers, and real wages fell by 17.4 percent for men and by 4.9 percent for women (Mishel et al., 2005).

These trends will be leveraged by the collective size of emerging economies, which will before long become centers of technology-based economic growth. Tom Friedman (2005) points out that in 1985 the 'global economic world' (North America, Western Europe, Japan, parts of Latin America and East Asia) was about 2.5 billion people. By 2000, with changes in India and China, and the collapse of the Soviet Union, the effective global marketplace had expanded to 6 billion people, including the addition of 1.5 billion new workers. As Friedman puts it, 'True, maybe only 10 percent of this new 1.5 billion-strong workforce has the education and connectivity to collaborate and compete at a meaningful level. But that is still 150 million people, roughly the size of the entire US workforce' (p. 183).

In the past, a *laissez-faire* approach to adaptation worked, albeit slowly. In the 19th century, the US economy made the transition from an agricultural society to one driven by manufacturing. Workers shifted out of agriculture as mechanization reduced jobs and demand for manufactured products increased. Thus, the argument goes, as manufacturing moves overseas, lost jobs will be replaced by other jobs, presumably in services.

The problem is that with the massive globalization process that has been in progress for the past several decades, the convergence of emerging economies is drastically shortening the available window for successful transitions by the leading economies. The large-scale transformation of 'nontradables' into 'tradables' as more and more economies become competitive in manufacturing and services technologies, means that *laissez-faire* approaches or, worse, resistance to change will cause more economic pain and do so faster.

The Core Policy Imperative

In counterpoint, transfer of technology is neither instant nor costless. This fact gives innovative economies the incentive and the potential to remain leaders across entire technology life cycles. Further enhancing innovative opportunity is that most manufacturing and service technologies are systems. This fact means that innovation is possible at the systems level as well as at the 'black-box' level. A technology-based economy therefore can create new and higher-valued-added product and service portfolios by supporting innovation at both these levels with targeted technical infrastructures.

Because such infrastructures are expensive and time consuming to imitate, the high-tech economy can remain so for some time – as long as it does not forget that the global economy is dynamic. However, industrialized nations are struggling to understand and implement responsive technology-based growth models. Currently, no nation is sufficiently high tech to succeed long term in the face of escalating global investment in R&D. The IT revolution is becoming what the quality revolution in the 1980s evolved into: more of a requirement for entry as opposed to an opportunity for competitive advantage. This premise creates an imperative to marshal resources toward the development of product, process, service and systems innovations and to do so across technology life cycles.

Success at this strategy requires a policy development and management methodology that is currently inadequate to varying degrees in most nations, in spite of successes in particular technologies for moderate periods of time. As the recent work of Arundel and Hollanders (2005) and Porter and Stern (2005) demonstrate, 'innovative capacity' is the synthesis of a very broad-based set of public and private investments and attitudes toward economic structure and behavior. Nothing less than a comprehensive and integrated policy algorithm will work.

Unfortunately, in a situation of slow employment and income growth, 'quick fixes' are psychologically appealing. Thus, the short-term consumption benefit from the few extra dollars provided by a proposed tax cut is converted into unrealistic expectations for the redressing of fundamental structural problems. It is human nature to focus on current issues and put off dealing with long-term trends or, simply, to not want to face the pain and uncertainty of adaptation.

Most industrialized nations face these problems. However, the United States is the potential champion of the rude awakening, as its size and past success, evidenced by a high standard of living, have made it the target of export-oriented emerging economies. This 'global consumer' status plus the dollar's position as the world's reserve currency have inflated excesses to enormous levels. The larger the bubble, the greater the pop when it breaks. Unfortunately, as history has shown, such a 'pop' and the extended agony are usually required to force significant change.

The Bottom Line

The high-growth economy of the future will be comprehensively technology-based. It will be more fluid and adaptive than any before it. The successful economy will be based on a 'complementary-asset' growth model in that both the public and private sectors have essential and complementary roles.

More specifically, while competition in the private marketplace is good and, in fact, essential for long-term economic growth, it is no longer the sole force behind the composition of economic growth as the traditional law of comparative advantage predicts. In fact, the dynamic character of global markets caused by the increasing pace of technological change and the ability of governments to influence it means that competition among national governments is also occurring. This increasingly important dimension to the global economic growth model will contribute to economic efficiency and, just like the private sector, competition among public sectors will result in winners and losers – even as aggregate global economic welfare rises.

The imperative to shift to such a growth model is being inhibited by institutional barriers in the US economy just as much as its private-sector dynamism has been an asset during its long period of leadership.

NOTES

1. 'A Survey of America: Centrifugal Forces', *The Economist*, July 16, 2005, p. 6.
2. Unfortunately, a number of definitions of a 'high-tech sector' are used. Any reasonable definition should include both manufacturing and service industries grouped into four major categories: IT-based manufacturing (electronics, communications and medical devices, plus process equipment such as robotics),

pharmaceuticals, communication services, software and computer-related services, and engineering and related services. The National Science Foundation does not have an official definition but publishes indicators compiled by others using several different definitions. A common means of designating an industry as high-tech is to use 'R&D intensity' (R&D as a percent of sales) as a discriminator. The Bureau of Labor Statistics (BLS) uses a 'technology-oriented occupation' intensity metric to classify industries, with data collected at the establishment level and then assigned to NAICS industries. Several 'levels' of high tech are defined by the BLS based on multiples of the average intensity for all industries. The Census Bureau uses a product-based approach in which imports and exports of 'product fields' are subjectively determined to be high tech based on the degree of new or leading-edge technology content. Because most trade is still product-based, services are largely ignored. Finally, definitions of high tech can be based on *use* of technology, as opposed to its source (innovation). The Bureau of Economic Analysis (BEA) has produced data that permit the calculation of the proportion of an industry's investment in equipment, software, and structures that consists of the output of 'high-tech' industries.

3. The term 'supply chain' refers to vertically-integrated industries that add value, beginning with raw materials and eventually produce a final product or service. Each tier (industry) in a supply chain adds value until final demand is met. The sum of the value added by the several tiers is the supply chain's contribution to GDP. An example of a first tier in a supply chain would be silicon and other materials. These materials are used to manufacture semiconductor devices, which are combined to form electronic components such as circuit boards, and ultimately equipment such as computers. Various types of equipment are further combined to form 'technology systems', such as an automated factory that manufactures a product or a telecommunications network that provides a service such as electronic funds transfers.

4. A 'cluster' is an economic development concept, first assessed in detail by Michael Porter at the Harvard Business School. Increasingly, 'technology clusters' are appearing across the global economy. These high-tech clusters are predicated on geographical concentrations of high-tech firms supported by technical infrastructure supplied by combinations of universities, government research institutes, and other government support services.

5. Evidence includes a doubling of patent rates among small R&D firms that are located in innovation resource-rich clusters (Feldman, 1994).

6. The US share of global R&D is 25 percent in purchasing power parity terms.

7. 'Dark Days for Volkswagen', *The Economist*, July 16, 2005.

8. As an example of such tax subsidies, customers in China pay just a 3 percent tax on semiconductor devices designed and produced in the domestic economy, whereas they pay a 17 percent (value-added) tax on imported chips, a violation of World Trade Organization rules.

9. The phenomenon of the relationship between the technology life cycle and vertical integration was first examined by Joseph Stigler (1957).

10. http://www.nemi.org/roadmapping.

11. Nasscom is India's software services industry association.

2. Indicators of Decline

Sooner or later, we sit down to a banquet of consequences

Robert Louis Stevenson

Developing and using technology requires considerable investment of several types. Understanding the broad trends in savings and investment is, therefore, essential, even though much of the flow does not involve technology directly. As the first section of this chapter demonstrates, the US economy is being threatened by excessive consumption. One of the negative manifestations of this imbalance is increasing dependency on foreign sources of capital to finance domestic investment. Although this macroeconomic issue is seldom discussed in S&T policy arenas, it is extremely important for long-term R&D and technology assimilation investment trends.

In the globalization of the late 19th century, surplus savings in Europe financed investment opportunities in the United States. As befitting the richest country in the world at the time, the UK averaged a current-account surplus of 5 percent of GDP between 1880 and 1914. Such flows from rich countries with abundant capital to developing ones with meager capital and hence greater rate-of-return potential are what economic text books predict. However, the US economy with its current-account deficit around 6 percent of GDP is a partner in a reverse flow of capital that is inhibiting US public investment in future growth, including technology-based growth.[1]

THE ENVIRONMENT FOR TECHNOLOGY INVESTMENT

If a patient terrorist set out to devise the optimal long-term strategy to bring down the US economy, a better plan could not be conceived than the promotion of record budget and trade deficits manifested in excessive consumption. The result has been a national savings rate that hovers around zero. The 2006 World Economic Forum, which ranks the competitiveness of the world's economies, lowered the US position from first to sixth, primarily because of mediocre scores for its public finances. The consequence is underinvestment in economic assets.

Among alternative investments, technology is one of the most volatile and risky. Investment in technology development and deployment therefore requires access to risk capital. Yet, the macroeconomic savings and investment environment is all but ignored in S&T policy circles. In this arena, the case for greater investment in R&D is asserted without considering the broader context of the national supply of savings that provides the funds for such investment. Further, this policy community gives little attention to the need to balance R&D investment with the requirement for adequate funds to assimilate and use the new technologies resulting from the R&D.

However, the macroeconomic stabilization policy apparatus (the Treasury and the Federal Reserve Board) gives inadequate attention to the economy's long-term investment needs. This segmented government policy structure negatively affects industry's demand for technology investment (both R&D and subsequent deployment).

In the private sector, industry's investment decision making weighs competing uses of retained earnings, including development, production and marketing of existing technologies. Retained earnings have been shown to be the dominant source of funding for most corporate R&D; thus, the collective corporate balance sheet is a critical factor in funding private-sector R&D. Further, for smaller firms that often must supplement retained earnings for investment purposes, the cost of external financing is an important influence. These determinants of private technology investment are affected by stabilization and other policies.

Budget and current-account deficits, interest on the national debt, entitlements and competing major spending programs collectively have an adverse effect on S&T policy. That is, excesses in these other areas of government policy constrain allocations to public support for R&D and the assimilation of new technology.

The Savings and Investment Imbalance

No one argues with the proposition that investment is the critical determinant of long-term growth. However, the optimal amount and composition of investment is inadequately addressed. In the 1990s, recognition of the growing dominance of communications and other information technologies led to a large influx of foreign investment into the US economy where many of these technologies originated. In the current decade, however, globalization of technology-based manufacturing and services has directed increasing amounts of investment elsewhere. At the same time, the surge in worldwide economic growth has created an increasing level of global savings. As an example, global pension, insurance and mutual-fund assets under management were estimated at $46 trillion in 2004, up a third from

The Economics of Decline

2000 (International Financial Services, London).

However, the US economy is the antithesis of this trend, with an aggregate national savings rate that actually became negative by mid-decade.[2] As indicated in Figure 2.1, the United States has the highest consumption rate among leading economies. In stark contrast, emerging Asian economies save at extremely high rates, for example, approximately 30–35 percent in India

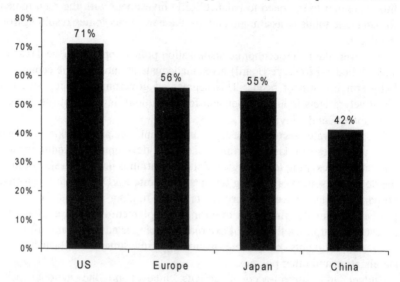

Source: Morgan Stanley Equity Research.

Figure 2.1 Comparative Consumption Shares of GDP

and 40–50 percent in China (Roach, 2007). Yet, growing consumption in these large economies and the fact that their continued fast rates of growth will draw down on these savings means that the debt-ridden US economy's need to import ever-larger amounts of foreign savings over time will eventually run into the proverbial brick wall.

The history of financial markets offers an additional insight into these trends. In 1913, the UK was the world's largest creditor. Within 40 years, after two costly world wars and economic mismanagement, it became a net debtor and the dollar replaced the pound as the international reserve currency. Today, the dollar is in the process of losing its status as the sole reserve currency for exactly the same reasons: costly wars and, most important, economic mismanagement. Following the same pattern as the UK, the US economy was the largest creditor nation after World War II and until 1989 it was still a net creditor. Since then, its foreign debtor status has mushroomed to the point that US net foreign debt is approaching 30 percent of GDP.[3]

Unfortunately, global imbalances have allowed the apostles of denial to fantasize away the inevitable collision with reality. Central banks, especially in Asian countries like China, Korea, and Japan, have been willing to absorb increasing amounts of US debt. In fact, they have done so as part of deliberate economic growth strategies that respond to their own domestic high savings rates (and hence inadequate consumption). Buying US debt keeps the major source of global consumption – US consumers and their government – financially afloat.

Japan, which has been mired in more than a decade-long economic slump, has indirectly provided a huge amount of capital to the US economy by keeping their domestic interest rates near zero. Intermediaries use these largely costless funds to buy higher-yielding investments, such as US debt (the so-called 'carry trade'). China's growth strategy is dominated by exports and export-oriented fixed-asset domestic investment. These two sectors now account for more than 85 percent of Chinese GDP and continue to grow at nearly a 30 percent annual rate. By contrast, the Chinese consumption share of GDP reached a record low of 42 percent in 2004. This dependency on exports induces China to maintain an artificially low exchange rate with the dollar to leverage their export-led growth model. Currently, 35–40 percent of Chinese exports go to the United States (Roach, 2005).

Developing countries can justify running international payments deficits because they have immature economies and therefore cannot internally finance the domestic investments necessary to industrialize and accelerate their growth rates. A developed economy can get away with payments deficits when structural change or adaptation to evolving world economic conditions is needed on a major scale. However, when such borrowing is used primarily to increase consumption over long periods of time, the end result is not pretty. From the mid-1980s, US consumption has been supported by an ever-increasing mountain of debt. The national debt doubled in just 15 years (from about $4 trillion in 1992 to an estimated $9 trillion in 2007).

For most of the past 100 years, the ratio of credit market debt to GDP stayed in a fairly narrow band of 140–160 percent of GDP. However, two decades of explosive growth has increased this ratio to stratospheric levels that exceeded 300 percent by the end of 2004, as shown dramatically in Figure 2.2. The only other spike of this magnitude was during the Great Depression when the ratio reached 287 percent in 1933. However, this earlier spike was due to a precipitous 33 percent drop in GDP, rather than an increase in debt, which is driving the current spike.

This spasm of relentless debt accumulation is all the more serious because foreigners now supply 40 percent of new borrowing by the US economy.

Demand by foreigners for new US debt will be affected by alternative global investment opportunities, exchange rates and expectations for currency trends. None of these factors is exhibiting favorable trends.

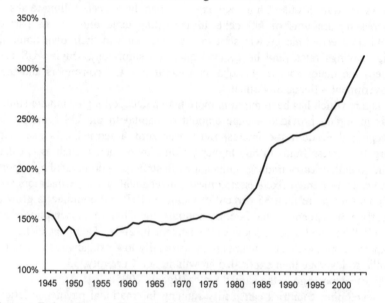

Sources: Federal Reserve Board and Bureau of Economic Analysis.

Figure 2.2 Total Credit Market Debt Relative to GDP, 1945–2004

The expanding US debt cannot continue. No individual, company, or national economy can get away indefinitely with deteriorating balance sheets. The current account deficit reached 5.5 percent of GDP in 2004 and stayed in this range for the next two years. Such levels historically have triggered currency crises. In fact, the dollar has been in decline during this period. The important point for long-term investment in technology is the fact that a declining currency leads to inflation and increases in interest rates. Higher rates raise the cost of investment and a depreciated currency raises the cost of imports, thereby reducing pressures on domestic firms to restrain price increases.

By 2004, private investors around the world were beginning to show reluctance to accumulate more US debt of any type. Foreign central banks are increasingly diversifying their currency reserves. In mid decade, a number of countries, including China, Russia and South Korea, announced plans to diversify their foreign currency reserves, which was a nice way of saying that they planned to slow or stop accumulating dollar reserves.

In the 1980s and again in the current decade, supply-side economics has rationalized large budget deficits by asserting that lower taxes (one major cause of the deficits) will stimulate the economy to grow and therefore so will the tax base, with the result that the deficit cures itself. The fatal flaw in both philosophies is that true supply-side growth strategies must be investment driven and deficit spending does not guarantee an emphasis on investment.

The Composition of Investment

While incentives for aggregate domestic investment are clearly important for long-term economic growth, so are incentives directed at specific categories of investment. These incentives are implemented primarily through tax laws and affect private-sector investment over long periods. For example, in 1996 the government changed the tax treatment of real-estate capital gains to favor investment in housing. With a few exceptions, it is now virtually impossible to pay capital gains taxes on a real-estate sale. Moreover, housing is the only

Source: Federal Reserve Flow of Funds Accounts, Table B.100; Bureau of Economic Analysis, NIPA Table 1.5.1.

Figure 2.3 Household Real Estate Assets as a Share of GDP

investment for which the interest on borrowed funds is tax deductible. An added incentive is the deductibility of property taxes from personal income subject to tax. So, if an asset class is both tax preferred on its sale and tax preferred on its holding period, funds will flow out of other asset categories and into the favored asset class.

Of course, that is exactly what has happened, as indicated in Figure 2.3. Real estate accounts for the largest share of household assets at approximately 30 percent. Only toward the end of the stock-market bubble in the late 1990s did household financial equity temporarily exceed real-estate assets. This situation was quickly corrected by the Fed's aggressive monetary policy. By 2004, American households owned approximately $14 trillion in real estate, which was almost double their total financial equity holdings and also a rapidly rising share of GDP. This trend in real-estate assets as a share of GDP is shown dramatically in Figure 2.3 and is a response to this set of strong incentives. The multiple tax incentives that create a bias for allocation of household assets toward real estate at the expense of other forms of savings that finance investments in productive capacity have a negative long-term impact on growth.

As discussed at length in later chapters, investment by government is an increasingly critical variable in long-term competitiveness in the emerging global economy. However, Figure 2.4 shows that this category of national

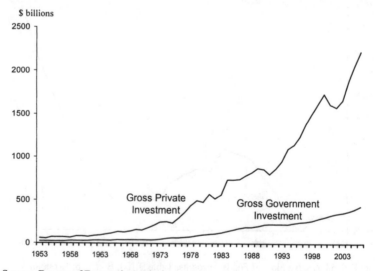

Source: Bureau of Economic Analysis.

Figure 2.4 Public and Private US Domestic Investment Trends, 1953–2006

investment has grown much more slowly than private investment. Thus, the problems for domestic growth policy are (i) the amount of domestic investment that will take place in the future and (ii) its composition.

To some extent, the higher growth rate of private-sector investment reflects the growth of the dynamic and highly successful private-market economy growth model that the United States pioneered. In fact, the US growth model has come to be viewed as so strongly private-sector dependent that only recently has a public–private technology-based growth paradigm begun to be discussed among significant numbers of economists and policy makers.

This very slow progress in overcoming denial persists, in spite of the ascendancy of the Japanese economy in the 1980s, the steady restructuring of the EU, and more recently the high growth rates of a number of Asian economies – all of which have benefited from substantial public investment. Even though a consensus on the complete growth model does not yet exist, these other countries have forged ahead. They have been willing to experiment with various growth strategies, including many forms of partnerships with industry, and thereby learn by doing.

Ironically, the United States has thrived on a public–private technology-based economic growth strategy for the entire post-World War II period – without admitting and hence understanding that this is the case. In fact, government investment was responsible for the early development of most major technologies driving the US economy today. Coupled with a broadly accessible public education system, such investment in breakthrough technologies has been one of the main drivers of US economic supremacy.[4] Today, however, only some state governments seem willing to experiment with ways of updating the original model.

Without doubt, US corporations have been the main agent for developing market applications of breakthrough technologies. Yet as Figure 1.4 indicates, domestic companies on average did not benefit as much relative to labor. For the first 40 years after World War II, the fact that the US economy owned most of the world's technology assets and much of its skilled labor meant that it had relatively little competition in most industries. Thus, labor was able to form strong unions and extract large and regular pay increases. In R&D-intensive industries, lifetime employment philosophies and the ability to price aggressively led to little resistance to substantial pay gains for technically oriented employees and minimal attention to overall cost containment. As a result, corporate profits' share of GDP declined for decades.

Beginning in the mid-1980s, three factors have been at work to reverse the negative relative performance of US industry (Figure 1.4). First, increasing foreign competition in manufacturing followed by services began to restrain domestic labor wage gains. Second, the shift to a service-based economy increased corporate profits, both due to greater use of productivity-enhancing information technologies and the relative insulation of this sector from foreign competition. Third, global competition meant that US companies' business models had to respond to mounting competitive pressures. They did this by moving first production and then R&D to other economies, which reduced unit labor costs and thereby boosted profits.

However, no matter how cash rich domestic companies are, if the government sector is investment deficient (Figure 2.4), the 'complementary-asset economy' model predicts lower returns for private investment within the domestic economy. Clearly, if investment opportunities become more attractive in other economies, major outflows of resources will occur with resulting loss of domestic income and employment.

It was once the case that outward investors were mainly looking for sources of raw materials to supply domestic operations. Today, however, more and more outward investment goes into not just materials and conventional manufacturing, but also into high-tech manufacturing and services. The OECD estimates that in 2005 foreign direct investment (FDI) by OECD countries reached $622 billion, a 27 percent increase over the previous year.[5] For the global economy, annual FDI most certainly passed $1 trillion.[6]

OFFSHORE OUTSOURCING

The third of the above three factors affecting corporate shares of GDP, offshoring, has become a defining characteristic of the current convergence process. Unfortunately, the offshore outsourcing of increasing amounts of high-value-added economic activity means that a growing proportion of corporate profits is being generated outside the domestic economy. In fact, BEA data show that profits of US corporations earned in the United States increased 7 percent in 2004, while US profits generated in the rest of the world grew by 26 percent.

The Outdated Law of Comparative Advantage

An economic historian might be puzzled by the shock and dismay over offshore outsourcing expressed by workers and their representatives in Congress because ever since trading between nations began around 3,000 years ago (that's 30 centuries), jobs have shifted among trading partners in response to the emergence of new comparative advantages. Conventional economic theory states that this is a good situation for the global economy because all nations invest more resources in the economic activities in which they are relatively more efficient.

For some time, such relative advantages were concentrated primarily in natural resources (arable land, minerals). Over the past three centuries, differences in manufacturing capabilities have driven shifts in investment. Today, services and knowledge capital have become increasingly important targets of resource reallocation.

The aggregate effect on US competitiveness of shifts in comparative advantage in manufacturing is shown dramatically in Figure 1.3, which depicts not only the large and still escalating trade deficit in goods generally but also the emergence of a deficit in the high-tech product portion of this trade. Thus, even if resource allocation across economies in response to changing comparative advantage is a good thing because overall global economic efficiency increases, at the very least the transition is not pleasant for many workers and businesses. For the US economy, those connected with less-productive industries point to the estimated 3 million manufacturing jobs lost between 2000 and 2004 as a sign of serious deterioration in competitive position.

During this same period, productivity has grown above trend. Defenders of a *laissez-faire* approach to global resource allocation point to this fact as proof that the traditional law of comparative advantage is working. In fact, the above-trend productivity growth in the current decade is to a significant extent the result of offshoring of labor-intensive and lower-value-added production, which, in turn, is yielding cheaper imports from converging economies. Most job losses are then due to the predicted reallocation of resources to economies with comparative advantages in using these resources.

However, as more economies create competitive (absolute) advantages in technology-based, high-value-added industries and shift resources into those areas, the remaining economies that are standing still find themselves shifted into lower-value-added sectors.[7] Thus, although global efficiency is increased, some countries gain and others lose. Although this may have always been the case to some degree, such impacts took place more slowly and were less widely distributed than is the case today.

In ignoring the likelihood of a 'winners and losers' outcome, the apostles of denial characterize the resulting US unemployment as 'frictional', assuming that it is only temporary until new jobs appear in more capital-intensive and technology-intensive sectors. That is, the increasingly strong assumption is that new absolute technological advantages will be created in the domestic economy (as opposed to in another economy).

A somewhat more sophisticated version of this argument is that even though investment in technology frequently increases the capital intensity of manufacturing processes that remain in the domestic economy, thereby extending 'temporary' unemployment, the net efficiency gain should eventually increase the number of jobs as the narrower focus on select competitive assets yields increases in sales and profits. Equally important, expanded volume based on more-focused and technology-driven investment causes a derived demand for more skilled and hence higher-paid labor.

This second version of a more dynamic law of comparative advantage is certainly feasible. However, for the first time, all economies are pursuing the same general strategy of creating new technology-based advantages rather than following the traditional mechanism of responding to existing differences in relative efficiency and, in some cases, accepting declining relative economic welfare. In fact, the National Association of Manufacturing points out that manufacturing employment has shrunk in all countries, even in China, as competitors create or adopt new automated processing technologies. In other words, many economies are pursuing approximately the same absolute advantages in manufacturing technology, which makes establishing and maintaining any competitive advantage, especially a large one, increasingly difficult.

The amount of diffusion and especially the speed of diffusion are likely to be greater among industrialized nations due to greater absorptive capacity. For this reason, most outsourcing of R&D by global companies is still to other technology-based economies. However, the technology imperative is clearly driving emerging economies and some of them are already making substantial advances in markets for advanced technology products previously the province of the traditional industrialized nations.

A rationalization for not being concerned about the loss of markets for manufactured goods is that advanced economies are becoming largely service-based and that such a shift is solving the unemployment problem. This view is exemplified in a 2006 report from the US–China Business Council, a trade group of primarily large companies doing business in China.[8] The Council argues that 'the long-term benefits' of US trade with China 'are substantial and likely to endure' and 'the projected loss of 500,000 manufacturing jobs over the next four years' due to outsourcing to China 'will be made up by the gain of 500,000 service sector jobs.' In summary, the US–China Business Council argues that 'the overall impact should be a continuing and increasingly positive boost to US output, productivity, employment and real wages.'

In following the traditional view of the law of comparative advantage, the Council is assuming that the negative effects on demand for US-produced goods will be overcome by productivity gains on the supply side, which lead to higher output, income and employment. The assertion is that a positive comparative advantage shift occurs in the outsourcing economy. That is, the static model assumes that (i) untapped resources exist that are both available or easily made available after a short transition period, and (ii) these resources are at least as productive after reallocation as the ones offshored. Under these assumptions, equal- or better-paying jobs will quickly be created to replace those lost. This is the win-win version of the law of comparative advantage.

The problem with this model in today's global economy is that the 'supply-side effects' are being changed at increasing rates by countries applying the public–private technology-based growth paradigm. For example, the assertion by the US–China Business Council that service jobs will automatically replace lost manufacturing jobs ignores the potentially negative impact of rapidly increasing capabilities in high-tech services by other economies (for example, Ireland, India and other countries' ascendancy in software). That is, the compensating shift into existing, relatively more productive economic assets that has taken place in the past when other assets were outsourced is now increasingly suppressed and truncated by aggressive technology-based economic growth strategies in competing economies. The degree and speed with which this process of global asset creation takes place depends on the number and effectiveness of other economies' growth policies. And, once established, the more effectively structured and managed processes by which these policies produce competing assets also eventually produce new and even more productive assets.

Most important for economic growth policy is the newly emerged paradigm in which economic assets – existing and new – are subject to manipulation by governments. Because industrialized economies are not about to accept lower salaries and wages to retain advantage in traditional industries, the only long-term investment strategy is to produce and use new technology at a faster rate than competing economies. Thus, in an era of globalization, if the requisite public and private investments in new technologies and the ability to assimilate and use them are not forthcoming, the domestic economy cannot adapt. That is, it no longer can draw upon resources created in the past because they have become obsolete. New industries and jobs will not magically appear as implied by past growth models.

In the face of this reality, the only remaining recourse for the apostles of denial is to argue that comparative advantages really have not shifted. Rather, it is asserted that trade barriers are blocking the realization of existing advantages. Thus, a number of trade-related factors are seized upon, such as misaligned exchange rates, technical barriers to trade, goods counterfeiting and intellectual property theft, as the causes of long-term trade imbalances. In addition, the 'superiority' of the American economy and hence its higher consumption capacity is asserted as a major explanation of the trade deficit.

These trade barriers are real problems and should be addressed, but even collectively they do not determine long-term comparative advantage. Trade impacts are increasing relentlessly for all countries, and comparative advantages will shift over time primarily based on relative innovative capacity. Morgan Stanley estimates that, in the 1987–2004 period, the expansion of global trade accounted for 35 percent of the cumulative growth in world GDP – essentially double the 17 percent share in the 1974–86 period (Roach, 2005). Thus, the undeniable fact of economic growth is that if the value added lost to the domestic economy due to offshore outsourcing is not replaced by new domestic comparative advantages, domestic growth slows and can even come to a halt.

So far, the maintained hypothesis has been that newly created jobs must be superior to the ones lost or the standard of living fails to improve. In other words, while trade does allow comparative advantages to be realized and thereby global economic efficiency to increase as traditional economic theory predicts, the other undeniable fact is that such shifts are today more volatile and produce both winners and losers with greater frequency. Thus, while individual companies can benefit from offshore outsourcing, the domestic economy in which they are headquartered is often not so fortunate.

Strategic Issues in Global Markets

Creating competitive advantage in a technology takes considerable time. An example is biotechnology. For a century, the US pharmaceutical industry prospered by discovering new drugs following a 'faith-based' model where numerous compounds were screened by chemists to achieve the end goal: a marketable drug. Pursuing this goal was guided largely by intuition acquired through experience.

With the deciphering of the human genome and the emergence of associated techniques such as recombinant DNA, a radically new paradigm for drug development emerged in the late 1970s. In this science-based approach, the structure and function of the development target was largely known (in contrast to the traditional approach of looking for a compound that 'worked' by trial and error). Over the ensuing 30 years, this drug-discovery paradigm has evolved as the basis for the increasingly dominant biotechnology industry (Conway, 2005).

The economic policy issue arises from the fact that most biotechnology firms are not yet profitable and depend on partnerships with traditional pharmaceutical companies to finance clinical trials and/or market newly approved drugs, while at the same time, many other countries are now nurturing domestic biotechnology industries. Europe has an established pharmaceutical industry, which to some degree at least can provide the same complementary assets to an infant biotechnology industry as is the case in the United States. For example, in Ireland, once a country hallmarked by unemployment and emigration, most of the major pharmaceutical companies now have a presence, along with over 200 biotech and related companies. The Irish government has established a €2.5 billion ($3.45 billion) fund for a five-year program targeted largely toward biotechnology supplemented by a venture-capital fund to support start-up companies. Finland has 110 biotech companies in the Helsinki region alone. The Sixth European Framework Program targeted €2.25 billion ($3.10 billion) for genomics and health-care research. Asian governments are putting substantial funding into biotechnology research infrastructures to attract foreign researchers and intellectual capital. Singapore has become the leader in Asia, generating $16 billion in sales of biomedical science-based products in 2005.

Because of its sizable lead in biotechnology, it is the US economy's competitive advantage to lose. But, other countries are not willing to concede US dominance and allocate resources to other technologies, as the traditional law of comparative advantage implies. Instead, they are aggressively striving to converge and then create innovative capability in various segments of this emerging industry. A major component of these strategic thrusts is the provision of incentives to foreign technology leaders to move investment to the local economies.

In response to such strategies, the potential for reallocation of corporate resources across national borders is increasing. Globalization is extending beyond simply the pursuit of additional markets and access to low-cost manufacturing and services. It includes opportunities to conduct R&D, including breakthrough technology research, at an increasing number of locations around the world. This means that it is not only value added at the manufacturing and marketing stages of economic activity that is moving offshore, but the sources of knowledge creation that formerly occurred mainly in the United States and Europe are rapidly diffusing globally as well.

The PC industry is a classic example. Originally an American monopoly from components to finished product, the PC is now truly international in terms of value added. A Hewlett-Packard Pavilion may still be designed in terms of performance specifications in the United States, but its hard disk drive is more likely to be made in Japan, China, or Singapore than in US plants. Its power supply and magnesium casing come from China. While memory chips are still manufactured in the United States, they are increasingly likely to be supplied by Korea, Taiwan, or Germany. Virtually all liquid-crystal displays (LCDs) are made in Asia (South Korea, Taiwan, Japan or China). Graphic processors are still designed in the United States or Canada but are manufactured in Taiwan. Only the microprocessor market remains under US control (Dean and Tam, 2005).

These components must then be assembled into the final product. This last step has been offshored for some time. The HP Pavilion is assembled from components obtained from all over the world by Quanta Computer Inc. (a Taiwanese company) in Shanghai, China.

Does this distribution of value added make a difference? Well, it depends on one's perspective. Business consulting firms such as the Boston Consulting Group are outspoken in support of globalization of both R&D and production. To a corporation, it makes little difference whether it outsources R&D to a network of domestic or foreign firms. It is simply trying to make rational decisions with respect to the most efficient strategies for acquiring needed technology.

The larger and more diverse are the capabilities of firms making up such networks, the greater is the speed and efficiency of technology and subsequent product development. Thus, global networks should be more efficient than single-economy ones, even large economies like the United States, as high-quality research capacity becomes more prevalent around the world.

However, from a domestic economic policy point of view, outsourcing in response to changes in comparative advantage poses a major threat. The new supplier in another country gains experience through performance of its value-added activity. The resulting learning curve progression enables growing capability for expansion into adjacent value-added activities in that supply chain. Thus, a negligent domestic industry and a negligent supporting domestic technical infrastructure often wake up one day and find that the value added from domestic firms has been 'hollowed out' to the point that domestic profits and employment have declined precipitously.

How much of the value added by PCs accrues inside the US economy? Obviously, only a small fraction of that from the components plus the marketing activities of domestic PC firms, such as HP and Dell. And, while the US economy is experiencing the largest economic losses from offshore outsourcing due to its size and long-standing pre-eminent position as the world's technology leader, this process is accelerating everywhere. Taiwan may be a leading supplier of memory chips and LCDs, but its assembly operations are increasingly outsourced to China.

Because the US economy is still the single largest in the world, US companies are able to retain some control of the supply chain. In technology-based markets such as PCs, design is a critical competitive attribute. However, as the percentage of value added moves relentlessly elsewhere, even large companies like HP and Dell must fight to control design, especially at the component level. US companies that have ceded virtually all but marketing to the global PC supply chain survive only as long as the US market is still dominant.

However, with less than 5 percent of the world's population, current marketing leadership is destined to erode. Even when the US company maintains titular control over design, this activity and hence its value added increasingly is moving to the other country to be near the manufacturing operation. For example, Dell set up a design center in Taiwan in 2002 with

50 people. By 2006, the facility had grown to 330 employees (Lee, 2006).

The characteristics of convergence become more pronounced as major technology life cycles mature. The US economy – the innovator of most major technologies currently driving the global economy – is therefore suffering the most as this process of convergence evolves. Even more threatening, radically new technologies that perform the same marketplace functions more efficiently than the existing ones will appear, and new cycles will start. The innovators in these new technology life cycles will reap the large early rewards from being first movers of new major technology life cycles. Increasingly, these first movers will be in different countries from the innovators of the previous life cycle, which means the United States.

There are several ironies in this debate over outsourcing. One is that lower-skilled manufacturing jobs will increasingly be done by robots and by highly flexible and automated production lines, while an increasing number of service jobs will be done by computers. Many of the jobs in these two categories are currently outsourced. Thus, lower-skilled jobs will continue to be lost no matter where they are located. Jobs requiring face-to-face contact to iterate job requirements and performance are probably relatively safe for the foreseeable future, but production and clerical jobs – ones that are increasingly being outsourced – will be increasingly automated (Levy and Murnane, 2004). A second irony is that no one in the US economy complained when jobs were being insourced at a high rate. During the 1980s and 1990s, foreign manufacturers in industries such as automobiles set up numerous factories in the United States, bringing many jobs to the domestic economy. Inflows of R&D via domestic affiliates of foreign-owned companies were similarly impressive. That is, insourcing was a significant contributor to domestic economic growth.

Third, in a growing economy that is creating new, higher-paying jobs, the loss of low-paying jobs should be welcomed. This condition unfortunately only applies to economies that are creating new, higher-paying jobs to replace the ones lost. The US economy is not doing this, thus the angst over job losses. More disturbing is that even some categories of medium- and higher-paying jobs are being outsourced because of the rapid global convergence that is increasingly technology driven. Finally, the fourth irony is that many industries today have relatively low labor content. Thus, other economic assets will be more important in the future in determining which countries attain comparative advantage in those industries. As President Ronald Reagan once said, 'There are those who make it happen, those who let it happen, and those who wonder what happened'. The first of these increasingly applies to countries other than the United States.

CORPORATE R&D STRATEGY SHIFTS

In response to globalization, corporate R&D strategies have changed in a number of significant ways that have profound implications for economic growth policy. In the mid-1970s, US firms began to realize that competitors in other countries, with the support of their governments, were acquiring R&D and technology assimilation capabilities. US industry responded by substantially increasing the rate of growth in R&D spending. For example, in the six-year period from 1969 to 1975, the average annual real growth in industry R&D spending was 1.7 percent. In the next six-year period, 1975–81, the average annual real increase jumped to 7.7 percent, and from 1981 to 2004 it was 8.8 percent.

However, the same pressures that have led to increased total R&D spending by US industry have also resulted in shifts in composition of R&D with negative implications for long-term competitiveness. These shifts are a

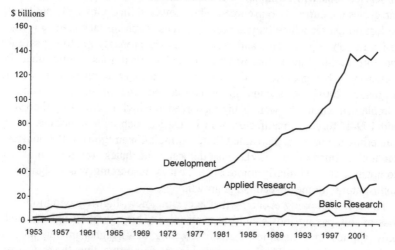

Source: NSF, *National Patterns of R&D Resources.*

Figure 2.5 Composition of Industry-Funded R&D by Major Phase, 1953–2004 (billions of 2000 dollars)

response to shorter technology life cycles caused by increasing foreign competition. As a result, most of the increase in industry R&D spending was for development, as indicated in Figure 2.5. The strategic goal has been to maintain market shares within existing life cycles.

Another result of the increasing technological capabilities of other economies is the steadily increasing offshoring of R&D. NSF data on global R&D investment make the direction of these trends abundantly clear.

Between 1994 and 2002, R&D spending by majority-owned foreign affiliates (MOFAs) of US multinational companies (MNCs) grew more than 50 percent faster (9.8 percent average annual rate) than that of their US parents (6.3 percent).

Incentives to Outsource R&D

The globalization of what for decades was largely a US monopoly – R&D capability – is now rapidly expanding in many nations. Because of their large collective size, these nations are attaining significant shares of global MNC R&D investment. In 2005 alone, Intel ($1 billion), Cisco Systems ($1.1 billion) and Microsoft ($1.7 billion) announced major multi-year investments in just one emerging economy, India. Approximately three quarters of these investments were for R&D.

There are two reasons for investing in R&D overseas: (i) to support local market strategies and (ii) to acquire technical knowledge. NSF's *Science and Engineering Indicators 2004* describes these two strategic motivations as 'market seeking' and 'asset seeking'. The second is the worrisome category because rising foreign investment for the purpose of acquiring R&D assets implies an increasingly attractive environment to conduct 'R' overseas. A more 'attractive environment' includes superior talent and, as Cherry Murray, senior vice-president of Lucent Technologies' Bell Labs, put it, 'the world's best talent doesn't necessarily come to the US'.[9]

Corporate strategy determines what a company does to succeed in the marketplace and how it goes about doing it. Its shareholders and board of directors demand that this strategy be conceived and executed at a high level. If the company succeeds in doing so, it grows and produces income for its shareholders and jobs for the economies in which it invests.

But here is the major growth policy concern: companies have an increasing number of options with respect to countries in which they can profitably conduct R&D. Thus, to devise a successful strategy for dealing with global convergence of all three stages of economic activity – marketing, production, and, finally, R&D – the convergence sequence and the motivations for the distribution of corporate investment among converging economies need to be analyzed and appropriate policy responses adopted.

In the period following World War II, the dominant technology-based industries led by those located in the domestic US economy developed and produced sophisticated products and then marketed them to customers around the world. Part of the marketing effort typically has included providing technical support in the local market to teach customers how to use and maintain these products. As an export market expands, local suppliers in the target economy are usually required in order to reduce costs and service local demand more efficiently.

China's semiconductor industry is an example of this convergence process. Its domestic market reached $25 billion in 2003, with annual growth rates in the 15–20 percent range. Increased domestic capacity is needed to feed efficiency-enhancing vertical integration with its expanding consumer electronics industries that use a huge number of semiconductors. Chinese manufacturers produce an increasing variety of electronic products, including PCs, cellular phones, flat panel displays, digital cameras, and DVD players. In fact, by 2005, China was the third-largest semiconductor market in the world and is projected to become the second largest by 2010. In that same year, it became the largest exporter of IT products. Domestically, China is already the world's largest mobile phone market and second-largest PC market (Scalise, 2005b).

Critical to understanding the process of convergence and its long-term impact is the fact that a company exporting into a foreign market of any size must at some point establish manufacturing operations in that country. Such a step includes a local laboratory to provide technical support for the manufacturing operation. Over time, larger sales and closer customer relationships create opportunities to adapt product design to the particular needs of the local market. Eventually, demand differentiation in this market results in a transformation of the laboratory's role from the initial focus on tactical support to strategic new product and service development. And, while this process is evolutionary, it is taking place relatively rapidly.

As part of this transformation, the expanding laboratory begins to support research in local universities and partner with domestic companies. The hiring of domestic scientists and engineers further increases the range and depth of partnerships. Large and fast-growing economies like China can offer foreign companies a substantial and growing R&D infrastructure with which to interact. In fact, a number of US companies now regard their Chinese laboratories as 'equal partners' in the development of technology platforms, as well as products and services. Several of these labs have come to be viewed by their parent American companies as having unique competences, unmatched by company labs located elsewhere.[10]

As one example, Chinese semiconductor manufacturers have been recognized as a growing force in world markets for a number of years. However, more surprising and perhaps more important for an assessment of shifts in long-term competitive position is the fact that in 2005 Chinese chip-design work was estimated to account for 14.8 percent of the global market, just behind the second-largest source of chip design, Japan, at 15.5 percent of the world's total and ahead of the fourth-largest chip designer, Taiwan, which had a 10.1 percent share.[11] One Chinese semiconductor firm, Vimicro, holds some 400 patents and is the world's leading supplier of PC camera chips (Silverthorne, 2005).

In summary, this backward integration in the Chinese semiconductor industry to include a substantial share of design work is being driven by the rapid double-digit growth rate of the domestic market for semiconductor devices (approximately $40 billion in 2004, which is about one-fifth of the world's semiconductor market), the emergence of skilled design engineers, and simply the desire to move up the value-added ladder. The next and final step in the convergence process is to become a world class exporter.

An important point for policy analysis is the mistaken belief that decisions to offshore R&D operations are largely a matter of cost. In fact, multiple factors contribute to R&D location decisions. The most important factors are market-growth opportunities, quality of R&D talent, collaboration with universities, and intellectual property protection. Of these, collaboration with universities is a particularly relevant factor for expanding into emerging economies, even though these countries provide lesser degrees of intellectual property protection (Thursby and Thursby, 2006). Cost was not identified as a major decision factor.

Similarly, complaints in the United States with respect to rapid expansion of semiconductor manufacturing in Asia focus on lower labor costs and tax and funding subsidies. However, in advanced manufacturing industries, automation has reduced labor costs as a percentage of total cost. The Semiconductor Industry Association (SIA) estimates that Chinese government policies, not lower labor costs, are the major contributor to a cost differential of $1 billion over 10 years for building and operating a semiconductor plant in China compared to the United States. About 70 percent of the cost difference is due to tax benefits, 20 percent is due to direct funding subsidies, and only 10 percent is attributable to lower labor costs (Scalise, 2005a).[12]

Even when substantial salary differentials appear, the resulting international shifts in resources bid up the cost of highly skilled labor in the emerging economy. For example, Romania's software industry has grown rapidly in the current decade, with major companies such as Microsoft, Alcatel, and Hewlett-Packard doing substantial business in that country. As a result, the salaries of Romanian programmers have risen rapidly and will soon approach such small discounts to those in Western economies that the existing competitive advantage will disappear.[13] The same narrowing of salary differentials appears to be occurring for software programmers in India. In general, therefore, labor costs – whether for R&D or high-tech production – will be a decreasing long-term factor in global resource allocation. Salaries for each category of skilled labor will move toward an average, and resource allocations will depend more on relative skills and other investment-inducing attributes across countries.

Asset-Dependent Investment Strategies

In Part Three, the key elements of a national strategy for technology-based competitiveness will be presented. One critical principle underlying such a strategy is that R&D investment is not as easily moved as are other categories of investment (production, marketing). This difference is due to R&D's dependency on a set of critical domestic infrastructures that are difficult to assemble and manage effectively. Once in place, however, these infrastructures attract foreign R&D investment as well as R&D funding from domestic sources.

The multiple asset character of R&D has meant that the erosion of the dominant US position has been sufficiently slow and uneven to allow the apostles of denial to argue that the current US research infrastructure is still far superior to that of the rest of the world. This contention is supported by fairly recent data. For example, the ratio of 2000 R&D spending by the MOFAs of US firms to the foreign employment and sales they generated was approximately half the domestic ratio of the parent companies and a little more than half the comparable ratio for R&D spending relative to gross product (value added). The reverse is the case for majority-owned US subsidiaries of foreign MNCs; they fund approximately twice the percentage of US domestic R&D relative to their percentage contribution to US employment and sales, as is the case in their home countries.

In other words, as of 2000, the relative R&D intensity of foreign affiliates operating in the US economy is greater than the R&D intensity of US affiliates in other economies. The implication is that the US research environment is relatively more attractive than other locations, in spite of the increased investment in research infrastructure by other countries. More generally, most international R&D investment flows are between industrialized nations where the majority of R&D capacity still resides. Thus, the anecdotes featured in the media with respect to R&D spending by US MNCs in developing nations (India, China, and so on) are currently an indicator of future impact.

As a result, it is still relatively easy to deny the warning signs of shifting R&D investment among industrialized nations and increasingly to developing economies. However, current distributions of foreign-owned R&D assets are a legacy of past investment in domestic R&D and, more broadly, innovative capacity. Global investment trends are decidedly in the direction of ever-wider diffusion of such capacity.

R&D employment trends reflect this legacy of past R&D investment strategies. NSF data (Moris, 2004) show that between 1994 and 2001, R&D-performing companies in the United States increased their R&D workforce at a faster rate than the growth of overall employment (38.8 percent versus

17.2 percent). US affiliates of foreign companies increased their R&D employment by almost the same rate (34.8 percent). This period approximates the emergence of the so-called 'New Economy' phenomenon, which has been characterized by high levels of investment in the development and use of information technology. Rapid acceleration of the National Institutes of Health (NIH) budget and the emergence of a biotechnology industry also contributed to the growth differential.

However, the same NSF analysis points to a trend that emphasizes the emerging process of globalization of R&D. R&D employment in US MNCs is still concentrated domestically, but during approximately the same period (1994–99) overseas affiliates of these MNCs increased their R&D workforce at a faster rate than their US parent companies did within the domestic economy (21.1 percent versus 6.0 percent). Increasingly, skilled scientists and engineers are available globally to enable such reallocation of resources, and this foreign technical human capital pool is increasing much more rapidly than in the United States. Because this subgroup of US firms is global in strategic scope, their lower domestic growth rate of R&D employment raises a warning flag with respect to the future.

Moreover, strategy shifts by large MNCs are particularly important because their R&D expenditures are proportionally much greater than their share of GDP. For the United States, the BEA points out that US MNC parent companies accounted for two-thirds of R&D spending by all industrial R&D performers in the United States in 2000 compared with about one-fifth of US industry's contribution to GDP in that year (National Science Board, 2004). Yet, it is this group of companies that is moving R&D offshore at a fast rate.

Although sometimes characterized otherwise, corporate managers, boards of directors and stockholders have loyalty toward the country in which their company was founded. Companies develop political and social preferences, which influence their corporate cultures and sense of comfort with political and social systems. However, the marketplace forces rule and a company must respond objectively and even ruthlessly or it will not survive. Craig Barrett said it best:

> As CEO of Intel, my allegiance is to the shareholders of Intel and to the success of the company. We go after the most cost-effective resources around the world, no matter where they are. As an American citizen, I would have to be worried about whether jobs are created outside the US . . . As a citizen, I see all these [foreign] resources and I think this puts my country in danger. (Heim, 2004)

Yet, the reality is that Intel is doing progressively more R&D and manufacturing in other countries. Ten percent of Intel's approximately $30 billion in annual sales now comes from production in China. The company has 2,400 employees in that country and is approaching $1 billion in total investment. Most important is the fact that Intel is moving increasingly sophisticated operations to China. The company has progressed from an initial assembly plant for data-storage chips in 1998 to plants producing more complex chip sets in 2001 to top-of-the-line Pentium microprocessors in 2002. Intel has invested in 30 Chinese startups and it runs three R&D labs working on next-generation product technologies.

In 2006, Intel announced a new architecture designed for its 64-bit microprocessors. The architecture will be used in all segments of its microprocessor business (for desktops, laptops and servers). However, this major advance was developed at Intel's two R&D centers in Israel. In response to co-location synergies between R&D and manufacturing described earlier in this chapter, Intel is building a $4 billion semiconductor manufacturing plant in Israel to implement the new technology. The Israeli government is subsidizing one eighth of the construction cost. Intel's combined R&D and manufacturing operations make it one of Israel's largest employers (6,700 workers) and the company accounts for 14 percent of that country's IT exports.

Intel describes its corporate strategy in terms of three major thrusts: product design, manufacturing and process development. The first two are increasingly distributed globally. So far, process development – probably the most critical for a mid- to late-cycle technology – remains entirely within the United States. Management explains this in terms of still superior domestic research assets and the need to protect critical intellectual property. However, this strategic area employs the fewest people of the three thrusts. And, of course, it is subject to eventual offshoring, if research assets elsewhere become superior and conditions such as intellectual property protection improve in target economies. Moreover, economic studies (for example, Thursby and Thursby, 2006) indicate that companies will offshore R&D, even to emerging economies where such protection is deemed inadequate, if attractive research infrastructure, particularly universities, are available for collaborative research.

Michael Marx, the CEO of Flextronics, one of the world's largest ODMs, estimates that 80 percent of engineers in product development do tasks that can be easily outsourced – like 'translating prototypes into workable designs, upgrading mature products, testing quality, writing user manuals, and qualifying parts vendors'. He also points out that most of the 'core' (generic) technologies in today's 'digital gadgets' are available to anyone (Engardio and Einhorn, 2005). In other words, by the mid- to late phase of a technology's life cycle, the generic technology assets upon which market applications (innovations) are based are frequently widely diffused. Today, such diffusion is global.

Intel means what it says when stating that it goes anywhere in the world where it can access the most cost-effective resources. To maintain flexibility to initiate large-scale production of new products in multiple foreign locations, the company has a 'copy exactly' strategy, which involves measurement-based quality control techniques that enable multiple plants in different countries to go to high-volume production simultaneously and shift production from one factory to another in response to local market demand or available capacity. The efficiency gain is not having to qualify each plant individually and thus most likely sequentially.

Companies rationalize domestic or foreign outsourcing based on cost savings and R&D cycle compression (up to 60 percent less time to get a product concept to market, according to some estimates). These companies also claim that outsourcing applied R&D and product engineering allows them to focus on the higher-value-added R&D (presumably the more disruptive and potentially more valuable next-generation or radically new technologies). Certainly, if core technologies are rapidly diffusing, thereby hastening technological convergence, focusing on being the innovator in the next technology life cycle is even more essential than in the past.

In fact, companies all over the world cannot be satisfied with relatively low-margin design and imitation strategies. Among other risks, such strategies leave them open to convergence by new competitors. Thus, technology-based companies face increasingly difficult strategic issues: (i) the range of technologies that may be applicable to solve a given problem is constantly expanding, which presents difficult R&D portfolio management problems; and (ii) the range of technical problems is expanding, arising from the growing complexity of technology. To some extent, these two trends explain the pressures on corporate management to retreat to core competences, that is, specialization in a few technologies where the firm hopefully has an advantage in understanding the underlying science and developing and applying derived generic technologies. Yet, such lack of diversification creates new risks.

Motorola is an example of the struggle to maintain competence in a select number of technologies and markets. In 2004, the company spun off its semiconductor unit (now Freescale Semiconductor). Such strategies are rationalized by the need to respond to a growing number of technologically competitive firms around the world in all markets and therefore the increasing R&D effort required to remain competitive in each market.

Focused corporate strategies can work, as long as innovation is the key driver. A strategic emphasis on innovation obviously requires R&D capability, even as the technology life cycle matures. Motorola basically invented the cell phone when it developed the world's first 'radiophone' in the 1970s. The company used its 'first-mover' advantage to become the dominant supplier. However, failure to react to emerging competition from Europe (Finland's Nokia) and Asia (Korea's Samsung and LG) led to a drastic demise in market share as the technology life cycle progressed.

But, adaptation is possible if a company has the necessary technology assets. By drawing upon its R&D capability and updating its business model to reduce production costs, Motorola once again gained a leadership position in 2005.[14] However, the window of opportunity to recover from strategic mistakes is steadily narrowing, as the average technology life cycle shrinks due to global convergence. In fact, Motorola failed to provide a timely successor to its ultra-thin Razor cell phone for the next product cycle and, by late 2006, the company's profit margins on cell phones narrowed and the company's overall income statement swung to a loss.

Shifting R&D and Market Strategies over the Technology Life Cycle

Both Nokia and Motorola – as do most large high-tech MNCs – now target emerging markets. The volume potential is huge. However, these markets also have lower price points, which put pressure on competitors to cut costs. Such a strategic imperative for competing on price reflects competitive requirements in the later phases of a technology's life cycle.

This does not mean that innovation stops, as the above example of Motorola underscores. But, cost-based strategies mean lower profit margins and eventually this trend dominates and sets up the entry of a new, disruptive technology. Ongoing efforts to maintain competitive positions in existing technology life cycles by all industrialized nations is evidenced by the fact that about two-thirds of R&D funded in the United States by foreign firms was in three large and maturing industry groups: chemicals and pharmaceuticals, electronics and computers, and transportation equipment. Interestingly, overseas R&D spending by US multinationals has been concentrated in the same three groups (National Science Board, 2004).

But, technological life cycles come to an end. Motorola and Nokia have succeeded largely based on internal innovation capabilities. Transitioning to the next life cycles based on new, disruptive technologies is a more complex strategic matter that increasingly involves multiple collaborations with public and other private institutions all over the world. Microsoft, for example, spent more than $750 million in China in 2002–03 on cooperative research, technology for schools, and other investments that enhance domestic innovative capacity. One objective certainly is to help ensure access to and ultimately attain significant shares of the huge Chinese market.

However, Microsoft also established an $80 million research center in Beijing that employs nearly 500 engineers, PhD students and visiting professors. The center is certainly not a market-entry payment for current technologies. It has become a key element in Microsoft's strategy to move company investment farther back in the R&D cycle and thereby develop new technology platforms in areas such as computer graphics, handwriting recognition and voice synthesizing. The ultimate objective is to become more innovative – that is, be a leading innovator in new technology life cycles. So far 72 innovations have been produced by the research center and incorporated into Microsoft products.[15]

Other large R&D-intensive companies are following the same strategy of acquiring the globally distributed research assets necessary to both manage the current life cycles and also be at the forefront of new ones. IBM has major corporate labs in China, Israel, Switzerland, Japan and India. General Electric (GE) has refocused on innovation as a corporate strategy by spending $100 million on upgrading the company's research center in Niskayuna, NY (Brady, 2005). However, the company has 27 research facilities in China working on projects from composite materials design to molecular modeling (Garten, 2005). GE also has cutting-edge research centers in Bangalore, India and Munich, Germany.

Trends in Corporate R&D Strategies that Require a Government Policy Response

From the above assessment of corporate R&D investment trends, a number of economic growth policy implications arise with respect to feasible company- and industry-level R&D strategies and the necessary government support:

1. *R&D Productivity:* A 2003 Boston Consulting Group survey of 236 senior executives across a wide range of industries in 30 countries identified innovation as a priority. Some 69 percent of these managers ranked innovation as a top-three priority and 64 percent planned to increase R&D spending in response to the technology imperative for competing in the global economy. However, 57 percent of the respondents stated dissatisfaction with the return on investment in innovation.[16] A Forrester Research Inc. study found a similar frustration with the productivity of R&D. Even more striking, data from the Dublin Group, a consultancy to high-tech firms, show a miniscule 4.5 percent success rate for R&D projects across all industries (success determined by firm-specified hurdle rates for acceptable rates of return). The implication is that increasing R&D productivity within the domestic economy will draw private investment.

2. *Global Distribution of R&D:* In spite of the enthusiastic support for global R&D networks among business consultants and the apparent initial

success by multinational firms who participate in them, managing such participation presents substantial challenges. Among them is efficient integration of the various parties contributing R&D assets to the network. Internal (to the firm) supplier units know well in advance what types of product are coming and can, therefore, work on developing the required process technologies. Extending such synergies to an external network is a more difficult task and requires an efficient supporting infrastructure. For example, Texas Instruments maintains its leading position in the $5 billion market for digital signal processing technology critical to mobile communications and consumer electronics by networking with around 100 IT-related companies all over the world. This disperses the value added from the R&D stage of economic activity that once would have been wholly contained within the domestic economy. Broader R&D incentives and supporting technical infrastructure in the domestic economy can repatriate at least some of this R&D activity.

3. *Intellectual Property Management:* Although technical knowledge does not flow freely around the world as many believe, foreign investment in domestic R&D facilities provides the host countries with prolonged and direct exposure to external sources of technology and research capabilities. Direct personal contact has been demonstrated by numerous studies to be the most effective way of diffusing technical knowledge, especially in the early phases of a technology's development. Realizing this, host countries provide incentives for FDI in R&D and, in some cases, require such investment as part of a deal with the foreign company to conduct business within their economies.

4. *Intellectual Property as a Tradable Asset:* Knowledge assets have become useful for negotiating cross-licensing agreements and serve as currency for buying into R&D collaborations. When large vertically integrated companies were more common and domestically focused, intellectual property rights were not a major issue. The central corporate lab developed the proofs of concept for new technologies and the lines of business absorbed this generic knowledge through internal tech transfer processes and then conducted the applied R&D to develop market applications (innovations). Today, however, the multi-faceted problem for a nation's innovation infrastructure is who creates, who owns, who uses this intellectual property, and therefore to what extent does the domestic economy benefit.

5. *R&D versus Technology Acquisition:* Many companies and their consultants have responded to the R&D efficiency issue by simply scouring the world for the right intellectual property and then purchasing it with the idea of adding value through complementary applied R&D.

6. *First-Mover Rationale:* An imitation strategy entails significant risk because it depends on the creativity of others who may license this intellectual property to competitors or use it themselves to produce competing innovations. Also, it stands to reason that the most valuable intellectual property will not be sold by its creator, constraining firms following a 'technology purchase' strategy to either attempt to compete with less valuable intellectual property or to pursue imitation/reverse engineering strategies. In the latter case, the technology may be acquired later in the life cycle than what is optimal. In summary, the strategy of outsourcing major components of a technology-based product to focus on one high-value-added component or simply be the system integrator leaves a company vulnerable to declining profits and significant barriers to remaining competitive in the next technology life cycle. This problem can be attenuated to an extent through measures to increase domestic R&D efficiency and thereby stimulate both greater amounts of R&D and more diversification of R&D portfolios.

7. *Amount and Stability of R&D Infrastructure Support:* An increasing challenge is sustainability of R&D support over the often lengthy gestation period required for emerging disruptive technologies. If enough R&D in a particular technical area moves offshore, the supporting knowledge infrastructure begins to erode. Government agencies may actually initiate the downward spiral by reducing long-term research funding. As university professors move on to other more lucrative fields and corporate research labs decrease their own domestic research budgets, universities have less incentive to invest in curricula in the subject area because lower domestic R&D investment means less domestic employment opportunities for scientists and engineers. The net result is a non-competitive innovation infrastructure. Clearly, the several-decade relative decline in US government funding of S&T research needs to be reversed.

8. *Investment Incentives over the Entire Technology Life Cycle:* Sustained economic growth requires considerably more government support for technology-based companies than simply direct incentives for some types of R&D. Specifically, the long-term question for domestic growth policy is how does a domestic industry create *and* then maintain a technological lead; that is, how much of its intellectual property will be developed within the domestic economy *and* be put to use there in the production and marketing stages of economic growth? The implication is that a comprehensive technology-based growth policy is needed.

9. *Investment Location Incentives:* What causes a domestic company to move value added to another country can only be explained by identifying

the several investment incentives it faces. Conducting R&D overseas means that innovation infrastructures exist that contain desirable technological expertise. This expertise is not only attractive for the conduct of R&D and its associated value added, but it is also available for the succeeding stages of economic activity in that country. Specifically, once an innovation is produced, commercialization requires investment in production facilities. Co-location of R&D with production matters, especially early in a technology's life cycle when much tacit knowledge must flow among early innovators. As a result, value added at the production stage often will be located in the economy where the critical portion of the R&D occurs. This fact is not only an argument for more R&D but also for more efficient innovation infrastructures.

How these issues can be addressed through specific policy instruments will be addressed in Part Three. For policy makers, the overall message is that as companies increasingly become more global at all stages of their operations – R&D, production, marketing – so will their strategic behavior become more global and hence less country specific. Even US industry and trade associations are becoming global. Examples are SIA and iNEMI. These trends cannot be stopped, nor should they be. Research has shown that global companies are more productive innovators because they have greater access to complementary R&D resources and sources of technical knowledge (Criscuolo et al., 2005).

Of course, this raises the question of what globalization of knowledge production does for domestic economic growth. As discussed in the previous section, moving production resources offshore, especially when accompanied by knowledge transfers, frequently acts as an engine of growth in the host country. US companies benefit from globalization of their supply chains and the resulting efficiency gains create higher profits. To the extent that these profits are repatriated to the domestic economy, at least some in that economy (shareholders) benefit. However, the only way this phenomenon works for long-term domestic growth is if the increased efficiency leads to increased domestic investment, thereby creating new and higher-paying jobs to replace those offshored. How this last impact turns out should be the crux of technology-based economic growth policy.

HUMAN S&E CAPITAL

In the boom years of the IT economy, from 1994 through the recession year 2001, corporate R&D investment increased 86.4 percent. This increased spending was reflected in R&D employment, which grew at twice the rate of overall employment during this period (34.1 percent versus 17.2 percent).

However, in spite of such spurts in R&D employment growth, NSF data show that, as of 2001, only 1.05 million FTE (full-time equivalent) R&D workers were employed in the United States compared to a total of 109.1 million workers in all industries in the nonfarm sector (industries other than agriculture). The broader category of 'high-tech' employment is estimated in AeA's *Cyberstates* at 5.6 million in 2005. This not-so-high-tech economic structure is characteristic of other leading economies of the past several decades, as well. Thus, the United States is not the only industrialized nation facing an inadequate high-tech focus in the face of global convergence.

The High-Tech Labor Force

American society has always prided itself on its skilled labor force, which is the product of a philosophy of widely available public education. Due to globalization over recent decades, this system has come under increasing pressure. Labor skill levels are being equaled or exceeded by those in other countries. Based on data for 2002 or the most recent year available, about 78 percent of natural science and engineering doctoral degrees awarded worldwide have been earned outside the United States. The US share will fall further, as the number of such degrees awarded in China, South Korea and Japan continue to rise, while the number in the United States continues to fall. Surprising to some is the fact that Europe awarded 60,000 S&E doctoral degrees, compared to the United States' 27,000 and Asia's 26,000 (National Science Board, 2006a).

The labor issues getting the most attention in the United States are those involving the lower end of the labor income range, such as offshoring of manufacturing jobs and unmanaged immigration. US-based companies have complained about the lower-skills-for-higher-pay problem for some time. Achieve, Inc., a business-backed education reform group reports that only 68 of every 100 American ninth-graders will graduate from high school. Of that number, only 40 will enter college with 27 remaining enrolled in their sophomore year, and only 18 will graduate 'on time' (no more than two years late from either a two-year or a four-year college).

Numerous surveys and testimonies by executives of technology-based companies continually make the point of skilled-labor inadequacies. A 2005 survey of 815 US manufacturing companies of varying sizes by Deloitte Consulting LLP and the National Association of Manufacturers (2005) found that the most highly skilled jobs were the most difficult to fill. Eighty percent of respondents projected a shortage of skilled production workers over the next three years, while 35 percent expect a shortage of scientists and engineers.

At the high end of the skilled labor category, a debate continues over the issue of whether shortages of scientists and engineers exist. The apparently conflicting data presented by the two sides in this debate result from complex relationships between the demand and supply for S&E labor and R&D spending. In particular, the demand and supply relationship is not a matter of counting jobs versus available workers. The S&E labor force comes in an extremely wide variety of skill levels and skill mixes. Thus, shortages can and do occur, even when aggregate numbers imply an approximate balance between supply and demand.

In response to the more dynamic global competitive environment, a domestic labor force that is sufficiently skilled and mobile is a tremendous asset. Broader sets of available skills make a labor pool more flexible (less additional training is required to adapt workers capabilities to changing requirements). However, labor mobility means reduced ties between companies and workers and hence reduced incentives for companies to provide sufficient training. Public education reform is therefore the long-term answer, but, although the phrase 'lifelong learning' is bandied about, the educational infrastructure is not coming close to responding and incentives for workers are not sufficient to create demand–pull for such infrastructure.

New industries, and, even more so, entirely new supply chains of related industries, have created enormous value added (profits and earnings) over the post-World War II period. The jobs created have not only been higher skilled and higher paid, but they have compensated for the less-skilled and lower-paid jobs lost to converging economies. Such newly created jobs are the answer to the offshore outsourcing trend that has generated so much concern.

A Bureau of Labor Statistics' study found that the median wages in all 29 BLS 'high-tech' industries exceeded the median for all industries. In 10 of these industries (including six of 10 'high-tech-intensive' industries), wages were more than 50 percent higher than the median for all industries. Moreover, median wages in seven of the 12 BLS technology-oriented occupations were more than twice the median for all occupations. Even for technicians, the lowest paid of the high-tech occupational categories, the median wage was about one-third higher (Hecker, 1999).

However, more recent BLS employment analysis indicates a weakening of skilled labor's contribution to industrial renewal and sustained growth. The BLS defines 'high-tech industries' as those with a percentage of total employment in 'technology-oriented occupations' that is at least twice the average for all industries.[17] In 2002, this average was 4.9 percent. Forty-six out of a total of 311 NAICS industries (15 percent) qualified. Recognizing that this definition of high tech might conflict with other commonly used criteria (R&D intensity, technology purchasing intensity and technology orientation of the industry's output), the 46 industries were divided into three 'levels'. Level II and Level III industries had technology-oriented worker intensities ranging from approximately two to five times the average for all industries. Many of these industries did not meet the other criteria for high tech, such as high R&D intensities, indicating that they were primarily users of technology. Level I industries, which had technology-oriented intensities of at least five times the average, were generally R&D intensive (Hecker, 2005).

The surprising fact emerging from the BLS study is that, for the 46 high-tech industries as a group, employment increased only 7.5 percent over the 1992–2002 period compared with 19.7 percent for the economy as a whole, and accounted for only 5 percent of total employment growth. As a result, high-tech employment's share declined 12.2 percent to 11 percent of total employment. Further, BLS projects that high-tech employment will continue to grow more slowly than the economy as a whole, at 11.4 percent compared with 16.5 percent through 2012.

Employment growth in Level I industries, on the other hand, grew 23.0 percent in the 1992–2002 period (above the average for the economy overall) and was projected to grow 15.6 percent in the following 10 years, which is slightly below average. The message is that the very high-skilled workers are still in demand within the US domestic economy, but companies are increasingly able to replace the next several tiers of skilled workers with foreign labor.

Although in any 10-year period, employment in a few industries will decline due to technological obsolescence (for example, wired communications), an examination of the 46 'high-tech' industries makes clear that the slow growth in overall high-tech employment in the 1992–2002 period was due to substantial reductions in employment in high-tech manufacturing industries (computers, communications, aerospace, video, chemicals, and measuring and control instruments), as domestic IT supply chains were hollowed out through offshore outsourcing. In contrast, the eight industries with the highest projected rates of employment growth are high-tech service industries.

Even among Level I industries, four manufacturing industries are projected to experience declines in technology-oriented employment over the 2002–12 period, while two of these industries (computer and peripheral equipment and communications equipment) are among seven IT-related industries projected to have the fastest growth in output (the other five are service industries).

Such an apparent anomaly is occurring with greater frequency for individual industries that outsource to other economies. The efficiency gains that can occur via this strategy lower costs and facilitate output (sales) expansion but with fewer domestic employees. That is, less of the total value added in these supply chains' final products is occurring in the domestic economy. To the extent that the service tiers in the relevant supply chains benefit from these manufacturing productivity gains, aggregate supply-chain profits should expand. However, for overall employment to grow within a domestic supply chain, the productivity gains must be sufficient to drive much larger domestic volume expansion and hence demand for additional workers.

The job markets for scientists and engineers, as a critical subset of 'technology-oriented employment', show similar trends. One factor affecting the recent slow growth in the US domestic supply of S&E labor is the relatively greater opportunity in the United States to earn higher salaries in other occupations. Freeman (2005) points out that pay deficits between doctoral scientists and engineers and highly educated workers in other US industries, combined with the fact that S&E PhDs must complete more years of education and post-doctoral work than other categories before beginning to earn a full salary, significantly reduces the incentive to choose science or engineering as a career.

A second supply-side factor is the growing pool of scientists and engineers in other countries. Surveys have shown that MNCs choose locations for R&D based to a significant degree on the availability of skilled researchers (Thursby and Thursby, 2006). The actual number of equivalent-skilled scientists and engineers graduating annually in large emerging economies such as India and China has been debated. However, the law of large numbers is clearly against the US economy, which has only 4.5 percent of the world's population. Thus, even if only a fraction of annual foreign graduates currently have skill levels equal to that of the average US graduate, the US share of the global S&E labor pool will decline over time, creating competitive pressures on salaries.

Industry groups such as the AeA and numerous corporate officials of high-tech firms have repeatedly argued that the US education system is not producing enough skilled workers, especially in view of recent declining enrollments and post-graduate employment of foreign students. The options are to import the needed workers or to move R&D and production offshore to locations where these skills are in ample supply. The latter option is becoming increasingly available.

Limits on H-1B visas, designed to meet temporary shortfalls of high-skilled workers, were increased substantially from a fixed annual level of 65,000 in the 1990s in response to perceived shortages of skilled IT workers. The annual quota was raised to 115,000 in 1998 and to 195,000 for the 2001–03 period. However, Congress returned the limit to the 65,000 level in 2004 to 'protect' American technology workers, as concerns increased over offshore outsourcing of jobs. These concerns arose largely because of the temporary decline in domestic demand for such workers in the aftermath of the excessive investment of the late 1990s and the consequent recession in 2001. By 2005, demand for technically skilled workers was increasing again and the protectionist pressure subsided. Still, the H-IB quota has remained at 65,000 in spite of efforts to raise it.

Because of the complexity of the newest and potentially highest growth technologies, a wide range of skills is needed by domestic firms. Biotechnology is one such example. US biotechnology companies have complained that domestic universities have turned out scientists with training in basic science. However, these companies also need workers skilled in clinical trial design, quality control, computer science applied to life sciences, and so on. Increasingly, other countries are training workers with these skills. Thus, biotechnology firms, which are constrained by the low H-1B visa quotas, have begun to move R&D operations offshore (Saminather, 2006).

The high-tech workforce problem is even more complicated than the required set of traditional skills. Companies have moved to flatter organizational structures in which workers are increasingly empowered to analyze and solve problems. The Deloitte-NAM survey found that this change is creating a demand for broader and deeper engineering skills. Moreover, the consequent declining role for middle management means that these workers must deal directly with other engineers as well as with salesmen and senior managers. Thus, such workers need communications skills, as well. Sixty-five percent of the survey respondents said that they could not find qualified engineers with the evolving mix of required job skills. Significant for the current focus on cost differentials across the global workforce is the finding that with respect to strategic imperatives, being the low-cost producer ranked third behind having a high-quality workforce and taking advantage of innovation opportunities. (Eisen et al., 2005).

Primary Education

US industry complains correctly that high-school graduates are not trained for most skilled vocations. The bottom line is that the US educational system is grossly out of date. The K-12 school system has not changed measurably for over a century. In fact, it has remained largely unchanged from its origins in an agricultural economy through the manufacturing era to the current information and service-based economy. The educational system still basically seeks to provide a general and largely abstract liberal arts education.

National standardized testing has been implemented to hopefully provide an incentive to better student performance. But, more than anything else, what these tests have done is reveal the gross structural inadequacies of American education. The 2005 national average test scores in reading and math showed that, for 4th graders, the number of students demonstrating math proficiency increased to 36 percent of all students compared with 32 percent in the 2003 test. Only 41 percent of US 8th grade students received instruction from a mathematics teacher who specialized in mathematics, considerably lower than the international average of 71 percent. In the context of 'you get what you pay for', the proportion of 8th graders showing proficiency in math increased from 29 to 30 percent.[18]

Such abysmal performance is even more worrying when American students' academic performance is compared to students in other countries. The Program for International Student Assessment ranks the United States 24th out of 29 industrial nations in math literacy; US students also ranked 24th out of 29 in problem solving. In fact, the study indicated that a large number of high-school students can barely do math at all. One-quarter of US 15-year-olds scored either at the bottom of a six-point scale or, worse, scored so low that they did not even make that lowest level. At the upper end, US scores also lagged. On average, about 4 percent of students across the 29 countries who took the test scored in the top of the six-point scale; in the United States, only 2 percent scored in this category.[19] This performance hardly predicts future technology-based competitiveness and economic growth.

In an international test of 12th graders for general knowledge in mathematics and science, US students performed below the average for 21 countries. In addition, an advanced mathematics assessment was administered to US students who were taking or had taken precalculus, calculus or advanced placement calculus and to students in 15 other countries who were taking or had taken advanced mathematics courses. Eleven nations outperformed the United States and four countries had scores similar to US scores. No nation scored significantly below the United States (National Science Board, 2004).

As evidence of the persistent pattern of denial by US education policy, a 2006 National Science Board report on K-12 education observed that nearly a quarter of a century ago, an NSB Commission on Pre-college Education assessed the state of K-12 science and math education and found it decidedly inadequate. Clearly, in the intervening 25 years, the country has failed to raise the achievement of US students commensurate with the goal articulated by that Commission – that US pre-college achievement should be 'best in the world by 1999'. By the time US students reach their senior year, the 2006 report states, 'even the most advanced US students perform at or near the bottom on international assessments.'

Not only has student achievement on international comparisons slipped, but over the last decade, teachers' salaries have remained nearly flat, averaging $44,367, just about $2,598 above what they were in 1972 (after adjusting for inflation), and 15 states experienced a decline in average teachers' salaries between the 1993–94 and 2003–04 school years, adjusted for inflation (National Science Board, 2006b). Once again, the market mechanism works and skill levels over time adjust to pay levels.

A vestige of the former agricultural society is the length of the school year. American K-12 students average 180 days, compared with 190 to 210 days in Europe and 240 days in Japan. In fact, the US has a shorter school year than all but two industrialized nations. Even with better curricula, teaching methods, and teachers, US students would likely not sufficiently improve current poor international rankings due to the inadequate number of available teaching days. Obviously, with agriculture accounting for approximately 1 percent of GDP and employment, this historical limitation on the US educational system is absurd. Over a 12-year academic career, this shortfall means that American students finish nearly a full school year behind their international counterparts.

Secondary Education

An important impetus to rapid ascension of the US technology-based sector to world leadership was the so-called 'brain drain' from European and Asian economies that began after World War II. Opportunity abounded in the more dynamic US economy and its superior university system. Thus, many scientists and engineers emigrated to the United States. Foreign students, once educated at US universities, remained permanently to work in domestic industries. The US university system still attracts large numbers of foreign students. For example, in 2005, Stanford University awarded 88 PhDs in electrical engineering, 49 of which went to foreign-born students. More generally, Department of Education data show that foreign nationals earn large percentages of all S&E degrees (Figure 2.6).

In fact, over most of the last half-century, the US economy was able to skim off the cream of foreign scientists and engineers. Many of these foreign students became leaders of innovative companies. Among the most notable are Andrew Grove, co-founder and Chairman of Intel, Vinod Kholsa, co-founder of Sun MicroSystems, Jerry Yang, co-founder of Yahoo!, and Sergey Brin, co-founder and President of Google (AeA, 2005).

Today, however, globalization and associated technological convergence are rapidly changing these patterns. NSF data show both lower enrollment by foreign students in US universities and higher repatriation rates after foreign students complete their education. Degrees to US citizens are certainly not taking up the slack. Moreover, the rise in the number of research universities in other countries is substantially reducing the number of foreign students coming to the United States to study in the first place.

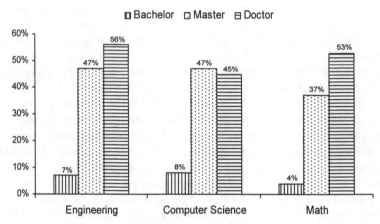

Source: US Department of Education, AeA (2005).

Figure 2.6   Shares of US S&E Degrees Awarded to Foreign Nationals, 2002

Tertiary Education

The doctoral segment of S&E degree trends is important because PhDs work in the early phases of the R&D cycle where breakthrough technologies are first demonstrated. They also provide essential consultation to startups and other R&D-intensive companies. It is, therefore, hard to believe that the economy that invented semiconductor technology, the digital computer and many new high-performance materials over half a century is experiencing flat to declining numbers of new PhDs in the physical and engineering sciences in the face of growing technological opportunities and competitive pressures.

Doctoral degrees in the physical sciences awarded by US universities to US citizens remained flat in the 1980s and 1990s at roughly 2,050 per year, but dropped to 1,861 in 2003 – the lowest in the past 20 years. PhDs in this area awarded to all students peaked in the late 1990s at around 3,800 but also dropped in this decade to a low of 3,185 in 2002 before rebounding somewhat to 3,647 in 2005. Engineering doctorates awarded to US citizens increased in the 1990s to a peak of 2,739 in 2001 but then declined precipitously in the next two years to 2,140 in 2003. Total engineering doctorates awarded peaked at 6,309 in 1996 and then also declined to a low of 5,076 in 2002 before finally attaining a new high of 6,404 in 2005.[20]

The trend for all S&E doctoral degrees is hardly better. From 1996 to 2005, the number of US degrees awarded annually increased from 27,240 to 27,974, an increase of 2.7 percent. Moreover, all of the growth in annual S&E doctorates in this decade (2001–05) has come from foreign students (25.0 percent). The growth rate for US citizens was –0.9 percent (Hill, 2006).

During this same period, the number of doctoral degrees in science and engineering produced outside the United States rose sharply. In 2001, the EU granted 40 percent more S&E PhDs than did the United States. Extrapolation of this trend predicts that the EU will produce nearly twice as many S&E doctorates per year as the United States by around 2010 (Freeman, 2005).

The apostles of denial can argue that Europe does not spend as much on R&D relative to its aggregate GDP as does the American economy. However, the EU has a target of a higher R&D intensity than the US economy. It will have to make progress toward that goal to employ this expanding S&E human capital pool. If it succeeds, the European economy will once again be a major technology-based force in the global economy.

In 1975, China produced a negligible number of S&E PhDs. But in 2003, that country graduated about 9,000. Overall, the US share of global S&E PhDs will fall to about 15 percent by 2010 (Freeman, 2005). Thus, the prognosis for the future adequacy of the US S&E labor pool is not good.

The Bottom Line

An analysis of surveys of employer labor needs indicates that for a large percentage of the US labor force growth in skill levels has not been sufficient to overcome the factors that are leading to offshoring. For the S&E subset of skilled workers, a telling indicator is the fact that the number of S&E degrees around the world is growing rapidly relative to the rate of growth of such degrees in the US economy. Given the export orientation of all emerging economies and the increasing share of exports in world GDP, the growing high-skilled global workforce is clearly resulting in ever-larger high-tech exports to the US economy.

In the broader context of labor markets generally, the low-skilled end of the labor force in all industrialized nations is being replaced by low-cost workers in developing nations or by automation. Even reductions in real wages can at best only retard this trend. The high-skilled end of industrialized economies' labor forces is still competitive to varying degrees but is being forced increasingly to compete on a global basis.

The bottom line is that higher-skilled and higher-paid jobs will only grow in the US domestic economy if greater demand is created through increases in R&D spending and if the skills of the labor supplied for R&D and other high-tech jobs are hard to find in other economies.

PRODUCTIVITY GROWTH

A Conference Board study calculated that the United States continues to maintain a large lead in per capita income over the rest of the OECD countries (41 percent in 2002), and 76 percent of this income advantage is explained by a significant gap in productivity. In fact, the productivity gap with the rest of the world explains 96 percent of the income gap (McGuckin and van Ark, 2002). Economic research has consistently shown that technological change accounts for the majority of long-term productivity growth. Thus, productivity growth and the technology investment that drives it are critically important indicators for economic growth policy.

However, the current leadership status of the US economy is increasingly challenged. Being the leader means that everyone else is copying your business model and, being behind, the imitators are more desperate than the economy in front. This lack of urgency on the part of the United States is exemplified by the tendency to compare this country to regional blocs of economies. But using averages for geographic regions, such as the EU, can mask the process of change in comparative advantages that eventually becomes painfully apparent. For example, although American productivity is higher than the average for the OECD countries, six European economies had higher productivity than the United States in 2002, up from four in 2001.

Most economic studies have indicated that the sources of recent productivity growth are limited to the IT-producing industries and, to varying degrees, the most intensive users of IT. For example, a Federal Reserve Board study estimated that the one percentage point increase in the productivity growth rate in the last half of the 1990s resulted about equally from increased investment in IT (computers, software and communications equipment) and innovation in the design and production of computers, including components such as semiconductors (Oliner and Sichel, 2000).

A study by the McKinsey Global Institute (Baily et al., 2006) confirmed this focused source of productivity growth over the past decade. Their analysis showed that all of the net productivity growth in the 1995–99 period was accounted for by six of the economy's 59 sectors. From 2000 to 2003, the major contributing sectors broadened somewhat with the top seven sectors accounting for 75 percent of net productivity growth.

Two major sources of productivity growth – technological change and capital deepening – have different roles in determining long-run economic growth. Both sources contributed significantly to the IT-driven resurgence in productivity during the late 1990s. However, this impact was a long time in materializing. Much of the acceleration in IT investment in the 15 years from 1980 to 1995 suffered from the so-called 'productivity paradox', which refers to the fact that the expected productivity gains from individual IT investments such as computers, software and telecommunications equipment did not show up in national productivity statistics. The potential gains were thwarted by the substantial difficulties encountered in integrating individual components into efficient and hence productive systems.

System-level productivity has only recently begun to improve enough to drive aggregate productivity at a faster rate. BLS data show that after increasing 1.5 percent per year in the period from 1991 to 1995, labor productivity (output per hour) increased at an annual rate of 2.7 percent in the 1996 to 2000 period. The acceleration in labor productivity growth elicited glowing commentary on the US economy.

Many economists project this trend to persist and therefore expect continued relatively high rates of productivity growth. However, dependency on a few industries for sustained productivity growth is risky at best. Jorgenson (2001), for example, estimates a sharp reduction in multifactor productivity, if the semiconductor industry's product cycle simply returns to three years from the more recent two-year pattern. The dependence of future productivity growth on a reduction in the product-life-cycle for a single industry that accounts for 0.8 percent of GDP is truly a 'razor's edge' economic growth path. Even if one attributes long-term productivity growth more broadly across all of what is commonly called the 'high-tech' sector, the US economy's growth is largely dependent on industries that account for a small fraction of GDP.

An important consideration in assessing productivity trends is the fact that virtually the entire debate over the sources of productivity growth has been based on analyses of trends in labor productivity. It is understandable that analysts and the media focus on this measure of economic efficiency. Labor productivity is relatively easy to calculate, so estimates are available relatively quickly.

However, labor constitutes just one input to economic activity. Consequently, the relationship of labor to overall productivity growth is affected by the magnitude and nature of investments in other inputs. Specifically, the amount of investment in capital and the amount and type of technology embodied in this capital (plus so-called 'disembodied technological change') are critical determinants of labor productivity. In fact, for periods of time, providing labor with more efficient (technology-endowed) capital will increase 'measured' labor productivity, even if the quality of labor (average skill levels) does not change. Similarly, reorganizing production processes will increase measured labor productivity by virtue of achieving greater efficiency at the system level, again without

The Economics of Decline

necessarily requiring a significant change in labor's skill levels.

For a more accurate understanding of economic efficiency, especially over longer periods of time, a more comprehensive and accurate measure of productivity that relates output to the combined effects of the major inputs of capital, labor, and technology, is required. The productivity measure used by economists to achieve this end is multifactor productivity, or MFP (also called total factor productivity or TFP). Whereas labor productivity is available on a quarterly basis a short time after the end of a quarter, MFP is estimated annually approximately 18 months to two years after the fact.[21]

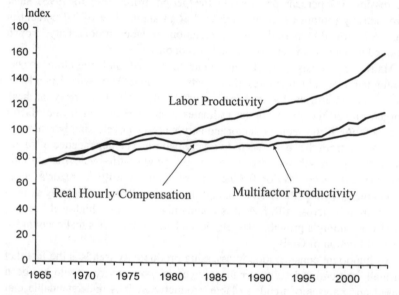

Source: Bureau of Labor Statistics.

Figure 2.7 Trends in Productivity and Income, 1965–2004 (Nonfarm Business Sector)

Figure 2.7 compares 40-year trends in the more comprehensive measure, MFP, along with average labor productivity and real compensation. The important observation is that real hourly compensation has tracked MFP over the past 25 years. Companies obviously have to pay for all inputs, not just labor, and it is the relationship of output to the weighted average of these inputs that determines true (multifactor) productivity and ultimately profits. The fact that MFP has grown at a decidedly slower rate than average labor productivity raises questions about the magnitude and staying power of the New Economy's impact, especially as the post-1995 resurgence in MFP has not fully re-established the annual growth rate in the 1948–73 Golden Age

(Tassey, 2004).[22] Perhaps most important, the growing divergence between measured labor productivity and real compensation likely reflects the cost advantages being realized by US-based producers from offshoring component development and production rather than actual increases in productivity by domestic workers.[23]

The Bottom Line

Productivity is an efficiency measure and thereby provides vital information on the relationship between investments and the resulting portfolio of products and services. However, no matter how efficient an economy becomes, at some point this portfolio becomes obsolete and must be replaced with new, innovative products and services. This requirement for long-term growth has significant implications for R&D policy. First, new technical knowledge must be continually embodied in both labor and capital, so that MFP can grow at an acceptable rate. Second, the concentration of productivity growth in relatively few sectors implies an unsustainable growth path because either these few sectors will have to maintain substantial above-average rates of productivity growth and drive the rest of the economy or other sectors will have to contribute to overall increases in efficiency. The prospects for either scenario occurring and maintaining sufficient leverage is steadily declining.

REFUSING TO ADAPT

The current process of technological convergence is not a new phenomenon. In the Second Industrial Revolution (late 19th century), Western European economies that had lagged behind the UK began to converge on British levels of per capita income (Harley, 2003). Economic historians have emphasized technological diffusion as the driving force behind this convergence (Landes, 1969; Pollard, 1981).

The US economy's surge to world economic leadership in this same period is particularly instructive because it demonstrates not only the process of convergence but also the potential – so real today – for a challenger to first catch up and then to develop a new and improved growth strategy that allows it to take over as the new leader. In 1870, America's real per capita income lagged that of the UK by nearly a quarter, although it exceeded the European average by a fifth. The simple convergence model would predict that US per capita income would grow faster than the UK's but slower than the rest of Europe. However, by 1900, American real per capita income was not only well ahead of continental Europe but had surpassed the English standard of living (Nelson and Wright, 1992). By 1950, US per capita income was 40 percent above that of the UK and approximately double that of the average of the European economies (Harley, 2003). The net result was first convergence and then a trading of competitive positions.

The major reason for this phenomenal performance was the fact that America succeeded in implementing a new growth paradigm based on developing and widely applying new process technologies, specifically mass-production techniques. An industry structure evolved characterized by large, vertically integrated firms that were able to capture economies of scale and scope (Chandler, 1990). Extensive investment in economic infrastructure (railroads, telephone networks and electrical power) unified regional markets and helped achieve economies of scale through specialization. Further, American industry pioneered standardization of parts, beginning with gun-making and woodworking in the mid-19th century and really accelerating in the Henry Ford era of mass production. Finally, rates of investment were high, even relative to the rapid population growth during the late 19th and early 20th centuries, resulting in a near doubling of the per capita capital stock (Harley, 2003).

Convergence and occasional change of leadership are threats that the pursued seldom recognize and react to in time. Today, the rise and fall of technology-based comparative advantage in domestic industries based on specific technologies is particularly insidious for two major reasons. First, the process of scientific discovery followed by developing or acquiring new technology and finally learning to use it effectively is a long process, usually spanning several decades. Second, the progressive cycle of science to technology to market success is incredibly complicated, involving multiple private and public institutions networked in multiple patterns. For both reasons, signs of competitive decline are frequent but dispersed and typically small, so the cumulative effect is not obvious until the former leader one day realizes it is no longer competitive.

In the 19th century when the UK was the dominant economic power, it had an economic growth model based on technology, access to cheap raw materials, and an effective market system. The result was economic power beyond its relatively small size. Although the details are different, the US economy followed the same general model to become the world's leading economic power in the 20th century. Moreover, while much larger than the UK, America is still small relative to the global economy of the near future. The explosion of increasingly skilled workers in emerging economies should bring home the point that the days of US economic hegemony are rapidly disappearing. Even if the United States were currently undertaking the necessary steps to adapt its economy to globalization, its future competitive position would be in doubt.

In the early 1990s, a few economists (in particular, Nelson and Wright, 1992) described the process of technological convergence and the implications for the decline of American technology dominance. A few others (Kodama, 1991; Tassey, 1992) described how government and industry strategies combine to achieve technological convergence and, in many cases, eventually to leadership positions. However, for most of the next 15 years, little was heard about these negative trends, even as convergence accelerated and became more pervasive across high-tech supply chains.

Warnings of this deterioration are increasingly frequent. However, *adaptation failure* is a common problem for the leader. The inability to understand and the unwillingness to set about responding to the causes of decline are due largely to the 'installed-base' effect, whereby accumulated assets create vested interests in the status quo. The consequences of this 'lock in', as Brian Arthur (1988, 1989) has called it, becomes more severe as the previously successful set of assets and associated technology infrastructures disperse globally to support their use by competitors.

An important dimension of the installed-base effect in technology-based industries is the tendency to expand along constrained paths or technology trajectories (referred to as 'path dependencies' by Nelson and Winter, 1982). This phenomenon results from the learning process, which contributes to the accumulation of assets. The specific character of the expanding knowledge base (especially tacit knowledge) creates the path dependency. All this makes the leading economy more resistant to change and hence vulnerable to convergence by others as the technology life cycle evolves and ultimately as new technology trajectories (paths) evolve.

The Bottom Line

Economists have made frequent use of the law of comparative advantage to explain offshoring of American jobs and to assert automatic and relatively painless adjustments. Unfortunately, in this modern world of public–private investment paradigms, adjustments by individual economies do not happen solely through market forces. This is especially the case when structural deficiencies in both the public and private sectors are allowed to become so suboptimal that major elements of the economic system have much to lose from the needed restructuring, thereby leading to resistance to change. In contrast, today's global trends require an ongoing commitment to the long, complex and temporarily painful process of re-creating comparative advantage, which is the only option for providing high-skilled and high-paid jobs and facilitating globally competitive companies.

However, creating comparative advantage will have to be accomplished in the context of ongoing globalization of corporate strategies. With the highly concentrated patterns of R&D investment and resulting productivity growth in recent years, such trends will likely mean continued offshoring of R&D and production by US companies and by companies all over the world. This evolutionary trend will be characterized by specialization and by R&D networks that make more and more companies partners as much as competitors. The result will be reduced loyalty to any one economy. This trend creates the need for a new class of competitor in this era of global markets – national governments.

Thus, while convergence is occurring with a vengeance and both broadening and 'flattening' the global economy, many of the competing economies – new and old alike – are planning and working determinedly to 'un-flatten' competitive arenas with new technologies and new supporting infrastructures. The important policy questions therefore are how does an economy identify the roles and mechanisms of its public and private sectors and then determine the adequate amounts and types of technology investment for each sector?

The bottom line is that higher-skilled and higher-paid jobs will only grow in the US domestic economy if greater demand is created through increases in R&D spending and if the skills of the labor supplied for R&D and other high-tech jobs are hard to find in foreign workers.

NOTES

1. 'A Topsy-Turvy World,' *The Economist*, September 16, 2006.
2. Apostles of denial argue that the conventional income-based measures of saving derived from the national accounts are incomplete and therefore claims of zero household net saving are incorrect. Saving also occurs in the form of accumulation of assets (stocks, real estate). In fact, household net worth spiked in the late 1990s (stock-market bubble) and in the early 2000s (real-estate bubble). However, bubbles by definition burst and thereby force a return to long-term income-based saving.
3. 'The Future of the Dollar', *The Economist*, December 4, 2004. In fact, the Chinese are accumulating such large foreign exchange reserves ($1.2 trillion as of 2006) that they are able to make huge investments in technology-based assets. For example, in 2007, the Chinese announced that $300-$400 billion of these reserves will be allocated such investments (McCormack, 2007).
4. The one exception is semiconductors, where government technology research funding was more piecemeal and limited.
5. See http://www.oecd.org/dataoecd/54/58/370 10986.pdf.
6. UNCTAD data for 2005 showed global FDI at $897 billion, a 29 percent increase from 2004. Thus, a growth of only one-third the 2005 rate will result in global FDI that surpasses $1 trillion in 2006.
7. In a simple two-country, two-technology model, the traditional law of comparative advantage allows trade between the two countries, even if one country has an absolute advantage in both technologies. The country with the superior technology in both cases specializes in the technology in which it has the greater absolute (that is, comparative) advantage and allows the other country to specialize in the second technology. Under these assumptions, global efficiency is maximized.

8. The report is available at http://www.chinabusinessforum.org/pdf/the-china-effect.pdf. See also 'China Trade Will Boost US Wealth, Argues China Council', *Manufacturing & Technology News*, March 17, 2006.
9. 'Scouring the Planet for Brainiacs', *BusinessWeek*, October 11, 2004, p. 106.
10. See Armbrecht (2004) for a summary of the experiences of 27 companies with laboratories in China.
11. Source: iSuppli, Inc. US design operations still lead all economies with a 40.2 percent share.
12. Such a relatively small advantage in labor costs may seem surprising, given the widely publicized huge wage differentials between average Chinese workers and those in the United States. However, as the SIA points out, semiconductor fabs are capital and technology intensive, so even an 80 percent differential in labor rates results in barely a 10 percent difference in total costs.
13. 'Brains Boxed In', *The Economist*, March 1, 2007.
14. Veverka (2005). In 2005, Motorola introduced a line of advanced cell phones characterized by their ultra-small footprint. Their small size was made possible by Motorola's leadership in antenna technology.
15. *BusinessWeek*, October 11, 2004.
16. Boston Consulting Group, *64% of Global Companies Will Increase Spending on Innovation in 2004, Research Shows*, January 2004.
17. Technology-oriented occupations are defined by the BLS as those needing an 'in-depth knowledge of the theories and principles of science, engineering, and mathematics underlying technology'.
18. Testing done under the National Assessment of Educational Progress. Test results are published by the National Center for Education Statistics, *Trends in International Mathematics and Sciences Study* (TIMSS).
19. Conducted every three years by the Organization for Economic Cooperation and Development (OECD), this assessment focuses on 15-year-olds' capabilities in reading, mathematics and science literacy.
20. National Science Board (2006a, Appendix Table 2-30) for degree awards to US citizens and NSF *InfoBrief* 06-301 for awards to all students at US universities.
21. MFP is defined as the ratio of output to the combined effect of all conventional inputs (capital, labor, energy, materials). However, a portion of the growth in output is not accounted for by these conventional inputs. This residual (called the 'Solow residual' after the Nobel Laureate economist Robert Solow) is attributed to technological change. When this concept was first advanced by Solow 50 years ago, technological change was much slower and therefore representing its impact by a residual was more acceptable. Today, the rapid pace of technology and its central role in competitive position and economic growth requires an explicit knowledge production function to explain the nature and pace of technological change. See Romer (1990) and Tassey (2005b).
22. During 1995–99, characterized as the take-off period for the New Economy, labor productivity accelerated to an average annual growth rate of 2.1 percent, while MFP grew at less than half that rate (1.0 percent).
23. Michael Mandel, 'The Real Cost of Offshoring', *BusinessWeek*, June 18, 2007.

PART II

R&D in the Modern Economy

3. The Technology Paradigm

Everything should be made as simple as possible, but not simpler.

Albert Einstein

In 1978 the book value of physical assets (property, plant and equipment) owned by publicly traded non-financial corporations was 83 percent of the average company's capitalization (the value of outstanding bonds and common stock). The remaining 17 percent was in the form of intangible (knowledge) assets. By 1998, 69 percent of assets were intangible and only 31 percent were physical (Blair and Kochan, 2000). This trend clearly indicates the rapidly growing economic role of technical knowledge in the modern economy and therefore its strategic importance in the future.

If technology is, in fact, the driver of long-term productivity advance and output expansion and hence real income growth, R&D investment is the key enabler. Unfortunately, the majority of those involved in innovation policy development and implementation simply assert the importance of technology, expecting others to accept the relationship with economic growth as obvious. Even more lacking is an understanding of the major elements of the typical industrial technology and how they interact to determine technological progress and economic growth. The next two chapters address these concerns.

TECHNOLOGY'S IMPACT

To make the case for technology as a critical investment, the policy analyst has to collect impact data and find ways to display it for various audiences. Basic concepts such as how technology drives productivity growth need to be portrayed. At the individual technology level, which is most important because that is where investment decisions are made, representations of impact such as cost reduction are an essential tool. For example, Figure 3.1 depicts an estimate of the considerable economic benefits from the steady advances in semiconductor technology on the cost of computing. If advances in this technology had stopped in 1995, government purchases of computers over the succeeding 10-year period would have cost $353 billion more than was actually paid (assuming that demand remained constant).

More broadly, the vast majority of participants in growth policy debates are at best only vaguely aware of the decades of economic research that have attempted to explain and quantify the relationships between investment in

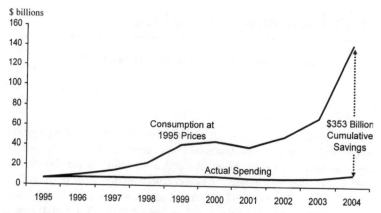

Source: Bureau of Economic Analysis and Semiconductor Industry Association
Note: Consumption data include federal, state, and local governments

Figure 3.1 Impact of Technological Change: Government Computer Purchases in Actual and 1995 Prices

technology and its economic impacts. A review, therefore, is necessary to provide a substantive justification for focusing national growth strategies on technology investment and utilization and, most important, on the nature, size and timing of specific policy actions.

Macroeconomic Impact Studies

At the macroeconomic (national) level, growth accounting studies have estimated that technology accounts for more than one-half of economic growth in all OECD countries except Canada (Boskin and Lau, 2000). Other economic studies have consistently shown a strong relationship between R&D investment and both productivity and output growth (Cameron, 1998; OECD, 2000; Oliner and Sichel, 2000). The contribution of R&D investment to productivity growth is critical because the productivity advantage of the United States over OECD countries as a group has been shown to account for three-quarters of the per capita income difference (McGuckin and van Ark, 2002). In fact, changes in technology are the only source of permanent increases in productivity (Basu et al., 2001).

An important observation with implications for future investment strategies is that many of these studies show that a small number of IT-related industries account for a majority of the productivity gains elsewhere in the economy. This concentration of the source of productivity growth is due to the fact that the IT sector is where the majority of technological innovations have occurred in recent decades. For example, Dale Jorgenson (2005) observed that, while three-quarters of US industries contributed to the acceleration in economic growth in the late 1990s, the four IT-producing industries were responsible for a quarter of that acceleration while only accounting for 3 percent of the GDP. IT-using industries contributed another quarter of the growth resurgence and about the same proportion of the GDP. In contrast, non-IT industries with 70 percent of value added were responsible for only half the economic resurgence. Obviously, the impact of the IT-producing industries was far out of proportion to their relatively small size. Such findings underscore the substantial leverage that technological change can supply to an entire economy.

Equally revealing are studies that emphasize the negative growth impacts of underinvestment. Specifically, technologically stagnant sectors experience slow productivity growth and, therefore, above-average cost and price increases. The rising prices actually increase these sectors' measured share of GDP, thereby lowering national productivity growth. This effect, known as 'Baumol's disease' (Baumol, 1967) was thought by some to have been cured by the increasingly pervasive effects of the IT revolution (Triplett and Bosworth, 2003).

However, in contrast to what some 'New Economy' advocates believe, Baumol's disease seems to have actually progressed over a 50-year period. Nordhaus (2006) found that industries with relatively low productivity growth experience higher rates of inflation. In fact, long-term differences in productivity growth explain around 85 percent of the variance in relative price movements. Thus, the positive role of technological change in reducing prices and increasing real output stands out clearly.

Microeconomic Studies

Analyses of industry-level impacts of R&D are critical because the 'industry' is a major target of government R&D policy. In particular, such studies reveal the role of 'spillovers' (loss of intellectual property by researchers and innovators) in explaining underinvestment, especially for certain types of R&D. The existence of spillovers – measured as the difference between the private and social (industry or national) rates of return on investment in technology – has been the main rationale for government funding of R&D for decades.

These microeconomic studies seem to support the macroeconomic analyses that about one-half of output growth and three-quarters of productivity growth are attributable to R&D investment (Griliches, 1995). Regarding spillovers, Griliches (1988) concludes from a survey of the relevant research that the social (usually industry-level) rate of return (RoR) to R&D is between 20 and 50 percent. As one would expect, these estimates are considerably higher than economists' estimates of the private (innovator) RoR for R&D, which has clustered around 10–15 percent (Hall, 1996). Obviously, such a rate-of-return 'gap' can be a significant deterrent to R&D investment.

These analyses fall into a class of studies called partial equilibrium analysis, which means that the impacts are estimated for only a segment of the economy (one or several industries and/or specific factors of production). Jones and Williams (1998) therefore argue that such estimates are actually a lower bound to the true social RoR because a national or macroeconomic estimate, derived from so-called 'dynamic general equilibrium effects', would lead to even higher estimates due to the multiplier effects of the original investment throughout the economy. Such broader social-rate-of-return estimates are in the 100 percent range (Griffith, 2002). Comparing rates of return across major types of investment led Jones and Williams (2000) to conclude that the optimal level of investment for the US economy is at least four times greater than the current rate.[1]

The case-study approach has also been used to estimate the social and private rates of return from R&D investment. In a famous NSF-sponsored study, Mansfield et al. (1977) used a measure for the RoR borrowed from the corporate finance literature (the so-called 'internal' rate of return). They found a median private RoR for 17 innovations of 25 percent and a median social RoR of 56 percent. Because of the attention the results received, the NSF sponsored a second study by Tewksbury et al. (1980). This study analyzed 20 innovations and estimated a median private RoR of 27 percent and a social RoR of 99 percent. For the most part, both studies examined average innovations (as opposed to radical or breakthrough ones) and the time series of benefits for each innovation was truncated, which meant that some of the benefits were not captured in the calculations.

For policy purposes, the relevance of these studies has been verification of the gap between the private and social rates of return. This differential has been used as the main rationale for government funding of R&D. However, as discussed in Chapter 5, the underinvestment phenomenon is not quite that straightforward and, in fact, requires both modification and elaboration for effective policy management. As a result, although the relationship between public and private investment in R&D has been studied and debated for decades, a consensus still does not exist on the respective sectors' funding roles. Moreover, because technology is not a black box, a number of unresolved issues exist regarding investment in specific technology elements. Important examples are the roles of the underlying science base, the creation and use of generic technology platforms upon which private-sector innovations are based, and the adequacy of supporting technical infrastructure. As discussed in following chapters, failure to agree on the correct technology-based growth model may be the single most important constraining factor in managing competitiveness and economic growth.

Significantly overlooked is the fact that private-sector technological change depends greatly on a varied and ubiquitous technical infrastructure. Over a 15-year period beginning in the early 1990s, the National Institute of Standards and Technology (NIST) conducted quantitative economic impact assessments of industry's use of the technical infrastructure produced in its labs by utilizing the same corporate finance approach as the Mansfield and Tewksbury studies. Because technical infrastructure is commonly used by competing firms and by buyers and sellers in specific markets, only a social RoR is estimated. Given the broad use of such public-good technology, frequently in the form of standards, one would expect fairly high social rates of return. In fact, 29 studies of NIST infratechnology research programs covering a wide range of technologies and industries yielded a median social RoR estimate of 128 percent.

THE HIGH-TECH SECTOR

The label 'high-tech economy' connotes a pervasive role for technology. In reality, although the impacts of technology diffuse widely, the industries that create it constitute a small portion of GDP. What is commonly called the high-tech sector or, more accurately, the R&D-intensive sector is a small and geographically concentrated portion of the broader US economy.

The collective share of GDP by this group of industries is 7–10 percent, depending on the precise definition of high tech. Moreover, six states account for almost one-half of national R&D and 10 states perform almost two-thirds. One might speculate that these 10 states are the most populous so that R&D spending is simply correlated with population. However, as Table 3.1 shows, a definite skewing exists with respect to location of R&D relative to population. Such geographical concentration is becoming increasingly important as the less-technology-intensive sectors of all industrialized nations suffer economic decline in the face of convergence by emerging economies and general shifts in comparative advantage.

Even if a state has a relatively large share of national R&D, technology-based growth is not guaranteed. Several states that have high ratios of R&D to state GDP are recipients of large amounts of federal research funds but which have not been accompanied by many of the other essential private and public technology assets necessary to leverage private-sector innovation. Such incomplete innovation infrastructure is pronounced in a number of less-populated states that have large federal research institutions.

Table 3.1 R&D and Population Shares: 10 Largest R&D Performing States

State	% of Population	% of National R&D
California	12.0	20.7
Michigan	3.5	8.1
New York	6.7	6.1
Texas	7.4	5.4
Massachusetts	2.3	5.3
Pennsylvania	4.4	4.6
New Jersey	3.0	4.6
Illinois	4.4	4.2
Washington	2.1	3.6
Maryland	1.9	3.5
Total	47.7	66.1

Source: National Science Foundation.

A growing number of state governments have realized the imperative to expand the high-tech economy locally through the promotion of regional technology-based clusters. These clusters are designed to provide the needed complementary assets. As discussed in the next chapter, this regional growth strategy reflects a disaggregated conceptual model of industrial technology development based on complementary public and private technology assets.

NSF analysis shows that industrial R&D support for academia is concentrated in the top 100 research-intensive institutions (defined by total R&D performed). In 2004, these elite universities received 76 percent of industry R&D support. The next 100 institutions received only 17 percent of these funds (Rapport, 2006). Thus, state promotion of technology-based clusters, which include R&D-intensive companies as partners, is limited by the availability in the target region of a top research university that can attract funding.

In support of a technology-based growth strategy, evidence can be presented that the portions of an economy currently defined as high tech have on average increased their share of manufacturing output across the global economy. Figure 3.2 shows that the high-tech share of global manufacturing value added has increased from 10 percent in 1980 to 19 percent in 2003. The impact on global trade has been even more dramatic. Over this same period, the high-tech share of global manufacturing exports has risen from 10 to 29 percent. Obviously, the global convergence process described in Chapter 2 is increasingly being driven by investment in high-tech products.

A major question for a nation's R&D investment strategy is the potential for R&D and the resulting technology to leverage productivity across an entire economy. Some research has indicated significant variation across

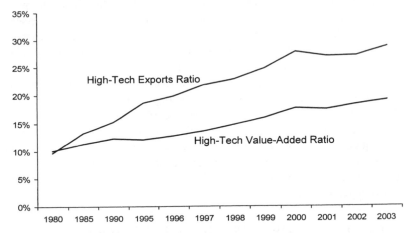

Source: National Science Board, 2006a, Appendix Tables 6-3 and 6-4.

Figure 3.2 Global Manufacturing Trends: Ratios of High-Tech Exports to Total Exports and High-Tech Value Added to Total Value Added, 1980–2003

industries in the effect of R&D on TFP growth. However, no evidence has been produced to indicate diminishing returns from increased R&D across the range of R&D intensities found in manufacturing industries (Cameron, 1999). Thus, no support exists for the argument that some industries need less R&D than others.

Nevertheless, in spite of this strong empirical support for technology's role in economic growth, doubts remain, even among policy makers in advanced economies where technology has been demonstrated to be the single most important ingredient of sustained growth. One frequently cited reason for such doubt is that technological change results in unemployment. Moreover, even when the importance of technological change is accepted, support for investment in R&D is often muted by the belief that at least some types of innovation occur independently of any formal R&D process.

Typically, the first problem is most intense during a recession. In such cases, unemployment increases as companies attempt to cut costs in response to decreased demand. One of the main ways to cut costs is to invest in productivity-enhancing technologies, which are most often labor saving.

Because sales are stagnant at best at this point in the business cycle, a company making such investment can maintain the same level of sales with fewer employees (see Figure 1.1). Moreover, incorporating new technology often increases the capital intensity of production, thereby reducing the relative demand for lower-skilled workers.

The second problem is a legacy of the past when technology was less science based and less complex. These conditions allowed inventions to occur by individuals without necessarily advancing the underlying science (the so-called Pasteur's quadrant). Today, the role of the independent inventor is being reduced by the growing influence and complexity of the typical science base underlying innovation.

The message is that over 90 percent of the US economy and thus most state economies are medium-to-low technology intensive. This is a 'strategy' that other countries are increasingly capable of imitating. In fact, more and more countries are combining some R&D, a skilled labor force, increasingly high-quality technical infrastructure, and lower wages to take market share away from US domestic companies. Under the 'if-you-can't-beat-them-join-them' theory of competitive survival, US companies are increasingly outsourcing to these foreign locations.

A DIFFERENT VIEW OF THE NEW ECONOMY

The emergence of the 'information' or 'knowledge' economy has led many to believe that the resulting higher productivity growth rates and subsequent higher incomes will continue unabated for the foreseeable future. In fact, because technologies evolve in cycles and because comparative advantages shift among nations, such an outcome is not guaranteed. In fact, as globalization progresses, it is less and less likely.

Most economists agree that the process of geographic reallocation of economic assets is inevitable but also a good thing. In recent years, emphasis has been on the gains in productivity available to outsourcing firms. In fact, such a strategy has increased corporate profits. Greater profitability implies eventual increases in the demand for labor, including in the home country where both higher productivity and innovation combine to create new and higher-paying jobs. Such a theory of 'rolling comparative advantage' relies on US economic history where new jobs have seemed to automatically appear to replace the ones that are offshored or replaced through automation.

The Threat of the Technology Life Cycle

While it is true that for the past several decades new technology-based industries have emerged to create higher incomes for some workers, no theory exists that guarantees leadership and hence economic rewards for the original innovating economy over the entire technology life cycle. Moreover, the outsourcing of resources does not assure higher incomes for a majority of workers. The data in Table 1.1 and associated discussion indicate both stagnant income growth for large numbers of workers and growing income inequality in recent decades.

In the typical technology life cycle, a burst of disruptive technologies imparts significant and broad economic gain. However, as these technologies become increasingly obsolete, the stakes in the status quo resist adaptation. The installed wisdom cultured by past success fights to rationalize business as usual. Today, such resistance is manifested in a passive response to changing technology-based global competition. As a result, attained competitive positions are susceptible to erosion by converging economies as the life cycle evolves.

The current case in point is IT. By virtue of being the innovator, the US economy has experienced significant economic benefits. However, before these benefits were realized, the slow maturation of IT resulted in several decades of constrained productivity gains and hence sluggish growth in real incomes. In spite of the enormous impact of digital electronics, Table 1.1 clearly shows that this sector by itself was too small to stem the declining productivity growth resulting from supply shocks in the 1970s and the onset of substantial foreign competition in the 1980s. Thus, IT investments, while growing rapidly, started from such a small level that only in the late 1990s did the installed base reach sufficient size and productivity to measurably affect national income (Oliner and Sichel, 2000).

This pattern is characteristic of radically new technologies whereby the economic benefits are realized only after substantial maturation in the first part of the technology life cycle. The takeoff in productivity growth for IT was due to the evolution of information systems and the growing ability of consumers of IT to take advantage of its potential benefits. Radical technological changes are not easily absorbed and utilized. Major modifications in the organization of work, industry structure and supporting infrastructure have had to occur in past technology life cycles. In the case of the current IT life cycle, these changes have taken place slowly and thus only in the past 10 years did growth in both productivity and output reach rates not seen for several decades.

However, once the productivity benefits became apparent, huge investments in IT ensued to further expand economic impact. A transition from an R&D strategy focusing on the development and use of stand-alone computers to an increasing emphasis on R&D at the systems level, particularly based on linking computers through communication networks, has greatly increased the productivity impacts of IT (McAfee, 2000). This occurrence is characterized by the inflexion point in the traditional S-shaped growth curve.

The policy concern raised by such long technology life cycles and their investment and learning requirements is that the global convergence now in process is truncating the portion of the life cycle in which the innovator in the past has been able to appropriate the majority of the rewards. The increasingly global distribution of the economic benefits from the current IT-based technology life cycle casts doubt on the future returns from emerging biotechnology and nanotechnology industries.

Given that all industrialized nations, including the United States, have relatively small high-tech sectors, each of these nations is now vulnerable to economic decline during the reshuffling that occurs as a new technology emerges. The installed-base effect and the turbulence in market leadership that accompanies the initial investments in the emerging technology act to inhibit investment. Needed investment can also be constrained by overestimates of the new technology's short-term benefits, the requirements for its assimilation and delivery to target markets, and a passive attitude by government toward the provision of the technical infrastructure necessary to accelerate maturation and market penetration.

The 'New Policy Issues'

To understand how to sustain and broaden the initial gains in innovation and productivity from new technology, four policy questions need to be answered about future economic growth potential in a global economy:

1. Is an economy high tech in an absolute and/or relative sense and therefore can it both create and assimilate new technology at superior rates compared to competitors?

2. Is IT the only truly important long-term growth trajectory?

3. Are current R&D investment patterns (amount and composition) adequate for sustained growth?

4. What are the sources of R&D investment and performance and how can they be effectively managed and sustained?

In formulating growth strategies based on answers to these questions, policy makers must realize that disruptive technologies, while essential to long-term growth, do just what their label implies. The major impacts are the creation of some new industries, restructuring of many established industries, and shifts in types of jobs and work location. Such structural impacts are obviously traumatic, but they are essential for future competitiveness.

These same categories of impacts resulted from the Second Industrial

Revolution in the late 1800s and early 1900s, when major investments in new infrastructure in the United States integrated largely isolated regional markets into a single national one. New communications technologies greatly increased the flow and timing of information, and standardization facilitated the emergence of the factory system for manufacturing. Investment in transportation infrastructure meant that geographically dispersed factories could specialize in components, which were integrated into more complex products at yet another location, and, because of standardization, could be used to repair a product at a remote location from the site of the product's manufacture. This restructuring of the economic system caused major changes in job content and location. The period was also characterized by a distinct lack of pricing power in the key technology-driven markets, which spawned a survival-of-the-fittest corporate environment.

The same process is underway today, but this time the resulting technological competence is spreading globally. The impact is that the price wars of today's global markets are the result of new national economies whose acquisition and development of technology are expanding global capacity and eroding market shares of established industrial economies. The persistent US trade deficit strongly exemplifies this trend.

In addition to the global diffusion of IT, an important point for economic growth strategies is the fact that IT, while pervasive and profound in its impact, in the long run will not be able to drive economic growth by itself. A major portion of the effects of IT is in the areas of market transaction efficiencies and corporate processes and operations. Because the US economy was first to invest intensively in IT infrastructure, it realized the benefits ahead of competing nations. However, the resulting IT-driven productivity growth advantage will not persist as IT investment across the global economy accelerates. Thus, the lasting leadership typically realized by the innovator after a long gestation period seems likely to become mainly a pattern of historical interest, not only for IT but for all emerging and future technologies.

Most important is the fact that other countries have not only imitated the US investment strategy in IT infrastructure but by some metrics have exceeded the US economy in deployment. Thus, IT infrastructure is no longer an optional strategy for attaining comparative advantage but rather has become a cost of entry into the high-tech global marketplace, just as quality became a strategic mandate 20 years ago. OECD data show that the United States ranks 12th among the 30 OECD member countries in terms of broadband subscribers per 100 inhabitants – a surprising situation, given the fact that the United States created the Internet and was the early clear leader in overall IT investment. More troubling is the fact that this mediocre position is considerably worse when deployment is adjusted for quality of broadband. An increasing number of countries, such as Japan and Korea, have much higher capacity broadband with even more advanced systems planned.

A limited US infrastructure will inhibit emerging multimedia IT services and ultimately restrict the competitive position of the US domestic economy. In the near future, telephone, television, radio and web services will all be delivered to business and individual customers by a single broadband connection. Thus, in terms of a critical infrastructure driving economic growth, broadband will play the equivalent of electricity's role in driving the manufacturing economy of a century ago (McChesney and Podesta, 2006). Yet, according to some analysts, the US broadband infrastructure ranks near the bottom among developed economies (Bleha, 2005).

The policy issue is that from a long-term economic growth perspective, final demand is not satisfied by infrastructure. Consumers do not buy infrastructure, they buy products and services. IT has opened up new vistas for innovative products and services provided by hardware, software and their integration. Thus, no matter how much IT infrastructure advances, the end points of high-tech supply chains (final demand) will continue to be products and services that consumers everywhere want. The message for economic growth policy is that investment in IT is a necessary but not sufficient condition for future competitiveness and economic growth.

As discussed in Chapter 8, the relationship between an industry's technical infrastructure and market innovation is a complex, iterative one, or, as sometimes characterized, it exhibits the 'chicken-or-egg' phenomenon. That is, private investment in innovation will be restrained if adequate technical infrastructure is not available because risk and cost both rise in its absence. Conversely, private investment in infrastructure will not be forthcoming because of its public-good content, while public investment is often postponed until sizable markets appear that create visible demand for the infrastructure. To deal with this economic gridlock, both Japan and Korea have forged way ahead of most other countries in broadband deployment by forcing a highly competitive communications infrastructure and providing subsidies through tax breaks, loan guarantees and direct payments to localities investing in municipal broadband systems.

This widespread investment in advanced broadband is leveraging private-sector investments in new products and services. The result is lower cost for much higher capacity, reflecting the understanding that such infrastructure has large positive externalities. For example, Korea has become a leader in online video games. The speed of DSL in Japan, has risen from 8 megabits per second in 2001 to as high as 40 megabits per second in 2005. In comparison, until recently most US broadband connections, whether DSL or cable, were still 1.5 megabits per second. Moreover, the cost of use to Japanese citizens and businesses is considerably lower. This understanding of the economic relationship between technical infrastructure rates of innovation in products and services has placed Japan in a superior competitive position. In 2005, one in 25 Japanese telephone calls was made over the Internet (VoIP).

Because advanced infrastructure at reasonable cost makes innovative market applications more feasible, Japanese companies are leaders in introducing new mobile Internet technologies that offer high-definition-television reception (IPTV), movie downloads and more sophisticated games. With the rapid penetration of advanced broadband, creation of websites specifically designed for mobile-phone use can be rationalized, providing consumers with news, financial services, weather, and so on. (Bleha, 2005). The US economy is moving in these directions but more slowly due to inadequate policies for overcoming the chicken-or-egg problem.

The policy problem results from the fact that the interactive nature of advances in infrastructure and innovations is not fully understood or appreciated. Not focusing on this complementary-asset relationship in an increasingly aggressive global economy will surely mean loss of comparative advantage or failure to attain it in the first place. In the case of IPTV, Japan's NTT is one of the earliest adopters of the next generation Internet Protocol (IPv6). Having this new standard in place is enabling NTT to deploy IPTV more efficiently. Service delivery is simplified by allowing each set-top terminal to be authenticated independently as soon as the user connects it to the network, which contrasts with the more complex and less efficient NAT (Network Address Translation) processes used with the current standard, IPv4.

Adequate infrastructure needs to be in place for investment in new products and services to be rationalized, but the infrastructure is not going to come totally from private-sector initiative when these new applications are not yet in the market. In the past, the inefficient interactive investment process between infrastructure and private-market innovations in the domestic US economy was able to evolve piecemeal over time because global competition at the high-technology end of the economic spectrum did not exist. That situation is no longer the case.

Some have argued that the deployment models being implemented in these other countries do not necessarily apply to a large and geographically dispersed economy such as the United States. Different types of infrastructure have different degrees of public-good content. Thus, a trade-off between relying on private-sector competition and public subsidies exists and can vary across economies with different characteristics. OECD data show that most of the economies ahead of the United States in broadband deployment are relatively small. These small economies are often more densely populated, which facilitates provision of IT infrastructure.

However, no matter how the infrastructure is provided, its availability enables competition in the provision of value-added services, as is evident from the success of such a policy model in smaller countries. Thus, the imperative is to find the infrastructure investment strategy that fits the structure of the domestic economy.

In fact, the optimal policy may not be straightforward. Two competing competition models have emerged in IT-based industries: (i) unbundling the infrastructure and applications providers within a technology platform, or (ii) relying on the emergence of multiple but integrated competing technology platforms. One of the greatest barriers determining the correct model seems to be the inability to distinguish between the economics of the technology-based infrastructure and the market applications that depend on it.

In the United States, companies are typically allowed to bundle the infrastructure with applications. The incumbents therefore have a strong incentive to resist competition at the applications level, leaving them with a virtual monopoly on service provision for their particular IT infrastructures. The policy rationalization for this approach is that sufficient competition exists from alternative technology infrastructures, so that service competition exists at the aggregate industry level. In reality, however, such competition often fails to materialize in many local markets and even nationally due to effective monopoly control by the owner of the installed base.

The Bottom Line

Strategies of companies in all sectors of the economy reflect the transformation to knowledge-based investment. However, the future centers around the global economy where knowledge is developed and applied to domestic economic advantage are only beginning to be determined.

Higher growth rates cannot be sustained by just riding the information highway. The evolving IT infrastructure has the capacity to leverage a diverse range of final consumption services, as well as many types of manufactured goods. The implied synergies are real. Therefore, technologically advanced economies are limiting their long-term growth potential, if policies allow investment to be channeled into just a few sectors. Diversification not only has the advantage of stabilizing long-term growth, but, when large economies of scope exist, the economic impact can be especially significant. Finally, capturing the synergistic effect of parallel investment in technical infrastructure and private-sector innovation raises the rates of growth in all sectors.

NOTE

1. Given that macroeconomic models theoretically produce national and therefore higher estimates of rates of return from technology investment, one might ask why economists do not use this approach exclusively to study technology's impact. In fact, macro models are much less accurate due to traceability erosion and the aggregation of multiple technologies embodied in a single impact estimate. The latter prevents analysis of specific investment strategies and hence the mechanism of innovation.

4. The Public–Private Growth Model

*If the US doesn't get its act together, Du Pont is going to go to the countries
that do, and so are IBM and Intel. We'd much rather be here, but we have an
obligation to our employees and shareholders to bring value where we can.*

Chad Holliday (CEO, Du Pont)

Through common sense, moderately constructive policy change can
sometimes be effected. However, like every other aspect of economic growth
strategy, the growing competition among governments to provide superior
support to private-sector technology development and utilization demands
systematic and rigorous development of policy instruments. Yet, every
innovation policy initiative of the past 25 years has been largely a guess,
devoid of an underlying consensus model and data to drive that model. The
result is policy that is at best poorly matched with actual market failures.

At a general level, everyone agrees that technological innovation is
essential to long-term growth. Unfortunately, this general relationship is
often where understanding of the role of technology and the investment
patterns that produce it ends. As such, economic growth policy frequently
experiences gridlock because stakeholders cannot discuss the complex policy
issues, let alone move toward informed consensus policy decisions. Simply
stating that R&D produces innovations and therefore more of it is required is
neither sufficiently specific to make intelligent policy nor is it convincing
enough to attain needed levels of resources.

The most significant weakness of existing growth models is adherence to
the black-box characterization of technology. In this framework, technology
is regarded as a homogeneous entity, which thereby prohibits consideration
of the existence of distinct technology elements. Incorporation of the major
elements is critical because each responds to distinctly different investment
incentives and therefore needs to be addressed separately by policy analysis.
Crude, uninformed attempts to remove perceived market barriers at some
general level will either miss the investment incentives that should be
targeted or provide too much coverage, thereby wasting resources and
creating opposition to the policy initiative.

For historical reasons, US innovation policies are more wedded to the black-box model than are many other economies. Competing nations do not have the correct model completely worked out, but to varying degrees they at least sense the major elements of the required one. These emerging models, based on 'multi-element' and 'public–private' characteristics of industrial technology, are the focus of this chapter.

R&D AND INNOVATION

To develop an efficient policy-relevant growth model, several specific factors affecting the productivity of investment in R&D must be taken into account:

1. *R&D is essential for two reasons.* The first is the obvious one, namely, such investment is necessary to create new technology. However, a second reason is the fact that an internal R&D capability is essential to effectively absorb technology from external sources, whether embodied in hardware or software or disembodied in the forms of methods, techniques and fundamental understanding (so-called 'tacit knowledge'). In fact, research has shown that the use of advanced technologies by manufacturing plants belonging to multi-plant firms is correlated with firm R&D spending (Dunne, 1994). Such capacity to absorb technology is particularly important, given that more than 90 percent of the US economy is not R&D intensive and must therefore 'import' much of the technology needed to compete effectively.

2. *Innovations based on radically new technologies come from very different R&D investment processes than do innovations within the life cycle of an existing generic technology.* The implication is that innovation policy must be segmented to allow the optimal mix of R&D incentives to be applied to each unique category of barriers that typically arises in each case.

3. *Incremental innovation is far more integrated into the management practices of existing corporate lines of business than is radical innovation.* Investment in incremental innovation typically requires some degree of publicly supplied technical infrastructure to enable assimilation by customers and therefore provide attractive expected rates of return, but the R&D investment decisions are largely made by the private sector. Disruptive technology R&D, however, suffers from a range of severe barriers and therefore needs multifaceted and sustained government support.

4. *Some elements of industrial technology and hence some types of R&D have an infrastructure (public-good) character and therefore suffer from*

persistent underinvestment. Technology-based growth policies must recognize this heterogeneity of R&D and structure funding policies accordingly.

5. *R&D intensity is correlated with the productivity of R&D.* A large study of 2,253 French manufacturing firms found that a company's R&D intensity has a significantly stronger effect on innovation output than a company's size.[1] The researchers calculated that a 1 percent increase in R&D intensity in 'high-tech' firms increases the probability to innovate by 20 percentage points for all five of the innovation indicators used in the study.[2]

6. *Increasing R&D intensity in low-tech industries appears to improve those industries' ability to compete.* For such industries, a 1 percent increase in R&D spending per employee increases the propensity to innovate in new-to-the-firm products by about the same amount as in high-tech industries, but it also increases the propensity to introduce a new-to-the-industry product, a new process, or the probability of holding a patent by twice the amount found for the high-tech sectors. Interestingly, in the low-tech sectors, the study found that R&D increases the share in total sales of new-to-the-firm products more than the share of total sales from new-to-the-industry products (7.9 to 2.2 percentage points). The implication is that while firms in low-tech industries may not be a source of radical innovation, they can bootstrap themselves up to a higher competitive position in their markets through increases in R&D intensity and hence R&D productivity.

7. *R&D productivity is affected by scale factors besides firm-level R&D intensity.* Larger industries with many R&D-intensive companies combine to produce a larger pool of spillovers, thereby enriching the technology base for all industry participants. Similarly, the supporting technical and other infrastructures for large industries benefit from research economies of scale and scope and therefore tend to be more efficient.

8. *Private R&D spending by itself will not yield a high rate of innovation.* In fact, left unsupported, it will decline over time due to lower rates of return. Policy makers should, therefore, be concerned not just with the amount of private R&D investment but also with that amount relative to public R&D and other types of investment (physical capital, management and organization) and with the efficacy of multiple supporting infrastructures (education, venture capital, entrepreneurship, competition policy). All three categories are critical indicators of an industry's and, in fact, an entire economy's long-term potential for economic growth.

The US economy became the dominant technology-based economy after

World War II because it combined public and private R&D investment with above-average technical infrastructure support, especially from universities whose structure and operating philosophies allowed relatively free flows of human and intellectual capital to the private sector. Applications of the results of R&D (innovations) have been enhanced by a dynamic industry structure that facilitates the entry of new firms into most R&D-intensive industries and accepts high levels of risk taking.

Whether or not individual economies match or exceed the US innovative capacity in the next several decades, the collective impact on US competitiveness and hence shares of global markets will be increasingly negative. Several small economies have already evolved models that appear superior. The apostles of denial try to ignore these nations because of their size, but the progress toward a truly unified European economy and the emergence of the Asian regional economy is creating comparative advantages for these economies in current technology life cycles and imply increasingly distributed technological leadership in the decades ahead.

The Bottom Line

From an economic growth perspective, four key productivity factors must be considered: the amount, composition, and timing of R&D investment, and the quality and accessibility of the supporting R&D infrastructure.

The concerns are that R&D policy is (i) not addressing the eight R&D productivity factors, instead treating technology basically as a 'black box', (ii) ignoring the fact that corporate R&D will not yield high returns over entire technology life cycles and (iii) positive returns can disappear completely during transitions between life cycles.

MAJOR ELEMENTS OF AN INDUSTRIAL TECHNOLOGY

The critical elements of an industrial technology are distinguished by their varying degrees of public-good content and their distinctly different roles in the innovation process. However, they also interact synergistically to determine the efficiency of an economy's R&D establishment.

Proprietary Technology

The application of existing science to develop new technologies is viewed in a very general way and frequently constitutes the entire conceptual model driving what passes for innovation policy. In such a black-box framework, the only policy problem is how to encourage enough 'applied R&D' to produce the black boxes that represent the desired flow of innovations.

Such a homogeneous technology growth model says that, given an adequate science base, only a few policy instruments are needed: tax incentives to promote risk taking by entrepreneurs and protection of the intellectual property rights that result from innovative activity. As originally pointed out by Nathan Rosenberg (1982) who coined the phrase 'black box' to describe this homogeneous view of industrial technology, reality is considerably more complicated than most analysts acknowledge. Therefore, so are the issues that policy makers must deal with.

Generic Technology

A critical early phase in the R&D cycle is the demonstration of commercial feasibility of new technologies. The end point of this phase will be referred to as 'generic technology' or the 'proof of concept'. The importance of the research that produces generic technologies stems from the fact that the proof of concept is the bridge between basic science and the considerable private-sector investment in applied R&D necessary to spawn the innovations and subsequent productivity increases that a modern economy must have to grow.

This transition phase between scientific research and innovation research is a major barrier to the emergence of radically new technologies. The perception of significant investment barriers at this initial phase of *technology* research shows up in characterizations such as the 'valley of death,' used in a 1998 House Science Committee report. Such labels have come to emphasize the high risk faced by the private sector when contemplating investments in the generic technology research phase of the R&D cycle. Not only is the technical risk high, but also the market risk is substantial because, at this early phase of the R&D cycle, potential market applications (innovations) typically are a long time from actual commercialization. Years to market requires companies to discount the potential profits from any successful innovation in part to allow for the time value of money. Further, the size or even the existence of future markets for a candidate innovation are in considerable doubt due to rapidly changing market demand and unknown potential competition. This fact results in further discounting of potential profits.

Once the proof of concept is in hand, sufficient risk reduction has generally been achieved so that the necessary large amounts of product- and process-specific applied R&D are forthcoming. Corporations are adept at managing these later phases of the R&D process. Therefore, given appropriate risk taking, industry structure, financing, and intellectual property rights infrastructures, innovations can be expected to flow forth – once the generic technology concept has been demonstrated.

However, a successful flow of innovations is not the end of the growth policy imperative. Time does not stand still and no technology life cycle lasts forever. Thus, critical questions for both corporate and government planners is where will the generic technologies come from in the next cycle and what is the required timing to enable the development of new products and services that companies need to remain competitive in global markets.

From a growth policy perspective, these questions cannot wait for a response until after a new radical technology has appeared somewhere else in the global economy. The frequently cited 'tire-tracks chart' (CSTB, 2003) shows that 10–15 years of 'fundamental research' by universities and private industry has typically been required to get all components of an emerging technology to the point that productive private commitments of applied R&D can be made. Such a lengthy gestation period requires systematic technology assessment and long-term economic and market research by both industry and government to effectively manage this phase of the R&D cycle.

A major barrier to effective R&D policy for emerging technologies is the fact that the international taxonomy for data collection does not explicitly recognize generic technology research. Instead, this phase of R&D is buried in the definition of applied research, which is therefore too broad to provide needed insights into funding issues for truly breakthrough technologies.

Companies, on the other hand, recognize this strategic distinction by dividing their internal R&D budget between a central research facility, which in the past at least has done largely generic technology research, and their lines of business that conduct applied R&D. Under the R&D taxonomy used by all national governments, the content of the central research facility has to be classified as either basic scientific research or applied research, while line-of-business units will classify some research as applied and other spending as development.

From a policy perspective, separating generic technology research from applied research is necessary because of significant differences in both technical and market risk. Companies do not even use the same project selection and evaluation criteria for these two phases of the R&D cycle. The policy significance is large, as investment behavior is quite different in the two cases.

A second important barrier to effective policy analysis is the difference between the term 'generic technology' and what is called 'pre-competitive technology'. Some policy makers and analysts prefer the latter because the term connotes the desired rationale for government funding. That is, the term 'pre-competitive' implies that such technology is both 'non-rival' and 'non-excludable,' which means that assignment of intellectual property rights is as difficult as is the case for scientific knowledge.

However, the implied distinct division between pre-competitive and proprietary research oversimplifies reality. Unlike proprietary research, which is excludable and hence fundable by industry, generic technology is partially excludable. Because property rights are partially attainable, this R&D phase therefore elicits some industry funding and should be called a 'quasi-public' good (Tassey, 2005a). This attribute along with long times to commercialization explain the complicated set of funding patterns involving both industry and government that address this early phase of technology research. The multidisciplinary character of such research and the frequent need for unique research facilities explain the multiple arenas for its conduct, such as universities, industry central research labs, government research facilities, and, increasingly, combinations of these three. However, its quasi-public good character means that intellectual property rights are a significant issue, so the term pre-competitive obfuscates serious policy issues.

Infratechnology

Another critical but often unrecognized element of an industrial technology is the set of 'infratechnologies' that constitutes an industry's technical infrastructure (hence, the prefix, 'infra'). Infratechnologies leverage the development and efficient use of technology at all three major stages of economic activity: R&D, manufacturing and commercialization (Tassey, 1997, 2005a).

In most truly high-tech industries, a large number of infratechnologies are needed. Many measurement and test methods are required to efficiently conduct R&D, control production, and execute marketplace transactions. For example, achieving efficiency for technologically advanced production systems requires process-control techniques, the critical evaluation of engineering data to execute the process control, and methods and reference materials to calibrate complex equipment.

Infratechnologies also provide the basis for technical and functional interfaces between products that make up a system. For example, an automated manufacturing plant can only function efficiently through the availability of seamless physical and functional interfaces for the components of that system. Beyond the single traditional market interface for product transactions, companies today share data with multiple tiers in their supply chain, which requires interoperability protocols.

Finally, at the point of commercialization, customers demand to be assured that a technology-based product performs as specified. This requires product acceptance testing protocols and standards and even specialized facilities for determining compliance with industry standards.

In summary, if you cannot measure, you cannot do R&D; if you cannot test, you cannot control the production process for yield and quality; if you cannot pass a variety of complex data from machine to machine and from company to company, you cannot control cost or schedule; and, if you cannot provide a customer with standardized test data for a product, you cannot assure that buyer that performance specifications have been met.

A public policy problem arises because such infratechnologies have economic utility only if they are uniformly and widely used, that is, as an industry standard. This characteristic creates systematic underinvestment due to free-rider problems. That is, if one company invests in the underlying infratechnology for a standard, everyone else (customers, suppliers and competitors) can 'free ride' on that one company's investment. This free-rider problem is often exacerbated by the fact that the research process for developing an infratechnology is capital intensive and requires specialized research skills. Hence, no one company has sufficient investment incentive, and underinvestment occurs at the industry level. Further, even when an infratechnology evolves, the associated standard often requires technically complex protocols and expensive test beds for determining compliance. Often such facilities must be operated by a competitively neutral and technically sophisticated third party.

As this discussion implies, the majority of standards are not associated with a specific product attribute, such as the format of a DVD or the architecture of a microprocessor. Rather, most are product neutral and, in fact, disembodied from the product or service (Tassey, 2000). Because individual infratechnologies typically have a focused application and hence impact (for example, individual measurement and test methods are applied at specific steps in a production process), their economic importance has been overlooked. However, the complexity of technology-based economic activity and the demands by users of technology for greater accuracy and higher quality require increasingly large numbers of diverse research-intensive infratechnologies. The resulting aggregate economic impact of these infrastructure technologies at the industry level is substantial.[3]

The Internet, for example, depends on a large number of standards. Some of these are particularly complex (such as the Internet Protocol for data transmissions) and are based on a large number of infratechnologies. For IT service industries that rely on the Internet, infratechnologies help define output, interoperability, security protocols and intellectual property.

Ironically, in the late 19th century, American science and engineering associations pioneered standardization of such critical infratechnologies as measurement and facilitated physically embodying them in instruments and production processes (Nelson and Wright, 1992). Yet, today, a century later, the multiple roles of standards and their underlying infratechnologies are poorly understood in US policy circles. Without the availability of this technical infrastructure, especially codified as standards, the efficiency of and transaction costs for all economic activity would be much higher, significantly slowing the evolution of technology life cycles.

THE PUBLIC–PRIVATE TECHNOLOGY MODEL

In contrast to the black-box model, the above set of private and quasi-public elements are functionally linked in complex ways. This construct is critical because success of a public role in supporting industrial R&D depends on demonstrating both theoretically and empirically that public R&D is a complement rather than a substitute for private R&D. Contemporary economics has responded by disaggregating technology into publicly and privately funded components, which implies a dichotomous model consisting of a pure public good and a pure private good (David and Hall, 2000). Some of the required interaction issues (in particular, complementarity) can be assessed in such a model, but the quasi-public-good nature of several critical technology elements is obscured and therefore an assessment of investment incentives and subsequent underinvestment behavior is compromised.

The Multi-Element Model

Figure 4.1 shows the previously defined major elements of an industrial technology and, most important, their interdependencies. Several of these technology elements have varying degrees of public-good content, which approximate the degree of underinvestment by industry. The arrows show the direction of impact of each element. Double arrows indicate the quasi-public-good character of that technology element.

In both the black-box and multi-element models, funding of basic science is a relatively straightforward policy issue because scientific knowledge is generally regarded as a pure public good. Thus, basic research is mainly the responsibility of government to fund. This characterization of science simplifies policy management, with the only issues being the amount of funding and the distribution of this funding across fields of science.

Technology research, however, is much more complicated for two reasons. First, the 'quasi-public-good' elements of an industrial technology described above mean that industry and government each provide some of the investment funds and share in the research conduct. This fact greatly complicates underinvestment analysis and policy response management.

Second, risk becomes a major factor in determining technology investment behavior. In scientific research, the only risk is that the recipient of government research funding will not produce high-quality scientific knowledge. But, for companies contemplating the conduct of R&D, which they depend on for their future prosperity and even their existence, two major types of risk must be faced. One is a technical risk: the R&D program will fail to produce the advances required to meet market demand. The second is a market risk: either demand will be misinterpreted or it will

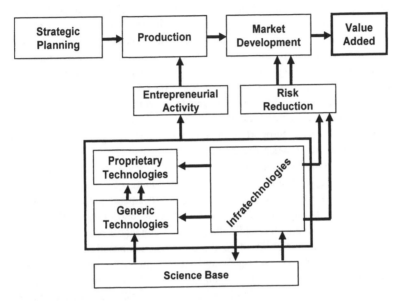

Source: Tassey (1997).

Figure 4.1 Economic Model of a Technology-Based Industry

change between initiation of the R&D program and the point of commercialization. As described in Chapter 5, these two types of risk combine to produce a 'risk spike,' which greatly inhibits private-sector investment. Thus, investment incentives adjusted for risk become the critical focal point of policy analysis.

In Figure 4.1, the first step in applying scientific knowledge (that is, in conducting *technology* research) is to prove the concept of the new technology. The resulting generic technology can take the form of a conceptual model or a more embodied form such as a laboratory prototype. Private-sector generic technology research is undertaken in central corporate laboratories, but increasingly universities and government research institutes are conducting such research, individually or as partners with industry in research consortia.

No matter where the generic technology is developed, if it is deemed to have sufficient potential commercial value and a company gains access to it, that firm assigns the substantial follow-on applied R&D to one or more of its line-of-business units to turn the laboratory prototype into commercial products. The outcome of applied R&D is represented by the proprietary technology box in Figure 4.1.

The importance for industrial competitiveness of investment in generic technologies is that this first phase of technology research provides the basis for 'next-generation' or, in some cases, radically new ('disruptive') products, processes and services. Developing new technology platforms (generic technologies) and market applications derived from these platforms (proprietary technologies) are two very different investments and are managed quite differently within large R&D-based companies.

For these reasons, failure to disaggregate the traditional 'applied research' phase of R&D precludes an appropriate focus on the generic phase of technology research. Support is thereby incorrectly given to the black-box model, which perpetuates the inaccurate view that entrepreneurial activity will draw upon basic science and directly create market applications (innovations). Although examples can be found of specific inventions appearing before a major science base and subsequent generic technology platforms have been established (the so-called Pasteur's quadrant), no major technology has advanced broadly that way in the past 50 years. The reason is that technology is becoming more and more science based (semiconductors, biotechnology, nanotechnology) and, consequently, fewer and fewer inventions can appear ahead of significant advances in the underlying science and the generic technology. Thus, the timely advance of generic technologies is a critical policy concern.

In Figure 4.1, the infratechnology element's broad economic role in the typical technology-based industry is indicated by the multiple arrows pointing to the other technology elements and stages of economic activity. Because many infratechnologies form the technical basis for standards, which by definition must be used collectively, the public-good content is obvious. In fact, the actual need for substantial spillovers in the form of standardization leads to major free-rider problems and underinvestment. The ubiquitous and diverse nature of an industry's infratechnologies means that their collective economic impact is both critical and large.

The Linear Dimension of Technological Advance

The above model is a static representation. Clearly, technological change is a dynamic process. As described in detail in Chapter 7, technologies evolve in a cyclical pattern. This life-cycle concept has critical implications for R&D strategies and policies.

Within a life cycle, the requirement to have sufficient generic technology in place in order to achieve efficiency in applied R&D implies a linear model of innovation. However, the R&D literature makes clear that feedback loops occur and 'cross links' develop between technology trajectories to fuse complementary technologies within technology systems.

Feedback loops are regular occurrences in which marketplace experiences become inputs for the redirection of R&D. In fact, some attempts at innovation may be necessary simply to provide feedback on the adequacy of the current development of the generic technology. Cross-linking necessary to evolve system technologies creates demand for advances in complementary technologies. In this regard, criticisms of linear models of innovation (basic science, generic technology, innovations – in that order) are justified.

Again, important innovations do occur and then the underlying science is developed to explain how the technology works. The most widely cited example is Louis Pasteur's invention of the vaccine. In the process, he and others discovered some new principles of microbiology. More recently, packet switching – the basis for computer networks including the Internet – evolved to a significant degree ahead of network theory (National Research Council, 1999). Parallel processing is another example of an innovation that did not follow the simple linear model. Demand in the 1980s for increased computing power and the widespread availability of microprocessors led to commercialization of multiple-processor computing, which preceded a good theoretical understanding of how processor combinations can work efficiently together (Office of Technology Assessment, 1995). These apparent iterative or recursive relationships between invention/innovation and the underlying basic science are referred to as being in Pasteur's quadrant (Stokes, 1997).

However, such cases are increasingly the exception. For example, it is hard to imagine apoptosis, antisense, RNA interference, monoclonal antibodies, or other generic biotechnologies being developed through experimentation or feedback effects rather than derived from previous advances in bioscience. In fact, the greatest difference between traditional pharmaceutical research and biotechnology research is that the former was largely trial and error, whereas the latter is based on fundamental science and a set of generic technologies that are evolving from this science. Faith-based pharmaceutical research may support the existence of a nonlinear model of innovation, but it is far less efficient than the more linear evolution of biotechnology research.

The increased research productivity of science-based biotechnology is indicated by the relative ability of the two industries to develop new drug 'targets.' Industry analysts estimate that the pharmaceutical industry today develops drugs for 500–600 'drug targets.' In contrast, within just a few years, the ability of biotechnology to isolate and focus on specific intercellular and intracellular mechanisms is projected to expand the number of drug targets by an order of magnitude to 8,000 to 10,000. The implication is that much greater research productivity is achieved when following the linear model.

Somewhat similar to feedback loops, policy priorities can have a 'demand-pull' effect backward in the R&D cycle, including the initial basic research phase. A number of policy analysts have made this argument. However, a needs-driven impact on scientific research is a portfolio-selection effect more than a research-productivity impact. Skewing of a nation's research portfolio is a serious policy concern, but it is a different issue from the knowledge–technology–commercialization sequence.

Thus, R&D-intensive economies with formal public–private R&D ecosystems are increasingly emphasizing a 'linearity' dimension to increasing the productivity of the R&D cycle. Figure 4.2 indicates this linearity to emphasize the need for recognition of the important public and private technology elements and the order in which they need to evolve, at least to a significant degree. Patterns of R&D by which technology becomes

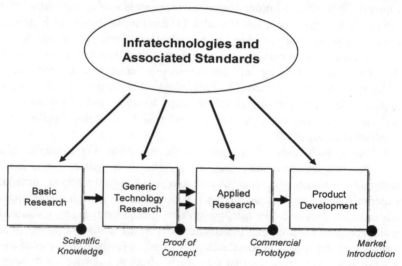

Figure 4.2 R&D Cycle Model

progressively more applied is evident in the life cycles underpinning the major technology drivers of the last 60 years, such as computers (Flamm, 1988), network communications (National Research Council, 1999), and biotechnology (Henderson et al., 1999). Understanding the degree and nature of public-good content in the output of each phase of the R&D cycle is critical to identifying and characterizing underinvestment and hence choosing the correct policy strategies.

TECHNOLOGICAL COMPLEXITY

Technologies are often characterized as 'complex.' However, if the true complexity of technologies were understood, the black-box model would not exist. A somewhat simple measure of complexity has been defined as the degree to which one individual cannot have a total grasp of all elements of a technology (Kash and Rycroft, 1998). Certainly, most modern technologies are substantially beyond this threshold definition. The implication is that communication (including risk assessments) among specialists is important and research coordination is hard to achieve (that is, more tacit knowledge is involved). Determining and accessing needed technical infrastructures also becomes more difficult.

A major response to growing complexity has been specialization of private-sector R&D across firms and industries, which means focusing on specific components of the overall system technology. However, specialization can create inefficient R&D investment at the component level due to inadequate coordination of system-level specifications, which ultimately reduces effective integration and hence system-level productivity. In effect, these negative economic impacts result from the fact that such segmentation increases the public-good content at the systems level, especially in the form of interface specifications and associated standards.

Biotechnology: Impacts of Complexity on the Linear Model

Table 4.1 uses biotechnology as an example of technological complexity. Although 'bioscience' is commonly used as a singular label for the science underlying biotechnology, column 1 of the table shows that multiple distinct areas of science are actually being advanced to then allow a larger set of generic product and process technologies to evolve (columns 3 and 4). These generic technologies have been created over the past 25 years and are just now beginning to yield a significant number of proprietary market applications (new drug therapies in column 5). Column 2 portrays the varied set of infratechnologies (technical tools for characterization, measurement, integration and other infrastructure functions) that affect the entire technology-based economic process.

Clearly, the greater the targeted advance, the greater the technical risk. As the technology life cycle evolves, companies often are caught between inefficient R&D processes and the intense competitive dynamics of high-tech markets, with the result that products are rushed to market with multiple performance defects. In the biotechnology industry, the lack of recognition of the need for advancing complex generic technologies before attempting the development of specific innovations (new drugs) led to attempts to leap

Table 4.1 *Interdependency of Public and Private Technology Assets: Biotechnology*

Science Base	Generic Technologies			Commercial Products
	Infratechnologies	Product	Process	
• cellular biology • genomics • immunology • microbiology/virology • molecular biology • nanoscience • neuroscience • pharmacology • physiology	• bioinformatics • biomarkers • biospectroscopy • combinatorial chemistry • DNA sequencing, profiling • electrophoresis • fluorescence • gene expression • gene typing • bioinformatics • magnetic resonance spectrometry • mass spectrometry • nucleic acid diagnostics • protein structure modeling/analysis	• antiangiogenesis • antisense • apoptosis • bioelectronics • biomaterials • biosensors • functional genomics • gene delivery systems • gene testing • gene therapy • gene expression systems • high-content screening • monoclonal antibodies • pharmacogenomics • proteomics • stem-cell • structural drug design • tissue engineering	• automated cell based assays • cell encapsulation • cell culture • DNA arrays/chips • fermentation • gene expression profiling • gene transfer • immunoassays • implantable delivery systems • noninvasive imaging • nucleic acid amplification • recombinant DNA • separation technologies • transgenic animals	• coagulation inhibitors • DNA probes • drug delivery • inflammation inhibitors • hormone restorations • mRNA inhibitors • nanodevices • neuroactive steroids • neuro-transmitter inhibitors • protease inhibitors • vaccines

from advances in basic science to product development. In effect, development of major portions of the generic technology necessary for efficient applied R&D and hence innovation was skipped.

For example, a company may develop a drug candidate that is effective in terms of the intended impact, say, blocking a specific RNA pathway that influences unwanted protein production by a tumor, only to discover after multiple phases of expensive clinical trials that the specific pathway (one of many within the tumor cell) is not solely or even particularly instrumental in the growth of the tumor. The market failure results from the fact that the required generic technology research into the relationships between different pathways and tumor growth (antisense technology) is too broad and complex for individual companies to undertake efficiently. Because such generic knowledge is only the precursor to specific applications (new drugs), incomplete development leads to very inefficient applied R&D and low yields of innovative products. Moreover, the needed infratechnologies are frequently not adequate, further reducing the efficiency (and thereby increasing the time and expense) of conducting the applied R&D.

In the face of pressure to bring a new drug to market, the many small companies that populate the emerging biotechnology industry guess at the missing elements of the underlying generic technology (the overall pathway structure and the interacting roles of all proteins involved in the disease process being targeted). They further attempt to use or adapt existing infratechnologies developed for other technologies, which are not optimized for biotechnology. The result is lower efficiency of R&D at the industry level.

In the above example of antisense technology, virtually all first-generation drug candidates failed. More broadly, failure to address the linearity of science-based technology development and, more specifically, failure to recognize the importance and public-good nature of generic technologies and associated infratechnologies has resulted in a very low drug development rate for biotechnology firms. In fact, 25 years after Genentech became the first public biotech company, only 12 of the 50-largest companies are profitable and the industry as a whole is still losing money.

The NIH funds a significant amount of generic technology research. However, the lack of an explicit disaggregated R&D model with appropriate real-options or stage-gate progress assessment methods to both guide funding and make missing elements of generic technologies more visible have led to inadequate investment in generic technologies before substantial private-sector investment in attempted innovation occurred. The result has been wasted effort by biotechnology firms in new drug development. The significance of this life-cycle management failure will only increase as more economies expand their domestic biotechnology industries, increasing competitive pressures to reduce R&D cycle times.

Responses to Complexity

Those who support overly simplistic models of technology-based growth will argue that the above examples of alleged underinvestment are actually the 'invisible hand' of the marketplace at work. They propose that, if the technology is truly valuable to society, a viable industry structure will emerge along with sufficient external financing to fund the requisite R&D. Such a premise is incorrect for several reasons. First, the lack of profitability shows that the dynamics of the biotechnology industry is extremely difficult to address. The reasons are clear: a very complex technology (or, more accurately, set of technologies), a long R&D cycle with a demanding discovery phase and multiple and expensive testing phases (clinical trials), administrative costs associated with regulatory approval, technically challenging process and quality control issues at the production stage, and segmented, resistant markets. Second, each major technology element is increasingly the product of multiple disciplines. In the case of biotechnology, the underlying bioscience is supported by microbiology, chemistry, materials science, optics, nanotechnology, robotics and information technologies. Biotechnology is truly a system technology challenge.

The American economy prospered in the 20th century because it excelled at large-scale batch manufacturing and continuous processing technologies. For example, as chemists developed an increasing array of innovations such as processed foods, agricultural chemicals, fuels for engines of various transportation modes (auto, trains, airplanes), pharmaceuticals, plastics, and so on, the scale of processing became larger and the production processes more sophisticated. Thus, chemical plants were needed that were large enough to meet growing demand, controllable (for quality and safety) and cost efficient.

The chemists understood chemical reactions involved in product innovation, but they knew little about process engineering. Therefore, as complexity evolved and cost competition became more important, experts from a number of complementary disciplines were required to design processing components and then integrate them into an efficiently functioning plant. Civil engineers developed pressure-safe reaction vessels and plants. Mechanical engineers designed pumps, valves, piping, heat exchangers, and so on. Materials engineers created corrosion-resistant alloys. Electrical engineers developed sensing, monitoring and control systems. As computer control increased at the plant level, systems engineers were required (Messler, 2004).

An important competitiveness factor is that such complexity is not easily addressed by converging economies. Not only must all the disciplines be available in the workforce, but the industry structure must be capable of efficiently delivering product to the marketplace and the technical infrastructure must be capable of supporting the entire economic process of R&D, production and market penetration. Such an industrial structure, both public and private components, requires time to evolve and constant effort to maintain.

However, complexity is not that easily managed by leading economies. Currently, the pattern described above for biotechnology is repeating itself with nanotechnology. A survey in 2006 by the National Center for Manufacturing Sciences (NCMS) of 600 companies led to the conclusion that 'Large-scale, market driven investments have been somewhat inhibited due to the lack of broader, in-depth understanding of nanotechnology's complex material-process-property phenomena and its interactions with humans and the environment'. The potential consequence is an extended initial flat portion of the S-shaped performance-cost curve. The NCMS analysis concludes: 'Therefore, the near-term impact of nanotechnology is likely to be fragmented, product-specific, and evolutionary rather than revolutionary'.[4]

The market does attempt to adapt at all points in the technology life cycle. As individual entities, young biotechnology firms must rely on sufficient external financing to achieve success for a single product, which then provides the cash flow for subsequent portfolio expansion. The portion of these firms with enough cash can employ contract research organizations (CROs) and/or contract manufacturing organizations (CMOs), but frequently the lack of funds and expertise forces partnerships with 'big pharma.'

More broadly, R&D networks not only have increased in number over the three-decade life of the biotechnology industry but have grown in complexity as well (Hagedoorn and Roijakkers, 2006). Today, most biotechnology firms are involved in one or more types of R&D collaboration. These arrangements usually involve intellectual property sharing and various forms of combined manufacturing and marketing.

At first glance, this trend could be viewed as a forced response by biotech firms to the daunting array of financial and technical barriers that they face over the typical technology life cycle. In fact, the need for complementary technical expertise at all three stages of economic activity (R&D, production and marketing) is increasingly supplied by large, experienced pharmaceutical firms looking for product portfolio enhancement. Further, partnering with other biotechnology or pharmaceutical firms not only raises the probability of long-term success by enabling diversification at an earlier phase in their evolution, but the structures of many such arrangements give biotech firms the initial marketing experience to allow subsequent internal development of marketing expertise and thereby the ability to go it alone in the future.

In the past decade, collaboration has taken on greater complexity, evolving from independent bilateral agreements to structures in which large pharmaceutical firms have become nodes characterized by partnerships with many biotech firms. Some analysts have interpreted this trend as yet another example of the Schumpeterian thesis in which large firms' 'superior' innovation capabilities dominate (Hagedoorn and Roijakkers, 2006). However, the reality seems to be that the complexity of biotechnology plus its distinct science base and production requirements all combine to act as a formidable barrier to large pharmaceutical firms making the transition to the new generic technology and its life cycle, thereby making collaboration as essential for them as for biotech firms.

Finally, the increasing systems nature of modern technologies, including biotechnology, is pushing companies toward more-focused R&D and market strategies within technology life cycles. However, efficient technology systems require multiple components to be developed simultaneously and optimized so that maximum system performance is achieved. Hence, specialization can be a good thing, as long as the innovation infrastructure facilitates systems integration.

TECHNOLOGY AS A SYSTEM

As mentioned briefly in earlier discussions, a concept essential to understanding the public–private character of the technology-based economy is the systems nature of all modern technologies. Resulting inefficiencies at the system level negate considerable technological advance and innovation in the system's components.

Health care is an example of what can happen when an industry ignores the fact that its delivery mechanism is a system. The NIH budget is the dominant share of federal non-defense R&D spending. This spending has created a radically new technology (biotechnology) and, after several decades of research, is now beginning to pay off in a slowly increasing flow of new drugs and diagnostics. However, new drugs by themselves are not enough. One tier forward in the supply chain, the broader health-care system is in a terrible state. New technologies continue to become available but are either ignored or not effectively utilized. US spending on health care as a share of GDP continues to rise, reaching 14.5 percent in 2002 (source: OECD). This share is the largest of any country. Yet, one study estimated that 98,000 deaths occur each year due to medical errors (Health Grades, Inc., 2004).

Information technology, which would significantly reduce costs and improve the quality of health-care delivery, is acknowledged to be grossly underutilized. For example, the x-ray was the primary imaging technology for medical diagnostics for decades. Today, however, imaging diagnostics has expanded to include multiple techniques under the general label of 'biomedical imaging'. These include computed tomography, PET-CT, MRI and optical imaging.

The problem is that, like the x-ray, each of these diagnostic devices has been used as a stand-alone instrument from which the resulting image must be physically transported to the location of diagnosis and the resulting diagnostic information separately transmitted to the site of the consequent therapy. Diagnostic imaging could be significantly improved by treating the imaging instrument as part of a medical system. To do this requires an IT infrastructure based on software that has been tested and made interoperable across the elements of the system. However, such a step requires not only IT infrastructure but also both the ability and willingness on the part of the health care delivery system to use it.

Another major area of the emerging medical diagnostic system, biomarkers, is experiencing similar IT infrastructure problems. Biomarker techniques generate data, but these data must be detected and qualified by a supporting technical infrastructure that ensures their accuracy. The diagnostician must then review the data and interpret them according to standardized protocols. Because generic detection methods are, in effect, customized for each disease, the software tools for detection and analysis of the resulting data must also be adapted for specific indications according to established standards. Finally, as medical data are passed over a network, assurances must be provided that these data are not altered in any way. In general, open standards and measurement infratechnologies have not been developed at a pace required to attain the productivity gains expected.

The problem for public policy is that health care is not viewed as a technology-based system that needs as much investment or deployment assistance as do the individual technologies of which it is composed. Because health care and most other technology-based industries now require complex systems integration infrastructures, including integration with other industries in the same supply chain, policy makers must take into account the investment needs for developing and deploying such infrastructure when considering innovation support programs.

The National Research Council's Computer Science and Telecommunications Board defines IT-based systems integration as the 'wiring' together of islands of computer applications (hardware and software) into a coordinated enterprise-wide distributed network system. At the industry level, systems integration includes more than just physically allowing incompatible components to communicate. It is the synthesis of application domains such as finance, manufacturing, transportation and retail, as well as the supporting information infrastructure including databases, operating systems, architectures, networks, communications devices, and security measures (CSTB, 2000).

Computers embedded in various application devices are all networked in order to collect, receive and process information so that these devices can function effectively. The problem is that local networks are typically not compatible, leading to enormous ad hoc integration costs to users of multiple networks. As Bill Gates put it,

> You might participate in an audio conference call, use instant messaging and schedule meetings with your calendaring application. The irony is that rather than making it easier to reach people, the proliferation of disconnected communications devices often makes it more difficult and more time consuming. And, in an age when business success increasingly depends on how quickly people can share information, this is a critical issue.[5]

System integration services are a fast-growing part of an economy's IT infrastructure. However, as later chapters will demonstrate, the promise of substantial productivity gains is being held back by lack of systems research and supporting standards development. A NIST study estimated that the cost of IT implementation can be four to five times the investment in hardware and software (Leech et al., 1998). Moreover, linking systems together seamlessly adds requirements for additional system-level functionality. For example, security attributes such as authentication, integrity and privacy can only be provided by system-level designs. At the same time, the system must function with a high level of productivity to provide users with 'availability' (the timely and accurate access to information).

Thus, the increasingly ubiquitous use of information generation, transmission and processing demands an effective technical infrastructure that can provide system-level productivity. The United States was the first nation to implement such infrastructure. However, in spite of the fact that it is clearly a public good, public policy has struggled with alternative government roles and approaches to deployment.

ELEMENTS OF TECHNOLOGY POLICY ANALYSIS

In contrast to the black-box model, the public–private model requires a number of elements to be defined and characterized in a policy decision context. Further, the functional relationships among the major elements must be specified. Policy analysis then looks for inadequacies in the elements or malfunctions in their integration, which is the subject of the next chapter.

The conceptual model presented here emphasizes the complexity and timing of R&D investment and the consequent following set of analytical steps required to develop effective technology-based growth policies:

1. Understand industry's criteria for R&D portfolio selection, especially short-term improvement versus long-term disruptive R&D objectives;

2. Identify factors affecting the private rate of return on R&D, including relative RoR for major types of R&D (disruptive technology research, internal proprietary company R&D, externally supported R&D, infratechnology R&D);

3. Analyze intrinsic risk, time discounting, intellectual property rights, regulation and other factors affecting 'hurdle rates' (minimum acceptable rates of return) for industry R&D and consequently degrees of underinvestment that can be expected in different industries or technologies;

4. Characterize and understand the impact of growing corporate reliance on external sources of R&D (contract/grant, joint ventures, consortia, networks, suppliers, customers, and so on) and the consequent implications for the efficiency and location of R&D;

5. Estimate the effect of growing technological complexity on the need for better technical infrastructure (measurement, supply-chain integration, IT infrastructure, and so on);

6. Assess the impact of the greater distribution of R&D across tiers in supply chains on types of R&D conducted by each tier, scale and scope of the R&D, sources of financing, and coordination, integration and diffusion of results; and

7. Identify and characterize the types of innovation infrastructures (skilled labor, financial, technical, diffusion/transfer services, clusters, incubators, entrepreneurial training, and so on) needed to attract global private R&D investment to the domestic economy.

The Bottom Line

The United States achieved the greatest systems design and deployment of technology in history when it placed the first human on the moon. Yet, when it comes to managing its economic system, the historical bias against the public–private technology model is handicapping the needed response to the increasing complexity of modern systems technologies.

At the same time, the global economy is adopting and modifying the original US public–private technology model. Ironically, the original form of this model was created 50 years ago by the Defense Advanced Research Projects Agency

(DARPA). Yet, attempts to adapt it to the needs of economic growth objectives have met with persistent resistance.

NOTES

1. Mairesse and Mohnen (2004). R&D 'intensity' is defined in this study as the ratio of R&D spending per employee. R&D intensity at the company or industry levels is more frequently defined as R&D/sales. The latter metric may be preferable because R&D/employee is affected by the overall capital intensity of an industry and hence using this metric can inhibit cross-industry comparisons.
2. The five indicators used include three dichotomous (propensity) indicators for process innovations, product innovations new to the firm but not necessarily new to the industry, and product innovations new to the industry. The other two indicators used are quantitative (intensity) indicators constructed as ratios of the share of new products in total sales for the two categories of product innovations.
3. Economic impact studies of infratechnologies are discussed in Link and Scott (1998) and Tassey (1997). For summaries and individual studies, see (http://www.nist.gov/director/planning/strategicplanning.htm). For economic impact assessment methods, see Tassey (2003).
4. 'Nanotechnology Is Not Quite Ready for Prime Time,' *Manufacturing & Technology News*, April 4, 2006.
5. Bill Gates, 'The Unified Communications Revolution'. Microsoft, June 27, 2006.

5. Underinvestment in R&D

The first step toward improvement is to face the facts.

Oliver Wendell Holmes

An assessment of the adequacy of US R&D investment must be placed in the context of the following general trends:

- The United States has a declining share of the world's population, which is now less than 5 percent.
- The US workforce is becoming a smaller share of the global workforce as large-population countries enter the world's economy with increasingly skilled labor.
- Within the US workforce of about 110 million, approximately 1.2 million are engaged in R&D.
- The US share of global R&D is steadily shrinking.
- The 'high-tech sector' is a small fraction of the US economy.
- The R&D intensity of the US economy is below its peak of 40 years ago; since then, the R&D intensities of many other economies have risen steadily and some are now higher than the US ratio.

Of these trends, R&D intensity is the most important, in part because it represents the degree of reinvestment of current national income in the future and in part because such investment creates demand for skilled and thus higher-paid labor. Thus, an important focus for economic growth policy is the *amount* of R&D investment relative to GDP.

Policy analysis must also focus on the *composition* of R&D. The economic growth paradigm that has served the US economy so well for decades is based on a stream of 'technology platforms' (generic technologies) funded in part by government and originating in industrial laboratories such as AT&T's Bell Labs, Xerox's PARC, RCA's David Sarnoff Research Center, and other large corporate research laboratories. Those days are gone, so the question is what will be the sources of the portfolio of breakthrough technologies, which will create the new markets, industries and jobs that will enable the US economy to continue to provide a high standard of living.

In the United States, considerable generic technology research is now funded at universities. The Bayh–Dole Act of 1980 has encouraged academic institutions to augment their traditional role of basic research. DARPA provided a large share of this technology research funding for decades, while more recently, the NIH has been a major source of such funding in biotechnology.

However, uncoordinated funding across universities is not an efficient model for producing new technology platforms. That is, if such funding is not managed in a 'portfolio' sense, comprehensive and integrated technology platforms will not emerge in a timely fashion. Although the concept of the research portfolio model originated in the United States, today various versions of the basic concept are emerging in Europe and Asia and are being implemented either on a national level or through technology-based clusters as part of regional economic growth strategies. The United States certainly no longer has a leadership position in developing and implementing such R&D investment strategies.

Finally, private investment is directed largely at specific marketplace objectives, whereas public investment is focused on technology platforms and various types of infrastructure that support private investment. Clearly, some balance must be maintained that reflects the complementary interaction of the public and private elements of an economy's technology capital. However, this policy issue is barely on the table in the United States, as indicated by the skewing of national R&D toward development and a limited set of technologies.

AMOUNT OF R&D

The most frequently discussed technology policy issue is the *amount* of R&D conducted in an economy. Assessing the adequacy of aggregate R&D spending requires comparing rates of return from R&D with alternative categories of investment, such as physical capital and marketing.

To many, the US position with respect to total R&D investment still appears enviable, accounting for slightly less then one-third of the world total of $1 trillion. The OECD countries collectively account for approximately 80 percent of the world total, which for many observers implies that the developing economies are not immediate threats as technology-based competitors. However, as emphasized repeatedly, trends are the important indicators. Corporations certainly realize that the global spread of R&D is one of these trends. Foreign R&D investments in China grew from $5 million in 1994 to $506 million in 2000 (OECD, 2005).

China's R&D intensity is still only 1.5 percent (the same as the United States in the 1950s), but their total R&D now exceeds Japan's spending and the growth rate is high. In fact, Chinese R&D investment is now second highest in the world and is projected to match that of the entire EU in 2009 or 2010. Other Asian economies, such as India, Korea and Taiwan, spend significant amounts on R&D.

R&D Intensity

Although the amount of R&D spending is more frequently discussed, the most important indicator for economic growth policy is R&D intensity (the ratio of R&D to GDP). This is because current output of goods and services is driven by past R&D and therefore current R&D spending relative to the size of the economy is a predictor of future economic growth. By comparing current R&D to current economic output, one gets a rough assessment of an economy's commitment to competing in the future based on technology.

Long-term economic decline is always the result of structural problems that manifest themselves over decades. Such problems arise from domestic economic policies and they are usually exacerbated by changes in global markets. The single best indicator of the long-term problems facing the US economy is its failure to increase its R&D intensity in the face of steadily increasing global competition.

The way by which the pattern of R&D intensity evolved is instructive. The Cold War was already driving up military R&D investment in the 1950s when the Russian launch of Sputnik in 1957 provided the first technology wake-up call for America. This event was followed in 1961 by the first man in space – also a Russian (Yuri Gagarin). Sputnik and Gagarin's flight were not economic threats, but they did serve notice that the rest of the world was becoming technologically capable. Russian military technology plus the achievements by the Russian space program showed that another country was capable of developing and using state-of-the-art technology.

In response, President John Kennedy in a famous 1961 speech called for greater investment in science and technology. For a brief period, budgets for S&E research continued to grow beyond the rapid military R&D expansion of the 1950s, major increases in scholarships for S&E students were implemented, and the S&T focus of the nation was galvanized by the establishment of the goal to put a human being on the moon before the end of the decade.

As indicated in Figure 5.1, national R&D intensity reached a peak average of 2.83 percent during 1963–67. However, the increased emphasis on science and technology petered out in the 1970s. National R&D intensity declined steadily to an average of 2.15 for the period 1975–79, just as new threats from inadequate technology investment – economic this time – were becoming apparent.

The 1980s brought a more pervasive and market-oriented technology-based threat from Japan in electronics, optoelectronics, advanced materials

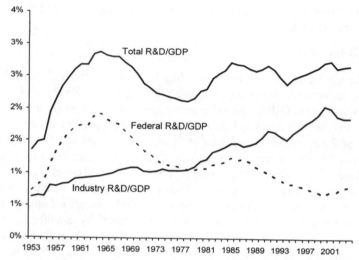

Source: National Science Foundation.

Figure 5.1 R&D Intensity: Funding as a Share of GDP, 1953–2004

(ceramics) and advanced manufacturing (robotics, quality control). This second shock led to sustained higher growth rates in R&D spending by industry and raised national R&D intensity close to its 1960s peak. However, due to continued slow growth in government R&D spending, this critical ratio today is still below the peak average of the mid-1960s.

A bright spot in the post-1960s period is the late 1990s, which benefited from decades of investment in network communications and other information technologies. This period experienced a surge in productivity and subsequent economic growth. Ironically, at the same time, an explosion in technological capability and investment was occurring in other parts of the world, especially in Asia, which is causing a rapid attenuation of the productivity advantage gained through this relatively short surge in domestic IT investment.

The current decade is witnessing an acceleration of global R&D capability well beyond past experience. The apostles of denial have rationalized this trend as being relegated to applied R&D at the lower end of the R&D value-added spectrum. However, this global expansion can no longer be characterized simply as the acquisition of late-phase R&D and product engineering capabilities to support domestic manufacturing. Other countries – developed and developing – are bringing on line new research portfolio management strategies, in particular, the use of technology-based regional economic growth clusters that are capable of conducting state-of-the-art research and facilitating rapid utilization of scientific and technological advances by the local economy.

Comparisons across national economies are revealing because different intensities reflect different national commitments to compete in global markets in the future based on technology. Figure 5.2 presents OECD data showing the distribution for a selection of industrialized economies, as well as average intensities for the expanded European Union (EU-25) and all OECD countries.

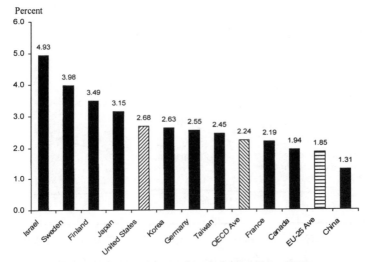

Source: OECD, *Main Science and Technology Indicators*, May 2005.

Figure 5.2 National R&D Intensities: Gross R&D Expenditures as a Percentage of GDP, 2003

The US R&D investment rate certainly does not reflect an adaptation to the growing global R&D capability. In fact, four countries now have significantly higher R&D intensities. The major reason for the long-term stagnation of this ratio is government R&D funding, which has declined steadily as a percentage of GDP from a peak of 1.92 percent in 1964 to 0.68 percent in 2000. An increase in federal R&D spending for defense raised the federal R&D intensity slightly to 0.80 percent in 2004, but that level is still only 42 percent of the peak intensity. Moreover, this defense spending has modest economic growth impact.

Emerging economies have lower intensities, but their growth rates in R&D investment are much higher. OECD data show that China doubled its R&D intensity between 1997 and 2003. Moreover, because of the huge size of emerging economies such as China and India, even a low intensity means that a lot of R&D is being conducted.

EU governments, whether the original EU-15 or the expanded EU-25, spend on average about 0.65 percent of GDP on R&D compared with 0.76 percent for the United States. However, the difference in R&D investment intensity is significantly greater for the private sectors, with US and European businesses spending 1.84 percent and 1.02 percent of GDP,

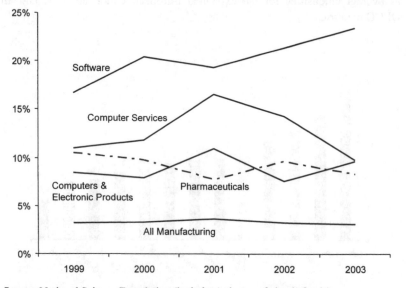

Source: National Science Foundation (includes 'other nonfederal' funds).

Figure 5.3 R&D Intensity: Company Funds for R&D Relative to Sales, 1999–2002

respectively (Dosi et al., 2005). The historical difference in the industry ratios is likely the major reason for the difference in past innovative performance and the productivity differential that favors the US economy.

Barriers to Increasing R&D Intensity

Only a small fraction of the US economy is R&D intensive. For example, Figure 5.3 indicates that most of US manufacturing is at best only moderately R&D intensive. In fact, only a few industries have R&D intensity ratios that predict long-term global competitiveness. Specifically, most industries do not have the high ratios (in the 8–12 percent range) that seem to be required for sustained world-class innovation. Unfortunately, the industries that are R&D intensive together account for only 7–10 percent of GDP.

The policy implication is that the remaining 90+ percent of the US economy, including those industries that are moderately R&D intensive, is vulnerable to the increasing R&D intensity of a broad array of industries in other countries. Industries with moderate-to-low R&D intensities must rely on technology supplied by other industries – domestic or foreign. In a closed economy (no foreign trade), suppliers of technology would obviously be domestic and purchasers would not fear cheaper and higher-quality imports. However, the increasing ability of foreign industries to acquire or develop modest amounts of technology allows them to compete very effectively with their US counterparts.

Due to downsizing in the face of growing import competition, especially in less-technology-intensive areas, US manufacturers' sales grew slowly in the 1980s. The resulting increased proportion of this sector's sales from R&D-intensive industries raised the overall R&D-to-sales ratio for the entire manufacturing sector in the first half of the 1980s from approximately 2.5 percent to 3.0 percent. However, manufacturing R&D grew more slowly over the next decade and the R&D-to-sales ratio remained flat from 1985 to 1995. In the 1996–2000 period, both R&D spending and sales accelerated with R&D spending growing slightly faster, resulting in the ratio increasing to 3.3 percent.

Thus, downsizing and restructuring by many manufacturing firms and even entire industries have resulted in a manufacturing sector that has continued to increase output but is smaller relative to the overall economy. However, a 3.3 percent R&D-to-sales ratio is not adequate for this sector to maintain long-term competitiveness in a global economy that is rapidly expanding its R&D capability. The wide disparity in R&D intensities among manufacturing industries (Figure 5.3) implies that not all manufacturing firms or even entire industries have adapted to the demands of global, technology-based competition.

Future improvement in real output growth rates for this sector will have to come from sustained real growth in R&D sufficient to further increase R&D intensity. Research has shown that a minimum amount of R&D must be conducted by companies just to maintain the capability to absorb technology effectively from external sources (Cohen and Levinthal, 1989).

However, more economies are emphasizing the innovation objective of R&D (as opposed to a technology absorption objective) as the primary strategy for maintaining high rates of economic growth (Griffith et al., 1998). Such strategies require considerably more investment in R&D than that required for imitation strategies.

Moreover, no evidence has ever been produced that increasing R&D intensities to levels found among the most R&D-intensive industries encounters diminishing returns (Cameron, 1999). In fact, estimates of rates of return among major investment categories indicate that at the national level the amount of R&D spending is only about one-quarter the optimal amount (Jones and Williams, 1998, 2000). More than any other single policy instrument, it is R&D investment that will have to lead the structural changes required by the US economy.

The difficulties in achieving acceptable R&D intensities and establishing effective R&D networks are increasing as R&D becomes dispersed across tiers (industries) in the supply chains making up the US economy. The greater complexity of modern R&D and its increased dispersion is creating a need for a more diverse technical infrastructure to support the necessary private R&D investment. To this end, analyzing R&D expenditures at just one tier (an industry) in a supply chain will be increasingly inadequate for assessing economic growth potential, as will a singular focus on private or public R&D.

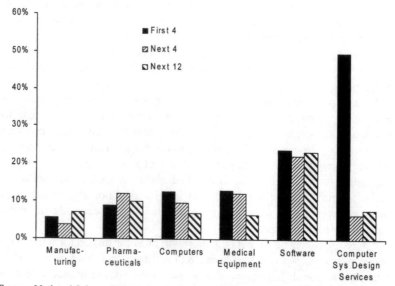

Source: National Science Foundation ('other nonfederal' as well as company funds)

Figure 5.4 Distribution of Industry R&D by Size of Company, 2002

Moreover, entire industries need to be R&D intensive in order to maintain competitive position broadly and thereby achieve maximum contribution (value added) to GDP. Figure 5.4 indicates the distribution of R&D among large and small firms in a number of high-tech industries and for the entire manufacturing sector. With one exception (software and computer services), these industries have reasonably even distributions of R&D. Absolute size and distribution of firm size are important attributes of high-tech industries for policy analysis.

Thus, a policy objective must be efficient R&D networks supported by public and private investment to maintain competitive positions in multiple linked industries. However, although much attention is being given to 'global' R&D networks, research has shown that significant portions of knowledge spillovers from R&D are localized, so that a technology-intensive industry needs to be more clustered geographically than other industries.[1] Such a constraint on R&D spillovers is evidenced by the fact that the performance of R&D is concentrated geographically within the US economy. In fact, NSF data show that the top 10 R&D-performing states account for almost two-thirds of national R&D, much larger than their 47 percent share of the population. As discussed in Chapter 10, technology cluster models are becoming increasingly recognized for their R&D efficiency effects, a majority of which derive from interactions among co-located public and private elements of the innovation infrastructure.

COMPOSITION OF R&D

While analyses of the amount of R&D spending and its distribution across companies and supply chains provide important indicators of the adequacy of aggregate R&D investment, the ever-advancing complexity of technology and the greater risks associated with long lead times mean that almost any distribution of private-sector R&D over time is likely to be inadequate with respect to investment in next-generation and especially radically new, disruptive technologies. The latter are the basis for new industries and major international shifts in competitive position. 'Inadequate investment' therefore also reflects problems with the composition of R&D.

R&D is viewed as a relatively long-term investment compared to other uses of corporate resources such as investment in productive capacity and marketing. However, because the source of funds, as opposed to the performer, controls the composition of R&D, it is significant that most of the nation's R&D is paid for by private industry. Almost three-quarters (72 percent in 2000) of corporate R&D expenditures are allocated to the 'D' in R&D, and industry's share of national R&D has grown steadily for decades. Most industry R&D also is relatively short-term. Many corporate development projects take less than one year to complete (Rajagopalan et al.,

138

R&D in the Modern Economy

2004). An IBM official stated that 50 percent of the company's hardware revenues come from new products introduced in the past six months. IBM now describes its product cycle in 'web years' of 90 days (Kingscott, 2001).

Moreover, industry R&D is both cyclical and subject to secular shifts in overall risk taking. Table 5.1 shows the variability in industry-funded R&D growth over successive six-year periods. In addition to occasional structural shifts in risk taking, the influence of the downward portions of business cycles on corporate R&D spending includes a decline in risk taking as well as an overall drop in total R&D.

Table 5.1 Growth Rates of Industry-Funded R&D for Six-year Periods

Period	Average Growth Rate
1969–1975	1.5%
1975–1981	7.7%
1981–1987	6.8%
1987–1993	4.6%
1993–1999	9.0%
1999–2004*	1.9%

Note: * Five years of available data
Source: National Science Foundation.

Such variability in both amount and especially composition is not conducive to the generation of radically new technologies. Yet, the need for breakthrough technologies is increasing as more economies converge on existing markets and develop innovative capabilities. Moreover, new technologies depend increasingly on the availability of new science. Biotechnology and nanotechnology are prime examples. Figure 5.5 indicates the trend in greater dependency of invention (patents) on scientific research. This uptrend is more than a correlation with the growing rate of patenting. NSF data show that between 1994 and 2003 the number of scientific literature citations per patent more than doubled from 50.8 to 116.2.

The implication is that the composition of R&D must be managed to ensure that (i) adequate scientific progress occurs to support disruptive technology research, (ii) this early-phase technology research takes place, and (iii) the production of new technical knowledge diffuses to later phases of the R&D cycle in a timely manner. Achieving these R&D efficiency goals requires adequate and stable funding of scientific and generic technology research over the early phases of the R&D cycle.

Investment by Phase of the R&D Cycle

The time dimension of R&D investment is critical because competitive pressures are shrinking technology life cycles, thereby forcing industry to increasingly concentrate its R&D resources on shorter-term projects that

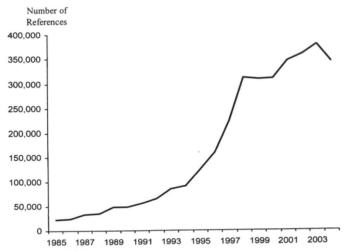

Source: Francis Narin, Research & Equity Markets; McMillan et al. (2000).

Figure 5.5 References to Scientific Publications in US Patents

yield the incremental improvements in the time periods necessary to defend current product or service markets. In essence, industry is being forced to adjust risk–reward profiles at each phase of the R&D cycle. Overall, such calculations are compromising investment in next-generation generic technologies and certainly in radically new technologies.

That a balance is required between short-term improvement and long-term disruptive technology research is evident from case studies of major breakthrough technologies. Such radically new technologies decimate existing competitive positions that have been based on the defender (existing) technology. In the past, such breakthroughs typically have had long gestation periods and frequently have appeared unimportant or at least not an immediate threat when they were first introduced. Thus, their advent was not only not planned for but also often ignored for considerable periods of time by the installed base. With more and more countries pursuing breakthrough technologies (nanotechnology is a current example), the policy imperative is to promote an optimum balance of investment across the phases of the R&D cycle.

The importance of this policy objective is supported in a study by Kim and

Mauborgne (1997). R&D-intensive companies in the United States and Europe were surveyed to obtain sales and profits data on investments in incremental improvements based on the current generation of technology

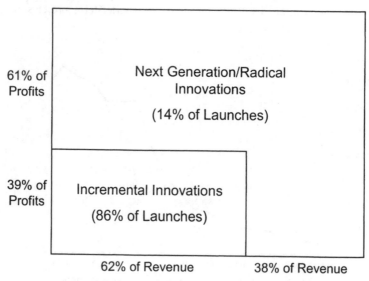

Source: Kim and Mauborgne (1997).

Figure 5.6 Profit Impact of Major and Minor Innovations

(product line extensions) and in products based on new emerging generic technologies. As Figure 5.6 shows, for the average firm responding to the survey, product-line extensions dominate both in terms of number and sales. This result is hardly surprising, as companies focus most of their resources on extracting value from their current technology portfolios. However, a majority of profits were found to be attributable to the relatively few 'discontinuous' innovations (that is, innovations based on radically new generic technologies).

Econometric studies have also demonstrated that the earlier phases of the R&D cycle yield the higher RoRs. Griliches (1995) concluded from a comprehensive review of microeconomic studies that the RoR on basic science is about three times that of applied R&D, which, in turn, is about double the RoR on physical capital. However, note that because an important phase of R&D between basic science and applied R&D, namely generic technology research, is not part of the NSF data collection scheme, companies responding to R&D spending surveys are forced to allocate funds for breakthrough technology research either to basic science or applied research. Much of this research is aimed at neither scientific knowledge (basic research) nor a commercial prototype for a specific product line (applied research). Rather, its target is a laboratory prototype or proof of concept to justify follow-on applied research.

Trends in the Composition of R&D

A major national R&D trend has been the increasing dominance of industry funding. The federal share peaked at 66.8 percent of all US R&D in 1964 reflecting the post-Russian space technology response. However, the federal share dropped steadily in succeeding decades, reaching a low of 24.9 percent in 2000. The main impact of this change has been greatly reduced federal funding for industry. The federal share of industry R&D dropped from more than one-half in the late 1950s and early 1960s to less than 10 percent by 2000 (National Science Board, 2006a). A good part of this trend is the result of American corporations developing considerably more R&D capability and funding R&D as a major business strategy. In fact, as Table 5.2 shows, industry is now the dominant national funding source.

Table 5.2   Shares of Funding by Phase of R&D for Major Funding Sectors, 2003 (percent)

	Basic	Applied	Development	Sector Share of Nat'l R&D
Industry	16.4	58.4	80.9	63.3
Federal Government	61.7	34.7	18.0	30.1
University and Other Nonprofit	21.8	6.9	1.1	6.6
National Share by Phase	19.1	23.9	57.0	100.0

Source: National Science Foundation.

Up to a point, the dominance of industry as a source of R&D funds is not a problem because each succeeding phase of the R&D cycle requires more R&D resources than the preceding one. However, the timing, amount and content of the early phases of R&D are critical to an economy's long-term competitive position. Thus, the sources of funds and their risk preferences must be analyzed to identify barriers to their availability at appropriate points in the R&D cycle. For example, while industry funds the majority of national R&D, most of these funds are allocated to applied research and development (95 percent). Government, on the other hand, while supplying less than one-third of national R&D funding, accounts for over 60 percent of national funding for basic research.

This separation of funding emphasis creates a major policy issue, namely the funding for 'the gap' or 'the valley of death,' as the generic technology research phase is often called.[2] Considerable anecdotal evidence has accumulated over the past decade indicating a secular shift in the composition of industry-funded R&D toward short-term development projects (Corcoran, 1994; Duga, 1994; Geppert, 1994). *R&D Magazine* summarized a survey (conducted jointly with Battelle) of industry's projected R&D spending plans for 2000 by stating that industrial support of basic industry R&D has largely disappeared, replaced mostly with support of high-tech development (Studt and Duga, 2000). In other words, the funding gap has widened, or, as described in Chapter 4, the risk spike has become larger.

Looking at a technology-based economy more broadly, most small companies do not even attempt generic technology research, relying instead on assimilating the required technical knowledge from external sources. Large companies have undertaken more of this type of research in the past, but a number of factors such as generic technology's public-good content and higher corporate discount rates are resulting in growing underinvestment. Firms are increasingly 'takers' with respect to the longer-term and higher-impact 'natural trajectories' that sustain high R&D intensities (Nelson and Winter, 1977). These trajectories usually derive to a significant extent from sources external to the private sector (Klevorick et al., 1995).

This literature leads to the model proposed here. Once a technology life cycle is initiated (that is, proof of concept is established), subsequent applied R&D investments are driven by the generic technology. Even though the generic technology evolves to a degree over successive sub-cycles, it provides the platform that determines the trajectory of applications. Thus, the multi-element taxonomy is essential for R&D policy analysis because it has implications for the sources of these new technology platforms, access to them (property rights issues), and the transaction costs associated with access (diffusion issues). Today, the systems nature of most technologies further complicates the model by creating multiple component trajectories that must evolve in concert for system innovation and productivity to grow over time.

Observers of traditional industries, such as automobiles, are often misled by these companies' large R&D budgets. While substantial amounts are still spent on R&D, very little of it is allocated to longer-term, disruptive-technology research. Such a strategy is inefficient because these industries are forced to rely on external sources to develop and deliver new generic technologies. It is not necessary that individual firms conduct all such research. However, without an adequate internal long-term research capability, companies in these industries not only lose control of the portfolio of new technologies, but they also have trouble evaluating and absorbing research results from the external sources (universities and government laboratories).

Figure 5.7 shows the overall national trends, at least to the extent possible with public data. Applied research, which contains the critical generic technology research expenditures, has grown the slowest of the three major phases of R&D over the past 15 years. This research provides the transition

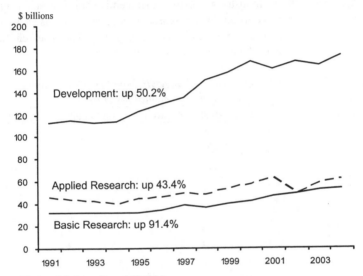

Source: National Science Board (2006a).

Figure 5.7 National R&D by Major Phase, 1991–2004 (in constant 2000 dollars)

between scientific research, which has no market objective, and technology development, which is totally focused on specific market applications. The multiple market failures interfering with this transition are several and increasingly severe; hence, the label 'valley of death.'

As described in Chapter 4, in the early portion of applied research, market risk enters the calculation for the first time and technical risk takes on new meaning for corporate R&D managers. With increasing global technology-based competition, discount rates applied to potential R&D investments rise for companies to reflect greater combined technical and market risk. As a result, risk adjustments for projects that are longer term, potentially higher payoff, and, in most cases, necessary for long-term survival are considerably higher than for shorter-term projects, which are focused on achieving improvements to existing product lines based on the current generic technology and, as Figure 5.6 indicates, yield lower profits over time. And, as Chapter 7 will describe, profits from the current technology life cycle will eventually disappear as the underlying generic technology reaches its physical limits.

The combined effect of these investment barriers is reflected in the slower growth of applied R&D. In 2002, US R&D declined by 4.1 percent. This drop was the first since 1953 when R&D data began to be collected (Shackelford, 2006). Industry's relative disincentive to invest in next-generation or disruptive-technology research is indicated in this year by a much greater decline of 35.2 percent in its funding of applied research. Such a large drop accentuates the longer-term trend in Figure 5.7.

Table 5.3 IRI 'Sea Change' Index: Changes in Member Firms' Annual Planned Investments for Major and Incremental R&D Projects

Forecast Year	Directed Basic Research	New Business Projects
1993	-26	+18
1994	-26	+18
1995	-19	+31
1996	-6	+39
1997	-26	+28
1998	-14	+24
1999	-23	+31
2000	-9	+34
2001	-21	+44
2002	-13	+31
2003	-21	+7
2004	-17	+1
2005	-21	+8
2006	-8	+31
2007	-6	+31

Source: Industrial Research Institute.

Unfortunately, data on industry generic technology research expenditures are virtually non-existent. The only trend data that illuminate the relevant investment patterns come from an annual survey by the Industrial Research

Institute. From this survey, the IRI calculates 'sea change' indices for R&D investment planning data collected from its member companies. Each index is the difference between the number of responding companies that indicate plans to increase a category of spending by more than 5 percent (less than such an increase is considered only to account for inflation) and the number of companies planning to decrease such spending.

One of the R&D expenditure categories is 'directed basic research', which approximates generic technology research. The data in Table 5.3 show that the index has been negative for the past 15 years, implying a secular shift in corporate R&D strategies toward less-radical/disruptive-technology research. Further supporting this observation is the trend in the index for 'new business projects' (investments focusing on R&D aimed at new or improved products within the current technology life cycle), which has been positive for every year.

These trends beg the question of where the new breakthrough technologies will come from. In recognition of the eventual consequences of its increasing focus on current technology life cycles, US industry has increased its research funding at universities by 312 percent over the 20-year period, 1984–2004. However, such funding is a tiny part of overall industry R&D funding, amounting to 1.0 percent in 1984 and barely increasing to only 1.1 percent in 2004. Moreover, this funding accounted for only 5.0 percent of total university research funding in 2004. Perhaps most significant for the future, the amount of industry funding of university research in constant dollars has declined from a peak of $2.18 billion in 2000 to $1.97 billion in 2004 (National Science Board, 2006a).

Non-Corporate Sources of Generic Technology Research Funding

Throughout most of the post-World War II era, the federal government, primarily through DARPA, has been the dominant source of funding for generic technology research in the physical and information areas. However, DARPA funding has been flat in constant dollar terms for two decades, while total Department of Defense (DoD) R&D funding increased substantially. Thus, the early-phase technology research by the DoD that spawned so many spin-offs into major commercial innovations has become proportionately smaller not only compared to total DoD R&D but, most important, relative to total national R&D and the GDP growth it supports.

In response to these indicators of underinvestment in the early phases of R&D, the apostles of denial have grasped at potential alternative sources of funding to justify the cutbacks in government support for breakthrough technologies. In addition to embracing the black-box model, which by regarding technology as a homogeneous entity allows rationalizing the equivalency of industry and government technology research funding, venture capital (VC) has been cited as the private-sector equivalent of government risk capital.

However, the majority of venture capital is invested significantly later in the R&D cycle than is the type of government research funding provided by DARPA in the DoD, NIST's Advanced Technology Program (ATP), and similar programs in other government R&D agencies.

In venture-capital taxonomy, the earliest round of funding, called 'seed' capital, is the equivalent to generic 'proof-of-concept' research. Only $55 million was allocated by venture capitalists to this phase of technology research in 2005, down from a peak of $519 million in 1999. Currently, less than 1 percent of private venture capital goes to this phase of technology research (VentureSource).

The reality is that the risk-adjusted RoR model used by venture capitalists provides very little justification for proof-of-concept research funding. In fact, Figure 5.8 shows that venture capital has shifted toward even less-risky investment options in recent years in response to the global competitive

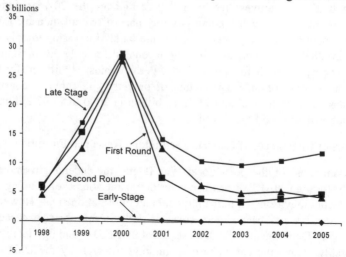

Source: VentureSource.

Figure 5.8 US Venture Capital Investment by Funding Stage, 1998–2005

pressures faced by industry, as indicated by the increasing share of venture capital allocated to late-stage investments. Further, while venture capital thrives in risk-tolerant economies with dynamic industry structures (that is, new-firm formation encouraged), such risk capital is quite cyclical. Finally, even to the small extent that VC funding goes to proof-of-concept research, no portfolio management overlay can be applied by VC firms operating independently to identify and fill gaps in the generic technology. Thus, the 'valley of death' remains inefficiently addressed.

As Figure 5.1 shows clearly, the federal government's share of national R&D has been declining for decades. This is a problem because government (i) has a lower discount rate than industry (that is, it does not have the short-term profit pressures and hence a strategic imperative to emphasize relatively limited-scope development projects) and (ii) can allocate substantial resources across the needed complementary research projects of a generic technology research program.

The lower discount rate allows sustained funding across business cycles for the duration of the time required to prove the concept or to determine that a technology does not have sufficient economic potential to warrant follow-on applied R&D by industry. The potentially large resource base allows spreading risk through the funding of a diversified portfolio of early-phase technology research projects.

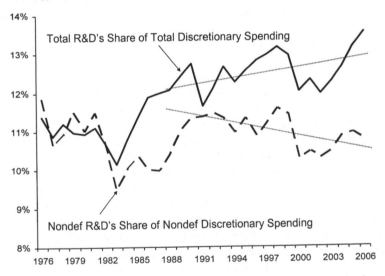

Source: NSF, Federal Budget FY2006; compiled by American Association for the Advancement of Science (AAAS).

Figure 5.9 R&D's Share of Federal Discretionary Spending

Whether the US government is performing this role to a degree adequate to provide the risk capital for future technologies is a critical policy question. Overall budget constraints can be cited as a factor in the current suboptimal R&D funding for emerging technologies (other than life sciences). This problem is reflected in Figure 5.9, which shows that after a dip and recovery in the 1980s, the nondefense R&D budget's share of nondefense discretionary spending has declined, while total R&D's share of total discretionary spending, bolstered by defense R&D, has increased. Because this growth has been for military applications rather than for general S&T, this long-term trend does not indicate an adequate strategic adaptation to the technology imperative being created by rising global competition.

Portfolio Composition

A large economy such as that of the United States or a bloc of economies such as the EU has the ability to allocate R&D investment funds across a broad range of technologies. The significant advantages of R&D diversification are: (i) competency in a broader range of technologies, which mitigates the negative consequences of surges in competitiveness by other economies in a particular technology; (ii) mitigation of the negative impact of decline in the R&D productivity associated with a particular technology, as that technology approaches the end of its life cycle; (iii) R&D synergies from domestic co-location of adjacent tiers in high-tech supply chains; and, (iv) enablement of regional growth strategies with distinctly different technology foci.

Without an adequate diversification philosophy, a few social objectives can come to dominate the national R&D portfolio and thereby unbalance the economy's 'seed' capital for future technology-based growth. The biopharmaceutical industry is the current example of a skewed weighting. The NIH budget has grown at an average annual rate of 12 percent in the first half of this decade to $27.8 billion in FY2005. If the collective budget for all other nondefense R&D funding had been increased to equal that spent on health-related research, NSF data show that the aggregate spending on nonhealth R&D would have had to have been $8.75 billion greater than was actually the case. This imbalance is evident in Figure 5.10. Growth in federal R&D spending in this decade has been driven by military R&D and the NIH budget. Federal spending targeted at other objectives, all of which potentially contribute to future economic growth, has been flat for 15 years. In fact, nondefense R&D spending, excluding NIH (and DHS), was actually 7.8 percent lower in constant dollars in 2005 than 25 years earlier in 1980.

Skewed government R&D spending has leveraged considerable investment by industry in biotechnology. Information technology, farther along in its life cycle, also has benefited from decades of substantial government research support and now is being driven by enormous private-sector investment in R&D. The same pattern is unfolding in biotechnology, as private venture capital and industry-funded R&D have increased dramatically in the past 25 years in response to a growing array of new technology platforms supported by NIH research funds. The economic impact will be as profound as has been the case for IT. Such investment

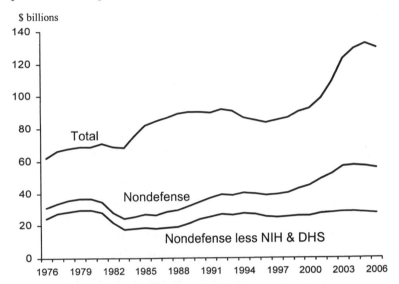

Source: AAAS (DHS is Department of Homeland Security).

Figure 5.10 Defense and Nondefense R&D, FY1976–2006 (constant FY2005 dollars)

creates demand for skilled labor and this derived demand induces larger numbers of students to choose the areas of science and technology as careers that receive the most federal support. Capital markets also respond. The highest shares of venture capital currently go to life sciences and IT.

This public–private investment-driven growth is reflected in Figure 5.11 by the much higher inventive output in these two areas of technology, as indicated by patent award rates. While these trends bode well for IT and biopharmaceutical industries, other technologies will not be so fortunate under current strategies. A large economy like the United States needs a much more diversified portfolio of emerging and mid-life-cycle technologies to drive high rates of economic growth. More recently, regional economic growth strategies have been focusing on specific technologies to convey comparative advantage and hence growth opportunity. However, this specialization strategy will only result in a diversified national technology portfolio if a number of generic technologies are sufficiently supported to provide enough new technology platforms to leverage economic growth across all regions.

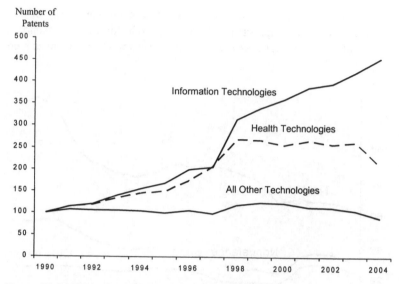

Source: Francis Narin, Vice President, Research & Equity Markets.

Figure 5.11 Growth in US Inventor Patenting by Technology Area

One of the most critical emerging technologies is nanotechnology, which is clearly a 'general-purpose' technology with enormous economic potential. The US government has increased funding for both nanoscience and generic nanotechnology research in recent years. However, in contrast to past funding histories for IT and biotechnology, where US funding dominated world spending, the current US nanotechnology program is just one of a number of significant programs around the world, particularly in Europe and Asia. Thus, the dominant monopoly positions achieved in IT and biotechnology will not be repeated in nanotechnology.

THE CAUSES OF UNDERINVESTMENT IN R&D

Based on the trends cited so far, a better understanding of the determinants of underinvestment in R&D is a critical policy imperative. To analyze underinvestment phenomena effectively requires an accurate model of technology-based growth, including the nature of technology and hence the range of possible investment barriers and incentives.

Patterns of Technical Knowledge Development

The microeconomics literature assumes a continuous, steady-state stream of 'technological opportunities' that, in turn, drive an optimal R&D intensity.

The result of such a model is that a 'stock of knowledge' grows steadily over time in response to a homogeneous R&D process.

This framework is an overly simplified view of reality, but macroeconomic models were even less specific with respect to technology's economic role. For several decades, these growth models (Solow type) did not address the source of technical knowledge or its explicit role in driving growth. Technology was assumed to simply appear from some external source to be magically embodied in the economy's capital stock. Only in the past 15 years have Romer-type general equilibrium models appeared that explicitly include a knowledge variable, although these still project a steady-state growth path at the national economy level.

While such patterns might be rationalized at the macro level, knowledge creation for individual technologies is far from a continuous flow and thus so are its contributions to economic growth. In particular, advances in generic technical knowledge appear only periodically and then drive applied R&D for periods of time, after which diminishing returns set in. Obsolescence requires refurbishment of the generic technology base or the optimal R&D intensity will decline, resulting in slower rates of economic growth.

Overall, a life-cycle model of technological change is implied. The richness of the underlying science base, the pattern of refurbishment of the generic technologies derived from this science base, and the efficiency of the process of creating market applications (innovations) combine to determine the optimum R&D intensity over a technology's life cycle. Case studies of the major technologies driving modern economies show this pattern quite clearly.

As described in Chapter 4, the resulting multi-element and life-cycle-based conceptual model is more complicated than the black-box version, which has dominated economic growth policy for decades. Nevertheless, understanding and using this more complex but more accurate model correctly is essential for effective economic growth policy. Particularly important is the concept that the generic technology base of an industry provides the platform for a large number of applications.

Within a life cycle, the rate of change in the generic technology, that is, the refurbishment of the opportunity set, determines the range of expected rates of return from investment in innovations and therefore the optimal R&D intensity of the industry that draws upon this technology base. It is not surprising then that pharmaceutical and biotechnology firms currently have very high R&D intensities because the huge flow of NIH funds for basic science and generic technology research has provided multiple generic technologies and hence enormous innovation opportunity.

However, even though the generic technology can be improved over its life cycle, diminishing returns eventually set in. For example, in semiconductors, generic integrated-circuit (complementary metal–oxide–semiconductor or CMOS) technology will eventually reach its physical limits and have to be replaced by some radically new technology.

A central challenge for R&D investment theory, therefore, is to explain the differences in incentives to invest in the basis for a new opportunity set versus applications of this set (actual innovations) and to incorporate these incentives within a cyclical R&D investment policy. This challenge is created in large part by the discontinuous character of new generic technologies. Such discontinuities make the potential market applications from an emerging technology highly uncertain for corporate managers, greatly increasing technical and market risk (Tassey, 2005a).

From 11 case studies of radical innovation efforts within major corporations, a team from Rensselaer Polytechnic Institute concluded that the life cycle of a 'discontinuous innovation' research project is significantly different from an incremental improvement project. The 11 projects studied exhibited several of the categories of market failure described in the next section. In eight of the 11 case studies, the researchers found that government was a major source of funds (Rice et al., 1998).

The Nature of Technical Knowledge and Underinvestment

Because of the characteristics of technical knowledge, barriers or market failures occur that lower the private sector's expected RoR calculations causing systematic underinvestment. Economists have explained underinvestment in R&D largely by the concept of spillovers, which refers to the tendency of knowledge either to directly leak (spillover) from the originating source or for its producer to be incompletely compensated for the additional value added in marketplace transactions.

While such phenomena constitute an important characteristic of technology-based markets, in reality, such economic activity is much more complicated and suffers from additional barriers not so commonly identified or understood. Specifically, the following five sources of 'market failure' and hence underinvestment occur across technologies and at specific points in a technology's life cycle:

1. *Technical Complexity:* Complexity and thus technical risk increase with the magnitude of the targeted advance and the complexity of a technology's interfaces with other technologies within a broader technology system.

2. *Timing:* R&D investment time horizons, determined by a combination of acceptable technical and market risk, are often shorter than those required to successfully develop radically new technologies.

3. *Economies of Scope:* Some R&D is capital intensive, which unbalances or limits diversification in R&D portfolios. This accentuates the tendency of R&D strategies to focus on achieving scale efficiencies to reduce both technical and market risk associated with specific applications at the expense of pursuing other potential market applications enabled by an emerging technology. Further, companies frequently focus on those market opportunities presented by the new technology that most closely resemble currently targeted markets. In both cases, the result is reduced incentives to invest in generic technologies with multi-market potential.

4. *Spillovers:* Leakage or spillover of technical knowledge to companies that did not contribute to the research project creating the knowledge frequently occurs and is typically greater the earlier in the R&D cycle an investment is undertaken. The inability to appropriate the intellectual capital produced thereby increases market risk. In addition to 'knowledge' spillovers, 'market' spillovers occur due to buyers' ability to command a price for the new technology that does not fully reflect its value.

5. *Infratechnologies and Standards:* Technical tools, methods and techniques, S&E databases, and the technical basis for interface protocols have a public-good character and frequently require uniform and widespread use as standards. As a result, ability to appropriate the property rights for such technical infrastructure is low and therefore subject to underinvestment over most of the technology life cycle.

Any one of these five barriers can have serious negative impacts on private-sector R&D investment. Moreover, the severity of the barriers imposed can vary over technology life cycles and among levels in supply chains due to differences in industry structure and behavior. For policy analysis purposes, it is necessary to understand how these barriers translate into excessive risk and therefore underinvestment.

The Risk Spike and R&D Investment Incentives

Economists have for some time identified the public-good nature of basic research, which has been traditionally interpreted as meaning that the resulting science is expensive to produce relative to its cost of diffusion and assimilation by others ('free riders'). That is, appropriation by the developer of the benefits of such knowledge is highly limited. In fact, basic scientific knowledge is close to a pure public good and government therefore easily rationalizes funding the research that produces it. In contrast, generic technology is a mixed or quasi-public good, meaning that a portion, but certainly not all, of the intellectual property resulting from this early phase of technology research can be appropriated by its creators. Low estimated rates of return from generic technology research means that knowledge and market spillovers, failure to capture economies of scope, and high discount rates applied to lengthy R&D cycles are significant deterrents to private-sector investment. Policy makers face a difficult task of ensuring adequate levels and composition of investment because the private and public shares of the results of generic research are hard to determine.

Technology Investment Risk

Economists have demonstrated empirically that the aggregate (industry or 'social') RoR on investment in R&D exceeds that for the innovator (or 'private') RoR (Mansfield et al., 1977; Griliches, 1992; Hall, 1996). This so-called 'gap' between the social and private rates of return has been related in a relatively vague way to risk and, therefore, somewhat incorrectly used to explain underinvestment in R&D.

Specifically, a differential between the social and private rates of return does not by itself accurately predict underinvestment. A more accurate characterization is that significant underinvestment occurs when the gap becomes large *and* certain factors suppress the private RoR below existing hurdle (minimum acceptable) rates of return (Tassey, 2005a). Further complicating analyses of underinvestment is the fact that a number of the five investment barriers described in the previous section are typically present, thereby affecting corporate R&D investment decision making in complicated patterns.

Counteracting these innovation investment barriers to some extent is the fact that imitators face barriers, as well. Technical knowledge does not flow freely and costlessly from its source to other potential users, as is often assumed. Purchasers, re-inventors and 'free riders' all incur costs to acquire technical knowledge from innovators and other external sources and then to assimilate this knowledge into their activities.

Part of the reason for these acquisition costs is the fact that technical knowledge is often tacit in nature, meaning that it cannot easily be disembodied from its source (von Hippel, 1990). This fact works in favor of the innovator, but economic history is full of unsuccessful attempts at innovation as well as initially successful innovators who failed later in the technology life cycle. Thus, companies face risks from attempting to be industry leaders and they face risks from being slow to innovate or to imitate. The innovator or 'first mover' strategic option must to a significant extent be selected early in the R&D cycle when both technical and market risks are highest, but investment barriers are typically greatest at this point, as well.

The Risk Spike

The distinction between scientific research and technology research is important for market-failure analysis. For scientific research, which seeks to create *knowledge*, the concept of risk is relevant only in the sense that funding decisions are based on the expectation that scientific knowledge will be advanced. In contrast, risk assessments are continually made by industry over the remainder of the technology life cycle based on estimates of the probability distributions of future market returns. These estimates drive R&D investment decisions. Here, risk has two components: (i) the probability of not achieving the technical objectives perceived to be required for the target markets, and (ii) the probability that if innovation is attempted, the market will not be receptive.[3] As long as reward-to-risk ratios exceed private and social hurdle rates, R&D funds will continue to be allocated by both the private and public sectors, respectively.

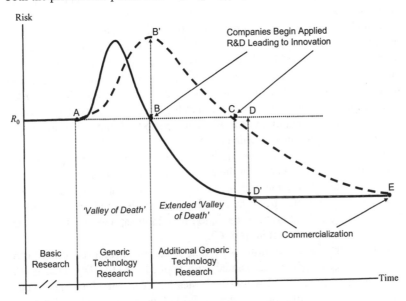

Figure 5.12 The Innovation Risk Spike (Valley of Death)

The technical complexity of the proof-of-concept objective of generic technology research, its frequent mismatches with existing corporate market strategies and internal research capabilities, and its distance in time from potential innovation, combine to cause a spike in overall risk whenever technology research aimed at commercialization is contemplated. By occurring early in the technology research cycle, this 'risk spike' can block the substantial private R&D investment that ultimately produces innovations and subsequent industry growth (Tassey 2005a).

This spike is portrayed in Figure 5.12 and consists of the two types of risk defined above. First, based on the body of scientific knowledge previously developed, the decision making process might be said to face an initial 'technical' risk, R_0, that summarizes estimates of the probability that a technology could be developed to perform some generalized marketplace function. That is, consideration of investment in innovations based on a new technology requires an assessment of the risk that the generic technology platform can be developed and then adapted to the specific technical needs of consumers. Thus, an additional amount of technical risk must be estimated and added to R_0 because the scientific principles presented now have to be proven capable of conversion into specified technological forms with specified performance attributes at maximum costs that meet market demand. Several of the factors cited in the previous section can raise such technical risks.

Second, a 'market' risk also must be estimated to allow for the significant probabilities that demand for the new technology will be overestimated, that market penetration will be slower than projected due to improvements in the defender technology, and that competitors will produce similar innovations from spillovers of the new generic technology. Constrained market penetration will also likely mean that production costs will be high relative to the defender technology for a longer period of time due to slower realization of economies of scale or scope.

In Figure 5.12, the risk spike (*BB'*) might be thought of as the 'public' risk component because it occurs in the early generic technology research phase, which has the public good dimensions described in Chapter 4. As such, this risk must be eliminated by some combination of public and private funding. Only then will individual firms begin to invest in the applied R&D necessary for innovation to occur (point *B* or *C*).

Without the risk spike, firms would be faced only with a reduction in the 'private' risk component associated with applied R&D (*DD'*). That is, the risk curves in Figure 5.12 would have steadily declining slopes and would support proponents of little government R&D funding beyond basic science.

Even with the risk spike, a longer early phase in the R&D cycle (represented by risk curve *AB'CE*) was not a major policy issue in the past. Long and relatively inefficient proof-of-concept research phases for emerging technologies were not a problem in the sense that whichever firm or firms eventually pursued the new technology the innovators were domestic companies.

Today, more globally competitive markets, inadequate research capabilities, higher time discounting, and corporate strategy mismatches mean that the old US model of funding generic technology research by mission-focused agencies with consequent indirect spillover paths to commercial market penetration is now highly inadequate. This R&D inefficiency effect is indicated in Figure 5.12 by the extension in time (*BC*) of the generic technology research phase and subsequent delayed commercialization (*D'E*). Increased global research efficiency and resources are shortening the proof-of-concept phase of the R&D cycle (*AB*), so that today such delays in producing new technology platforms can mean loss of markets to foreign competitors.

In the absence of the risk spike, conventional R&D investment criteria would deal with technical risk because acceptable reward–risk ratios would be the norm. This latter situation is what the black-box model predicts is reality. Thus, if at the level of pure technical risk (R_0) conventional corporate R&D criteria would result in private investment based on risk-adjusted RoR estimates, the policy problem is to overcome the risk spike so that corporate investment criteria can be applied.

The importance of overcoming the risk spike for a major disruptive technology is increased by the fact that the economic potential of such a technology is relatively greater than for most technologies. Although technical and market risk during the applied R&D phase will also be higher (including organizational and technical infrastructure risk), achieving technical success can mean that market risk will actually be lowered to a greater extent than for lesser technological advances because of the disruptive technology's superior performance attributes. Thus, the total private risk associated with developing such a technology may actually decline by a greater amount than that for less-radical technologies.[4]

Such a situation is indicated in Figure 5.13. Here, R&D project *A* is more radical than project *B* and thus its risk spike RS_A is higher. But, once having overcome the risk spike, successful reduction of the technical component of private risk also reduces the market risk to a greater degree. Such an impact could lead to a larger reduction in total private risk, RP_A, reflecting project *A*'s greater economic potential. Of course, the higher RoR from *A* will only be realized if industry can get by the higher risk spike.

Responding to the Risk Spike

For most of the post-World War II period, the US economic growth model dealt relatively effectively with the risk spike in two ways. The federal government funded not only scientific research but also considerable generic technology research through mission-oriented agencies, such as the DoD, the Department of Energy (DoE), the National Aeronautics and Space Administration (NASA), the NIH and so on. Corporate America also funded

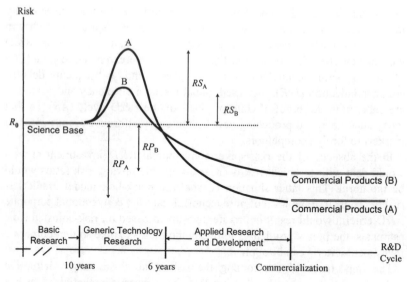

Source: Tassey (2005a, 2005b).

Figure 5.13 Risk Reduction in the R&D Cycle

generic technology research. For the first half of this period, the United States was the only technology-based economy of any significance in the world. Companies like AT&T, IBM, Xerox, RCA and DuPont became dominant in their domestic markets and had little global competition to be concerned with. Therefore, they could project realizing substantial rates of return from investments in proof-of-concept research, even though under more competitive market conditions such research presented significant investment disincentives, such as high technical risk, free-rider potential with respect to intellectual property, long times to commercialization, varied but vaguely defined potential markets and requirements for new technical infrastructures. Market dominance reduced the potential market risk from these barriers and resulted in low discount rates being applied to such investments. For example, free riding was not a serious problem because relatively few competing firms existed capable of developing market applications. Decisions to target new markets could be contemplated for some time with relatively low risk of competitors taking first-mover advantage.

These factors did not prevent many successful companies from eventually declining, but risk-adjusted market opportunity was sufficiently significant to eventually bring forth considerable private investment in radically new technologies from new domestic sources. The dynamic character of the US economy encouraged the formation of small firms that, once having gained access to the generic technology, either started new industries or entered niche markets in the middle and later phases of an existing cycle to further expand the economic returns to the generic technology.

Eventual spillovers of new generic technologies and the entrepreneurial character of most US industry structures provided a motivation for a large venture-capital market. The subsequent development of innovations was therefore enhanced by diversified and constantly renewing industry structures. This was the Schumpeterian process of creative destruction at work and the subsequent global shifts in comparative advantage always favored the US economy. As discussed in Chapter 2, this paradigm is increasingly malfunctioning. Yet, many economists still assert that offshoring of intellectual and manufacturing capital is an automatic win for the domestic economy.

Equally important, government funding of early-phase technology research in the first part of the post-war period was large relative to industry R&D spending and therefore had a substantial catalytic effect. The combination of government-funded and large-firm-funded generic technology research drove multiple technology life cycles. Even when an industry finally declined due to the emergence of a disruptive technology, the new industry was also domestic, so that the value added (profits and jobs) remained in the US economy.

However, global convergence in most high-tech industries has changed the calculus. Current R&D policy tools do not fully recognize (i) the large discontinuity in the risk-reduction process occurring at the transition between science and technology research, which industry increasingly will not fund, and (ii) the significant reductions in windows of opportunity due to shorter technology life cycles.

In summary, the advancement of basic science sufficient to allow technology development to begin does not guarantee immediate or even eventual commitment of adequate private-sector funds. Reducing risk spikes through early-phase generic technology research is necessary to enable optimal private-sector R&D spending. However, the fact that specific elements of an industrial technology are quasi-public goods means that their efficient development over the entire life cycle requires a mixture of public and private funding, with funding responsibility distributed according to the magnitude and duration of various market barriers.

Case Study: Risk Spikes in Biotechnology

Advances in bioscience in the 1970s led to an understanding that the surfaces of different cells were distinguishable by unique distributions of 'receptor' proteins (antigens). Even though the same receptor molecule can appear on the surface of more than one cell type, the frequency varies to the point that scientists began to imagine drugs that would target receptors that are expressed (appear) more frequently on the surfaces of, say, cancer cells. In the 1980s, researchers therefore tried to leap from the science to actual drugs that would kill tumor cells by differentially locking on to the receptors more prevalent on the target cells' surfaces.

Technically, such therapies required identifying the target receptor and then developing an antibody that would lock on to it in order to disrupt the cancer cell's metabolism, causing it to die. By structuring the antibodies to only latch on to receptors dominant on the surface of cancer cells, collateral damage to healthy cells would hopefully be minimized. The specificity of so-called 'monoclonal antibodies' (MABs) therefore offered a significant potential advantage over the brute force approach of conventional chemotherapy where collateral damage is extremely high.

In 1982, Dr Ronald Levy and colleagues at Stanford University succeeded in treating a chemotherapy-refractory patient with low-grade follicular lymphoma by using high doses of MABs. This initial success created hopes that the 'magic bullet' against cancer had finally been found (Morrow, 2005).

However, subsequent efforts at developing therapeutic MABs for various cancers failed. The problem was that the generic mechanism of action was not adequately understood. Many guesses were made in order to rationalize proceeding with drug candidate development. For example, some researchers thought that the monoclonal antibody somehow activated the patient's immune system because successful treatment provided protection long after the antibody was eliminated from the patient, but no proof of this conjecture was developed.

Such guesses were forced by the fact that the generic technology of MABs was only vaguely understood. Without the underlying technology platform in place, subsequent drug development efforts failed. The result of multiple failures was that both companies and investors lost interest in MABs as a promising therapy. The risk of further failure for additional drug candidates was prohibitively high and therefore they became unattractive targets for venture capital. In effect, the risk spike remained a barrier to innovation.

Approximately 10 additional years of government funding by the NIH were required to eventually advance the generic technology to the point that once again private capital was induced to flow into antibody drug development. The major advances were the introduction of recombinant antibody technologies and the development of human and humanized antibodies.[5] These advances in the generic technology led in the late 1980s and 1990s to successful drugs, such as Genentech's Rituxan, which treats B-cell lymphomas and is directed against a particular protein (CD20) present on the surface of more than 95 percent of these cancer cells.

Yet, as has been the case for all drugs of this type, only a subset of patients was successfully treated. For Rituxan, a major clinical trial leading to the drug's approval showed that 48 percent of patients responded instead of the expected 95 percent, implying that the generic mechanism was still not completely understood. Approximately 20 years after the first success with an antibody drug, further research by Dr Levy and his colleagues determined that a genetic polymorphism (a variety of similar proteins) exists for the target receptor. Because drugs typically bind to a portion of the receptor sub-types, only a fraction of patients benefit. The implication was that antibody drug candidates needed to be modified to achieve a broader binding motif within the receptor 'class' (in the case of Rituxan, the CD20 surface proteins). Using this approach, recent research has developed antibodies with modified binding attributes that appear superior to Rituxan (Morrow, 2005).

One could argue that it is unrealistic to expect the generic technology to be completely developed before attempting innovation, and that feedback loops in the R&D cycle will eventually redirect or expand generic technology research. To an extent, at least, the argument has merit. In fact, for this reason, the risk spike is depicted in the previous section as a distribution of risk levels rather than an instantaneous single-point spike. It takes some research just to understand the approximate nature and levels of technical risk. For example, improved antibody design concepts led to the realization that physical limits exist with respect to the degree that affinity that can be engineered into a single molecular species. This finding has led to efforts to develop multiple antibody cocktails.

However, the major point for R&D efficiency and hence time to market is that without sufficient advances in the underlying generic technology, the subsequent applied R&D productivity is so low that private risk capital is not forthcoming. In the case of antibody technology, without sustained funding by the NIH over the past 25 years, the obviously large risk spike would not have been overcome. Only because the US biotechnology industry did not have significant competition during this period was R&D inefficiency not a major issue in determining which economy became the innovation leader.

The R&D cycle management problem is complicated by the fact that generic technology is only one of two major technology elements with public-good content and hence high investment risk for individual companies. The other is the technical infrastructure that enables the different phases of the R&D cycle to occur efficiently and thereby reduce the cost of R&D and the time required to achieve the desired results. Cost and time are clearly critical factors in private-sector estimates of R&D investment risk.

For example, in the 1980s, laboratories screened vast numbers of candidates in the search for cancer-specific monoclonal antibodies. However, the screening systems were slow and cumbersome and most failed to demonstrate the level of specificity necessary for selecting anticancer drug candidates. Eventually, improved techniques were developed to identify and isolate antigen–antibody binding pairs with improved affinity (that is, interactions that do not result in cross-reactivity with non-cancerous cells). Infratechnologies for accomplishing these research efficiency enhancements, such as fluorescence-activated cell sorting, were an important tool in this effort.

A current and perhaps even more compelling example of the risk spike and the difficulty in overcoming it is stem-cell technology. In contrast to monoclonal antibodies, which has evolved through several generations of generic technology and has finally reached levels where significant commercialization is appearing, stem-cell research is at the same point in its life cycle as antibody research was 20 years ago. Like antibodies, which were billed as the 'magic bullet' that would eliminate cancer as a health risk, stem-cell technology has experienced periodic bursts of investor euphoria in anticipation of its enormous potential not only to cure disease but also to regenerate damaged or diseased tissue and even re-grow complete organs.

Stem cells, at least embryonic ones, need to be cultured to the right stage of differentiation to avoid rejection or to ensure that the introduced stem cells will continue to mature while integrating with surrounding tissue and then remain viable for extended periods (Dutton, 2005). Without having answered these fundamental questions, biotech companies nevertheless formulated business plans in the 1990s, obtained venture funding and attempted to develop specific therapies. Once again, the proof of the concept was not sufficiently advanced and, as such, the subsequent attempts at applied R&D failed. Most biotech firms and investors recognized the existence of a substantial risk spike and avoided this area of research.

The existence of such barriers does not mean that no progress has been made. Even inefficient research strategies will yield a few successes. A small biotech firm, Geron Corp., demonstrated dramatic improvement in spinal cord injuries by injecting embryonic stem cells directly into the injury site. However, because so many diseases need effective R&D programs in the face of limited funds, efficiency across all funding programs is essential. In the case of stem-cell research, many years of government funding of both scientific and generic technology research will be required to sufficiently overcome the risk spike and thereby attract the large amount of private-sector applied R&D needed to produce comprehensive and effective therapies. As more is learned, major shifts in research will occur until the generic technology can efficiently spawn viable commercial applications.[6]

INFORMATION MARKET FAILURES

The technical knowledge resulting from R&D investment will have relatively little impact on domestic economic growth if it is not widely disseminated and, in today's shrinking technology life cycles, rapidly assimilated and used. Applied technical knowledge can diffuse by licensing, imitation R&D triggered by the innovation, or reverse engineering (a related form of imitation). Diffusion of technical knowledge is, in effect, built into R&D when undertaken through multiple-firm partnerships. However, whatever the diffusion mechanism, rapid and effective assimilation requires internal technical capability to understand the technology and to determine how to integrate it into a company's existing technology portfolio.

The fact that generic technology, as a quasi-public good, can be patented and licensed results in some degree of diffusion. Large R&D-intensive companies, especially those with central research labs, have considerable capacity both to evaluate externally produced generic technologies and to assimilate them, thereby overcoming these barriers to an extent. However, even large firms can be precluded from access to a generic technology, if it is patented and licensed on an exclusive basis.

Technology acquisition is especially difficult for small firms. They typically do not have the internal capacity to conduct the required evaluation and assimilation functions. Because small firms are less likely to capture economies of scope from generic technology, it is harder to rationalize the investment in the minimum efficient scale of research capability, which in turn provides the technical expertise needed to find, evaluate and then assimilate technical knowledge, especially tacit knowledge. As a result, these firms must be co-located with the sources of tacit knowledge, such as universities and government laboratories. This fact constrains the number of such firms that can start up and eventually succeed.

More generally, because much generic technology has a public-good character, the sources of the research are often separate from the would-be innovators. The major public-sector performers, universities and government research institutes, are institutionally and often geographically separated from most potential users of their research output. These issues are becoming increasingly important as technology becomes more science based.

A major global response has been increased emphasis on research consortia, especially within the 'cluster model,' that involves public support and conduct of generic technology research. As described in Chapter 10, not only can clusters increase R&D efficiency, but they also speed up technology diffusion. Private-sector participants in a cluster either are engaged themselves in the research, which provides a built-in transfer mechanism, or their geographical proximity facilitates assimilation of fundamental technology as it is created.

However, most of an economy's high-tech sector still operates within traditional non-clustered industry structures, which means slow and ineffective diffusion of generic technical knowledge. Small firms, in particular, suffer from poor access to such knowledge and therefore can benefit from location within clusters. Many small firms are spin-offs from universities within a cluster and thus have the direct personal contacts necessary to transfer tacit generic knowledge. In such cases, these startups are often the first to attempt to develop innovations based on new generic knowledge.

Infratechnology diffusion has a somewhat different but equally serious set of barriers. Infratechnologies often arise from a separate science base than the generic technology they support. They also often have applications in multiple industries; that is, they exhibit significant economies of scope. Measurement-related infratechnologies are a prominent example. For example, a fundamental measurement method called isotope dilution mass spectrometry (IDMS), developed by NIST scientists and others, led to infratechnologies and associated standards in such divergent applications as measurement of sulfur in fossil fuels for compliance with environmental regulations and test methods for cholesterol and other blood elements.

The different science base and frequent research economies of scale and scope mandate a few large and often capital-intensive government research facilities for much of the required infratechnology research. They are thus geographically separated from a majority of private-sector users. Yet, the use of these infratechnologies by individual industries requires industry-specific joint strategic planning and local delivery. The result is often information asymmetries between industry and government that lead to underinvestment or at least poor timing of the investment and diffusion. This situation implies that R&D efficiency and subsequent diffusion can be increased by embedding at least some infratechnology research within technology clusters.

The Bottom Line

The amount, composition, and public–private nature of R&D investment are critical policy variables that must be much better understood and managed. Failure to do so will increase already serious underinvestment and misallocation problems, so that providing a diversified national portfolio of emerging technologies will be significantly constrained. The problems caused by the above three investment characteristics are being exacerbated by:

- increasing emphasis by companies on short-term payoffs from investments of all types, including R&D;

- wider distribution of the sources of R&D across the typical industrial supply chain;
- relentless increases in the complexity of industrial R&D, particularly its greater multidisciplinary character;
- growing importance of the integration phase of R&D in response to technologies' increasing system character; and
- rapid globalization and increasing efficiency of R&D investment strategies around the world, supported by multiple investment incentives with equal emphasis on attracting domestic and global sources of investment capital.

In summary, not dealing with the risk spike lengthens the time to initial investment in innovation (applied R&D). Even then, companies are often forced to attempt to apply an incomplete technology platform supported by an inadequate technology infrastructure. Industry structure and behavior play important roles in the degree of underinvestment in innovation, but the inadequacy of public-private policy models will prevent even the optimal industry structure from competing effectively in today's global marketplace.

NOTES

1. Rosenberg (1982), Jaffe et al. (1993), Acs et al. (1994), Feldman (1994), Audretsch and Feldman (1996), Keller (2000) and Porter (2000).
2. The term 'valley of death' first appeared in a Congressional report, *Unlocking Our Future: Toward a New National Science Policy*, House Science Committee, September 24, 1998. It has been used repeatedly as a metaphor for the funding gap often experienced in the transition between the scientific research and applied technology research phases. The gap results from the high risk and long time to market at this point in the R&D cycle.
3. The relationship between technical and market risk was defined and examined empirically by Mansfield et al. (1971, pp. 50–54). The probability of commercialization of an R&D investment (innovation) is determined by the product of the probability of technical completion and the probability of commercialization (given technical completion).
4. For example, Mansfield et al. (1971) found that the probability of commercialization was higher for 'large or medium' technical advances than for 'small' ones.
5. One of the problems with first-generation antibodies was that they largely derived from mice and hence were attacked by the patient's immune system before reaching the target cancer cells. Humanizing antibodies greatly reduced this problem.
6. For example, research is currently shifting from molecular biology to cell signaling.

6. Strategic Shifts in the IT Economy

Not everything that counts can be counted, and not everything that can be counted, counts.

Albert Einstein

To the extent that R&D investment and other innovation policies are analyzed by the limited government analysis infrastructure, the focus remains on manufacturing and, in particular, on individual manufacturing technologies. This historical artifact is yet one more example of the lack of systematic, forward-looking and broad-based analysis of trends in technology and their economic implications. While a case can be made for a strong domestic manufacturing sector and hence continued R&D support for individual manufacturing technologies, major trends are at work that demand much greater focus on technology systems, not only in manufacturing but increasingly in services.

TECHNOLOGICAL CONVERGENCE

Chapter 1 discussed the accelerating convergence of overall technological capability among competing national economies. From a more microeconomic investment perspective, another convergence is taking place, namely an integration of functions previously performed by standalone products based on distinctly different technologies. Semiconductor devices are a prime example. The 'chip' has evolved from individual transistors to integrated circuits to the current trends toward multiple integrated circuits, each performing a distinct function on the same silicon wafer.

Twenty years ago, the cell phone was a 'brick' that had to be hauled about for one function – voice communications. Today, it is being replaced by physically more compact devices, which are true systems in that, in addition to voice, they provide a camera, instant messaging, Internet browsing, address or date book, and wireless email.[1]

Moreover, at the end of IT supply chains, previously isolated and locally delivered services are increasingly converging into integrated collaborative systems spanning the entire global economy. Open source software systems are reasserting the textbook definition of infrastructure and creating more competition through greater opportunities to enter multiple markets.

But, until recently, the complex chips that are the basis for these applications were still hardware, which therefore must be integrated with software to form the system that performs the manufacturing or service function. The emerging technology is to embed software in the hardware components, that is, integrate hardware and software as a single entity and thereby realize much greater productivity.

The message is that, because of successive degrees of integration and increasingly seamless work-flow infrastructures, the potential for individual companies, industries and national economies to gain or lose shares of supply-chain value added is increasing. These trends are a huge leveling factor for global competition. Every economy must, therefore, adapt its economic growth model toward increasing not only component but system-level productivity, thereby enhancing competitiveness at both levels.

As described in detail in Chapter 7, part of the adaptation process is the recognition that technologies evolve in cycles with each cycle based on advances in generic or fundamental technology. The first-mover economy, by virtue of having funded the basic science and the subsequent technology proofs of concept, provides its industries with technology platforms and supporting research infrastructures that allow its industries to become global innovators.

However, both convergence and the installed-base effect conspire to erode leadership positions as life cycles age. In the current decade, these processes are at work as never before with imitator economies increasing both public and private R&D investment. Competitive battles are being fought in both the emerging IT-based service industries and the longer-standing but still important manufacturing sector. The most important trend is the integration of components and subsystems into complex systems. These systems are generating increasingly larger shares of supply-chain value added. One implication is that RoRs on traditional product innovation strategies will become constrained, as their value added is more rapidly bid down by the growing number of global competitors who can participate in the same supply chain.

R&D STRATEGIES IN A SERVICE ECONOMY

Services have become the largest component of most advanced economies. Private-sector (68.2 percent) plus public-sector (12.4 percent) services contributed 80.6 percent of US GDP in 2005 (Bureau of Economic

Analysis). The long-term reason for this dominance is that growth in real incomes has provided individuals with greater capability to pay for more services (including public services through taxes on these incomes).

However, with the knowledge content of services increasing rapidly and the growing capacity of the Internet to facilitate work flows instead of just information dissemination, high-tech and hence high value-added services have become tradable. Thus, fears in industrialized nations over the loss of manufacturing jobs now must be expanded to include the increasing potential for offshoring of higher-paid service jobs.

The Increasing Role of High-Tech Services

To respond to this new dimension of globalization, policy analysts must realize that services' share of GDP has increased for three additional reasons. First, the growing complexity of modern technologies has created the need for new service functions to operate and maintain these technology-based systems over their life cycles. Thus, an increasing portion of the life-cycle costs of delivering modern technologies is due to supporting services. For example, less than 20 percent of the $6,300 annual average cost of owning a PC is for hardware. The total cost of operating a railroad locomotive is more than 20 times the cost of the locomotive itself. The purchase price of a new car is only 20 percent of the total $6,100 annual cost of ownership (Ralston, 2005).

Second, as measured by the national income and product accounts, services' share of GDP has grown in part because of the effect on the accounting framework of manufacturing companies contracting for activities they had traditionally performed themselves. As such, the supplying firms are classified as 'service' companies. For example, the trend by cell-phone companies to contract for the design of handsets means that what was once manufacturing R&D is now classified under 'R&D services'. The result is that, in the national accounts, some value added is transferred from the manufacturing to the services category simply by virtue of the fact that it is now outsourced by the traditional manufacturing firm.

Third, the explosion of IT has facilitated this specialization by providing a new and highly versatile infrastructure that has enabled innovative services. Most of these new services operate on the Internet and are driving the knowledge-based economy. In 2004, approximately $2.4 trillion was spent on Internet services. These trends have not been lost on large high-tech manufacturing companies. Many have invested increasingly larger fractions of their resources in IT-based services, which now account for almost $1 trillion (23 percent) of total e-commerce (Census Bureau e-commerce data).

The Nature of High-Tech Services

Integrated-service strategies by manufacturing firms yield potentially large advantages. Such firms not only have intellectual capital accumulated through experience with previous system integration projects, but they also have access to the technology being developed by the manufacturing divisions of their company and to the researchers leading these activities. This ultimate co-location business model is the source of much of the growth in value added by these companies.

IBM now attains more than one-half of its revenues from services. The highest value added is coming not only from integration of hardware and software into specific services but also from integrating multiple functions into broader service systems (RTI International, 2005). IBM's Global Services unit has anthropologists who specialize in researching the way professionals in different industries use information to maintain complex business operations. Although the study of human behavior is a social science, the end use is to increase the effectiveness of IBM's integrated service products.

In terms of national economic growth strategies, governments who hope to attract investment to their domestic economies must provide supporting research and technical infrastructures, which respond to the fact that the nature of service R&D is conceptually and substantively different from manufacturing R&D. For example, consider performance attributes that count the most in designing complex information-based service systems (CSTB, 2000):

- *Scalability:* As markets for such services expand, the underlying system technologies require more components and are expected to support a larger number of users simultaneously. This complexity creates interoperability and system management problems.

- *Complexity:* The number of required components, lines of code and elements that interact and share information, combined with the accompanying feedback loops, causes increased difficulty in understanding the underpinnings of system functionality.

- *Interoperability:* When systems are designed, the components come from a wide array of vendors who use different object-oriented coding. Seamless functioning among system components and applications in other systems requires that the computer science community develop a well-understood methodology to avoid system design failures. Currently, no accepted method or standards exist for attaining interoperability other than by trial and error.

- *Flexibility:* IT-based systems are characterized by long life spans once they are put into use. Individual components will therefore require frequent upgrades to the most recent technology without having to restructure the entire system with the introduction of every new component. This life-cycle management requirement has become more complicated with the trend toward embedded software.

- *Security:* As industries such as health care and e-commerce develop a larger need for passing personal information over networked systems, breaches in the security of such systems will cause accidental disclosure of financial, medical and other records, ultimately resulting in huge financial losses and reduction in consumer confidence. Complexity is the enemy of security and IT-based service systems operating over networks are extremely complex. As the amount of 'critical infrastructure' becomes dependent on networking, opportunities are created for corruption of systems by outside sources.

- *Availability and reliability:* While large-scale systems have enormous potential functionality and hence economic importance, ensuring that such systems are available and functioning when needed is a demanding system design challenge. Distributed computing services, for example, must develop algorithms that ensure delivery of data packets despite changing conditions affecting the performance of the network.

The value added by IT-based services depends on these attributes. They hardly sound like the performance requirements that drive manufacturing R&D. However, they evolve in the same linear development process over time as do manufacturing technologies. That is, each area has a technology platform or generic technology and a set of supporting infratechnologies.

Largely because of their complexity, modern services require a sophisticated IT infrastructure. As a result, it has become one of the key differentiators across high-tech economies. Because the Internet provides the infrastructure for globalization and hence convergence of IT-based services, the same economic growth policy imperative presents itself to governments as it does for manufacturing. Today, businesses must rely on the efficient and reliable transfer of data internally and externally across an entire supply chain. Types of data include design, supply logistics, production, distribution and marketing.

System integration also requires a large number of standards. In the first decade of the Internet, most standardization focused on formats for organizing, displaying, storing and disseminating data. Doing so enabled the innovation of portals through which multiple sites with myriad different types of information could be accessed. More recently, the management of 'work flow' has become the focus. 'Work' is the progressively higher value added of a series of stages from raw data from multiple sources to an eventual final user who will consume an electronic package of information tailored to that customer's specific needs. This next 'generation' of Internet applications requires standards that enable value added to occur at multiple locations by independent parties. This value added will be the result of progressive assembling and processing until final demand has been met. In effect, a seamless service supply chain is being created (Friedman, 2005).

An important policy issue with respect to these emerging integrated global service systems is the fact that the current competitive advantage in high-tech services enjoyed by the US economy is being eroded through functional segmentation of the elements of the typical IT-based service, which in turn has allowed geographic distribution of value added. This process is little different from what has been happening to manufacturing, which has been increasingly disaggregated into components and phases of production and assembly.

In fact, because no need exists to move physical product, as is the case with manufacturing, geography is potentially even less of a barrier to convergence and more services will become 'tradable.' Improving standardization enables seamless flows of information and then integration into the final service, which then can be delivered anywhere in the world. Interface standards allow this compartmentalization, but automation of processing and integration (work flow built on an additional set of standards) makes the design and delivery processes even more efficient and potentially widely distributed.

The policy message is that the evolving IT infrastructure will enable value added from high-tech services to be distributed all over the world. The proliferation of research and production networks is great for companies who can substantially improve efficiency by moving assets globally. However, labor assets are not mobile and consequently the net shift of resources from one economy to another can have a substantial negative impact on employment and income without substantive planned responses by economic growth policy. This phenomenon is occurring not just between levels in a supply chain but also horizontally across heretofore integrated components of a particular tier in the production and delivery of a technology system.

THE CONTINUING IMPORTANCE OF MANUFACTURING

The economies of industrialized nations have gone through major sectoral shifts over the past two centuries. In 1820, agriculture accounted for about 70 percent of the US economy. Today, that sector's share is under 2 percent.

Manufacturing's share increased through the two industrial revolutions to a peak of 30 percent of GDP in the 1950s, but has declined to less than one-half that peak share. The decline accelerated in the past decade due to two major factors: rapid productivity growth in services and accelerated offshoring of many manufactured products.

The Case for Manufacturing

An indigenous high-tech manufacturing sector is still critical to an advanced economy. As indicated in Figure 6.1, one reason is that a disproportionate share of technology still originates in manufacturing relative to its share of industry's contribution to GDP. Equally important, the service sector is the primary purchaser of this technology. As pointed out in Chapter 5, systems technologies are both increasingly complex and dominant in the modern economy. Because the design of service systems requires integration and optimization of diverse hardware and software, the flow of manufacturing

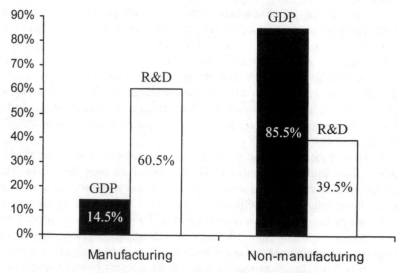

Source: Bureau of Economic Analysis, National Science Foundation.

Figure 6.1 Sector Shares of Industry's Contribution to GDP Compared with Sector Shares of R&D Performance, 2003

technology must be closely integrated with the development of high-tech services. Effective integration is essential to realizing productivity gains from technology-based services. In fact, the cost of IT implementation can be four to five times the investment in hardware and software (Leech et al, 1998). The higher the technology content, the more important is the role of tacit knowledge. Such knowledge can be most effectively transferred through person-to-person interactions, which makes co-location of suppliers and users important. It is not a coincidence that India, which is emerging as a provider of high-tech services, also has substantial competence in software development.

Unfortunately, instead of focusing on the synergy between manufacturing and services, the shrinking manufacturing base in the US domestic economy (in relative if not absolute terms) has brought forth two distinctly different responses – neither of which has been constructive. One group has denied or at least ignored the causes of declining manufacturing and simply demanded that something be done about the problem. The implied desired response is some form of protectionism. A second group, mainly economists, invokes the traditional version of the law of comparative advantage. As described in Chapter 2, this basically static version implies automatic adjustment, so that the trend to offshoring is therefore not a problem and even desirable. Even if offshoring and declining competitiveness were to continue, they assert, resulting in an economy almost totally reliant on services (implying an equally large reliance on imports for manufactured goods), such a scenario should not be viewed negatively but rather simply as the efficient reallocation of global resources.

The view of the first group has to be rejected outright because protection has proven over several centuries to result only in lower productivity, slower growth and higher prices. These trends in turn result in stagnant employment at lower real wages – the very events that protectionism is asked to prevent. The second response, letting the law of comparative advantage raise global economic efficiency and thereby allegedly making everyone better off, is more complicated to address. First, in defense of letting comparative advantage be realized, the fact is that manufacturing output has increased at an average annual rate of approximately 4 percent since 1990. Manufacturing employment has declined during this period, but the decline is due more to automation than to offshoring. Moreover, output and employment declines have been more pronounced in the low-tech portion of manufacturing, which pays lower salaries and wages. The result has been an increasingly more technology-intensive and capital-intensive type of manufacturing – a trend that will not reverse.

In 2005, Chinese hourly compensation in manufacturing was 3 percent of that in the United States. Although Chinese wage growth is much faster than in the American economy (an incredible 25 percent annual rate in the 2003–05 period), Chinese compensation was only about 4 percent of comparable US levels in 2006 (Roach, 2006b). In other words, neither the US nor any other industrialized economy will again be competitive in labor-intensive manufacturing.

The remaining US manufacturing jobs are increasingly more skilled and higher paid, coming from high-tech industries such as software and pharmaceuticals and replacing some of the jobs lost in lower-skilled industries such as textiles and metal parts manufacturing. Thus, the law of comparative advantage works, but with a critical caveat: enough new higher-paying jobs must be created to provide the income to take advantage of the cheaper labor-intensive goods imported from other economies.

This is a major policy problem because aggregate manufacturing employment continues to decline. Thus, either these lost jobs will have to be replaced by service jobs (ones paying equal or higher wages) or manufacturing output must grow even faster to create more high-productivity jobs that can stand up to growing global competition.

The separate forces are seen clearly in an Economic Policy Institute study, which estimated that 59 percent of the decline in manufacturing employment since 1998 has been due to trade imbalances. However, the study also estimated that productivity increased enough to actually account for 111.5 percent of the net job losses. The negative productivity impact on employment is larger than the net job losses because demand growth during this period created jobs, which counteracted a portion of the estimated losses due to automation. These two domestic factors, demand and productivity growth, when netted out against each other account for 41 percent of the loss in jobs, which is significant but less than the trade impact (Bivens, 2005).

As already stated, a problem for policy analysis is to determine whether global demand for domestic manufacturing can have a nonlinear relationship with the growth in productivity. That is, if larger productivity gains cause a proportionately greater increase in demand, employment can increase in spite of the greater output per worker. On the surface, this prospect makes sense because the higher the domestic economy's relative productivity, the less the competition and the greater the consequent market share.

However, even if manufacturing output continues to grow but employment does not, Figure 6.1 implies that a domestic manufacturing sector is essential if co-location interactions with services are significant. That is, manufacturing is not important just because it still contributes a hefty $1.6 trillion of US GDP and employs 17 million workers. Much of the output of manufacturing industries is consumed as stand-alone products, but increasingly such output is integrated into systems of products that provide services as the final form of consumption (communications, operations management, financial management, wholesale and retail trade and so on).

The integration of hardware and software into service systems requires synergies among multiple levels in the relevant chain of supplier industries. Such interactions are frequent and occur over the entire technology life cycle. Hence, close proximity is an advantage, especially when the knowledge or information being transferred is not well structured and therefore needs to be iterated or explained in person. These conditions can be dominant in the early phases of a technology's life cycle and they are increasingly important in the design and assimilation of technology systems. In addition to the knowledge-related advantages of co-location, supply-chain integration occurs more efficiently within a single economy because of standardized technical infrastructures and simultaneous adjustment to new standards in hierarchical markets.

Even when manufactured products are consumed as final demand (they do not become components of service delivery systems), a case can still be made for domestic value-added strategies. High-tech products require considerable R&D and their production is increasingly capital intensive (which means low labor content). The labor in most technology-based products today accounts for around 10 percent of total production costs. As a result, output and value added, driven by productivity-enhancing product and process technologies, can continue to grow – even as employment declines. Such R&D- and capital-intensive characteristics make high-tech manufacturing an attractive element of an advanced economy.

A final point is that R&D and manufacturing are synergistic, as described in Chapter 2. This relationship is especially strong in the early phases of a science-based technology life cycle because tacit knowledge transfers require regular person-to-person contacts. Even in more mature technologies, this is the case. Dell, the world's largest PC manufacturer, has stated that over 50 percent of its notebook PCs are now designed in Taiwan by local contractors who coordinate closely with their manufacturing partners (Lee, 2006). Thus, when either R&D or manufacturing loses competitive status and is consequently offshored, the other follows relatively quickly. The combined loss of domestic value added is significant.

Creation of Comparative Advantage

A steadily increasing number of economies now develop high value-added products. Korea, for example, has risen to the world's 12th largest economy by steadily increasing manufacturing R&D. That economy's progress has been leveraged by major national projects, such as a 10-year, $200 million collaborative R&D effort involving six research institutes, 27 universities and 70 companies to advance computer-integrated, flexible manufacturing systems. The Koreans claim that the project has increased productivity growth for the involved companies by 300 percent. In addition to such process technology gains, Korea has emerged as an innovation leader in high-definition television and CDMA mobile phone technology. Korea's Hyundai has joined Toyota and Honda as the three leading global automobile companies with respect to quality, according to JD Power & Associates.[2]

Looking forward, nanotechnologies will drive future manufacturing innovation and process productivity. Developing these technologies will require major long-term R&D commitments by governments and their domestic industries. Separating R&D from manufacturing is likely to be an unsuccessful strategy. Generic technologies will likely be available for licensing at attractive rates in the early phases of nanotechnology life cycles. However, the value added in subsequent phases, where process technology experience feeds back into new R&D, will accrue to those economies that invest in both stages of economic activity (R&D and manufacturing). Staying competitive over the entire technology life cycle is essential to maintain domestic value-added growth, including growth in employment.

Whatever the particular manufacturing technology, private investment does not take place in a vacuum. In particular, an elaborate economic infrastructure is required. In competitive economies, economic infrastructures facilitate (1) the financing of investments in advanced manufacturing technologies, (2) the conduct of advanced manufacturing R&D, (3) the integration of the results of R&D into production systems, and (4) the provision of skilled labor to effectively use both the equipment and associated software. Such infrastructures are difficult to construct and maintain. Economies with efficient R&D networks, venture capital markets, integrated supply chains (virtual or actual), and education and training facilities have competitive advantages that are not easily established – or imitated.

Investment in technical infrastructure also plays a pivotal role in competitive position over a technology's life cycle. Significant increases in manufacturing productivity are being driven by IT-based integration of internal corporate activity and business interactions with companies in the corporation's supply chain. IT also enables substantial increases in the productivity of manufacturing processes. These processes are capital intensive, which implies considerable investment per worker.

Such capital-intensive industry structures offer the potential for substantial increases in labor productivity. As indicated, higher capital-to-labor ratios are resulting in a declining portion of total costs for labor in most areas of advanced manufacturing. For example, the amount of equipment required per worker in an LCD plant is about $1 million. Providing that labor has the requisite skills to perform the demanding operations in complex technology-based manufacturing environments, the resulting higher levels of labor productivity result in higher pay levels.

Perhaps most important from labor's perspective is the fact that robust domestic high-tech manufacturing leverages service-sector productivity due to co-location synergies. The result is that more high-tech service jobs are created in the domestic economy. This relationship is particularly evident in the growing forward-integration by R&D-intensive manufacturing companies into high-tech services. The economic impact can be large because many high-tech services are relatively labor intensive. For example, in software development, the equipment required can be as little as $10,000 per worker (Fingleton, 1999). Thus, even if manufacturing employment does not grow appreciably, pay levels should rise and the existence of a high-tech manufacturing sector should leverage many more jobs in the service sector.

SYNERGIES AND MAXIMUM DOMESTIC VALUE ADDED

The previous discussion indicates that the synergies between manufacturing and services are significant and an integrated manufacturing–services economic growth strategy is therefore desirable. Such supply-chain integration still occurs more efficiently within a single economy because of access to specialized labor pools, technical infrastructures and target markets. However, a number of economic factors must be understood and managed to realize these efficiency gains.

Within the manufacturing sector, a unique problem exists due to two countervailing sets of trends. One set is the movement toward reliance on 'core competences' – specialization not only in a reduced number of product categories but also in stages of economic activity. These strategies create problems for the second set of trends, namely the competitive pressures to achieve synergies among the three stages of economic activity within a particular tier in a supply chain through high degrees of communication among suppliers of component technologies, especially at the system integration tier.

The need for supply-chain synergies is often the result of an evolutionary process over a technology's life cycle. For example, when Hewlett-Packard started making ink-jet printers in the 1980s, it set up both its R&D and manufacturing divisions in Vancouver, Washington. HP wanted the product development and production teams to work together because ink-jet technology was in its infancy, and the biggest printer market was in the United States. When demand grew in other parts of the world, HP set up manufacturing facilities in Spain and Singapore to service European and Asian markets. Although HP continued to develop new printers in Vancouver, Singapore became the largest production facility because the company needed economies of scale to lower manufacturing costs as the technology life cycle evolved. However, by the mid-1990s, HP realized that printer manufacturing technologies had matured and that it could outsource production to vendors completely. By doing so, HP was able to reduce costs and remain the leader in a highly competitive market (Lee, 2004).

From a public policy perspective, while achievement of such synergies is a good thing in general and especially for individual companies and their shareholders, distribution of economic activity over a global supply chain means erosion of domestic value added in the innovator economy. The efficiency gains from globalization are being realized mainly by large firms, which have both the motivation and the ability to offshore. These large multinational firms have the capability to network R&D globally to a greater degree than do small firms.

Because of their size, decisions by large firms to outsource both R&D and manufacturing have significant negative consequences for the domestic economy. Analysis by the Department of Commerce's (DoC's) Economics and Statistics Administration (ESA) shows that large firms (more than 1,000 employees) account for 37.4 percent of total US employment. For this reason alone, they remain a critical element of the domestic economy. Because large firms are relentlessly expanding their global business models, domestic investment incentives, including an effective technical infrastructure, are essential to retain large fractions of these companies' global value added.

However, many other economies are providing an impressive array of incentives, which, along with the market expansion factors described above, will increasingly flatten the competitive global marketplace. Thus, an additional policy imperative is the need for a dynamic industry structure to facilitate new company formation and infrastructure support for the growth of young firms. New technology-based firms are important for three reasons: they are highly innovative, they maintain a largely domestic focus for some time, and they provide an attractive source of domestic supply for co-located multinational firms. ESA analysis shows that from 1992 to 2005 (a period of rapid globalization of technology investment by large US-based firms), small firms (less than 250 employees) accounted for 57.9 percent of net job growth compared to 42.1 percent for large firms.

The Bottom Line

High-tech services are critically important because they represent the largest growth opportunity for the modern economy. These industries are somewhat more labor-intensive than advanced manufacturing and increasingly pay high wages. Because of their increasing R&D intensities, high-tech services have the potential to continue to grow rapidly.

As a result, some predict that manufacturing's share of GDP will continue to shrink from the current 13 percent to possibly as low as agriculture's two percent share. Such a decline likely will not happen because high-tech services require considerable amounts of high-tech products. While this dependency does not preclude importing such products, three reasons argue for ensuring a robust domestic high-tech manufacturing presence: (i) the value added from high-tech products is significant, (ii) synergies exist between manufacturing and services, a large part of which can be most efficiently realized through co-location, especially at the system level, and (iii) the substantial requirement of both high-tech manufacturing and services for skilled labor means their co-location increases the total labor pool available to respond to shifts in industry demand.

NOTES

1. 'The World is Your Palm?', *Working Knowledge*, Harvard Business School, February 14, 2005, (http://hbswk.hbs.edu).
2. *Manufacturing & Technology News*, July 7, 2004.

7. The Technology Life Cycle

In the long run, we are all dead.

John Maynard Keynes

The above quote by the famous English economist of a half-century ago is somewhat of an exaggeration. While fundamental changes occur slowly, they do so well within lifetimes. Thus, mistakes in growth policy end up biting the perpetrators, as well as succeeding generations. Nowhere is this premise more true than for technology. As the engine of long-term economic growth, technology drives the creation of entirely new industries, adds substantial value to the economy, but eventually becomes obsolete and loses its value – the economic equivalent of being dead.

The villain is the installed base effect. Because of it, industries that dominate one cycle seldom lead the next cycle and, in some cases, are not even major players. In cases where a radically new technology underpins the new cycle, successful firms from the previous cycle not only underperform but frequently go out of business due to an inability to adapt to the new paradigm.

For 40 years after World War II, the United States was the overwhelmingly dominant technology-based economy. During this period, both the old and the new high-tech industries were largely composed of US firms. Thus, from an economic growth perspective, managing transitions between life cycles was not a serious strategic or policy issue. Moreover, innovative US firms and subsequent domestic imitators were not challenged significantly and therefore garnered most of the value added over entire cycles.

That is no longer the case, so life-cycle management is now an important attribute of overall growth policy. The shortest and most recognized is the product cycle. A series of product cycles based on underlying generic technology appear over the economic lifetime of this technology platform. Over much longer periods, a series of generic technology cycles evolve, based on an initiating major advance in the underlying science. Collectively, these latter cycles form a 'major' cycle (also called a 'grand cycle' or 'wave') that can cover decades (Tassey, 1997).

Management of product cycles is largely a private-sector problem, but understanding the determinants of both major technology life cycles and the intermediate generic technology-based cycles nested within each major cycle are imperatives for economic growth policy. If high long-term growth rates are to be maintained, the factors shaping the S-shaped growth curves, which characterize these cycles, must be understood and the barriers to efficient progression managed.

Initially, such a framework may sound abstract, but technology-based economies are increasingly focusing growth policies on accelerating the early phases of these cycles in order to attain first-mover advantage from breakthroughs in science. The effect of this competition among multiple technology-based economies is to make the bottom of the S-shaped growth curve steeper, that is, to shorten the early phases of a cycle and thereby accelerate innovation within the domestic economy.

As previously described, advances in solid state physics enabled a series of generic semiconductor technology cycles and advances in cellular biology started a wide array of generic biotechnology cycles. More recently, nanoscience has reached a level that is allowing the initiation of nanotechnology life cycles. For economic growth policy, the key foci are the factors that determine the pattern of growth within a cycle and also the factors that terminate one cycle and start the next one.

However, in the face of the acceleration of technology life cycles, the installed-base effect constrains the adaptation to new technology paradigms by incumbent industries that are based on existing technologies. One indicator of the installed-base effect is the striking contrast between business concerns emphasized by corporate managers in high-tech industries and those that are important to older, technologically stagnant industries. High-tech firms are concerned with amount and type of government R&D funding, intellectual property rights, cost of risk capital, and availability of scientists and engineers and, more generally, skilled workers. Older (and frequently declining) industries, on the other hand, typically cite taxes, regulation, health and pension costs, trade barriers and tort laws as their most serious problems.

To deal with these characteristics of long-term economic growth, policy analysis must recognize the fact that a series of product cycles are 'nested' within generic technology life cycles, which, in turn, comprise a major technology cycle. Understanding the dynamic character of such a technology-based growth model enables characterization and ranking of market failures as they change over time and therefore over the several types of life cycles.

NESTED TECHNOLOGY LIFE CYCLES

Business analysts have studied the product life cycle for decades (Abernathy and Utterback, 1975). A series of product cycles emerges from an underlying generic technology platform. In each succeeding product cycle, however, attributes of the product technology become progressively standardized and the rate of change in specific attributes slows, indicating approaching exhaustion of the generic technology's potential. The result is an increasingly commoditized product, of which the PC is a current example. At these later phases of the generic technology's life cycle, competition shifts from major product innovation to incremental changes and process innovation. The greater emphasis on process efficiency means that competition is increasingly based on price.

Generic Technology Cycles

Within a major technology's life cycle, significant innovations occur over time based on periodic advances in the generic technology. For example, the limitations of stand-alone transistors wired together (speed, heat, weight) became obvious once experience with a series of product cycles was in hand. The need to improve the performance of these three attributes led to the invention of a new generic circuit technology – the integrated circuit (IC). Subsequently, a massive explosion of product cycles based on the IC ensued.

However, the technology-based economy is even more complex. One generic technology cycle does not necessarily end when a new one appears. In the case of semiconductors, the generic technology underlying the transistor continued to advance, responding to technological opportunity and also to the fact that both the IC and the transistor remain complementary components of higher-level technology systems. The important point is that final-demand products and services are increasingly met by complex technology systems and, therefore, the performance of all system components must advance simultaneously.

Specifically, although the IC met much of the demand for digital electronics performance improvement, it is still a fact that computing power is related to intrinsic transistor speed; that is, the faster the transistors on a chip, the better the computing power. In previous generations of transistor devices, reaching terahertz speeds required current densities so large that device components would melt. Obviously, this limitation imposed a cap on computing power. However, in 2004, scientists at the University of Illinois at Urbana-Champaign created a new type of bipolar transistor that can operate at much higher frequencies with less current density than traditional devices, possibly opening the door to the terahertz marker. The specific demand–pull effect for a new bipolar transistor came from the fact that applications such as improved power amplifiers for future cell phones were already known to be needed. Thus, while nested generic technology life cycles for a system component are linear in time, such evolution occurs in parallel with other components of the technology system (in this case, the transistor and the IC).

More generally, life cycles for the generic technologies comprising these systems originate at different points in the major cycle and co-exist for periods of time before eventually being replaced by radically new ones based on new generic technologies. These interdependencies among generic technologies are displayed for information technologies by the well-known 'tire-tracks chart' (CSTB, 2003).

Such a mapping dramatically indicates the complexity of technology systems. For example, in response to the relentless need to increase microprocessor speed, Intel developed the first application of multiple-processor technology. In 2005, the company introduced a 'dual-core' chip (two processing circuits). The underlying generic technology will eventually yield chips with thousands of co-processors. However, as transistors have become smaller and are packed ever closer together on a silicon wafer, heat buildup, electrical current leakage from circuits, and electrical crosstalk between wires are increasingly serious problems (Service, 2005). Thus, the potential increased processing speed is unusable if the input–output function (the copper wires that move data to and from the processors) have insufficient capacity.

The generic solution for expanding data transfer capacity among multiple processors is the introduction of optical components, specifically the silicon laser. Potentially, input–output speeds can be increased at least a thousandfold. Unfortunately, at the time, available optical materials (gallium arsenide and indium phosphide) were prohibitively expensive. As pointed out in the discussion of the risk spike, part of the technical risk facing R&D resource allocation is derived from the need to develop the technology to not only perform as desired, but to do so at an acceptable cost.

Intel eventually solved the problem by several advances in silicon photonics. In 2005, the company developed a silicon modulator that performed on a par with other more expensive optical modulators.[1] However, silicon is a poor laser in that when its electrons are excited, it generates too much heat compared to light. As a result, a light signal from such a laser has to be 'pulsed' (delivered in discrete bursts to allow the electrons in the silicon atoms the millionths of a second needed to give up their excess energy and relax back to resting states, thereby 'cooling off').

But pulsed lasers (compared to continuous lasers) are inefficient for transmitting data. In response, Intel created a silicon waveguide with implanted electrodes that basically quarantined the electrons, thereby preventing heat buildup while allowing the flow of photons to build up until a continuous laser beam was achieved.

Several policy-relevant points are implied from these examples. First, once the generic technology is largely available, industry can innovate at the product level (as evidenced by the Intel examples). Second, the generic technologies for each component of a technology system (in this case, a communication system) must be available to allow parallel innovation to occur and thereby advance the system technology. This is the ultimate objective because it is the system that satisfies final demand.

These requirements underscore the policy imperative to ensure that a portfolio of generic technology research progresses to meet the system performance requirements. Once a major technology reaches the middle of its life cycle with resulting substantial markets and an established industry structure, large R&D-intensive firms, such as Intel or IBM, can and do conduct significant amounts of generic technology research.

However, not all generic technologies required for the advance of the system technology proceed at the same rate and even the largest companies cannot rationalize all of the needed early-phase technology research. For emerging technologies, major underinvestment is typical because of pronounced risk spikes. While government funding for such research based on a portfolio model has been used by DARPA (and for a short period of time by the ATP in the mid-1990s), most federal R&D project funding is weakly coordinated from a system portfolio perspective.

Major Cycles

Major technology life cycles are of paramount importance to long-term economic growth because they enable a series of nested cycles that encompass a spectrum of related technology trajectories. The cumulative economic impact is enormous. Unfortunately, the transitions between major cycles are usually traumatic. The general process of cycle transition was first characterized by Schumpeter (1950) who conceived the frequently cited concept of 'creative destruction'. He explained the cyclical pattern of technological change in terms of investments in capital stock and market relationships that lead to rigidity and decreasing returns on investment, setting the stage for a radically new technology to emerge and take over markets from the defender technology.

The most widely recognized major technology life cycle is silicon-based semiconductors, which receives considerable attention because of its extreme 'general-purpose' character. The progression of this major cycle has been characterized by 'Moore's Law', originally proposed by Intel co-founder Gordon Moore in 1965. Moore observed that the number of transistors on a chip and hence computing capacity doubles every two years, while the cost of producing a chip remained the same. Consequently, the unit cost of computing will drop by one-half. In 1965, a chip held just a few dozen transistors. Today, Intel's high-end chip contains more than 1.7 billion transistors, and that number is expected to exceed 10 billion by 2012. And, as Moore predicted, a transistor that cost about $1 in 1968 dropped to just under 10 cents in about five years. The cost continued to fall tenfold every four-to-five years until 1985 when the cycle lengthened to seven years. In spite of these variations, this law has been considered largely valid for decades. Most important, as long as the specified relationship holds, the silicon-based semiconductor life cycle will continue.

The length of a major cycle and the competitive position of the domestic industry over such cycles are particularly critical for general-purpose technologies like semiconductors because they spawn a host of innovative industries, such as computers and communications equipment, with huge collective economic impact. These two industries along with the software industry and the semiconductor industry itself (the four 'IT' industries) have been responsible for 25 percent of the increased rate of US economic growth since 1995, which once again demonstrates high-tech industries' tremendous leverage on growth in spite of their small size relative to the overall economy. The four IT-producing industries account for only 3 percent of GDP. In contrast, non-IT industries have been responsible for half the growth rate, but they account for 70 percent of GDP. And, the four IT-producing industries have had an even larger impact on multifactor productivity, contributing more to economy-wide productivity growth than all other industries combined (Jorgenson, 2005).

Unfortunately, global leverage by an initially innovative domestic industry is typically not maintained over an entire technology life cycle. In the semiconductor life cycle, individual companies have risen to prominence and then lost competitive position and retreated to narrower market strategies, abandoned the industry, or even ceased to exist. Entire domestic industries can follow similar patterns (Tassey, 1997).

Figure 7.1 shows that the US semiconductor industry, clearly the 'first mover' in the major cycle, lost market-share leadership to Japan in the 1980s, but then drew upon its superior R&D capability and research infrastructure to regain the leading position in the 1990s. Since then, convergence by a growing number of economies has resulted in a steady increase in the combined market share of the new entrants at the expense of both the US and Japanese economies.

As stated several times in previous chapters, the appropriate unit of growth for policy analysis should be the supply chain because of the interdependence of the tiers (industries) that comprise it and hence the

R&D in the Modern Economy

potential leverage on the total value added by synergies among tiers. Examination of earlier tiers in the US semiconductor supply chain show that the device industry (Figure 7.1) is not the only tier losing market share. The semiconductor equipment industry was also once the sole province of US

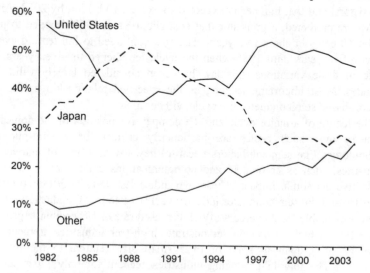

Source: Semiconductor Industry Association.

Figure 7.1 National Shares of Global Semiconductor Device Market, 1982–2004

firms. American companies still have the largest overall market share, but a 20 percentage-point lead over Japanese firms has been cut in half in recent years. Moreover, in a number of important equipment categories, such as lithography, US firms are no longer a factor. Farther back in the supply chain, critical materials and wafer production are largely performed in other economies.

The End of a Major Cycle

It is during the final phases of a major technology's life cycle that the barriers to transition to the next cycle exert their detrimental effects. When the transistor first appeared in the 1950s and promised to take over a large number of electronic component markets served by vacuum-tube technology, the vacuum-tube industry went into full-scale counterattack by trying to improve the functionality of its products and even asking for government research assistance. Such efforts may have extended the life cycle to a modest degree, but the inherent superiority of the generic technology underlying the transistor and subsequent semiconductor devices put an end to the vacuum tube's life cycle.

A more recent example is the TV picture tube. Quickly becoming referred to as 'old-fashioned tube televisions', the market share for cathode ray tubes (CRTs) is being steadily eroded by plasma display and LCD technologies. Yet, as with vacuum tubes 50 years ago, the CRT industry fought for its existence.

The advantages of the challenger technologies (especially LCDs) are lower weight and smaller footprint (much thinner), allowing easier placement in a room, including the option of wall hanging. At a time when the CRT market was declining at approximately 10 percent per year, a joint venture between the Korean firm LG Electronics and the Dutch firm Philips Electronics was formed to shrink the dimensions of the CRT. In 2005, the joint venture started selling a 35-cm 'thin' tube and announced plans to reduce the depth of a 32-inch (81.3-cm) TV tube further to as little as 25 cm. Another Korean electronic firm, Samsung, also introduced a 'thin tube' TV in early 2005 (van Grinsven, 2005).

Consumer research indicated that the thinner tube would attract a significant market. However, such assessments focused on the physical dimension attributes and seemed to make the unwarranted assumption that the CRT would maintain an advantage in picture quality compared to LCD displays. In fact, the picture quality gap was closing rapidly with respect to LCDs and was already closed with respect to plasma displays. Plasma technology had other limitations at this point in its life cycle, such as weight, 'burn-in' and higher cost (that is, it was still on the bottom of its S-shaped growth curve) and LCDs had size limitations and color purity issues. However, these problems were also being rapidly solved. At the same time, volume and increased competition led to steadily declining prices. Hence, the performance-price ratio, which determines where a technology is on its growth curve, was steadily increasing.

Virtually all technologies have multiple performance attributes. Collectively, these attributes determine competitive position and this complexity complicates technology and economic assessments. Uneven technological and cost improvements across attributes can give the defender technology hope. Over time, however, the challenger, benefiting from a superior generic technology, catches up to and eventually passes the defender technology. The segment of the global industry that achieves a balanced advance across product attributes (and interfaces with other system components) takes the dominant market share.

As the potential for applying the science underlying a major technology life cycle approaches its physical limits, development of new generic technologies becomes increasingly difficult.[2] Yet, projecting the end of a major cycle and hence determining the timing of major investments in breakthrough research necessary to be a leader in the next major cycle is not easy. In semiconductors, advances in chip-processing technology (lithography) have allowed the width of various circuit features to shrink from 130 nanometers (nm) in 2001 to 90 nm in 2003 to 65 nm in 2005, with a goal of 45 nm in 2007. This progress has convinced many that the silicon-based semiconductor technology cycle will be extended for some time. In fact, a plethora of product innovations, such as the advanced modulators and silicon lasers described above, and process innovations that address the problems associated with nanometer-wide circuit elements, such as current leakage, are extending the major semiconductor life cycle.

However, the processing equipment required to manufacture these advances is progressively more capital intensive and hence expensive, which means that economies of scale become increasingly important in determining profitability. As a consequence, production cost can only continue to be halved every two years if sales per plant reach levels sufficient to attain the needed production efficiencies.

In response to this increasing capital intensity, many domestic companies have ceased production operations, choosing instead to offshore manufacturing to locations where various incentives reduce these costs and, in some cases, where large potential markets would help achieve needed economies of scale. In an apparent contradiction, the number of global semiconductor vendors has risen steadily from 120 in the mid-1980s to roughly 550 in 2003, with most of this increase occurring in other economies. Two explanations for this trend are: (i) rapid global economic growth has expanded the demand for semiconductors providing a rationale for such investment, and (ii) emerging economies believe that this capacity is a necessary precursor to attaining the capability to domestically produce more advanced devices with higher profit margins.

The same competitive imperative applies to product technology. Currently, continued progress in device integration offers all the attributes necessary to extend the semiconductor life cycle: increased chip speed, lower power dissipation, greater functionality per chip, lower system cost and physically smaller equipment.[3] But, such integration and the resulting incredibly small dimensions of circuit elements, perhaps as small as 1–5 nm, are requiring intense and increasingly expensive research into radical materials, which, in turn, require equally challenging advances in supporting research infrastructure, such as sophisticated modeling and simulation capabilities, and advanced metrology to characterize candidate materials' properties and the interfaces among circuit components at the nanometer scale.

Slowly, the difficulty and expense of extending the major life cycle, coupled with too much global capacity expansion, will reduce the cash flow available to individual companies to fund more R&D. As a result, enthusiasm by capital markets for further investment will decline, which, in turn, will make investments more expensive for the entire supply chain. As Schumpeter observed a half-century ago, excessive asset accumulation characterizes the end of a life cycle and when declining profitability eventually sets in, the door is opened to new, disruptive technologies.

TRANSITION TO THE NEXT MAJOR CYCLE

The shrinking of the average technology cycle's lifetime requires that industry and government strategic planners more efficiently support potentially disruptive technologies in anticipation of the need to more rapidly and efficiently transition to emerging technologies. Such technologies typically struggle in their early phases of development, attempting to address the substantial technical and market risks that create the risk spike, before eventually moving toward market confrontation with the defender technology. In the case of semiconductors, such varied and seemingly exotic technologies as light-emitting polymers, carbon nanotubes, molecular transistors and protein-DNA logic circuits are currently being researched. Initially, they may co-exist with or even complement silicon-based semiconductor technology, but eventually some will evolve into formidable competitors.

In contrast, industries nearing the end of their underlying technology life cycles increasingly rely on strategies other than R&D, such as relentlessly reducing costs and spending more on maintaining demand through advertising. The pharmaceutical industry is a current example. Its out-of-date trial-and-error technology development strategy is rapidly being replaced by science-based biotechnology. Yet, its installed wisdom inhibits adaptation. For example, instead of converting their research infrastructure to biotechnology, traditional pharmaceutical firms have tried such research techniques as 'high through-put screening'. While superior to conventional chemical entity assessment, it is still only a high-speed trial-and-error research method.

However, as the experience of the biotechnology industry shows, emerging technologies experience difficulties in moving off the bottom of the S-shaped growth curve. Process technology innovations are required to optimize performance–price ratios and new marketing strategies are needed to effectively address customer segments and the interfaces with other components of the technology system. Such changes are complex and take time. For these reasons, giving up on the existing technology prematurely or allowing the emerging technology to languish are both mistakes.

With the rapid expansion of technology-based competition, the probability of an industry in a different economy becoming the technological leader and realizing first-mover advantage in the next life cycle is increasing. In the semiconductor supply chain, industries in Asia and Europe are gaining market shares at the expense of US industries. As Figure 7.2 shows for the semiconductor device industry, leading-edge manufacturing plants (that

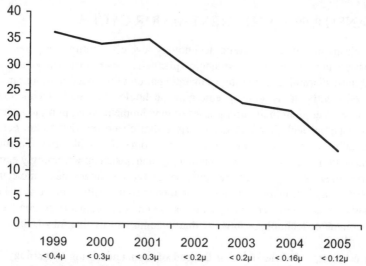

Source: SICAS/Semiconductor Industry Association (μ = microns)

Figure 7.2 US Shares of Leading-Edge Semiconductor Capacity

produce the smallest circuit features measured in microns) are increasingly being built in other countries, thereby setting the stage for further shifts in market shares of the design, equipment, and wafer tiers of the supply chain to these economies. This trend is clearly an ominous sign for US competitive positions in a forthcoming major life-cycle transition because, as previously discussed, achieving state-of-the-art manufacturing requires a commensurate supporting R&D capability, which, in turn, provides the basis for innovative product and process research. Thus, as these shifts in market share occur, so do shifts in the capacity to innovate in the next major technology cycle. The bottom line is that advanced manufacturing and the associated R&D tend to co-locate.

When the United States was the dominant technology-based economy, reshuffling of market leaders within an industry was not a serious concern. Those companies that did not adapt to the advent of disruptive generic technologies disappeared but were replaced by new, innovative firms from within the domestic economy. Resources were reallocated but always to a new domestic industry. Thus, the law of comparative advantage worked just fine for the US economy in that, while lower-skilled and lower-paid jobs were offshored, these jobs were replaced by higher-skilled and hence higher-paying jobs. Thus, the disappearance of most mainframe computer companies (Burroughs, Sperry Univac, NCR, DEC and so on) was not a problem for the domestic economy because the design and manufacture of succeeding generations of PCs and servers were dominated by other American companies.

For today's science-based technologies, innovating and then acquiring market share in the early phases of major life cycles require large numbers of scientists and engineers both in industry and supporting university and government institutions to advance and broaden the applications of the original innovation. For example, cell-based drug development has evolved as a research and manufacturing technique over the past 25 years only through the efforts of thousands of biologists, geneticists, and chemical engineers who perfected the fermentation systems that increased the capacity to produce recombinant proteins at least tenfold just in the past decade and 30-fold since the inception of biotechnology (DePalma, 2005).

As technology life cycles mature, opportunities increase for converging economies to pick off portions of the value added in a supply chain. In the modern-day version of Schumpeter's creative destruction, Christensen (1997) argues that firms reaching market leadership positions through innovation increasingly focus on maintaining that lead through incremental innovation targeted at preferred customer segments of the overall existing markets. At some point, new entrants appear who may first focus on imitation aimed at serving neglected market segments. Eventually, however, these challengers or even yet additional entrants introduce disruptive new technologies and take over the existing markets.

As previously described for semiconductors, the cycle transition begins in the form of a hollowing out of incumbents' positions within the current technology life cycle. Christensen et al. (2004b) characterize this process in terms of a 'decoupling point'. Typically, integrated manufacturers dominate the supply chain for a period of time until the interfaces between components are firmly established. These interfaces allow innovative specialists in individual components to enter the industry. The tier in a supply chain at which this vertical disintegration occurs is the decoupling point. This point tends to move backward over time from the final product toward subsystems and then to component tiers.

Christensen et al. cite a number of cases from the computer industry in which the establishment of a 'clean modular interface' led to segmentation of suppliers making up the supply chain. First, the decoupling point moved backward from the interface between the mainframe computer (integrated system level) and the system user to the interface between the disk drive and the computer, followed by further backward movement to the interface between the recording head and other components of the disk drive. As virtually all high-tech products and services are systems, this backward movement of the decoupling point opens the door to innovative firms specializing in particular components of the technology system.

Today, the backward movement of decoupling points as technology life cycles evolve increasingly includes foreign innovators taking shares of the total value added produced by global high-tech supply chains. Foreign-market shares set up these economies to be innovators in the next life cycle as their industries gain R&D, manufacturing and marketing expertise, and as their governments learn how to support emerging technologies. This distribution of value added is a normal part of the evolution of the typical technology life cycle, but it means erosion of the innovator's and often the domestic economy's previously dominant market position.

Because technology and market-share convergence is an increasing challenge, jump starting new technology life cycles within the domestic economy is essential. A major policy imperative is that if the innovating economy is going to reap a large share of the benefits, it must have sufficient technology-based capacity to move off the bottom of the S-shaped growth curve and thereby rapidly penetrate the target markets before significant imitation arrives. Doing so successfully requires (i) continued product innovation (improvements on the original innovation), (ii) innovation in process technologies as competition becomes dependent on ensuring quality and lowering cost, and (iii) new 'methods of inventing' that increase research productivity or actually make continued innovation possible.[4]

In the sigmoidal (S-shaped) pattern that characterizes a technology life cycle, the technological and infrastructural elements evolve slowly and unevenly, resulting in restrained market acceptance. This characteristic is found in all nested cycles from the major cycles based on new science to intermediate generational technology cycles to the shorter product cycles.

However, for new science-based major cycles, initial generic technologies can yield only small markets for some time. This phenomenon is due in part to the fact that the supporting infrastructures are typically not available, forcing entrepreneurs to adapt ones from other technologies. These borrowed technical infrastructures are suboptimal and remain so until markets become large enough to warrant their development specifically for the new technology. Thus, the relatively flat initial portion of the S-shaped growth curve can be stretched out in time, unless a competing economy overcomes the barriers (the risk spike) more rapidly.

Another reason why the economic impact of radical innovations is often constrained early in the life cycle is the fact that such technologies require very different assimilation and management approaches. Moreover, the complexity of all modern technologies, especially their systems nature, means that not all components advance at the same pace. This phenomenon leads to performance problems at the system level. Further, the functionality of the interfaces among components has a public–good dimension (as described in Chapter 8), which creates additional performance barriers until the needed infratechnologies and associated standards are provided.

The above factors (evolution of performance attributes, emerging industry structure, and amount and quality of technical infrastructure) conspire to create an initial performance–price 'gap' for the new technology. This gap is shown in Figure 7.3 by the vertical distance between points *A* and *B*. The size of the gap and the time required to mitigate the set of barriers causing it varies depending on the magnitude of these barriers.

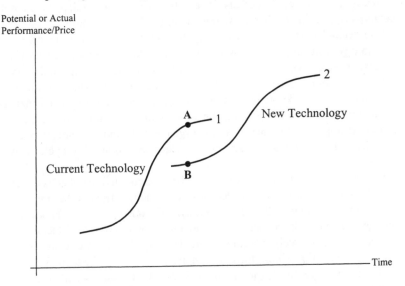

Source: Tassey (1997, 2005a).

Figure 7.3 Transition Between Two Technology Life Cycles

With enough time, a new technology becomes integrated with emerging process and organizational innovation cycles to yield large productivity increases. The development of electricity in the last half of the 19th century was a slow process, but one that in the first half of the 20th century had enormous economic impact. Economic historians such as Rosenberg (1976) and David (1990) argue that the development of electricity did not have an immediate payoff in higher productivity growth because (i) new production technologies based on electricity evolved and diffused slowly, and (ii) even after adopting this technology in new plants, learning how to effectively use it took considerable time.

The first of these two reasons is due largely to the installed-base effect. That is, companies who have invested time and money in current production systems are reluctant to scrap their accumulated assets and learned practices optimized for the existing technology system. Companies are faced with the prospect of replacing still-serviceable plants with totally new plant structures and organizational strategies to make use of the new technology. Managers must also deal with the fact that the considerable knowledge capital they and their workers have built up over time will be obsolete to a significant degree under the new paradigm, requiring considerable time and expenditure on technology assimilation and worker training. Finally, new technologies typically have inherent defects in addition to being foreign to existing businesses, and this further slows the rate of market penetration.

The second reason is evidenced by the series of advances in computer technology from the late 1950s to the early 1990s. These advances (nested cycles) progressively increased a range of manufacturing and service capabilities, but the economic impact remained muted. This 'productivity paradox' confounded analysts at first, but they eventually realized that the computers and, more important, the IT system as a whole would have its promised impact only when business organizations and consumers changed their behavior to take advantage of this major technology life cycle (David, 1990).

Only if technologies are considered to be disembodied (as major economic growth models assumed for decades) can their diffusion be immediate (Atkeson and Kehoe, 2001). In reality, of course, much technology is aggregated into systems, based on components with embodied technologies that must be effectively integrated. This fact can slow market penetration. It took 50 years for Albert Einstein's conception of the laser to become a reality as an 'invention' (for which a US and two Russian scientists shared a Nobel Prize). From that point, major quantum jumps in the generic technology (in particular, the semiconductor laser) led to a myriad of derived product-based cycles based on unpredicted innovations with huge economic impact. However, the rate of innovation was retarded by the fact that the laser did not interact well with other components of IT systems until optical-fiber cable became available; that is, the productivity of the system technology was muted.

A final complication for policy makers is the fact that many of the major technology drivers of the past century have an infrastructure character. Electricity and IT are the two most prominent examples. Not only does IT act as a facilitator for new products and services and therefore must evolve in tandem with innovative effort at the product and service levels, but this 'economic' infrastructure itself has a technical infrastructure base (in the form of standards), which clearly has public-good content. As the next chapter will demonstrate, the technical basis for standards can be as complex as the technologies they support and therefore the evolution of technology life cycles is usually inhibited by inadequate technical infrastructure.

LIFE-CYCLE LENGTH AND COMPETITIVE OPPORTUNITY

In the first part of the post-World War II period, the dominance of the US economy through technology meant that life cycles could be allowed to stretch out in time without concern for lost market opportunities. The only issue was which firms within the domestic economy would dominate the various phases of the new life cycle.

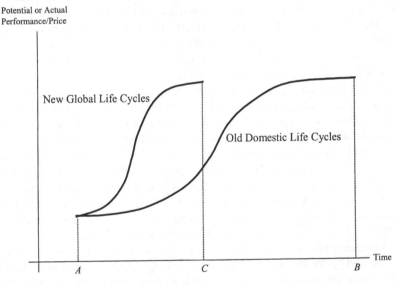

Figure 7.4   Technology Life-Cycle Compression

Constraints on Market Opportunity from Shorter Life Cycles

The time available to achieve market objectives is illustrated in Figure 7.4 where the initiation of technology research at time *A* eventually results in commercialization and a market that expands until obsolescence occurs, leading to the end of the cycle at time *B*. However, the advent of multiple technology-based economies has greatly expanded global resources available to develop new technologies and penetrate markets. The result is a significant shortening of the average life cycle, which can now be expected to end at time *C*. The windows of opportunity have been shortened at all phases of the life cycle because next-generation technologies appear sooner and push the end point of the current cycle forward in time (that is, from point *B* to point *C*). Further, imitation by other countries' industries erodes market shares of domestic companies earlier and more frequently.

The DVD player exemplifies the rapid market penetration and multiple cycles that now occur within a relatively short period of time. It became one of the fastest-adopted product technologies in history: the first players appeared in 1997 and around half the households in the developed world now have one, with the cheapest models costing a mere $40.[5] The first-generation DVD was read-only followed by rewritable, and soon the 'high-definition' generation will replace the original format – all in less than 10 years. Each generation of DVD players (product cycles) is nested within a set of generic technology cycles that contribute to the system technology (the DVD). This 'tire-track' system structure means that manufacturers must conduct or network with sources of the needed technology in a way which results in more efficient R&D cycles and then interface their products with others that together make up the technology system.

Multiple technology-based economies also mean multiple strategies with respect to competing over a life cycle. Moreover, these strategies evolve over time as countries target new comparative advantages. As China, India and other Asian nations are doing today, Japan bootstrapped itself into a position of world technological leadership in the 1980s by focusing on an imitation/incremental improvement strategy coupled with intense emphasis on process technology innovation. Having a large economy, the Japanese were able to apply this strategy to electronics, automotive, intelligent machine technologies (robotics) and certain areas of materials technology such as advanced ceramics and, more recently, solar cell technology.

Japan continues to pursue this mid-life-cycle strategy with a vengeance, as evidenced by the fact that the Japanese economy has one of the highest R&D intensities. Its national R&D is dominated by large companies, which has the effect of focusing the majority of R&D toward applications of existing generic technologies. These companies have excelled in the mid-to-late phases of technology life cycles where steady incremental product and process innovation can generate high rates of return. Their performance is indicated in US Patent and Trademark Office statistics, which show that five of the top 10 US patent award recipients in 2004 were Japanese companies (four others were American and one was Korean). Moreover, the Japanese economy has a much higher patent intensity than anyone else, including the United States (National Science Board, 2006a).[6]

In addition to specialization with respect to product technology (decoupling), globalization is also forcing companies to focus on specific phases of economic activity. For example, Christensen et al. (2004b) point out that, once the basic science was available, discovery, design/development (including clinical trials), manufacturing, and marketing have all been integrated into the same pharmaceutical firm. Today, however, the biotechnology industry, being an emerging technology experiencing growing global competition, exhibits large-scale partnering with other biotech and pharmaceutical firms for R&D, manufacturing and marketing – almost the antithesis of the fully-integrated (and rapidly declining) pharmaceutical industry.

The growing global competition for markets of existing technology life cycles gets considerable attention from growth policy analysts due to the risk created for the domestic economy's existing market shares. However, the front end of new life cycles is also under attack, which has significant implications for future market shares. The successful strategies behind this second phenomenon, which focus on more rapidly and efficiently overcoming the risk spike, are reflected in a steeper slope for the front end of the S-shaped growth curve. As described in detail in earlier chapters, many countries are now attempting first-mover strategies. They recognize that the innovating economy can attain substantial advantages in terms of initial high profit margins and also has the potential to maintain large market shares through major portions of the ensuing life cycle.

Even as they reached world-class status in terms of economic performance during the late 1980s, the Japanese realized that the imitation model did not provide for life-cycle transition capability. However, initial attempts at funding next-generation and even more-radical technologies were not successful (Tassey, 1992). Fifteen years later, while their rate of innovation has extended the middle portions of a number of life cycles, the installed-base effect still seems to be inhibiting adequate government funding of disruptive technology research and is perpetuating a rigid industry structure that makes new-firm formation and market entry difficult. Japan has also made little progress in forcing an isolated university system to assume an infrastructure role in support of new regional technology-based, economic-growth clusters.

Still, the imperative to adapt is a strong forcing function. Japan is finally pushing reforms such as integrating national laboratories and the public university system with domestic industries to facilitate life-cycle transitions. The Japanese government is implementing these reforms through matching funds for university–industry research partnerships, support for spin-off companies from universities (including funding and relaxation of restrictions on professor participation in these companies), and general promotion of technology-based clusters (Yoshida, 2004).

Opportunities for Sustained Competitive Advantage

In spite of the barriers that must be faced in responding to the factors that are compressing technology life cycles, the complexity of modern technology can actually convey sustained advantages to those economies that make the multiple simultaneous investments required to advance system-level technologies. A major reason is the fact that most economic growth policies are just beginning to understand the importance of managing R&D portfolios so as to efficiently produce a technology system. Thus, innovation in technology-based growth policies can create a broad-based set of comparative advantages.

Even at the component level, advanced R&D capability can yield technologies that are difficult to imitate. For example, while a simple machine tool can be fairly quickly re-engineered, one that has proprietary control algorithms and substantial technology embodied in its components is much more difficult to copy. More generally, the increasing importance of a science base for technological innovation means that the transfer of tacit knowledge is increasingly essential. The diffusion channels for such knowledge are local and require high levels of technical expertise and personal contact.

System-level technology also embodies a significant amount of tacit knowledge related to overall design and operation. Moreover, technology-based systems require several layers of technical infrastructure, as described in the next chapter, which demand a variety of public and private institutions to design and manage. Such infrastructure is not easily copied and has a significant impact on domestic productivity.

In summary, while the life cycle of the typical technology is becoming shorter as more players participate, it can never collapse to zero or even below some minimum length of time. Thus, while increased competition compresses the window of opportunity backward from the end of the cycle, finite amounts of time must elapse between innovation, imitation, industry growth and maturity, and finally decline. This phenomenon works to the advantage of the economies with greater technology development and utilization resources, the infrastructures to leverage the productivity of these resources, and the policy models to effectively manage the government's several critical roles.

MANAGING THE LIFE CYCLE

The critical issue for economic growth policy is how to support the domestic industry over an entire technology life cycle because total life-cycle competitiveness both maximizes and stabilizes economic growth. While the successful innovator attains a temporary monopoly and hence large profit margins, most economic growth occurs in the middle of the cycle when imitators have entered and markets have expanded to create substantial value added (employment and profits). Thus, a competitive domestic industry over the entire technology life cycle is an essential policy objective.

Cycle Dynamics

The initiation of a life cycle (innovation, manufacturing startup and early market-share leadership) usually occurs in the country in which the underlying advances in science occur. However, as described in Chapter 1, it is also the case that as a life cycle evolves, manufacturing can and does move offshore, even to a largely R&D-naive economy. Plants in the host country usually produce products with fairly mature technologies developed elsewhere, so an indigenous R&D capability is not necessary at first. Frequently, the host country makes the foreign owner give up some intellectual property for the privilege of manufacturing the product in its country. In this way, it gets some initial experience with the current generation of the technology and prepares itself for the second phase of its economic growth strategy.

In this second phase, the host country starts to train the skilled labor not only for high-tech manufacturing but also for R&D. Eventually, it will begin to invest in its own R&D, because (i) the growing manufacturing base needs the support, and, more important, (ii) the next generation of the technology has to come from somewhere and the host country would like to capture the additional value added from the intellectual property that results from the R&D, as well as realize the synergies with the co-located domestic manufacturing.

For the companies in the early phases of a technology's life cycle, competition can be particularly intense and business-model errors can be fatal. Companies, especially small ones, frequently react to such pressures by attempting to leap to the 'D' in R&D; that is, they emphasize getting products to market sooner to create cash flow and to attract additional financing. To some extent, such strategies are understandable because delays in commercialization can have a negative impact on future investment by reducing retained earnings and restricting access to external financing.

With respect to external financing, no matter how well the R&D cycle is going for a small company, the macroeconomic environment has significant influence on the timing of funding if not the amount (see Chapter 2). The implosion of the stock market, especially the high-tech stocks in 2000, led to several years of high risk avoidance by investors, including a significant reduction in venture capital.

The resulting truncation of R&D strategies to focus on short-term but less important R&D objectives compromises longer-term, potentially higher payoff research (the 'R'). In this decade, a combination of a shift in venture capital markets toward less risk and a low rate of clinical trial successes led biotech companies to modify their business models to attract investors. Even though venture-capital flows into biotech companies revived in 2003 to $1.3 billion, a 32 percent increase over 2002, the shift in risk preferences toward later-stage product development (that is, later-stage clinical trials) was clear (see Figure 5.8). This so-called NRDO (no research, development only) model attempts to reduce the risk of failure and long periods of inadequate profitability typically associated with biotechnology startups (Williams, 2005). In essence, this strategy seeks to truncate early-phase R&D (discovery) to get to development (clinical trials). Two negative consequences are reduced efforts at major (higher-risk) drug discovery and faith-based attempts to leap from scientific discovery to major drug development (in effect, truncating the proof-of-concept phase of the R&D cycle).

But implementing an NRDO business model has not solved the serious R&D cycle management problems faced by biotech firms. Many small companies have been compelled to form partnerships with either other biotechnology companies or large pharmaceutical firms to get access to needed funding and to clinical trial and manufacturing/marketing expertise that might have been acquired at lower effective prices under different financing conditions and with more time for proof-of-concept research. Although R&D networking has become common practice for reasons discussed earlier, the shortage of risk funding leads to premature partnering at less-favorable terms in order to get an initial drug through clinical trials. Companies have actually appeared whose business models are focused solely on negotiating favorable in-licensing deals from struggling biotech firms for drugs typically in early-phase clinical trials. In the process, the biotech companies give up some or all of the intellectual property associated with the drug candidate and hence still end up with risk-capital constraints for developing the remainder of their pipelines, even if the partnered drug is eventually commercialized.

In theory, at least, the evolving complex industry structure can improve the efficiency of the overall biotechnology industry by matching complementary assets distributed among two or more firms. Use of contract research organizations (CROs) and contract manufacturing organizations (CMOs) or various partnerships can take advantage of specialization in areas of R&D, manufacturing, marketing and bring more drugs to market to the benefit of both the industry and consumers – at least in the short term. However, the NRDO model, if widely adopted, will result in a meaningful shift for the industry as a whole to a later life-cycle mode of investment behavior at the expense of major drug discovery.

Case Study in Life-Cycle Dynamics: Battery Technology for Consumer Electronics

New generations of wireless devices and portable entertainment products are making power demands on batteries that existing technologies are finding difficult to meet. Reductions in operating voltage have done little to offset the problem as designers continue to enhance their products with extra features and capabilities. In addition to coping with increased functionality – such as color displays, speech-recognition capability and embedded MP3 players – batteries must cope with significant increases in voice and data traffic. Future generations of these products, such as location-based services, electronic banking and a plethora of information and entertainment services will increase the burden on battery life (SRI Consulting).

Disposable batteries are a mature $18 billion global market. Not only is a market of this size attractive but the proliferation of electronic devices means continuing growth in demand. Japanese companies, in particular, have excelled in making continual product improvements in the mid- and later phases of the life cycle of electronic products and combining such improvements with sufficient advances in manufacturing efficiencies to maintain target price points.

However, standardization imposed by device manufacturers on the current generation (alkaline) technology restricts even modest innovation. Specifically, options for new chemical compounds are constrained by the requirement to 'fit' the battery into the standard shape.

It is through such constraints in the later phases of a life cycle that the installed-base effect has its greatest and often terminating effect on the existing industry structure. While the market-share leaders are pouring enormous resources into minor improvements, a radically new technology is lurking in an unseen location elsewhere. The incumbents become victims of what has been called 'motivation asymmetries' (Christensen et al., 2004a).

This model was developed to explain how individual companies that become dominant find ways to ignore the inroads in their markets by new entrants who are both more desperate and uninhibited by the current technology and market focus. The new entrants may initially focus on the low-value-added market segments, which are beneath the dignity of the incumbents. However, through innovative technology and marketing strategies, these upstarts move up the value-added scale and encroach upon or, in some cases, grab large shares of the existing market. In the latter case, the incumbents frequently are put out of business.

In the early 1990s, lithium-ion batteries were developed as a challenger technology. A distinguishing feature is that they are rechargeable. As a result, they have become the standard for high-energy rechargeable battery technology. Moreover, they have four times the energy and twice the power capacity of nickel cadmium (Ni-Cd) batteries. They also do not experience a memory effect (partial discharge before recharging that reduces subsequent charge capacity).

However, the phenomenon of the installed base comes into play with its typical negative impact on the incumbent industry's ability to adapt to change. American companies, having succeeded in reaching the leadership position in disposable batteries through realization of economies of scale in production, brand imaging and superior marketing, have not been able to adapt to the new technology life cycles for rechargeable batteries. A disposable battery is a standardized commodity and hence so is its interface with the electronic products it powers. This situation allows battery manufacturers to operate in a non-integrated way within the device supply chains they serve.

This is not the case for newer rechargeable battery technologies, such as lithium-ion. Development of Li-ion batteries has required close contact with portable electronic device designers to adapt the battery to the performance attributes of the device. Large American battery manufacturers, such as Duracell and Eveready (now Energizer Holdings), began R&D efforts in the new technology in the early 1990s. Their intent was to ultimately commercialize and domestically produce Li-ion batteries. However, as Li-ion battery technology emerged, lack of scale and initial production inefficiencies discouraged these companies from investing in production facilities in the United States. Labor costs were not a factor in this decision. The highly automated unit cell production process for the new technology offset any labor cost advantage of locating production in East Asia (Brodd, 2005).

The lower profit margins typical of the early phases of a technology's life cycle coupled with the higher profit margins of mature disposable batteries acted as a disincentive to US manufacturers to invest in the capacity to produce the new rechargeable batteries (three of the five-largest disposable battery companies are in the United States). The installed-base effect was in full force.

In contrast, most producers of portable electronic devices are located in

Japan and are vertically integrated companies; that is, they are both producers and users of Li-ion batteries. Success in the rechargeable market requires knowledge of the electrical requirements for emerging products that require these batteries, as well as the ability to achieve rapid product improvements to meet changing device requirements and then to assemble the unit cells into battery packs for use in the specific device. Most US manufacturers lack the ability to integrate with upstream design firms and materials suppliers and with downstream customers; that is, supply chain integration is not present in the US market.

Moreover, effective supply-chain integration, in addition to communication, requires an understanding by large manufacturers that smaller suppliers need both adequate profits and some minimum level of orders during down portions of the business cycle to sustain R&D and update productive capacity. However, the strong profit-maximization focus by US companies, in contrast to a greater emphasis on market share and sustainability by Japanese companies, has led to further hollowing out of the US supply chain. Finally, even though several US companies have the capability to produce all the components and materials associated with Li-ion technology, no viable market exists in the US economy because all the manufacturing takes place in Asia (Brodd, 2005). Several small US firms have developed new battery technologies with financial assistance from DARPA and ATP, but with production capability largely offshored, the intellectual property tends to leak in the direction of the source of production.

Current disruptive technology research in battery technology is investigating the potential of a range of energy sources, including ceramic, kinetic, photovoltaic, electrochemical, thermal and biological technologies. Attaining the ability to deposit microbatteries directly onto printed circuit boards will provide a significant competitive advantage over stand-alone batteries – an advantage that manufacturers are keen to exploit. Other radically different battery technologies, such as 'beta voltaic', which uses beta particles from a radioactive source to generate a current in semiconductor materials, are also appearing. Samsung has developed a (direct methanol) fuel cell as part of a docking station that allows a notebook computer to run for eight hours a day, five days a week, for up to four weeks (Garrett, 2006). Thus, the race to the next technology life cycle is occurring and potential first movers are appearing in different economies. This pace of technological change with its increasingly varied global sources cannot be dealt with by old economic growth strategies that ignore early-phase R&D and supply-chain integration.

Case Study in Life Cycle Transition: Semiconductors

Early semiconductor technology was highly labor intensive. Going from a paper circuit diagram to creation of a prototype mask (the master circuit pattern) required physically inscribing each circuit feature, reducing it to chip size and constructing the final mask. This 'design' process was largely in engineers' heads (that is, tacit knowledge) and for some time after the initiation of a product life cycle produced initial yields in the 0–20 percent range. Yields were slowly improved over a life cycle by testing and re-testing chips to determine what design changes and process adjustments were needed.

However, with the advent of global competition in this industry during the 1980s, the average life cycle began to shrink. Labor-intensive design and slow ramp-up in yield at the production stage were no longer acceptable. The competitive solution appeared in the form of very large-scale integration (VLSI) technology. The major innovation was using the computer to design a chip. In this new life cycle (based on a new generic process technology), the companies that adopted computer-aided design survived; those that did not perished. Although VLSI era chips were more dense than the previous technology life cycle (100,000 transistors per chip), features were not too small to prevent computer-controlled production techniques from placing and routing wafers through the multiple steps of inscribing the desired circuit patterns without significant interaction between the design and production stages.

Thus, VLSI process equipment became the critical driver of competitive advantage. An entire process equipment industry sprung up. This industry replaced the test-equipment companies of the previous life cycle as the dominant equipment suppliers. The increasing ability to match computer-aided design with the manufacturing process pushed initial production yields past 50 percent in the early 1980s. American companies, of which KLA Instruments was the largest, initially dominated this new tier in the semiconductor supply chain.

As this second life cycle evolved through the 1990s, convergence resulted in American and Asian companies battling for market shares in both the chip and equipment industries. The more VLSI technology diffused, the more profit margins were squeezed. At the same time, the growing density of each generation of semiconductor devices increased the capital intensity of production, thereby making the cost of new manufacturing plants expand rapidly. These trends, typical of the last part of a technology's life cycle, made it increasingly difficult for companies, even those with substantial operations, to stay in the chip business. In fact, a number of large producers exited, as exemplified by Motorola's spin-off of Freescale Semiconductor in

2004 (VLSI Research Inc., 2005).

In the early 2000s, the VLSI cycle came to an end as nanoscale circuit dimensions ushered in a new major technology cycle.[7] 'The nanoelectronics era will once again revolutionize the semiconductor industry as we utilize new materials, new device structures and new assembly methods to extend Moore's Law', stated SIA President George Scalise.[8] For example, in 2005, Hewlett-Packard's Quantum Science Research group published a paper announcing an invention called a 'crossbar latch'. The inventors described it as a nanoscale device that provides the signal restoration and inversion required for general computing – without the need for transistors. Such a technology could result in computers that are thousands of times more powerful than those in existence today (Baker, 2005).

The new nanoelectronics cycle is characterized by a return to a design-dependent orientation like the original cycle in the 1960s and 1970s. That is, design-related defects are once again a significant threat to production yields, so design-for-manufacturing has once again become an essential element of R&D. The separation of R&D and manufacturing in the VLSI era has led to a dysfunction in the new nanoscale life cycle. Semiconductor companies, accustomed to starting a yield ramp at a 70–80 percent benchmark established under VLSI technology, suddenly are struggling to achieve 10 percent yields (VLSI Research, Inc., 2005). This drop in yield is an example of the early-cycle performance–price gap AB in Figure 7.3.

The cycle transition scenario is for nanoscale electronic devices to first supplement and eventually replace conventional silicon technology. The initial partial overlap of the two cycles will cause suppliers of the defender technology to be late to respond. Current life-cycle companies have succeeded in extending Moore's Law well beyond the predicted end of the silicon era. In 2005, the world's smallest transistor (produced by Intel) was about 50 nanometers – half the size of a flu virus. In early 2006, IBM announced the development of an improved optical lithography manufacturing process that prints the smallest, high-quality circuit lines ever achieved (around 30 nanometers wide).

Such advances are extending the life of Moore's Law. But, industry and government research agencies both know that the physical limit will be reached in the next decade. As this time arrives, a reshuffling of competitive positions across companies and entire industries will speed up, in spite of the fact that the initial process of transition has been deceptively slow.

In fact, the transition is already underway. IBM announced in May 2007 that the company had developed the first nanoscale, self-assembling material to construct a semiconductor device that is beyond the capabilities of conventional manufacturing. IBM used a plastic-like material that spontaneously forms into a systematic sieve-like structure with holes of just

20 nanometers in diameter. IMB claims this material will enable computer chips to run 35 percent faster or reduce energy usage by the same amount (Svensson, 2007).

Life Cycle Management Issues

Because of the installed-base effect, the most difficult policy challenge for innovation leaders is to commit to planning for the next life cycle. Over time, as young industries mature, consolidation and increasing average firm size tend to solve some of the problems identified for early-cycle participants by allowing more research to be funded out of cash flow and for risk to be diversified across larger-product pipelines. Moreover, attainment of a significant market share stabilizes cash flow and the integration of the product into larger system technologies adds to perceived continuation of demand for the product. In addition, successive improvements in both design and process technologies increase total market value, and a subset of firms that have participated in this market come to dominate.

Eventually, however, opportunities to apply the current generic technology decline, design volatility decreases, and the product's structure takes on a commodity character (the personal computer is an example). Competition shifts to efficiency in production processes and hence to price and service as increasingly important determinants of market performance.

These changes in competitive focus create opportunities for less-advanced and lower-cost economies. They can acquire the maturing product technology and combine it with cheaper labor and incremental improvements in process technology. Certain classes of semiconductors, computers and many types of software exhibit the maturing phases of life-cycle patterns and the resulting competitive convergence. Japan in memory chips in the 1980s and, more recently, India in software and Taiwan in laptop computers are examples of this convergence process.

Even in the face of such competition, the fact that the size of markets is increasing as the global economy expands cultivates the belief among incumbents that sales targets can be sustained. Thus, companies will invest huge amounts of time and money to extend a life cycle in which they are major players. In spite of the advantages accrued by the leaders in the current life cycle, including the cash flow necessary for the sustained R&D investment needed to take on higher risk but potentially higher payoff technologies, the installed-base effect restrains such investment.

The message is that timely development of radically new technologies comes from vision on the part of both industry and government, followed by the long-term commitment to fund the early proof-of-concept research. Furthermore, actual commercialization frequently requires significant changes in production technology and coordination among the entire supply chain. The research required for major technological breakthroughs takes years, but so does the retooling of manufacturing strategies and capabilities. A new technology infrastructure must also evolve simultaneously to enable the R&D to be conducted and then to launch commercialization. The first-mover advantage goes to those economies in which industry and government cooperate at all phases of the R&D and commercialization cycles to fund the long-term research and provide the technology infrastructure (infratechnologies and standards) that enable a domestic supply chain to enter the emerging markets and acquire market share.

Because government funds at least portions of long-term generic technology research that provide the foundations for new technology life cycles, the amount and composition of such research support *and* its timing are increasingly critical. Moreover, because infratechnology development and promulgation of associated standards constitute an infrastructure that must evolve with the technology life cycle, its amount, composition and timing are equally critical. In the example of semiconductors, the first cycle depended on testing so metrology was a key infrastructure. At least portions of this infrastructure receded in importance in the next (VLSI) cycle, but have now returned to the forefront with a vengeance as the nanoscale technology era accelerates. Global competition is forcing corporate strategies to deal increasingly with time compression and therefore plan for and execute the needed adjustments in R&D portfolios more efficiently in advance of each new technology life cycle.

Another factor affecting life-cycle management is complexity. On the surface, this issue would seem to be addressed by specialization. However, as the decoupling point is pushed back to initial tiers in high-tech supply chains, the burden on companies in the final tiers to perform system integration is increased. Motion Computing Inc. is the third-largest seller of slate-style tablet PCs, a market that is approaching $7 billion annually. Motion's product allows users to write directly on the screen, display articles as they appear in a magazine, and transmit documents over wireless networks. The company sources most of the technology's components from a number of suppliers scattered around the world. The digital pen comes from Japan's Wacom Co. and the software for digital sketches from Toronto's Alias Systems Corp. The 12-inch pen-based screen, which can be viewed in bright sunlight at a range of angles, was developed by Korea's Boe Hydis. The machines are made in China by Taiwanese contract manufacturer Compal Electronics Inc. Such supply-chain complexity puts pressure on the system integrator to monitor technology life cycles in multiple component markets. Thus, corporate strategies are increasingly shifting to 'distributed innovation models' that acquire and build on technological knowledge from a variety of sources (Bowonder et al., 2005).

Such models include in-house R&D, support of academic research, acquiring or partnering with firms embodying complementary technologies, in-licensing of technologies, and outsourcing to R&D service firms. These strategies are difficult to manage and, significantly, they distribute value added across a global supply chain.

Two key policy concerns based on the technology-life-cycle concept follow. First, *within* a life cycle, the amount and speed of technological advance achieved by a domestic industry is critical because these factors determine the realized economic return. Innovating industries with high R&D–sales ratios will usually do well, especially over the first part of the life cycle. However, slow adaptation of R&D capabilities over later portions of the cycle (which can cover extended periods) often allow foreign competitors to take significant market share and thereby establish the ability to be innovators in the next generation of a major cycle.[9]

Second, transitioning *between* technology life cycles is an even more difficult issue for both corporate strategy and the policy process to address. A number of high-tech companies manage transitions among successive product life cycles quite effectively. However, the transition between two generic technology life cycles, especially to a radically new generic technology (a major technology transition), is seldom achieved by the same companies. This process of 'creative destruction' is not a problem, as long as the new leaders reside within the domestic economy. Otherwise, value added (jobs and profits) is lost.

The Bottom Line

To be a technology leader, R&D must be the first investment priority. Later in the technology's life cycle, other economies become manufacturers by absorbing technology from the innovator. Imitation strategies work well, but only for converging economies. However, countries bootstrapping themselves up the economic ladder through imitation can only raise their income during the later phases of a life cycle. Thus, they cannot be one of the highest-income economies in the long run; that is, across technology life cycles. Becoming a high-income economy requires innovation leadership.

Over time, the greatest threat to the world leader comes toward the end of a cycle, when a challenger technology is on the horizon. The leader has invested enormously in maximizing the return from the defender technology and is naturally reluctant to shift focus from a cash cow to the considerable expense and risk involved in transitioning to the next generation of the technology. Yet, spillovers of generic technical and proprietary knowledge have accumulated to the degree that significant convergence occurs.

In summary, as life cycles compress, R&D at the company level can no longer exist in isolation of a supporting network and infrastructure. To raise R&D efficiency, corporations increasingly require access to R&D conducted by other firms and to the broader technology infrastructures provided by national innovation systems. If domestic R&D resources are not available, companies do not hesitate to form partnerships with foreign companies or outsource R&D overseas. These relationships often lead to follow-on manufacturing in the host country. Thus, the maintenance of an effective domestic R&D network is essential for attracting global R&D funds and subsequent manufacturing investment, which collectively increase domestic value added and hence economic growth.

NOTES

1. In fiberoptic networks, modulators break the laser-generated light beam into discrete bursts that represent the 1s and 0s of the digital world.
2. One dramatic piece of evidence of approaching physical limits is the fact that semiconductor device features, such as circuit line width, are reaching nanometer dimensions that are actually smaller than the mean free path of the electrons (average distance between collisions). The result is signal leaking that degrades data moving through these incredibly small circuits.
3. Gartner Dataquest Semiconductor Industry Summit, September 13–14, 2004.
4. For a discussion of the third requirement, see Darby and Zucker (2003). For example, polymerase chain reaction (PCR) – an infratechnology used to amplify the number of copies of a specific region of DNA – facilitates the production of enough DNA to conduct experiments, run tests and so on. PCR has thereby enabled applications ranging from detection of infectious agents to forensic applications.
5. 'An Unexpectedly Bright Idea', *The Economist*, June 9, 2005.
6. A caveat is that the Japanese seem to have a greater propensity to patent independent of all other factors.
7. According to VLSI Research, the nanoscale chip era commenced with the 130 nm node because physical gate lengths were reduced to 80 nm or below, which were too small for VLSI production methods.
8. 'Nanotechnology Market Study Planned', *Silicon Valley/San Jose Business Journal*, January 10, 2005.
9. The video cassette recorder (VCR) is one of the best-known examples, but there are many others. A major type of semiconductor manufacturing equipment called a 'stepper' was invented in the United States, but market share is now almost totally Japanese. Oxide ceramics, which every modern commercial wireless communication and detection system incorporates, was discovered in the United States, but Japanese industry today dominates commercial markets. Other examples include flat panel displays, robotics, semiconductor memory devices, digital watches and interactive electronic games (Tassey, 2004).

8. The Role of Technical Infrastructure

I'm terribly concerned ... that we're on track to a second-rate economy.

Pete Domenici (US Senate)

The Industrial Revolution would not have succeeded to the extent that it did in the United States without substantial investment in economic infrastructure. Public spending on roads, bridges, canals, railroads and telephone networks integrated regional markets, thereby facilitating specialization that greatly enhanced economic growth. A less-recognized infrastructure, standardization of parts, enabled the modern factory system to emerge. Overall, superior public investment contributed to the US rise to the top of the global economic ladder during this period.

Today, a number of distinctly new categories of infrastructure underpin the technology-based economy. Rules governing intellectual property, a number of sets of regulations (energy, environment and health), industry structure and capital markets are important examples. Particularly critical is the education infrastructure that produces the skilled labor needed by technology-based industries. Recently, innovation infrastructures to support regional economic growth strategies have emerged, including entrepreneurial training, incubators for new high-tech firms, formal technology transfer mechanisms, public venture capital and so on. The dependency of industrial innovation on such infrastructures has been demonstrated by a number of economic studies (Freeman, 1986; Dosi, 1988).

Moreover, the intense battle for global competitive position is increasingly affected by a complex and less-understood 'technical infrastructure'. It consists of a ubiquitous set of methods, techniques, protocols, standards and simply tacit technical knowledge that apply to the three stages of economic activity. Every technology currently driving the US economy is supported by such infrastructure. Economic studies of individual infratechnologies that make up this infrastructure have shown substantial net economic benefits, and collectively the economic impact at the industry level is huge in terms of productivity gains and lower entry barriers (see Chapter 4).

However, the public-good nature of the infratechnologies and related standards making up an economy's technical infrastructure results in underinvestment by industry. Unlike the case of the Industrial Revolution, today's infrastructure is barely visible to the many stakeholders in the technology-based economy. Whereas one can see a railroad or a telephone, drawing a picture of a test method or a process control technique or a database of a material's properties or an interface standard is difficult at best.

In addition to this technical infrastructure, high-tech industries depend on evolving economic infrastructures that are themselves technology based. The Internet is the most vivid and important example. However, many other IT-based infrastructures abound that support both high-tech manufacturing and services, for example, the communications interfaces for supply-chain integration. These infrastructures are incredibly complex and require large amounts of resources to develop and maintain. As a result, both technical infrastructures and the economic infrastructures that depend on them offer the opportunity for national economies to differentiate themselves from competitors through more aggressive investment and deployment strategies.

ECONOMIC ROLES AND IMPACTS

A major premise for economic growth policy is that some economic assets are less mobile than others. Investment in these immobile assets should, therefore, be emphasized. Among the most critical categories of assets, skilled labor and technical infrastructure are the least mobile. However, while the need for expansion and upgrading of the S&E labor pool is a relatively understandable issue, the concept of technical infrastructure, including alternative ways of accumulation and management, is both complex and highly heterogeneous. Hence, it presents a particularly difficult challenge for technology-based growth policy.

In general, the technology-based economy requires a diversified and pervasive set of technical infrastructures that support all three stages of economic activity: R&D, production and commercialization. Such infrastructure is ubiquitous and critical. In fact, in today's global economy it has increasingly become not only a basis for attaining competitive advantage but a cost of entry into the global marketplace.

Imagine trying to conduct R&D without accurate and consistent measurement techniques, or to control production processes to attain high yields and quality levels without sensors that instantly and accurately measure the performance attributes of a product as it is being manufactured, and then transmit critical process data to a computer-based control system. Similarly, the commercialization of a technologically complex product often requires agreement between the buyer and seller on five to 10 key performance attributes, which cannot be achieved without equally complex product acceptance standards.

For example, semiconductor design and manufacturing requires a large and diversified set of measurement infratechnologies that are applied directly to individual products and also to the highly automated production systems used in the modern semiconductor plant. The pervasive role of measurement infratechnologies is indicated by a study of this industry's investment in measurement, which estimated that industry spent about $2.5 billion in 1996, triple the amount spent in 1990. This expenditure was projected to continue growing at least 15 percent per year. Assuming that this rate of investment has continued, the semiconductor industry spent over $9 billion on measurement equipment and services in 2006 (Finan, 1998).

As technologies become more complex, the supporting infrastructure is following the same pattern. Semiconductor companies are now designing components where performance is affected by the placing of single atoms. To support the associated measurement requirements of nanoscale and molecular-scale electronics, techniques must be developed to both place individual molecules on a substrate in precise patterns and then verify the component's performance through appropriate testing procedures. As an example, NIST researchers have built the world's most accurate electron counter; it can place 70 million electrons on a capacitor with an uncertainty of just one electron.

In contrast, inadequate measurement infrastructure capabilities can slow or even bring to a halt innovative product development at a time when foreign competition is increasing and technology life cycles are being compressed. For example, in the biosciences the most powerful tool for studying gene expression is the microarray, but the technology is plagued by large uncertainties and variability in measurement. One assessment using three different microarray systems to measure the same sets of genes, found that the best agreement between any two systems was only 21 percent (Tan et al., 2003).

Such infratechnology inadequacies are typical of an emerging science-driven technology. For example, to enable highly sophisticated R&D and to control extremely complex production processes, the biotechnology industry spends $1.2 billion per year on technical infrastructure, according to a study for NIST by RTI International (Gallaher et al., 2007). Industry surveys conducted by RTI led to estimates that feasible improvements in this infrastructure could significantly reduce the huge average cost of developing a new drug. Given that the biopharmaceutical industry has already commercialized 260 drugs for 380 indications (Biotechnology Industry Organization, 2006), the potential for future gains in economic efficiency through improved technical infrastructure is substantial.

In another group of emerging markets based on nanotechnology, just one subset of issues confronting innovation incentives – environment, health and safety concerns– requires a wide range of measurement infratechnologies and standards:

- Methods for detecting nanomaterials in biological matrices, environment, and workplace;
- Methods for standardizing particle size and size distribution;
- Standardized tools for assessing nanomaterial shape, structure, and surface area;
- An inventory of engineered nanomaterials and their uses;
- Methods to quantify and characterize exposure to nanomaterials in biological matrices;
- Understanding absorption and transport of nanomaterials throughout the body;
- Understanding the properties of nanoscale materials eliciting biological responses; and
- *In vitro* and *in vivo* assays and models to predict *in vivo* human responses to exposure.[1]

Moreover, the trend in most industries toward increased specialization ('core competences') is creating more market interfaces and thereby raising the importance of technical infrastructure that enables the specification of interoperability standards. For most of the last century, original equipment manufacturers (OEMs) were vertically integrated firms. Henry Ford's company even owned the sources of raw materials for the steel it made that went into its cars. Today, automobile OEMs increasingly specialize in general vehicle design, final assembly and marketing. The rest of the manufacturing process, including much R&D and most component and subsystem manufacturing is now done by independent tiers in the automotive supply chain.

Deregulation of the electric utility industry effectively broke up historically integrated production, transmission and distribution of electricity, creating new market interfaces. While specialization and ensuing competition were expected to reduce prices for consumers, the new markets created significant measurement problems that needed to be solved before the sale of electric power among independent electric utilities and their customers could occur efficiently.

These multiple roles for technical infrastructure, along with their impacts by stage of economic activity, are depicted in Figure 8.1. The examples of technical infrastructure from the semiconductor industry are only a small fraction of the total number of infratechnologies and associated standards that support this industry.

In the global economy, two cross-cutting factors will determine competitive outcomes. One is the relative ability among economies to determine and implement the complementary private and public investments to deal with the increasing complexity of emerging technologies. The second

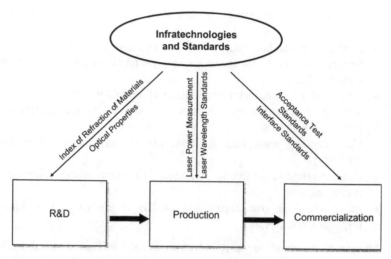

Figure 8.1 Technical Infrastructure Impacts All Three Stages of Economic Activity (Examples from Semiconductor Industry)

is the need to manage technology infrastructure effectively, which requires determining what is infrastructure as distinct from private goods and services, who should provide and own it, and to whom and through what mechanisms should access be allowed.

TECHNICAL INFRASTRUCTURE FOR THE KNOWLEDGE-BASED ECONOMY

All technologies of any economic consequence today are systems. Whereas once a radio or a TV was developed, sold and used largely as a stand-alone product with content delivered by a single network, audio and video are now delivered to a variety of devices by multimedia information systems based on multiple high-speed networks. Such system technologies are supplied by increasingly complex industry structures and supported by equally complex technical infrastructures.

IT Infrastructure

Without an elaborate technical infrastructure, only a fraction of current information flows would take place at anything approaching reasonable cost. For example, electronic funds transfers, which today dominate financial services industries, could not occur without conformance to standards that ensure accuracy and security. Similarly, information could not move across the Internet without standards to define and control the information flows. Almost everyone agrees that the Internet, along with the wheel, the internal combustion engine, the transistor and a few others, is one of the most important innovations of all time. The Internet has enabled instant access to vast amounts of information. These information flows have affected virtually every industry in the economy. Knowledge is created, transferred and used by millions of individuals and organizations who do not know each other. This last fact implies major social, political and economic change, which is already occurring.

The need to understand and manage this increasingly ubiquitous IT communications system is yet another example of the demands on a modern economic infrastructure. Consider that knowledge exists in two major forms. One is 'codified' knowledge, which is highly specified and available in a discrete form. Thus, ownership usually can be assigned and such knowledge can therefore be bought and sold. Codified knowledge is what moves so efficiently over the Internet.

The second type is tacit knowledge, which has been discussed in the context of analyzing factors affecting emerging technologies. It is a bit fuzzier and hence harder to deal with. Tacit knowledge, or 'know-how' as it is sometimes referred to, is quite the opposite of codified knowledge in that it is not explicitly described and written down. It is therefore hard to assign ownership and to move over an impersonal communications medium, such as the Internet. Instead, it diffuses largely through person-to-person contact. Studies have shown that strategic alliances, when embodying such contact, provide efficient transfer of tacit technical knowledge.

The message is that the conduct of innovation activity requires a diversified and pervasive set of technical IT infrastructures to provide access to the several forms of knowledge essential to the development and use of new technology. The number and variety of such infrastructures has grown steadily due to increasing complexity of modern technologies and the associated industry structures. Without them, technological progress in an economic sense would come to a halt.

Pervasive Measurement and Standards Infrastructure

At the apex of a modern economy is the capability to measure and control virtually all economic activity. For example, most people directly or indirectly benefit from highly accurate time and frequency signals every day, usually without realizing it. Cell phone networks must be synchronized to about one microsecond (millionth of a second) to function, as must long-haul telecommunications networks using fiber optics. So, every time a cell phone or long-distance landline call is made, accurate timing is being used, traceable in the end to a public-sector time and frequency information infrastructure (NIST in the United States).

Electric power grids spanning thousands of miles of transmission lines must be synchronized to about one microsecond to ensure that the approximately 10,000 generating stations spread across the United States are driving the alternating current in synchronization. Small deviations from synchronization result in loss of efficiency in both power generation and transmission and thus higher costs. Larger deviations can result in damage to the power generation or transmission systems. Again, in the end, such synchronization traces back directly or indirectly to an intricate system of measurement-based standards.

The Global Positioning System (GPS), consisting of about 24 satellites each with an atomic clock, relies on very tight synchronization to provide positioning and navigation information for a wide variety of military and civilian uses. GPS requires synchronization on the order of one nanosecond (one billionth of a second) to operate. In addition to the obvious military applications, civilian uses of GPS are expanding dramatically. Examples are recreational positioning and navigation, built-in systems in automobiles (coupled with mapping software), commercial airline navigation, and management of agriculture. The US Naval Observatory (USNO) provides the time scale for GPS and the 'size of the second' used in GPS traces back to NIST standards.

The NASD (National Association of Securities Dealers) requires that all computer-system clocks and mechanical time stamping devices be synchronized to within three seconds of the NIST atomic clock to provide a traceable and auditable record of electronic financial transactions, including NASDAQ stock exchange transactions. These rules govern millions of financial transactions each day carried out by the more than 5,000 brokerage firms with more than 660,000 registered securities dealers under NASD jurisdiction.

Regulatory Compliance

Technical infrastructure is also essential for ensuring compliance with a wide range of regulations designed to achieve environmental, safety and other social goals. The cost of compliance is high for both the regulator and the affected industries, so regulatory efficiency is essential. This is especially the case in today's global markets, where such regulations are frequently more lax and hence less costly for domestic industries in competing economies.

For example, a varied array of standard reference materials (SRMs) is required to calibrate sophisticated equipment that monitor compliance with government pollution regulations. In support of regulatory efficiency, NIST developed 29 sulfur-related SRMs that are used by an entire supply chain (instrument manufacturers, independent testing laboratories, industry suppliers of secondary standards, coal processors and petroleum refiners, and users of fossil fuels such as electricity generators and steel producers) to design and calibrate pollution monitoring and control equipment.

The issue of regulatory compliance becomes magnified in international markets. As trade has become more important to the world's economies, incentives to create barriers to imports that compete with domestic industries have increased. Traditionally, tariffs have been the main instrument for modifying competitive positions in favor of domestic industries. However, the importance of trade has created pressures to open domestic markets through tariff reductions. Consequently, countries have sought alternative means to alter the terms of trade in their favor. In the place of tariffs, the increasing complexity of traded goods has afforded opportunities to insert a range of non-tariff barriers to trade that are based on country-specific technical specifications for imported products.

Assessment of technical specifications as trade barriers is complicated. On the one hand, these specifications often have legitimate uses, such as ensuring efficacy, safety, environment quality and compatibility with interfacing products. However, on the other hand, technical requirements placed on imports are frequently designed to restrain trade. Examples of the latter are requiring detailed product data, including proprietary information, to accompany every batch of the same product from the exporting country, or requiring testing of each unit imported (as opposed to sampling or self-certification according to international standards). In many cases, the separation of legitimate uses from trade-restriction objectives within the same regulatory structure is conceptually difficult. Moreover, although some qualitative information can be collected on technical barriers to trade (TBTs), estimation of the economic impacts of these barriers is limited by the lack of uniform and sufficiently precise quantitative data.

A NIST-sponsored study of TBTs analyzed pharmaceuticals and automotive products. These case studies demonstrate the wide range of possible TBTs and also the difficulties in identifying, characterizing and measuring them. For example, the pharmaceutical industry is among the most highly regulated across all countries, but the variety of product offerings is great and the typical product is complex and becoming more so as biotechnology takes over as the driver of pharmaceutical innovation. Thus, a wide range of regulations and conformity assessment procedures are used. Many of those in the study were found to have TBT-like characteristics. For example, a number of countries write regulations in such a manner that they appear to discriminate against innovative pharmaceuticals for which the United States is the leading supplier. Differential regulatory approval intervals and inspection procedures, such as testing each lot imported or requiring certification documentation and other conformity assessment data, were found to have characteristics of TBTs (Popper et al., 2004).

The complexity of candidate TBTs makes accurate economic analysis for policy decision making quite difficult. Such analysis requires the development of metrics and measures that reflect both one-time costs and trends over time for barriers that impose repetitive costs. The anecdotal information in the two case studies indicates that the economic cost of TBTs is high.

Market Transactions in High-Tech Products

Even the act of buying a high-tech product requires a technically sophisticated infrastructure. For example, how would a communications services company determine whether the thousands of kilometers of ultra-thin optical fiber it buys meet specifications for such performance attributes as band width, rate of signal loss, core diameter consistency, insulation properties and so on unless technologically advanced acceptance testing standards are available? Without such infrastructure, the high-tech sector of the economy could not grow and prosper because prospective customers would be reluctant to commit funds for products whose performance is not assured. In economic terms, market transaction costs will be substantially higher without adequate supporting infrastructure. These costs include time delays, which obviously slow market penetration of a new technology and can eliminate or reduce the 'first-mover' advantage of innovating firms in the domestic industry.

As indicated in Figure 8.2, today's average high-tech product or service has a significant number of attributes. Some of these attributes are associated with the item being sold, while others are due to socially imposed regulations that seek to internalize negative externalities. In all cases, assurance to the buyer that the specifications of these attributes have been met requires a set of standards that permit unambiguous and efficient determination of acceptability. Otherwise, the market transaction either will not take place or will occur with a delay and at a higher cost. High transaction costs are common, especially in the early phases of a technology's life cycle, and act as a deterrent to market penetration. The result is slower diffusion of the new technology.

TECHNICAL INFRASTRUCTURE AS A PUBLIC GOOD

All advanced economies have technical infrastructures to support their high-tech sectors and the much larger sectors that utilize technology. Just as is the case with an economy's private sector, all levels of efficiency can be found across competing nations with respect to the management of this infrastructure. As a result, investment in technical infrastructure is a differentiator among competing technology-based economies.

Figure 8.2 The High-Tech Market Interface

Barriers to Investment in Technical Infrastructure

In spite of the pervasive and large economic impact of technical infrastructure, the roles and the consequent importance of the infratechnologies and associated standards that make it up are poorly understood. In contrast, the policy arena gives considerable attention to the major categories of information infrastructure. The reason is that the Internet and other communications networks are pervasive and interface directly and visibly with consumers. Thus, the economic impact is more evident. Ironically, information infrastructure itself depends on a wide array of infratechnologies and standards, which are not systematically analyzed. In fact, it was not until 2004 when the Council on Competitiveness released its National Innovation Initiative that the concept of technical infrastructure was included in a major policy document, along with the traditional categories such as R&D investment, intellectual property rights, human capital, venture capital, and also information infrastructure.

Ideally, the optimal pattern for investment in technical infrastructure and proprietary technology is an iterative or recursive one in which proprietary technology and technical infrastructure investments take turns leveraging demand for the other. However, the demand for technical infrastructure is more frequently derived from the demand for new products and services, and only becomes visible as markets for the new technology attain sufficient size to make inefficiencies significant and therefore more apparent. This phenomenon is accentuated as secondary and tertiary groups of consumers enter the market in the middle and later phases of a technology's life cycle when competition increasingly depends on cost. Thus, the early phases of a life cycle often suffer from substantial inefficiency, resulting in an extension of the initial flat portion of the S-shaped growth curve. A slower rate of market penetration is the result.

In some industries, underinvestment in information infrastructure as well as in technical infrastructure results in very high levels of inefficiency. For example, medical care was once provided by a single doctor operating largely independently from other sources of medical expertise and information. Eventually, that doctor might pass a patient along to another physician utilizing a different information base, but the process was strictly sequential and segmented. What supporting infrastructure existed was totally manual and crude. Today, individual medical tests are still developed, approved and put into use without a supporting information infrastructure to quickly transfer the resulting medical data among health-care providers and to integrate the data into a holistic analysis of the patient's health. Inadequate interoperability among medical information systems leads to time delays in diagnoses and treatment decisions.

In addition, the medical tests themselves suffer from inadequate technical infrastructure. Recent studies have shown that inaccurate or inconsistent (imprecise) tests lead to repeat tests, additional unnecessary tests, and wrong or delayed diagnoses. For just one medical test (blood calcium levels), a joint study for NIST by RTI International and the Mayo Clinic estimated that such testing inadequacies cost the US economy as much as $200 million per year (Gallaher et al., 2004a). Thus, the combined infrastructure inadequacies add up to a decidedly underperforming health services system.

Distinguishing Public and Private Technology Elements

The competitive dynamics of the US economy has long been one of its strengths. Never has the force of competition been more evident than in the last 15 years as global pressures have forced American firms to adopt information technologies to increase productivity and to focus more on core competences to achieve excellence in a reduced number of technologies. The latter step has led to the distribution of R&D backward in supply chains, with the result that more firms, large and small, are becoming co-dependent in their supply chains' innovation efforts. Efficiency in the R&D, production and marketing stages of economic activity within the current technology life cycle has become the mantra of American industry.

During this period, corporate R&D spending has steadily increased as a share of GDP, which has allowed proponents of the black-box model to succeed in reducing government R&D funding relative to GDP. Not surprisingly, therefore, the public-good character of technical infrastructure, which means reliance on government support, has contributed to systematic underinvestment in this element of industrial technology.

Moreover, disagreement over what is and what is not technical infrastructure has contributed to overall underinvestment. One of the most striking examples of the failure to distinguish technical infrastructure from proprietary technology is the operating system of a computer. This critical software element interprets demands from applications software for the central processing unit of the computer's hardware. The operating system therefore is the 'information highway' upon which independent vehicles (application software programs) execute their roles. Just as a road is a form of economic infrastructure upon which trucking companies move goods from factories to consumers, the operating system manages the inflow and outflow of business and personal data, audio and video between the computer's processor and an application software program or an external communication program.

Because these applications programs are developed and sold by competing companies, the operating system on which all applications depend should be competitively neutral. Otherwise, the owner of the operating system can influence and, in fact, control many of the application programs. The latter situation is tantamount to one of 10 trucking companies owing a road used by all of these companies. The owner can choose the locations of exits and, by knowing in advance where those exits will be, buy up choice land for commercial development projects (comparable to software applications).

By controlling the operating system of the PC, Microsoft had a significant advantage in developing and marketing applications software. The Justice Department's antitrust charges against Microsoft should have emphasized the more generic and hence broadly negative effects of this monopolistic control instead of the much more narrow focus on Microsoft's bundling of its Internet browser with its core operating system.

Browsers are sufficiently small and focused software programs so that competition is feasible, which was the conclusion of the legal proceedings. However, an operating system is much more central to the operation of a computer in that it determines the format of all applications that run on it. Hence, the supposition of a natural monopoly situation is relevant. Equally important for public policy is the fact that an operating system, by virtue of its enabling role in the operation of a PC, has the attributes of infrastructure.

Allowing one of several competing applications software companies to own the underlying infrastructure is asking for trouble in the form of economic inefficiency. However, the lack of a consensus on what should be infrastructure led to years of acrimonious debate between Microsoft and applications software companies, followed by unsatisfactory antitrust litigation. That is, the black-box model prevailed.

Defenders of the status quo argued that constraining Microsoft's monopoly was a restraint on innovation. Regardless of one's opinion of Microsoft's innovative capacity, history shows that eventually most monopolies disappear because the technology life cycles that they depend on come to an end. In this case, a number of observers pointed out that even if Microsoft had eventually been forced to spin off its Windows division from the rest of the company, such a step would have come too late because the open systems movement was gaining enough strength to significantly dilute the monopoly position.

In theory, at least, the evolving open operating system known as Linux meets the textbook definition of infrastructure both in function and by virtue of the fact that it is, to a degree at least, publicly owned. The large public-good content inherent in an operating system gives credence to the open-source model. As long as the operating system can be maintained and updated by a cooperative mechanism, giving it away as a free public good has several potential advantages.

Distributors, such as Red Hat and Novell, supply implementation assistance by providing users of open-source software with manuals, regular updates and customer service for an annual subscription fee. Computer makers benefit because they can sell computers with Linux without having to pay an operating system license fee, as is the case when a proprietary system such as Windows is used. With Windows, computer users pay an initial licensing fee of several hundred dollars for a PC and several thousand for a server. The total cost of a subscription for a small server used by 30 people, including licensing fees, support and upgrades is about $3,500 for Windows. However, implementation subscriptions for Linux with Red Hat are about $2,400 (Hamm, 2005). Thus, the distinction between a proprietary and an open-source operating system is not as clear cut as most assume. Certainly, neither is free.

In this context, hybrids of the pure open-source model have evolved, which offer some prospect for a workable infrastructure management system. The company MySQL, which develops a type of open-source database software by the same name, gives away software under an open-source license. At the same time, the company sells its software bundled with maintenance and support contracts. The 'free' segment of its business model is predicated on the fact that non-paying users provide valuable feedback on performance and may ultimately become paying customers.

Still, the bottom line is that this is a fee-for-service infrastructure business model.

Moreover, in spite of the open-source label, problems may arise over time due to ownership issues. Patents are deadly to an open-source system, as they can block improvements from diffusing freely. For software, copyright is a major issue, as the many 'voluntary' contributors can legitimately claim an ownership share.[2] An additional complexity with respect to characterizing the infrastructure character of an operating system is the fact that Linux, while publicly owned in the sense that its intellectual base is created and improved over time by a legion of independent programmers from all over the world, is nevertheless not publicly managed. As Linux evolves and more and more applications are developed to run on it, the management requirements become more and more complex. At some point, these demands are likely to become overwhelming for a loosely organized and volunteer management structure.

Thus, open-source systems will have to face the management problems that do not appreciably affect a single owner of the infrastructure element of a system, such as Microsoft. One of the most basic difficulties is that 'voluntary' contributions by individuals and, more recently by companies seeking to benefit from proprietary applications that run on an open-source infrastructure, are subject to spillovers (that is, benefits to free riders). In response, open-source approaches typically have to evolve into organized hierarchical management structures with controls on sources and quality of contributions.

Microsoft has attempted to counter the open-source movement by developing a strategy of expanding software services and integrating their capabilities across platforms to maintain long-term leadership and emphasize value added beyond the operating system. Microsoft recognizes that all software is now being written for a networked world, so the company is targeting communications across platforms as a major strategic thrust. This trend means that a system's architecture – its breadth and integration and hence the collective efficiency of programs that it supports – is becoming more important relative to operating systems, thereby changing the determinants of competitive success in the next life cycle.

Such an event might prompt critics of the Justice Department's antitrust suit against Microsoft to declare themselves vindicated, as they had argued strenuously that the market eventually solves all problems. The key word here is 'eventually'. If public policy had been using a reasonable model of technology-based growth that included accurate distinctions among private- and public-good elements of industry technologies, the problem of a single company owning both critical IT infrastructure and software applications that run on it might have prompted policy action when it might have had some positive effect, say, in the late 1980s. Launching an antitrust campaign against Microsoft a decade later was, in fact, too late. By then, any serious competition in the applications markets was gone (name one PC word processor, spreadsheet or drawing software vendor besides Microsoft with significant market share by the time the antitrust charges were filed).

Other operating systems exist as well, which, combined with Linux and Windows, create heterogeneous and incompatible networks. The result is higher cost of ownership for users. Over time, advances in information technology will relegate the operating system debate to a low level of importance, but other infrastructure issues will replace it. The point for public policy is that the complex nature of IT-based systems makes defining what is infrastructure difficult and therefore constrains policy actions. As long as operational definitions of infrastructure and applications are not developed and implemented, confusion and wasted resources will continue.[3]

EXAMPLES OF TECHNICAL INFRASTRUCTURE

Microeconomic theory states that goods and services can be classified as *rival* if one buyer's consumption reduces the amount available for consumption by others. Goods and services are considered *excludable* if the owners can prevent consumption by others. Pure public goods are defined as those that are neither rival nor excludable, with the result that private markets will not provide such goods. National defense is a classic example and the government rationale for providing such items is straightforward. In contrast, so-called private goods are largely rival and excludable.

However, some goods and services fall in between these two types in that they are partially rival, for example, too many cars on a public road cause congestion costs. Others provide only partial excludability, for example, technical knowledge spills over to non-owners. For such goods and services, individuals can obtain at least some of the benefits through the investment of others (that is, by acting as 'free riders'). In such cases, the level of investment without government support will be suboptimal. Because many market participants have the ability to free ride, the ability of investors to capture an adequate rate of return is difficult resulting in an insufficient level of private investment.

Ironically, from a public policy perspective large spillovers and non-rival conditions for certain elements of an industrial technology are desirable. This is clearly the case for technical infrastructure. A standard by definition must be widely and uniformly used to have substantial economic impact.

Industry Structure Efficiency: Supply-Chain Integration

Firms that emerged in the first few decades of the 20th century, including those in the automotive and electrical products industries, were very concerned about the performance of their supply chains. One of the most common organizational strategies was vertical integration, in which the entire supply chain was brought within the firm's ownership and hence management structure. Henry Ford built such an integrated company in the 1920s and 1930s, owning not only automobile parts production and assembly, but also car dealerships, steel mills, iron ore mines and even rubber plantations (Nevins and Hill, 1957). The advantages of vertical integration in centralizing decision making and maintaining coordination across a supply chain were sufficient to make it an organizational strategy of choice.

However, disadvantages to vertical integration can be substantial. Vertically-integrated firms often find themselves running operations in which they have little expertise, as Ford did with its rubber plantations. Such non-core businesses are likely to have inferior technology and thus higher costs than is the case for specialized suppliers. The divisional structures adopted by most firms after World War II tended to defeat the close coordination that vertical integration was intended to facilitate – two divisions of the same corporation might have as much difficulty communicating and managing logistics as separate firms in a similar supplier–customer relationship.

During the 1960s and 1970s, corporations invested heavily in information technologies to manage intrafirm planning and logistics. Information systems to control and optimize the entire production chain, from raw materials to customers, became possible. Decreases in the cost of computing and internal networking helped corporations realize benefits from vertical integration in financing, production, distribution and marketing.

However, the trend toward integration began to reverse by the mid-1980s. Faced with rapid technological change, increasing global competition and accelerating quality improvement expectations, many large enterprises found their agility in the marketplace hampered by the complexity of their corporate structures and the spread of resources across different technologies and markets. In order to concentrate on leveraging core competences, firms spun off lines of business.

Whereas initial advances in computing and communications within firms promoted vertical integration, the dramatic decreases in external communication and data transfer costs via the Internet in the 1990s removed much of the rationale for this strategy. The potential emerged for large numbers of firms to prosper by each specializing in one tier (industry) in a supply chain. These and other developments have encouraged new forms of organization that incorporate modern information technologies in all stages of a firm's operations. As a result, vertical disintegration has become the dominant trend in industrial organization (Besanko et al., 1996).

However, this evolutionary change has created a set of important efficiency issues: (i) corporate reliance on IT is mandating the movement of enormous amounts of information; (ii) more market interfaces are being created and hence more transfers of information among the multiple tiers of high-tech supply chains are necessary; and (iii) at the same time, competitive pressures are requiring increased speed and accuracy in transmitting this wide variety of business and technical data.

These trends raise the importance of interoperability of information exchanges.[4] This concept of seamless transfer of information requires several types of technical infrastructure:

1. standards for reliable and secure communication of sensitive information across companies;

2. standardization of interfaces (middleware) among proprietary information systems;

3. standardization of data formats to enable transmission and interpretation among firms of various categories of data; and

4. efficient methods for updating standards to accommodate the introduction of new technologies.

Such integration has turned out to be difficult for industry to accomplish. Companies have tended to try proprietary solutions to integration first, often as extensions of market strategies but just as frequently because an adequate infrastructure for industry-wide integration is not available. The most difficult technological issue is the multiplicity of communications methods, protocols and formats that exist among trading partners.

A large number of information categories exist within an extended enterprise – part descriptions, manufacturing specifications, requests for bids, purchase orders, ship notices, price and availability of information, sequencing instructions and order status. Therefore, even with the existing methods of achieving some degree of interoperability, a low probability exists that any pair of companies in a supply chain can communicate with each other in an unambiguous fashion without considerable negotiations and resource-intensive oversight.

If one interoperability system is better than another, one would expect migration to the more efficient system. However, in any modern economic system, life is more complicated. For example, in many manufacturing supply chains, the volume of information exchange among firms varies significantly, which affects the relative efficiency of different data exchange systems and hence their incentives to invest in specific solutions (White et al., 2004).

The automotive supply chain is a good example of the difficulties and consequent costs of not creating and effectively using integration infrastructures. Multiple proprietary systems exist for the transfer of both product design and operations data within this supply chain. In spite of industry efforts to standardize on a single infrastructure, little progress has been made. A NIST study estimated the costs from inadequate interoperability among tiers in the automotive supply chain for the exchange of just one type of data (product design) to be at least $1 billion per year (Brunnermeier and Martin, 1999).

When interoperability standards and the supporting infratechnologies are inadequate, companies must expend considerable resources to avoid compatibility problems or mitigate problems after they occur. One large supplier of auto parts and subsystems was described in the NIST study as having more than 20 home-grown planning systems in its plants, none of which could interoperate with the others. Not only do such incompatibilities significantly raise operating costs but they also result in delays with respect to product/service delivery, which adds additional costs. Organizations of all sizes across industries use 'informed' estimates rather than actual or production planning data in scheduling, materials management and delivery activities. A large number of firms, especially smaller ones in the initial tiers of a supply chain, simply operate without essential data.

Similar costs are incurred for attempted transfers of data relating to overall business transactions between companies. A second study estimated that interoperability problems in managing flows of a number of types of business data cost the transportation and electronics manufacturing sectors $9 billion annually (White et al., 2004). A third NIST study of the construction and building management industries estimated the costs of inadequate interoperability for this supply chain to be $15.8 billion per year (Gallaher et al., 2004b). In the case of the automotive supply chain, 1.25 percent of the total value of all shipments is lost each year due to the incompatibility of its information systems. For a large supply chain, this amounts to a considerable deadweight economic loss and is a significant portion of average profit margins. Obviously, the total cost for all supply chains making up the US economy is much greater.

Competitive pressures force companies' attention and available resources on constantly improving proprietary product and process technologies. This fact coupled with the public-good content of technical infrastructure results in inadequate and inefficient effort being devoted to improving the efficiency of supply-chain integration. However, underinvestment is clearly costly. Without a seamless communication format, one-to-one relationships must be developed between every pair of companies transacting business. When multilateral relationships are involved, the difficulties are even greater because business models have to be developed that expand the number of communication pathways and the resources needed to ensure unambiguous authority, responsibility, interpretation and security of information flows. Communication delays and inaccurate information lead to inventory fluctuations, which in turn lead to higher costs.

The complexity of this type of technical infrastructure makes it easy to understand how markets can fail to provide the necessary level and quality of infratechnologies and associated standards. This is especially the case if the size and technical capabilities of the partners are quite different. Small supplier firms in the early tiers may have a strong interest in improving their information infrastructure but may lack the financial resources or technical capability to make it happen. Their incentives to invest are further reduced if they believe that any cost advantages they obtain from increased efficiency will be quickly competed away through lower prices. The typically larger firms at the end of the supply chain, that is, the interface with the final consumer, might more easily take on the burden of developing improved information systems. If, however, most of the initial benefits accrue to their suppliers, these OEMs may conclude that their investment might not pay out over their required time horizons (White et al., 2004).

In summary, the several economic studies cited show that inadequate interoperability is a source of substantial economic loss. Virtually all firms in the US economy are negatively affected, but for small firms the lack of interoperability can be a life or death matter. Access to targeted markets by these firms increasingly depends on not only providing an innovative product but also having a technically sophisticated interface to other components of the product system. Engineering complex, non-standard interfaces, which often vary significantly among customers, adds both excessive costs and time delays that can be fatal for small firms. The supply chain and the entire economy then lose their innovative capacity.

R&D Cycle Efficiency: Software Testing

Most technology-based products require substantial amounts of testing during development. Yet, the testing infrastructure required to achieve high levels of R&D productivity is frequently not available. One of the best examples is software – both because of the critical importance to this industry of testing for quality assurance and the substantial inadequacy of the existing testing infrastructure.

Virtually every business in the United States now depends on software for development, production, distribution and after-sales support of products and services. Innovations in fields as diverse as robotics, pharmaceuticals and semiconductors have all been enabled by low-cost computational and control capabilities supplied by computers and software. In 2000, total US sales of software reached approximately $180 billion. Rapid growth has created a significant and high-paid workforce, with 697,000 employed as software engineers and an additional 585,000 as computer programmers. Software is clearly a dominant tool as well as an attribute of IT-based growth. Industry forecasts indicate that companies allocate roughly half their IT budgets to software.

Software, however, is an extremely complex product. Given its ubiquitous economic role, it is alarming that software products are shipped with such high levels of defects. In fact, the process of identifying and correcting errors ('bugs') during the software development process represents approximately 80 percent of development costs. Moreover, complexity is increasing. The size of software products is no longer measured in thousands of lines of code, but in millions. This greater complexity along with a decreasing average product life expectancy has increased the economic costs of errors. The media are full of reports of the catastrophic impacts of software malfunctions, but these high-profile incidents are only the tip of a pervasive pattern of failure that software developers and users both agree is causing substantial economic loss.

In a NIST study, inadequate testing was defined as failure to identify and remove software bugs in real time (RTI International, 2002). Over half of software errors are currently not found until somewhere 'downstream' in the development process. The farther the development process proceeds before error detection, the greater the economic costs. The NIST study identified a set of quality attributes and used them to construct metrics for estimating the cost of an inadequate testing infrastructure. In a case study of transportation equipment industries, data were collected from software developers (CAD/CAM/CAE and product data management vendors) and from users (primarily automotive and aerospace companies). Financial services were also studied with data collected again from software developers (routers and switches, financial electronic data interchange and clearinghouse services) and from users (banks and credit unions).

As indicated in Table 8.1, the annual cost to portions of these two major industry groups (manufacturing and services) resulting from inadequate software infrastructure was estimated to be $5 billion. Similarities across industries with respect to software development and use and, in particular, software testing labor costs allowed an extrapolation of this cost estimate to the entire US economy. Doing so yielded an estimate of approximately $60 billion per year from inadequate software testing infrastructure. Significantly, 64 percent of these costs are incurred by software users due to the fact that many errors are not detected until the product has been sold.

Some 300,000 workers are engaged in software testing and debugging activities, which represents approximately one-quarter of all computer programmers and software engineers. Clearly, software testing during development should be more efficient. Rather than do more testing, the analysis showed that more accurate and efficient testing was needed.

Unfortunately, testing methods have a strong infrastructure character because uniformly accepted approaches must be used to assure buyers that specified quality levels have in fact been achieved by suppliers. This requirement for common use (standards) coupled with competitive pressures to get new generations of software into the marketplace has led to substantial underinvestment in the infratechnologies underlying software testing. The complexity of the needed infrastructure is evidenced by the conclusion from the NIST study that standardized testing tools, suites, scripts, reference data, reference implementations and metrics that have undergone a rigorous certification process are all needed before a significant reduction in the inadequacies currently plaguing software markets can be achieved.

STANDARDIZATION

Standards are a pervasive and unique form of technical infrastructure and are essential to innovation and the effective use of technology. Embodying information in a standardized form not only increases its economic value but also greatly expands and accelerates its impact. The economic importance of standards is evidenced by the substantial efforts companies, industries and national governments make to influence the standardization process.

However, alternative content and forms are typically available to choose from when promulgating a standard. As a result, standardization can be highly positive or negative in its economic impact. When well designed and appropriately timed, standards facilitate innovations and their equally important market penetration. In contrast, poorly designed or poorly timed standards can impose barriers to R&D investment and market expansion of innovative products or processes.

Firms within an industry can put needed standards in place to support integration efforts in several ways, and each approach has implications for the efficiency and completeness of the resulting infrastructures. If the industry is dominated by one firm or if a statutory monopoly exists, that firm can create standards and impose them on an entire supply chain. AT&T assumed this role in telecommunications during the era of regulation, and developed most of the standards used within that sector. In the case of PC operating systems, Microsoft's dominance has allowed it to set standards that hardware and software firms alike are obligated to support. The US DoD has forced all military contractors to use its procurement specifications and procedures since shortly after its creation in the 1940s.

Table 8.1 Summary of Software Testing Infrastructure Study Results (billions of dollars)

	Annual Cost of Inadequate Software Testing Infrastructure			Potential Annual Cost Reductions from Feasible Infrastructure Improvements		
	US Economy	Transportation Equipment[1]	Financial Services[2]	US Economy	Transportation Equipment[1]	Financial Services[2]
Software Developers[3]	21.2 (36%)	0.37	2.34	10.6 (47%)	0.16	1.20
Software Users	38.3 (64%)	1.47	1.01	11.7 (53%)	0.43	0.31
Total	59.5	1.84	3.34	22.2	0.59	1.51

Notes
[1] Primarily automotive and aerospace industries.
[2] Distribution of costs in the financial services case study does not follow the national trend due to the inclusion in this case study of a manufacturing industry (routers and switches).
[3] Includes CAD/CAM/CAE and PDM in transportation equipment and FEDI (Financial Electronic Data Interchange), clearinghouse software, and software for routers and switches in financial services.

231

In an alternative scenario frequently found in imperfectly competitive markets, each large OEM can develop its own standards and insist that its suppliers comply if they want continued business with that company. This has long been the practice in the automotive sector where, for example, General Motors, Ford and DaimlerChrysler have routinely imposed their proprietary standards on suppliers in the preceeding tier of their supply chains. Many of these suppliers, in turn, require their upstream component and material suppliers to comply as well. Because many firms provide products to all three OEMs, as well as to Japanese-owned domestic automotive facilities, excessive costs are inevitably incurred under this regime from duplication of effort and lack of interoperability.

Theoretically, many or all of the firms in an industry can work together to create a mutually beneficial standards infrastructure, either by forming a consortium through an industry trade or technical association, or with the help of one or more standards development organizations (SDOs). Antitrust concerns have receded sufficiently over the past 20 years so that SDOs can develop standards without risk of adverse governmental attention. Still, it is difficult to manage power and influence issues within consortia and other voluntary organizations. Thus, success in creating efficient standards is not assured. In addition, incomplete representation of entire industry supply chains within these groups means that important suppliers and customers may be left out of the standardization process.

STANDARDS IN THE GLOBAL MARKETPLACE: THE INTERNET PROTOCOL

One of the most dramatic examples of both the complexity and the global competitiveness impacts of standardization is the Internet Protocol (IP). This standard, which is really many standards integrated into a single system of standards, controls information flows over the Internet and enables applications (software that provides various services to users of the Internet) to be implemented efficiently. It does this by providing a standardized 'envelope' or 'header' that carries addressing, routing and message-handling information. The information in this header enables a message to be transmitted from its source to its final destination over the various interconnected networks that comprise the Internet.

The IP is an excellent case study in the many requirements for modern technical infrastructure to complement private investment over all phases of the technology life cycle. The importance of the IP stems from the enormous global reach of the Internet. The worldwide IT market is forecast to reach $1.3 trillion by 2009. By that time, virtually all IT equipment and software will be networked, making the Internet the most important single infrastructure of all time. Thus, the IP is arguably one of the most important industry standards.

However, the complexity of the IP and other Internet standards presents extreme challenges for IT policy. The Internet is thought of by most as simply a set of connected communications networks. In fact, it is a highly structured combination of hardware and software, linked by a controlled and tightly specified set of standards that have considerable technical content. The complexity of this infrastructure becomes apparent when the standards infrastructure needs to be replaced by a new generation. Suddenly, the entire supply chain involved in developing and delivering market applications (that is, innovations) becomes active and various positions on transition strategies appear.[5]

Motivations for the Transition

For important standards like the IP, a generational transition has such potentially large economic consequences that inadequate government policy support can place the dependent domestic industries at a significant competitive disadvantage. One might wonder how this could happen if a single international standard is adopted. However, the technical complexity of many standards means that considerable time and expense are required by the domestic economy in accomplishing the transition to a new version of the existing standard. Thus, many levels of deployment and effective utilization are possible.

Currently, the global Internet supply chain is beginning the transition to a new version of the IP, version 6 (IPv6). The motivation derives from two major factors: (i) the need for additional address space for general growth of domestic IT infrastructures, and (ii) the projected emergence of new, advanced applications that need both large amounts of address capacity and network infrastructure efficiencies likely only attainable with IPv6.

Efficient network architecture means improved support for header options and extensions, simplified assignment of addresses, and rapid and efficient configuration options for communications devices. Such attributes are likely to be essential for emerging highly mobile and flexible communications systems. For example, Japan's NTT has been one of the earliest adopters of IPv6 for the purpose of accelerating deployment of IPTV. Having this infrastructure in place is enabling NTT to efficiently provide delivery of video content by allowing each set-top terminal to be authenticated independently as soon as the user connects it to the network, in contrast to the more complex Network Address Translation (NAT) processes used with the current version of the Protocol, IPv4.

Emerging applications, especially devices that are globally addressable so that they can be remotely accessed and controlled via the Internet, represent a potentially important application of IPv6 addresses. Specifically, automobile components or subsystems, refrigerators, cameras, home computers and even human body parts could be assigned IP addresses, linked together on networks, and connected to the Internet. Wireless sensor networks and machine-to-machine communications will eventually lead to a proliferation of devices that are remotely controlled. Additional benefits of remote access are the potential increased life expectancies of large ticket items such as automobiles and appliances (durable goods) through continual monitoring that will result in optimal servicing that minimizes life-cycle costs. Human organs could be monitored for symptoms of disease with the information transmitted to a medical facility to activate a preventive medical response. Such applications also require the flexibility to reconfigure the network automatically, as users connect and disconnect or simply move the point of connection.

Supporters of IPv6 argue that the impending exhaustion of discrete addresses as global growth of the Internet continues to expand will limit access to the Internet and possibly block many of these emerging mobile communications applications. As a result, many countries have begun to aggressively push their domestic industries to transition to IPv6, which has virtually unlimited address capacity and the potential for considerably more efficient network management.

Yet, in the face of the need for the US economy to plan for and begin to execute what will be a long transition to the new Protocol, several barriers have appeared. These barriers are common to transitions between generations of a complex standard and, to varying degrees, affect most users. However, their severity is typically greater for the technological leaders of the existing generation. Two of the most important barriers are the installed-base and chicken-or-egg effects.

The Installed-Base Effect

By virtue of being first to the party, the United States cornered a large share of available Internet address space and consequently has shown less concern over address capacity. Moreover, over time, the incumbent standard induces the accumulation of an installed base of hardware, software and an IT labor pool trained in maintaining the many applications that were designed for the current version of the standard. Continued investment in the current standard is perpetuated because of these sunk costs. As a result, IPv4 has been patched repeatedly. In particular, separate devices called 'middle boxes' have been concocted to deal with major performance weaknesses. These efforts have created an increasingly complex standards architecture and large application base that have managed to run reasonably efficiently with the current set of Internet applications, thereby reducing incentives to migrate to the next generation of the standard.

For example, the address limitation problem has been mitigated by the NAT device. A NAT is inserted at the interface between the public Internet and private networks that connect to it. Many private addresses can hide behind the NAT, which controls messages entering and leaving the private network through a single portal (in effect, a single address on the public Internet). Thus, by providing a single interface with the rest of the Internet, public address space is conserved. In some Asian countries, layers of NATs have appeared. Other middle boxes perform functions such as security (firewalls).

In general, the widespread use of middle boxes has created a perimeter between the public and private networks. This evolutionary event actually runs counter to the original concept of the Internet, which was to create a network that enabled direct end-to-end (or peer-to-peer) communications. However, necessity is the mother of invention. These middle boxes solved problems caused by the limitations of IPv4. Once such a 'fix' becomes part of the installed base, it is difficult to remove – not only because of the original need but because user behavior adapts to it. For example, some users have come to view NATs as providing not only security but anonymity, which they do not want to give up.

However, a major problem with NATs and other middle boxes is that they add complexity to the network structure. As a result, developers of applications incur significant costs in modifying software to 'transverse' NATs. A study supporting a DoC Task Force that examined the need to move to IPv6 estimated that expenditures for modifying software to transverse NATs are approximately $550 million per year. Moreover, network managers incur considerable additional cost in managing NATs and other middleware. The study estimated that these network management expenses are about $1.4 billion annually (RTI International, 2005).

The Chicken-or-Egg Effect

In addition to the installed-base effect, a recursive (chicken-or-egg) relationship exists between private investment in market applications and some combination of private and public investment in the standards infrastructure. On the one hand, improvements in technical infrastructure facilitate innovation and potential innovators take its availability into account. On the other hand, investment in this complex and expensive infrastructure may not happen without the pulling effect of demand from emerging innovations that require it.

A transition strategy for IPv6 has been developed over a number of years by an international standards body, the Internet Engineering Task Force (IETF). The dominant view expressed by US industry is that this transition strategy (a dual-standard approach) will mitigate an investment-blocking, all-or-nothing situation (that is, the entire new standard must be deployed and the old one turned off). However, while the proposed transition mechanisms largely avoid such a 'throw-the-switch' decision for both internet service providers (ISPs) and Internet users, the likely technical and economic deficiencies of early implementations of IPv6 coupled with the cost of the transition itself will slow the perceived natural market penetration rate.

Thus, American ISPs, some of which have constrained profit margins, seem unwilling to invest in IPv6 infrastructure until major customers request IPv6 services, but the emergence of this customer demand requires that IPv6 applications be available. One potential attribute of IT standards that might reduce this chicken-or-egg problem is the fact that IPv6 *capability* can diffuse into the market at relatively low cost to users and vendors. This is because the marginal cost to vendors of including additional functionality in hardware and software is relatively low. Similarly, the acquisition cost of such capability by users is also low, as long as it is acquired within normal hardware and software expenditure cycles. Hence, IPv6 capabilities will likely penetrate many aspects of the network infrastructure over the next few years. For example, most routers and operating systems currently sold already include IPv6 functionality, so as industry and government purchase new routers for various reasons, they will acquire IPv6 capabilities at little additional cost.

However, considerable transition costs still must be incurred to *enable* or turn on these capabilities, and the incentives to do so are not strong in the early phases of the transition. Specifically, a few modest IPv6 applications are not sufficient incentive to stimulate incurring these additional deployment costs (in particular, labor training and conversion of IPv4 applications to run on IPv6, both of which are expensive undertakings).

On the other side of the public–private technology interface, inadequate deployment of an active and fully functional IPv6 infrastructure will mean that application developers have reduced incentive to invest in R&D for potential IPv6 markets. That is, first-mover incentives are constrained. According to the RTI study, applications developers have been the slowest movers toward IPv6.

The fundamental economic reason for this situation is that small markets limit network externalities, thereby inhibiting increases in the performance/price ratio and thus in demand. Such investment barriers coupled with high transition costs contribute to the flatness of the initial portion of the S-shaped market penetration curve. In a highly competitive global market, an extension of the flat initial portion of the curve can place domestic industries at a disadvantage that, in some cases, is never removed over the entire technology life cycle. Therefore, addressing the chicken-or-egg problem in developing and implementing an effective transition strategy is a major imperative for both government and industry.

The Economic Impacts

The implication of the above analysis is that, in the early phase of market penetration, neither the available incomplete infrastructure nor the limited applications are strong enough to induce significant numbers of users to transition to the new IP. Individual companies, caught up in managing the current life cycle of their infrastructure equipment, lack the knowledge and vision with respect to networking technology to perceive the importance of the emerging life cycle and, therefore, the associated new standard. Instead, most users continue to attempt to modify new applications to run on IPv4, albeit inefficiently, while the unavailability of advanced applications requiring IPv6 slows testing and hence certification of IPv6 infrastructure.

Over time the new standards infrastructure will become more complete and applications will evolve that have sufficiently high need for constant connections and automatic network reconfiguration. At some point, IPv4 will be deemed incapable of further adaptation and its inadequacies will become apparent to a majority of Internet providers and users. Thus, the slow iterative pattern of investment in infrastructure and applications will eventually overcome the installed-base and chicken-or-egg effects and the rate of market penetration will accelerate, as represented by the steeper portion of the S-shaped growth curve. However, because the Internet is now global in scope, 'eventually' can mean that first-mover advantages will accrue to industries in competing economies where both the infrastructure evolution and the development of market applications have been facilitated.

Another policy concern is the potential for decline in domestic value added in initial tiers of the Internet supply chain when leadership of the pacing technology is lost. For example, current leadership by US router manufacturers could be at risk to the extent that the locus of investment in infrastructure and applications shifts to Asia. No currently available evidence suggests an immediate loss in comparative advantage to Asian manufacturers, but co-location is almost always a factor in private-sector investment decision making. Thus, significantly more rapid growth in IPv6 applications in Asia could induce some shift in initial tiers in the Internet supply chain to that region. As described in earlier chapters, converging economies use transitions between technology life cycles as an opportunity to attain more permanent competitive status.

In contemplating transition between generations of standards, a major hurdle is the time and cost of the transition itself. Major technology-based standards such as the IP are so complex that they can only be completed over a number of years. The IETF has written approximately 250 specifications for the standard during the past decade. To get technical input from as many sources as possible, the IETF issued approximately 70 'requests for comment' and held numerous workshops. Still, many more specifications remain to be developed. An incomplete standard infrastructure will attenuate the performance of innovative market applications.

One example of the multidimensional structure of a complex standard like IPv6 is the need to ensure interoperability among the myriad deployments. Although IPv6 is a 'standard', it can be implemented differently by different companies (for example, using proprietary functions in optional header portions of the standard's structure). In addition, interoperability will be required between IPv6 and IPv4 networks that some have predicted may have to last as long as 20 years. The IETF noted that poor IPv6 implementation practices during this transition can lead to connection delays, inadequate connectivity and network security deficiencies. Conformance testing standards can greatly reduce such problems. However, international interoperability issues can still result from strategic actions by foreign governments that, for example, restructure technical specifications and conformance testing or limit encryption capabilities.

Equally important, most technologies only appear initially in isolated pockets within the market space of the defender technology. These 'islands' of the new technology are thereby initially compromised by the inability to realize economies of scale or scope, further reducing their early net benefit relative to the defender technology. In the case of a standard such as IPv6, early implementations will have to cross Internet space controlled by IPv4. The IETF has evolved a transition strategy to deal with this problem, which includes ways to 'tunnel' through IPv4 space (basically, encapsulating the IPv6 application in an IPv4-compatible envelope) or using dual stacks of routers, switches and so on for each standard.

The problem is that running a dual standard increases the complexity of an already complex infrastructure. Doing so raises operating costs and creates other problems such as security risks, which must be addressed and which further increase costs. For example, in dual-standard infrastructures, two paths are available to attack protocol or applications, multiplying the complexity of security approaches. A new (and incomplete) standard will have security problems that will only be discovered with actual use. Moreover, in the projected lengthy transition stage, encapsulating IPv6 applications is the equivalent to creating a Trojan horse (its IPv4 envelope), in which cyberspace-threatening computer code can hide while transversing IPv4 space, only to 'open' at its destination (inside perimeter defenses such as firewalls) and unleash its mischief.

Policy Responses

The interactive nature of advances in infrastructure and innovations described above seems largely ignored in the United States. In contrast, Asian economies seem to have a better appreciation of this iterative relationship. The Japanese government has aggressively supported the development of an IPv6 infrastructure and, in return, Japanese IT firms have begun to commercialize applications. Video on demand, 3G cell phones and 3GPP (text messaging) services are three early examples. As a demonstration, Taiwan has installed a national educational IPv6 network for university campuses and a government network using the dual-stack transition strategy. Both nations have invested in domestic test beds and participation in international standards programs to certify domestic suppliers of IPv6 applications. China is also investing in a major IPv6 network. In the United States, Internet2, a high-performance network run by a consortium of 200 universities, has IPv6 capability but only modest efforts have been made to encourage its use.

Failure of policy makers to understand the complementary-asset relationship of Internet innovation and Internet infrastructure and the time and resources required to overcome the flat bottom of the S-shaped growth curve will likely mean loss of comparative advantage in future IT infrastructure and hence future IT-based services. The policy response should be a broad analysis of all potential technology infrastructure needs. Moreover, ongoing analysis is essential to determine the optimal mix of policy responses during each phase of the technology life cycle that the infrastructure supports. In this regard, projecting emerging application life cycles is a critical part of the required analysis. Future benefits must be predicted coupled with determination of the threat of foreign competition to justify accelerating the transition to the next generation of the infrastructure.

If competitive threat or opportunity is deemed to require an acceleration strategy, then a diverse set of policy options need to be considered to promote development and deployment of the infrastructure:

1. support research on relevant infratechnologies (R&D market failure removal);
2. facilitate industry's standards development processes based on these infratechnologies (information and coordination market failure removal);
3. provide industry with performance/behavior test methods and test beds for

determining compliance (technology diffusion barrier removal);

4. deploy and enable the new standard to meet internal government needs (initial market penetration barrier removal through procurement); and

5. continue to monitor and analyze technological and market trends in the global infrastructure and applications arenas (information market failure removal).

The policy analysis must also take into account the fact that compressing the front end of a life cycle can both increase transition costs and do so in the early part of the supported technology's life cycle. Table 8.2 summarizes analyses prepared for the DoC Task Force that indicate how escalation of transition costs results from transition time compression. Such a cost impact

Table 8.2 Cost Estimates for Acceleration Scenarios

Scenario	Present Value of Estimated Cost (billions of 2003 dollars)
Base Case: normal hardware and software upgrade cycles with use determined by emergence of market applications (so-called 'natural' rate of transition)	25.4
Scenario I: enabling ('turning on') of IPv6 capability accelerated by 3 years; impact is largely labor training costs	33.9 (25% increase)
Scenario II: hardware and software upgrades accelerated over natural rate by 1 year, which accelerates labor training costs by four years	72.0 (300% increase)

Source: RTI International (2005).

occurs for several reasons: (i) the transition costs are front-loaded (within the transition period) and moving these larger costs backward in time to the early years has a proportionately greater effect on the present value of total costs; (ii) the more this early transition period is truncated, the more types of costs are affected; and (iii) cost acceleration is proportionately greater than time compression because inefficiencies are encountered when transition activities are accelerated and undertaken more in parallel than is optimal. This last point is particularly important and implies a strong need for careful analysis of global trends and hence acceptable time-cost tradeoffs.

GOVERNMENT SUPPORT OF TECHNICAL INFRASTRUCTURE

The overall message of this chapter is that today's technologically complex infrastructures are not receiving adequate levels of resources due to a poor understanding of such infrastructures' roles in long-term economic growth. Several factors contributing to this situation are:

1. *Segmented and ubiquitous nature:* Any one infrastructure element and the associated set of standards frequently have modest economic impact, but a high-tech industry depends on hundreds of such infrastructure elements, so the collective impact is substantial. This fact is largely undocumented, except for the economic studies done by NIST.

2. *Invisibility:* Today's high-tech economy depends increasingly on measurement and test methods, scientific and engineering databases, process control methods, interface protocols, quality assurance techniques and so on, which must be integrated into systems of hardware and software. Such systems are difficult to visualize and understand and this problem will only become more vexing as software is embedded in hardware and these complex components are integrated into diverse systems technologies.

3. *Reliance on private markets:* More than its competitors, the US economy relies on private institutions to provide both infratechnologies and related standards. These institutions, such as SDOs, consortia and various associations, are funded at meager levels. They are also staffed by industry personnel who rotate to these organizations for brief periods, causing continuity, institutional memory and general management problems.

4. *Portfolio management:* The number and variety of infratechnologies needed to support each stage of the technology-based economic process constitute a very difficult portfolio management problem. Thus, even if public–private sector role issues were resolved, setting priorities, conducting research in a timely manner and deploying the resulting technical information through an efficient standards process present extremely difficult management challenges.

5. *Quasi-public-good character:* Although some of the needed infratechnologies are provided by industry, the requirement for common use through standardization means that this infrastructure suffers from free-riding and coordination problems, which consequently cause substantial underinvestment.

In summary, these barriers lead to several negative economic impacts that compromise technology-based economic growth: (i) underinvestment in infratechnologies; (ii) inadequate resources for the standards setting processes; (iii) inappropriate or ineffective standards, such as proprietary rather than open-source standards or simply low-quality standards; and (iv) poor timing and ineffective deployment of standards relative to market needs, including inadequate management of transitions to new generations of the same generic standard.

The last of these impacts, market timing, is increasingly important as growing global competition shrinks technology and product life cycles. Private markets may eventually provide the optimal infrastructure. However, by that time, foreign competition, with its own infrastructure in place, will have taken a larger share of global markets.

The Bottom Line

The types of infrastructure market failures described on this and previous chapters occur in all technology-based economies. The quasi-public-good character of the technical basis for standards creates free-rider and coordination costs that are not likely to be acceptable to individual companies. The resulting situation – large potential gains in economic efficiency at the industry level but underinvestment at the company level – rationalize support roles by government.

Many economies are copying the American 'strategy' of a diverse industry structure and reliance on competitive dynamics. As part of such efforts, these countries are promoting small firms, venture capital and more rapid deployment of technologies. But, in addition, they have evolved a more advanced view of the public–private asset growth model and provided incentives and institutional mechanisms to support the infrastructure functions that facilitate entrepreneurship, general risk taking, technology dissemination and more optimal timing of innovation investments. These trends are an increasingly critical dimension of global convergence and impose competitive challenges on all governments.

NOTES

1. Source: James Murday, University of Southern California (talk presented at the Industrial Physics Forum on Nanotechnology in Society and Manufacturing, Policy Session: Nanotechnology & Society, San Francisco, November 13, 2006).
2. 'Open, But Not as Usual', *The Economist*, March 18, 2006: 73–5.
3. For example, in 2006, Google complained to antitrust regulators that Microsoft was using its Internet Explorer to direct users toward Microsoft's new search engine via MSN. The implication is that a web browser is an element of Internet

infrastructure. This is a weak case at best because no inefficiencies result from the existence of multiple browsers, as is the case for operating systems.
4. Interoperability is 'the flow of information from one system to another without the need for human intervention' (Morell and Phelps, 2001).
5. The Internet supply chain consists of four levels: hardware and software developers, applications developers, Internet service providers (ISPs) and users of Internet services.

PART III

Technology-Based Political Economy

9. Assessing the Government Role

If one does not know to which port one is sailing, no wind is favorable.

Seneca (Roman philosopher)

The inadequacies of currently available sets of indicators for the technology-based economy have previously been identified and assessed. Even with better economic indicators, policy analysis does not use sufficiently accurate technology-based growth models and associated policy analysis tools. In terms of the policy process, 'science and technology' (S&T) policy and the relatively narrow scope of issues it implies exist on a largely separate track institutionally from economic growth policy. Yet, because technology is the acknowledged critical long-term investment for sustained economic growth, the two areas of policy should be highly integrated.

Science, technology, innovation, and finally market development through technology diffusion constitute the needed scope of policy analysis. Hence, science, technology, innovation and diffusion (STID) is a more-inclusive and appropriate label than is S&T and, most important, collectively yields the ultimate policy goal – economic impact.

Recently, some analysts have begun to refer to STI policy but the fourth element, diffusion and assimilation of new technology (the 'D' in STID), is still not included. Without the latter, the impact of innovations would be limited because it is through wide use that technology has the majority of its economic impact.

This broader scope is not new in the sense that none of the four elements is totally ignored by policy. A careful reading of the following Congressional statement reveals their recognition and implies the important interdependencies:

> The [Senate Appropriations] Committee noted that productivity growth, powered by new knowledge and technological innovation, makes the economic benefits of a comprehensive, fundamental research and education enterprise abundantly clear. New products, processes, entire new industries, and the employment opportunities that result, depend upon rapid advances in research and their equally rapid movement into the marketplace. In today's global economy,

continued progress in science and engineering and the transfer of the knowledge developed is vital if the United States is to maintain its competitiveness. (Senate Report 108-353 accompanying the NSF 2005 appropriations bill S. 2825)

The problem is the lack of an integrated and systematic analytical capability to identify STID barriers and then design and efficiently implement appropriate integrated policy responses. This situation exists in part because the black-box model still prevails in the policy-making process and in part because the complex relationships between technology and other forms of investment are not sufficiently recognized.

The imperative is to throw off the ideological baggage of the past and realize that future economic progress will require a true 'public–private' growth policy framework with multiple government roles. This philosophy recognizes the complexities of technology-based economic growth, in particular, the public and quasi-public nature of key elements underpinning the typical industrial technology, as described in previous chapters.

Given the wide range of public and private economic assets that drive long-term growth, a responsive national investment strategy must emphasize those incentives that entice investment in the most *productive* and *immobile* of these assets. It is important to understand that 'immobile' means assets that are difficult and costly to (i) acquire by companies operating in competing economies (highly skilled labor, R&D capacity), or (ii) accumulate and manage by the governments of these economies, such as support mechanisms for an emerging technology portfolio and a comprehensive innovation infrastructure. These technology-related assets are relatively immobile, even though different types of technical knowledge spill over to varying degrees and thus can be acquired by competitors. This is the case because successful imitation, legal or otherwise, only occurs at significant cost and over time. Such costs and time lags allow the innovating economy to remain ahead – as long as it efficiently manages the entire technology life cycle.

In focusing on highly productive and immobile technology assets, the policy framework must recognize the fact that a significant fraction of the public-good portion of STID investments exhibits economies of scale and/or scope and is therefore most efficiently managed at the national level. However, public technology assets are increasingly developed and deployed at the local or state level as part of aggressive regional development programs. For some time, states have bid against one another to attract production activity, but R&D has seldom been similarly in play. This is because private R&D assets were not as closely tied to public research and other infrastructure, as is increasingly the case today (that is, Pasteur's quadrant is shrinking). As the scientific basis for new technologies increases in importance and as growing technological complexity requires more integrated supply chains, regional clusters have become increasingly important for implementing STID strategies. These clusters collect diverse scientific, technological, human, educational, financial and physical assets, which, once in place, are actually more immobile than the previous less-integrated innovation system.

MODELS FOR GOVERNMENT R&D FUNDING

Unlike other areas of economic policy, almost no STID policy analysis capability exists in the federal government. The result has been low levels of largely ad hoc and disconnected research into needed models and empirical analyses for dealing with specific policy issues. President George W. Bush's Science Advisor, John Marburger, identified this inadequacy at the annual AAAS meetings in April 2005, calling for more theoretical and empirical effort to develop policy analysis capabilities. At the same conference, Martin Bailey of the Institute for International Economics (and former member of the Council of Economic Advisers) pointed out that in an environment of poor conceptualization of government roles and empirical analysis to support decision making, Congress tends to favor funding options in the 'pastor's quadrant'. That is, R&D programs with visible, easily understood, and politically attractive objectives get funded, others do not.

The Dominant Firm Model

In the early post-war period, a few large companies with significant market control and hence long time horizons could afford to invest in generic technology research to prove concepts for new breakthrough technologies. The best-known example is Bell Labs. AT&T's regulated monopoly status protected it from competition. Virtually guaranteed minimum rates of return enabled a much lower rate of discount to be applied to prospective R&D investments. As a result, Bell Labs researched and proved the concepts for a range of breakthrough technologies.

Unfortunately, the very factors that allowed such research to be rationalized and funded over the many years required to prove new technology concepts also provided disincentives to take such generic technologies forward into applied R&D and eventual commercialization. AT&T's main strategic focus was defending its dominant market position, enabled by being a regulated monopoly. In doing so, it gave up property rights to the transistor (invented by AT&T scientists) in order to stave off threats to break it up. The company made other inventions (Unix and cellular-phone technology) but never pursued them due to its singular focus on long-distance phone service (Rhoads, 2005).

However, even without the protection of economic regulation, many large US companies in the three decades after World War II failed to capitalize on the new technology concepts developed in their central research laboratories. Xerox's Palo Alto Research Center (PARC) produced many important technologies that were successfully applied, but by other companies. PARC is one of the most impressive examples of generic technology spillovers. Not surprisingly, as competition increased in Xerox's markets and its share of those markets eroded, PARC became an increasing burden. In 2002, Xerox gave up completely and spun PARC off as an independent entity.

Although companies frequently make successful transitions between technology life cycles and thereby continue to be competitive, these firms seldom have the inclination or the ability to diversify horizontally and thereby capture the often substantial economies of scope from major technology breakthroughs.

For example, although Xerox managed to convert its entire technology base from mechanical technology to electro-mechanical and finally to a fully digital electronic platform, the company ignored the much broader innovation potential of the emerging PC industry, which PARC-demonstrated generic technologies helped create. That is, Xerox followed what is called the 'closed-innovation' model. The company was only in the copier business. Management had no interest in and little expertise in evaluating the range of potential technologies emanating from this disruptive technology research program (Chesbrough, 2004).

Today, fewer companies have the market control, size, and diverse lines of business to capture the economies of scope necessary to rationalize investment in many breakthrough generic technologies with multiple market applications. That is, they cannot project adequate rates of return from a subset of the potential innovations that might flow from the core technology platform. Further reducing expected rates of return is compression of technology life cycles from the growing global competition, which focuses a company's resources on core competences.

In summary, companies find the strategic diversification required to capture the economies of scope available in many disruptive technologies beyond their capabilities – especially in today's global markets where a company's installed base is itself under attack. Thus, many firms no longer have the option of operating a large central research facility with a broad mandate to explore radically new technologies. Instead, these facilities conduct research focused more on extending existing lines of business, developing complementary technologies, and evaluating and helping assimilate new technologies from external sources.

In response, national governments are increasingly funding early-phase generic (proof-of-concept) technology research. The European Framework Program, individual European country programs and Japan's Science and Technology Basic Plan are the well-known examples, but a number of emerging Asian economies now have expanding programs of the same type. To provide full proofs of concept, these programs use a portfolio approach to fund the required research, organize consortia to acquire complementary research assets and, to assure rapid and widespread use of the research results, co-locate the research with a regional innovation infrastructure.

The portfolio characteristic is critical. Because earlier phases of technology research typically take place years ahead of significant commercialization, because the technical risks associated with eventual commercial potential are high, and, finally, because the specific application markets and their eventual sizes are uncertain, the overall risk of such investment is high. The expanding size of global technology-based markets with their growing number of players means that no single country will ever dominate these markets the way the US economy did during the last half of the 20th century. Certainly, no single company will dominate a specific technological arena the way a series of American companies did in this period. Thus, much more efficient, systematic management of an economy's generic technology research portfolio and other technical infrastructure is an imperative.

The Mission Agency Model

The US government has for decades intensively funded generic technology research when it could be rationalized as supporting a specific social mission. The DoD's DARPA is a good example of the implementation of this philosophy and also of the use of the portfolio management model. For decades, DARPA has been at the forefront of funding radically new technologies, many of which not only served national defense needs but eventually spilled over into commercial market applications with enormous economic impact (Bonvillian, 2006). The basic philosophy is stated by DARPA Director Anthony J. Tether as 'DARPA's only charter is radical innovation'. DARPA tries 'to imagine what a military commander might want in the future and then change people's minds about what is technologically possible'. Given the high returns on basic science and generic technology research, DARPA's $2.8 billion budget is a significant source of 'seed corn' for new, disruptive technologies (Carey, 2004).

The DoD has multiple programs aimed at advancing the early phases of technology development. It funds basic science (DoD research funding category 6.1) and uses that science base as a point of departure for its generic technology research portfolio (6.2 funding) and applied research programs

(6.3). The Departments of Homeland Security and Energy, NASA and the NIH also have significant budgets for these types of research.

A prominent current example of government support for generic technology research is health care. The NIH budget has exploded over the past two decades in large part because (i) the objective of improving health is easily understood and supported (that is, it falls into Martin Bailey's 'pastor's' quadrant), and (ii) pharmaceutical research is perceived to be largely 'science' as opposed to 'technology'. One need only look at the web sites of the major news media to see that this is the case. They have a 'high-tech' section, which is largely IT industries, and a 'science' section, where all pharmaceutical or biotechnology news is found.

In reality, the NIH funds a lot of 'technology' research in addition to bioscience research. By funding clinical trials, the agency even supports applied R&D. AAAS R&D funding data show that, in FY2004, the NIH funded $14.8 billion in basic research, making it by far the largest federal supporter of science. But, the agency also funded $12.1 billion in applied research, including a $600 million small-firm grants program (largely early-phase technology research).

Through such technology research funding, the NIH has, in effect, created the biotechnology industry. Yet, none of this activity raises even the slightest complaint from Congress or policy circles; no charges of 'industrial policy' or 'picking winners and losers' are made. In short, no one challenges the appropriateness of such a large and broad government role in supporting an improved health-care objective.

However, if economic growth is the policy focus, all of a sudden an ideological barricade goes up. Government support is resisted for emerging technologies even though history shows that such funding opens the flood gates for much larger private-sector applied R&D investment and consequently new opportunities for economic growth. This ideological inconsistency is evident in proposals to create DARPA-like funding functions in the DoE ('ARPA-Energy') and the DHS ('HSARPA'), while at the same time attempts continue to be made to shut down NIST's ATP with its broad civilian technology (economic growth) focus. By mid-2007, supporters of ARPA-Energy were projecting an eventual budget of $1 billion, while ATP limped along at $80 million.

For every major technology life cycle, something like the DARPA model is needed because of the risk spike. In computing and communications, government funding played a critical role in advancing generic technologies and achieving minimum thresholds of R&D capability necessary to stimulate takeoff in private-sector investment. Federal funding for electrical engineering in areas such as semiconductors and communications technologies has fluctuated between $800 million and $1 billion since the

1970s. Funding for computer science increased from $10 million in 1960 to approximately $1 billion in 1995 (National Research Council, 1999). These amounts represented major fractions of total funding in these fields for the early phases of the relevant R&D cycles.

The Public–Private Model

In the broader government-support models described above, funding went to industry and university researchers. The distribution of funding among phases of the R&D cycle and among components of the technology system shifted over time in response to assessments of progress in overcoming the risk spike. Network communications is an example. Before 1970, the federal government sponsored individual researchers who developed the underlying network technologies, such as queuing, packet switching and routing. During the 1970s, experimental networks, notably the ARPANET, were constructed. These networks were primarily research tools, not operational services. Most were federally funded because, with a few exceptions, the early versions of these technologies were simply proofs of concept (National Research Council, 1999). Such preliminary technology platforms were necessary to provide a generic knowledge base to which industry could apply their conventional investment criteria and determine to commit funds for applied R&D and eventual commercialization.

During the 1980s, networks were widely deployed, initially to support scientific research. The National Science Foundation became the major supporter of networking, primarily through the NSFNET. At this point in the technology's life cycle, industry finally began to see the enormous economic potential of networks, if not the Internet. Companies such as IBM, Digital Equipment Corp. and Compuserve established proprietary networks, which were rapidly utilized worldwide for email, file transfers and electronic funds transfers.

However, the public–private nature of the evolving network technology blocked broader commercialization. To be truly successful and thereby have large economic impact, systems technologies such as the Internet have to be based on open architectures. This requirement presented a negative investment incentive to firms with substantial commitments to proprietary networks. Moreover, telephone companies, whose lines carried the packet-switched information, also resisted because the nature of voice communications networks is strikingly different from the evolving computer networks that led to the Internet (the installed-base effect was strong).[1]

The interplay between private and public research is apparent in other areas of IT, as well. IBM developed the concept of relational databases but did not pursue commercialization of the technology because of its potential to compete with established IBM products. NSF-sponsored research at UC-Berkeley allowed continued exploration of this concept and brought the technology to the point that it could be commercialized by several startup companies. The demonstration of commercialization was strong enough to finally overcome the installed-base effect, providing sufficient investment incentives to established suppliers, including IBM, to bring relational database products into the market.

A similar pattern was evident in the development of reduced instruction set computing (RISC). Though the concept was originally developed at IBM, RISC was not commercialized until DARPA funded additional research at UC-Berkeley and Stanford University as part of its VSLI Program in the late 1970s and early 1980s (National Research Council, 1999).

Similarly, expert systems, speech recognition and image processing all required extended generic technology research support from government. Industry began to invest in these and other areas of artificial intelligence (AI) in the 1960s but scaled back when the long periods required to reach commercialization became apparent. Continued federal investments advanced the generic technologies over a decade or more until conventional industry R&D criteria could rationalize sustained investments in applied R&D. Now, private investment is finally driving the commercialization of many AI technologies.

This model is repeated time after time. The early phases of R&D for many other important components of IT system technology were funded by government, slowly building the basis for the much larger private investments in applied R&D required to move the generic technologies toward commercialization (AeA, 2005). Examples are the web browser (NSF), the mouse (DARPA), bar codes (NSF), fiber optics (NSF), routers (NSF), computer-aided design (NSF/DARPA) and speech recognition (NSF/DARPA).

THE NEED FOR A NEW POLICY FRAMEWORK

Japanese officials have characterized the motivation for getting the economic growth model correct as deriving from the fact that innovation is the sole determining factor for the future growth of Japan's economy. In recognition of this imperative, Japan and other economies are experimenting with various forms of the multi-element technology-based growth model described in Chapter 4. The budget of Japan's third Basic Plan for the four years beginning in 2006 is 25 trillion yen ($226.4 billion based on the exchange rate at the time the program was launched). In the first year, $12.8 billion was allocated to basic research but even more, $16.2 billion, was targeted at mission-oriented R&D.

In a sea of technology-based competitors, a country or bloc of countries of any size must adopt a portfolio approach to funding generic technology research and supporting infratechnologies in the same way that a mutual fund manager purchases a portfolio of stocks. Some of these investments will succeed, others will not.

However, one major difference between a national portfolio of generic technology research programs and a mutual fund's portfolio of stocks is the fact that the national research portfolio is not the end game. Rather, it fills the gap between advances in basic science and market applications (innovations). Thus, this portfolio has the appearance of stock options, where the price of the option is a year of research funding to produce information that contributes to an eventual decision to commit to the much more expensive applied R&D needed to produce innovations and subsequent market penetration. Overcoming this information gap means overcoming the risk spike (Chapter 5), which occurs at a point in the R&D cycle where technical expertise and investment time horizons are well beyond the capabilities of individual firms and even industries to manage.

A critical factor in managing such a portfolio is research efficiency. Significantly different approaches are used to overcome the risk spike. Thus, required critical policy decisions go well beyond selection of the portfolio to include: (i) design of a research infrastructure that includes the performers with the required complementary research assets; (ii) management of the resulting intellectual property to ensure the optimal trade-off between incentives for follow-on research and widespread use of the resulting new technology platforms; and (iii) mechanisms for fast and effective transfer of the research results to innovative companies.

Supporting Generic Technology Research

From an economic growth policy perspective, mission-specific funding of generic technologies is less efficient because the portfolios are optimized for those missions rather than for economic impact. In addition, the 'industrial base' that delivers the technologies that implement a social mandate will become oriented over time to support that mandate. To contribute to economic growth in the mission-oriented model, the resulting proofs of concept or even more advanced commercial prototypes from applied research must be spun off to separate private industry networks with commercialization motivations. This path is indirect, which means that industry input into portfolio management is diminished and technology transfer channels are less developed, if they exist at all. Moreover, the completeness of the resulting generic technology platforms is likely to be suboptimal for maximum commercialization potential. The indirect mechanism is therefore a less-efficient, lower-yield approach to providing a portfolio of commercially oriented technologies. At a minimum, this approach requires too long a period of time to produce the required portfolio.

Over the post-World War II period, first defense R&D and then the addition of several other socially mandated areas, particularly health, dominated federal funding. However, in the late 1980s, the growing recognition of the need for a broader range of technologies to directly support domestic economic growth led Congress to establish a civilian counterpart to DARPA – the Advanced Technology Program at NIST. ATP's mission was to co-fund private-sector generic technology research. Due in part to a lack of consensus over federal roles in supporting technology research, ATP's funding initially rose in the early 1990s to between $400 and $500 million per year but then declined dramatically until the program reached a marginally effective annual funding level of around $80 million in the mid 2000s.

Yet, the need for supporting a portfolio of generic technologies to drive long-term economic growth is increasing. The linkage between industrial technology (represented by patents) and science (represented by the citation of scientific papers in patents) has increased dramatically. Economic studies reveal that US patents preferentially cite the highest-quality research (indicated by the fact that a relatively small number of research papers are repeatedly cited). Moreover, the institutional origins of the papers cited in the patents were dominated by public-sector organizations. Analysis shows that 73 percent of the papers cited in US patents were authored in public-sector institutions, such as universities and government laboratories (Narin et al., 1997; Hicks et al., 2000).

The DARPA model reflects this reality. In FY05, DARPA provided $525 million to universities from a total budget of $2.8 billion. Grants for basic research fund what in the past was the sole university role within the national research establishment. However, DARPA funds only $150 million in basic research. Of that $150 million, $90 million goes to universities. The rest of DARPA's university funding goes to early-phase technology research (6.2 and 6.3 funding). This compositional shift in university research reflects both the increasing dependency of technology research on basic science and universities' ability to own the intellectual property produced by such research.

However, it is government mission-oriented R&D portfolios that are driving the increase in university generic technology research with the result that the resulting technologies are not optimized for industry's future competitiveness needs. In contrast, industry is funding progressively less university research. An NSF report shows that industry funding of university research fell each year from 2001 to 2004. In 2004, for example, private funding fell 2.6 percent, while federal spending at universities rose 10.7 percent (NSF *InfoBrief* 06-315).

Portfolio Management for System Technologies

One aspect of the portfolio bias from mission-oriented funding of technology research through universities is that the development of system technologies suffers. Innovation in components of system technologies creates demand for innovation in the remaining components to allow the productivity of the entire system technology to grow. Moreover, initial advances in some components cross-fertilize advances in other components. These phenomena were initially recognized in the 1980s by concepts such as the 'chain-link' model of innovation (Kline and Rosenberg, 1986) and the NRC tire-track framework.

For example, a National Research Council report states: '...development of magnetic core memory for computers did not flow directly from advances in materials research (although it certainly drew upon such research), but from the need to develop a memory system with short enough access times and high enough reliability to support real-time computing' (National Research Council, 1999).

Responding to the derived demand for a technology (that is, from needs at the system level) requires (i) science and generic technology platforms (the results of materials research) that enable a specific component technology's development (magnetic core memory), and (ii) an innovation infrastructure that can respond in the time frame dictated by trends in global markets. Clearly, technological advance at the system level (the computer) required advances in all components, including this one (magnetic core memory), and such component advances in turn require efficient life-cycle research to enable innovation at the component level. Understanding these relationships is an imperative for effective research portfolio management.

Portfolio Management for Diversified Economic Growth

At the technology level, the skewed pattern of the federal R&D portfolio toward two technologies – information and health – is evidenced by the distribution of federal funds in recent decades and, therefore by the distribution of research expenditures by major recipients, in particular, universities. For example, NSF data show that in 2003 approximately 50 percent of university research was in biological and medical sciences (Jankowski, 2005). On the output side, patent statistics compiled by Chi Research show that in the 1990s the number of IT patents filed annually increased by 250 percent and the number of health technology patents increased by 150 percent. In contrast, patents in all other technologies combined increased by just 25 percent (see Figure 5.11). This skewed distribution of inventive output should raise concern over the obvious lack of a diversified government R&D portfolio and consequent inability to ensure balanced and steady economic growth over time.

A large economy has the advantage of effectively distributing risk through investment in a diversified set of emerging technologies. Moreover, economic size enables the realization of efficiency advantages in the early phases of the R&D cycle, specifically, access to a set of centers of diversified research expertise in all three sectors: universities, industry and government. Finally, a large economy can on average project capturing economies of scope from investments in new generic technologies.

DARPA has evolved a research management model that utilizes both portfolio and interactive management techniques to take advantage of these considerable research assets (CSTB, 2002). A number of US companies use research management approaches with characteristics similar to DARPA's. Intel, for example, employs a concurrent research model to involve complementary research assets from university professors and its own researchers to more efficiently achieve proofs of concept in emerging technologies commensurate with Intel's strategic plan. Intel manages such efforts through what it calls an open collaborative research agreement that provides incentives to both Intel and its university research partners by mutually selecting and managing projects and, most important, assigning non-exclusive property rights to induce both parties to commit to a project's objectives. Intel also builds effective technology transfer mechanisms into these projects by moving researchers into follow-on applied research programs (Tennenhouse, 2004).

A major impact of this collaborative approach is to compress the traditional linear R&D cycle model. Unfortunately, the few large R&D companies capable of effectively managing portfolios of emerging technologies in this way cannot carry a large economy in an increasingly technology-dependent world. This is especially the case as these companies' business models are increasingly dispersing R&D investment funds across global networks. To reverse such trends, much broader R&D infrastructures that facilitate efficient early-phase research involving universities and many firms, both large and small, are essential as are effective built-in technology transfer mechanisms. This is the only path if an economy is to be truly technology based.

Being 'technology based' means that both a broad range of technology opportunities are developed and the results of such research are applied broadly and quickly enough to attain target rates of innovation and productivity growth. Equally important, the breadth and depth of such an investment strategy enables broader participation by small R&D firms, which is essential to provide for renewal of industry structures as the biotechnology industry is dramatically proving in pharmaceuticals.

When such research infrastructure is not provided, or if it is allowed to deteriorate, a competitive gap appears that is not easily removed. In the 1980s, advanced ceramics was being touted as an emerging 'general-purpose' technology with potential applications in electronics, heat engines, machine tools, sensors and medical devices. The Japanese were making increasing investments in the generic technology with both the Japanese government and its industry funding the long-term research.

In the United States, however, government funding was inconsistent and largely unmanaged. Most US ceramic companies were small and could not rationalize funding generic technology research. In fact, they were not motivated to do so as they focused to a large extent on single-application areas (no economies of scope potential). In contrast, the world's largest advanced ceramics company, Japan's Kyocera, targeted most of the major potential application areas. It could therefore rationalize funding proof-of-concept research, either independently or as collaborative projects with the Japanese government, because its market strategy was broad enough to project capturing the economies of scope that are characteristic of general-purpose generic technologies. Kyocera now controls about one-half of the world market for electronic ceramic packages (which also have critical defense applications). Meanwhile, US firms either quit the business or scaled back operations. Without sustained government research funding, academic research teams deteriorated or disbanded entirely.

The above assessment does not mean that the United States has no advanced ceramic research capability. Rather, the lack of strategic planning and a research portfolio management approach segments and underfunds generic technology research. Further, the lack of an integrated government–university–industry research (GUIR) infrastructure reduces research efficiency and the probability of a significant number of attempted innovations based on the evolving technology platform. Thus, the potential domestic value added from this technology is significantly reduced.

Of course, even without a formal research model in place, sufficient funding will eventually achieve results. The major and sustained government funding of IT and biopharmaceutical research created demand for scientists and engineers to conduct research, manage production and manage technology-based businesses. Such funding has not only enabled steady and broad research, but it has also had a demand–pull effect on students deciding on a career in science or engineering. As Figure 9.1 shows, the growth in degrees awarded in these two areas has dwarfed the growth in all other areas of technology in the last decade. In fact, the rate of degrees awarded in these other areas remains flat, further underscoring the problem of a skewed national emerging technology portfolio.

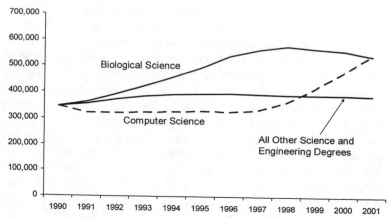

Source: National Science Foundation, *Science and Engineering Degrees: 1966-2001* (includes bachelor, master, and doctoral degrees).

Figure 9.1 Biological Science and Computer Science Degrees vs. All Other S&E Degrees, 1990–2001(normalized growth trends)

POLICY GAPS

Disruptive or breakthrough technologies radically change the technology platform for one or more markets. The most important of these are general-purpose technologies that exhibit economies of scope, meaning that they provide technology platforms from which a large number of markets can evolve with consequent substantial economic impact.

The Widening Federal Investment Gap

As previously discussed, the federal share of national R&D has steadily shrunk and the major victim has been proof-of-concept research for radically new technologies. In recent years, Congress has become increasingly alarmed at this trend. In February 2006, a number of senators wrote to the President urging a significant (10 percent) increase in DoD basic research (6.1 funding). The letter noted the past essential role of such funding in providing the scientific basis for the major technologies driving today's economy:

> Much of our nation's economic and military superiority has been built on past investments in basic research at the Department of Defense and the human talent

base that such investments have generated. Radar, digital computers, cryptology, wireless mobile communications, the Internet, lasers and fiber optics in communications and in medicine, composite materials, satellite navigation, and global positioning systems (GPS) are all technologies that came entirely or largely out of past Defense research investments.

However, the realities of growing global technology-based competition make the 'spin-off' model for creating major new technology life cycles inadequate. Thus, technology-based economic growth policies must adapt to this reality by shifting away from reliance on a skewed research portfolio managed by separate and uncoordinated mission-oriented agencies. Instead, the GUIR model mentioned in the previous section must be implemented for a portfolio of technologies with the greatest expected economic impact.

Total US R&D investment has increased at an average annual rate of 6.3 percent in real terms over the past 25 years (1979–2004). US industry spending has increased much faster at 10.0 percent per year over this period. However, this growth has succeeded in raising only a small fraction of US industries to the high R&D intensities that seem necessary to sustain competitive positions in expanding technology-based global markets. This situation is occurring in spite of the multi-decade increase in industry's share of national R&D.

A growing number of policy makers agree that some amount and type of underinvestment in technology research occurs. However, as discussed at length in previous chapters, techniques are lacking for identifying underinvestment phenomena and then selecting among alternative policy response mechanisms. Moreover, public subsidies for R&D (tax incentives, direct funding, or government laboratory research) have been based on rationales that are often non-economic, leaving the economic growth impacts as an ineffective trickle-down process.

In spite of these inadequacies, the federal government was the main provider of US R&D funds until the last 25 years – accounting for 54 percent in 1953 and as much as 67 percent at its peak share in 1964. The federal share first fell below 50 percent in 1979 and then stabilized in the 40–45 percent range in the 1980s. The rapid increase in industry funding of R&D during the 1990s coupled with the general restrictions on federal spending progressively reduced the federal share to an all-time low of 24.8 percent in 2000, as shown in Figure 9.2. The non-defense share of federal R&D increased from 18–19 percent in the 1950s to over 50 percent in 1980 before the defense buildup reduced its share to 35 percent by 1985. The non-defense share rose again in the late 1990s to around 45 percent before declining to 40 percent in 2006.

These periodic relative increases in federal defense R&D funding have benefited economic growth to the extent that the DARPA and other DoD S&T research budgets have increased with overall defense R&D spending. Over several decades, DARPA support has been responsible for the

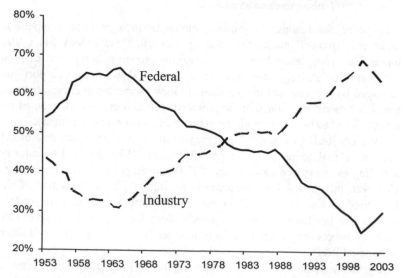

Source: National Science Board, *Science and Engineering Indicators – 2006*.

Figure 9.2 Federal and Industry R&D: Percent of Total R&D Expenditures, 1953–2003

emergence of a number of major new technologies. However, in recent years, a refocusing of this agency's budget on more applied military-specific objectives implies a reduction in its future role in stimulating new technology platforms, especially relative to the ever-expanding needs of the US economy for a diversified portfolio of economic growth-oriented technologies. Moreover, the non-defense portion of the federal R&D budget, while varying as a share of total federal R&D, has remained relatively constant in real dollar terms for 30 years (Figure 5.10). A static non-defense R&D budget is clearly a serious concern with respect to providing industry with a range of technology platforms to launch new industries.

Funding the Gaps

The composition of national R&D has an equally significant concern resulting from the declining share of federal R&D funding. Two critical elements of an industrial technology are shared among companies. These elements are the technology platform of an industry (the generic technology) and infratechnologies (techniques, methods, databases and so on). Because these elements are voluntarily or involuntarily shared, they take on the character of public goods, which imply underinvestment by private sources.

The more radical the technology, the more difficult it is for companies to (i) rationalize assuming the higher levels of technical and market risk (the risk spike is high); (ii) rationalize the commitment to the required long-term research (high corporate discount rates lower the present value of projected future earnings); (iii) make the adjustments to investment and organizational strategies necessary to diversify into the wide but often different range of new markets created by such a technology (economies of scope are not captured); and (iv) access the required multidisciplinary and often new required research capabilities (modern technologies are complex).

These market failure (systematic underinvestment) mechanisms collectively are having a strongly negative effect on the composition of private R&D investment. Yet, in the face of pressing R&D funding issues, federal policy lacks the ability to determine the correct target phases of the R&D cycle, select appropriate funding mechanisms for different underinvestment phenomena, and measure the impact and progress of existing funding programs.

As government funding is extended forward in the R&D life cycle, that is, to include applied research and especially development, the market mechanism is increasingly compromised. In contrast, early-phase generic technology research funding serves the role of providing industry with technology platform options and thereby increases the likelihood that industry will select a more optimal technology trajectory or simply select a trajectory sooner. In essence, a portfolio approach to government R&D funding is implied in that the early phases of the development of a technology's major elements and the sub-elements within them are funded with the realization that not all investments in the portfolio will eventually become part of the economy's industrial technology base. That is, average project risk is high so relatively high failure rates should be expected. The important metric is the higher expected long-term rate of return on the research portfolio.

Because of the complex and dynamic nature of the risk spike and the persistent public-good nature of technology infrastructure, annual funding decisions for emerging technologies should be viewed as a set of options on further research commitments with the results of each option being reviewed by all stakeholders before deciding to continue. Industry's conventional R&D decision process for applied R&D should kick in at the appropriate point in the R&D cycle and government's role should then diminish rapidly. That is, once proof-of-concept data are available, industry will either reject the projected technology trajectories or take over an increasingly large portion of total research funding. Case studies cited earlier have shown this pattern to be the case many times over.

Much of the NIH's support of biotechnology and DARPA's support of computer-related technologies and communications networking technology preceded and, in fact, enabled a much larger private investment. Additional support then leveraged the evolution of the technology base where private investment was too narrow in scope, too segmented, or too resistant to the more radical versions of the underlying technology. The result was world technological leadership, the creation of new industries and substantial economic growth.

Without an initial government role, few major commercial technologies would be developed. The appropriate combinations and the right funding time frames are the key policy variables. For example, Lerner (1996) has shown that Small Business Innovation Research (SBIR) awards are more effective in regions with substantial venture-capital availability. However, 40 percent of these awards have gone to two states (California and Massachusetts), once again emphasizing the skewing of R&D in the US economy in response to a geographically constrained innovation infrastructure. This situation demands wide application of a GUIR model as a centerpiece of regional technology-based growth.

A second policy point is that funding for generic technology and infratechnology research is small relative to the subsequent investments by industry in applied R&D. At the same time, the public-good character of this research creates formidable barriers to private-sector investment. Fortunately, the relatively small cost allows government to fund a broad portfolio of emerging technology and infratechnology research. The key requirements for successful government research programs are the targeting of the right technology elements at the appropriate phases in the respective technology life cycles and application of a portfolio management model that enhances research efficiency, including technology transfer.

Unfortunately, this basic policy framework is not easy to manage. Case studies reveal numerous pitfalls for companies and entire industries attempting to penetrate markets by moving up the S-shaped performance–price curve. This movement toward greater efficiency and hopefully greater competitive advantage is multifaceted and therefore subject to failure at any point in a technology's life cycle.

The US biotechnology industry is an excellent case study of both the potential success possible from large and sustained government funding but also of the difficulties in managing the relevant life cycles. In this case, a new and highly important industry has evolved not only because of federal research funding but also because of a risk-taking culture supported by an extensive venture-capital infrastructure. Yet, over its 25-year history, the biotechnology industry has experienced a number of peaks and valleys of investor enthusiasm. These pronounced capital market swings have caused R&D cycles to lengthen and many biotechnology companies to license their technology at unfavorable terms or even sell out to large domestic or foreign pharmaceutical firms at prices unattractive to their investors.

A specific example within biotechnology is monoclonal antibodies (MABs). Used in Chapter 5 to illustrate the effects of the risk spike, this technology platform with many potential therapeutic applications was first developed in the mid-1980s and was heralded as the magic bullet for treating cancer and possibly other diseases. First-generation MABs were not particularly effective for several reasons and investors quickly lost interest. Many companies in this area were acquired or went out of business. However, sustained funding by the NIH and a trickle of venture capital allowed research to continue. A decade later, second-generation MABs and even newer hybrid technologies that use MABs as targeting devices for other therapeutic agents have appeared. As a result, investor enthusiasm has returned.

Another previously described area of biotechnology with a similar pattern is antisense technology, which blocks the formation within cells of unwanted proteins by interfering with RNA messaging. In the early 1990s, antisense was a hot technology, but degradation and toxicity problems caused difficulties for the first-generation drug candidates. By the mid-1990s, hardly anyone was interested. Now, many of the earlier problems appear to have been solved and the technology is coming back into favor again based on second generation technology.

The R&D policy message is that when the time to commercialization is relatively short, perhaps a year or two, risk is relatively easily estimated and incorporated into corporate R&D decision making. For the longer early phases of the R&D cycle, estimated risk increases (spikes) and inconsistent company and capital-market support results. Federal research funding for basic science and for the generic technologies based on this science are critical to sustaining the innovation patterns that appear frequently in emerging technologies. In addition, the timely availability of infratechnologies can significantly improve the efficiency of the R&D process and thereby attain critical reductions in R&D cycle times and cost. Without the efficient and timely provision of these two major quasi-public technology elements (that is, generic technologies and infratechnologies), the initial flat portion of the S-shaped growth curve is extended in time. The result is wasted R&D resources, slower market penetration, and the possible loss of market shares to foreign competitors.

The Bottom Line

Technology and the public and private institutions that support its development and use are interdependent components of a national innovation system. This system is not easily replicated due to the complexity of the actors and institutions, including multiple infrastructures, which ultimately yield the market applications that produce the desired economic benefits. Thus, policies that are effective at stimulating such systems are to be highly valued.

However, managing the policy process is a demanding undertaking. Decision makers must be concerned with diversification of an economy's technology base and its myriad applications. To this end, both absolute size and composition of a nation's R&D investment are increasingly critical policy variables. Each area of investment is itself complex in that government funding must recognize the public-good character of the several major technology elements.

More specifically, (i) government funding roles must be implemented by modern portfolio management techniques applied in an integrated manner both for component technologies and technology systems; (ii) radically new technologies must be supported by major investments in technical infrastructure and standards; and (iii) a national innovation system must be created based on national-level public technology investment and regional growth research and innovation strategies. Unfortunately, the civilian – and hence economic growth policy – side of government is still relatively low on the R&D management learning curve, so these imperatives are not being addressed.

NOTE

1. For example, voice traffic is handled by a continuous connection (a circuit) for the duration of the transmission, while computers communicate in bursts. Unless a number of these bursts or 'calls' can be combined on a single transmission path (seldom the case in complex, high-capacity transmission systems), line and switching capacity is wasted. National Research Council (1999).

10. Elements of STID Policy

It is well to keep in mind how primitive the framework is that we use to evaluate policies and assess strength in science and technology.

John Marburger (President's Science Adviser)

The effectiveness of a government's technology-based economic growth policy is determined by how well it conceives and executes programs to support science, technology, innovation and diffusion of technology. Each area of STID policy must be constantly updated through institutionalized analysis to respond to the increasingly challenging dynamics of the expanding global economy. However, the required analytical tools and data to support effective STID policies are not available. Without analytical models, data, and a methodical decision-making process to identify needs, to design and implement appropriate programs and to measure results, no economy will remain competitive for long. In essence, if you can't measure it, you can't manage it.

Dwight Eisenhower once said 'plans are useless but planning is essential'. That is, decision-making processes are critical to success. Eisenhower also characterized the operational aspect of this philosophy with respect to military strategy by stating that no plan survives first contact with the enemy. Such a statement could not provide a better analogy to the challenges of managing the technology-based economy. From the moment an R&D program is begun in one company or industry, the rest of the world takes note. The act of innovation is a clarion call to innovative competitors and imitators everywhere. Until the end of a technology's life cycle, change is relentless and unpredictable. Clearly, as technology becomes more important for continued growth in industrialized nations, so does STID policy. As technology becomes more complex, so does the required policy analysis. Further, as a technology evolves over its life cycle, policy must anticipate and react in an equally dynamic manner. Finally, at the macroeconomic level, individual STID policies must be integrated and balanced to achieve economic growth objectives.

Remedying the previously identified deficiencies in STID policy analysis capability will require the establishment of a comprehensive policy analysis function, which is possible only in an institutionalized setting embodying the requisite analytical skills, access to data and functional interfaces with decision makers. Completeness from a policy research method perspective means addressing the following five steps: trend analysis, barrier identification and ranking, barrier source and cause analysis, development of policy options and, finally, measurement of impacts of these policies once they are implemented.

Unfortunately, the United States is a long way from having, let alone using, an S&T policy analysis capability of this scope and depth. Within the federal government (both legislative and executive branches), almost no analytical capability is available. What little capacity once existed has been largely disbanded. Small units established in the 1970s at the NSF and NIST (at that time the National Bureau of Standards) were terminated in less than a decade. More recently, the Technology Administration and its Office of Policy Analysis is being eliminated. Only a few economists with technology policy expertise have ever been appointed to the Council of Economic Advisers. In Congress, the highly respected Office of Technology Assessment (OTA) was shut down in 1995. Congress also suffers from a lack of technical and high-tech business backgrounds among its members.

The impact of this situation is predictable: two decades of debate over a still temporary research and experimentation (R&E) tax credit that does not appear effective, the lack of consensus over the roles of government R&D funding for economic growth purposes, and the continuing inability to agree when each of these two distinctly different policy instruments (tax incentives and direct funding) should be used for particular barriers.

In academia, normally an important source of policy analysis expertise, only a handful of university public policy programs have a reasonably comprehensive STID policy curriculum and research focus. Very few economists choose technology as their primary field of specialization. As a result, although some progress has been made over the past five decades in understanding the process by which scientific and technical knowledge is created and ultimately turned into commercial products, processes and services, the current models and empirical evidence have many gaps and distinct weaknesses that create problems for policy makers. A number of industry-supported think tanks and associations exist that have technology policy as one area of interest, but these operations are thinly funded and at most can undertake only a few ad hoc policy exercises that depend largely on external sources of expertise.

The first needed change in upgrading STID policy analysis is to discard out-of-date microeconomic theory that regards technology as a black box, that is, as a purely private good. In such a model, the required policy algorithm is quite simple: government funds basic scientific research and industry funds technology R&D. However, as argued at length throughout this book, the real world is more complicated. Technology evolves through a series of steps by which technical knowledge is made progressively more applied until the technology attains the performance and cost attributes necessary to achieve commercialization. The key attribute of this sequence for government policy is the fact that each major element of an industrial technology responds to distinctly different investment incentives. Mismatches in private-sector investment across these elements can and do occur.

The post-World War II history of the US economy shows clearly that government must play several complementary roles with industry in advancing new industrial technologies. Virtually every major technology driving US economic growth today (semiconductors, digital computers, software, advanced materials, network communications and biotechnology) has benefited from not years but decades of government support of both scientific research and early-phase generic technology development.

At the same time, the complex multidisciplinary character of modern technologies coupled with trends in corporate strategy towards a focus on core competences and R&D collaboration are creating large numbers of new market interfaces for the development and diffusion of technology. Technological complexity also requires an elaborate technical infrastructure to support R&D, production process control, information exchange among companies, and market exchange of technology-based products.

Such complexity is hardly explained by traditional neoclassical theory. In fact, this ongoing role and evolution of modern technology demands major change in the form of a sophisticated STID policy analysis capability that can identify underinvestment phenomena and match these investment barriers with the appropriate policy instruments and do so in the appropriate time frame. Economists have addressed the public–private issue for decades, but only recently has research begun to focus on this construct for R&D and other STID policy areas (Tassey, 2005a, b).

The second needed change is to provide models with appropriate data so that the policy analyst can identify and rank underinvestment phenomena, match high-priority policy targets with the optimal policy responses, and then measure the impact of these policies over time. The STID policy arena is just beginning to systematically assess data needs that expand well beyond the traditional focus on R&D investment (National Research Council, 2005a).

DEVELOPMENT OF POLICY OPTIONS

Analysis-based policy is no longer an option. All technology-dependent economies have set up and are expanding policy analysis capabilities to enhance the government role in supporting economic growth objectives.

The Current Policy Process

The advent of convergence among the world's economies has not been completely ignored by US policy makers. Beginning in the 1970s, the federal government began to take notice of such issues as the returns to federal R&D investments, industrial productivity growth, rates of innovation and overall competitiveness appeared to fall. These concerns continued into the 1980s, resulting in important legislation such as the R&E tax credit (1981), the Bayh–Dole Act (1980), the National Cooperative Research Act (1984), the Technology Transfer Act (1986) and the Omnibus Trade and Competitiveness Act (1988). Since then, little significant legislation has occurred, partly due to the surge in economic growth in the late 1990s, which allowed long-term structural problems to be temporarily ignored. Another major reason has been the inadequate scope and poor quality of indicators of technology-based growth, which has permitted denial of declining competitive positions in global markets.

In such a policy analysis vacuum, concerned stakeholders from all three major sources of R&D funding and/or performance (industry, academia and government) have been forced to assert the existence of specific problems (inadequate R&D, inadequate long-term R&D, shortage of skilled workers, shortage or inconsistency of venture capital, inadequate intellectual property right laws and so on). Based largely on anecdotal information, these groups then propose general solutions.

Over the past decade, a significant number of industry associations and government-sponsored advisory groups have issued reports urging policy changes. Unfortunately, ad hoc policy assessment exercises by virtue of their temporary nature are not supported by the resources, the time and the skills required to develop accurate and defensible policy options. In the absence of adequate scope and depth of data collection and the lack of a policy analysis capability within government, such exercises are limited to general problem assessment and speculative policy recommendations.

Finally, a degree of urgency to reform technology-based growth policies began to emerge in 2004. In one of the more thorough innovation policy development efforts, the Council on Competitiveness (2004) culminated a year of work on its National Innovation Initiative with the release of *Innovate America*. The National Academies of Science's (2005) *Rising Above the Gathering Storm* attained more attention than most reports partly because of the Academies' stature, but also because it contained a set of relatively specific recommendations. This report was followed in December 2005 by a congressionally mandated National Summit on Competitiveness, attended by senior-level officials from high-tech corporations, government, academia, and various industry and non-profit associations. A statement released at the conclusion of the summit outlined three major tasks: 'revitalize fundamental research', 'expand the innovation pool in the United

States' and 'lead the world in the development and deployment of advanced technologies'. The specific recommendations were:

- Task One: Revitalize Fundamental Research
  o 'Increase federal investment in 'long-term basic research by 10 percent per year over the next seven years with emphasis on the physical sciences, engineering, and mathematics'.
- Task Two: Expand the Innovation Pool in the United States
  o 'By 2015, double the number of bachelor's degrees awarded annually to US students in science, math, and engineering, and increase the number of those students who become K-12 science and math teachers'.
  o 'Reform US immigration policies to enable the education and employment of individuals from around the world with the knowledge and skill in science, engineering, technology, and mathematics to boost competitive advantage of the United States'.
  o 'Provide incentives for the creation of public–private partnerships to encourage US students at all levels to pursue studies and/or careers in science, math, technology, and engineering'.
- Task Three: Lead the World in the Development and Deployment of Advanced Technologies
  o 'Provide focused and sustained funding to address national technology challenges in areas that will ensure national security and continued US economic leadership, including nanotechnology, high-performance computing, and energy technologies'.[1]

The introduction in late 2005 of the National Innovation Act of 2005 (S. 2109) sought to legislate many of the recommendations from these policy exercises. The bill was comprehensive. It included provisions for increased funding for basic and high-risk technology research, tax incentives for R&D (defined broadly), increased support for S&E education and better coordination of policy. Provisions were also included to achieve improvements in existing technology transfer programs, specifically the DoD's Manufacturing Technology (ManTech) Program and NIST's Manufacturing Extension Partnership (MEP) Program. An emphasis on manufacturing technology and competitiveness showed the legislation sponsors' concern with the declining status of that sector.

In January 2006, the Bush Administration announced the American Competitiveness Initiative (ACI), which committed $5.9 billion in FY 2007 and more than $136 billion over 10 years, to increase investments in R&D, strengthen education and encourage entrepreneurship and innovation. 'The centerpiece of the American Competitiveness Initiative is the President's strong commitment to double over 10 years investment in key federal agencies that support basic research programs in the physical sciences and engineering: the National Science Foundation (NSF), the Department of Energy's Office of Science (DoE SC), and the Department of Commerce's National Institute of Standards and Technology (NIST).'[2]

While this policy activity is notable for the broad scope of its recommendations, its sense of urgency, and a willingness to specify specific initiatives, history predicts that most of the proposals will not be effectively implemented due to the absence of a consensus on the most important market failures and the supporting data that: (i) provide concrete evidence of the nature and magnitude of specific problems; (ii) rank the identified areas of underinvestment; (iii) conduct cause-and-effect analysis for each major market failure; and (iv) using such analysis, match market failures with the appropriate policy instruments. Without such supporting analysis, the typical policy initiative, no matter how passionately put forward, is forced to assume or assert the first three steps in order to reach step (iv).

If, in fact, such initiatives are maintained and funds are provided, federal agencies will develop strategic plans for their implementation. However, at best, the authorization and appropriation processes will be long and result in a largely arbitrary set of implementations and funding levels.

The Framework for Improved STID Policies

To determine which policy instrument to choose for a particular market failure requires comprehensive and systematic analysis. The disaggregated public–private model of technology-based growth presented in Chapter 4 (Figure 4.1) can be used to demonstrate the specific areas of impact for the variety of mechanisms available to policy makers. This mapping of government policies is shown in Figure 10.1. The complexity of the set of STID policy instruments currently in use derives from the multiple categories of market failure identified in Chapter 5. Each market failure mechanism affects private-sector investment in a different way and demands a unique policy response. The thinner arrows indicate the points of intervention. The thicker arrows represent transitions between phases of the technology life cycle. As in Chapter 4, the thicker double arrows indicate the quasi-public-good nature of those technology elements (one arrow for the private component and one for the public component).

However, even a well-developed static policy model that matches specific problems with specific policy solutions at specific points in the technology life cycle is not sufficient because, as the discussion of such cycles in Chapter 7 demonstrates, investment gaps change in size and character over time. Moreover, markets that support private investment in technology, such as venture capital, can vary with the business cycle, so the policy analyst must also separate cyclical patterns and their implications from any secular shift in the risk orientation of investment behavior.

In the context of this framework, the next two sections analyze two of the most important policy instruments in Figure 10.1, tax incentives and direct funding of R&D.

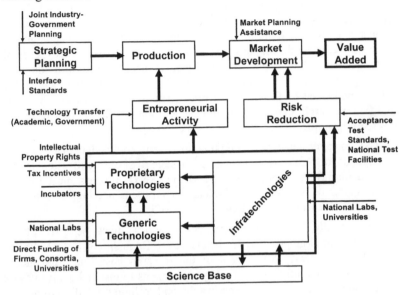

Figure 10.1 STID Policy Roles

TAX INCENTIVES

Many conservative economists and policy makers have argued that tax incentives should be used almost exclusively as the policy response to private-sector underinvestment in R&D. The reasoning is that tax policy is market neutral in contrast to direct funding, which targets particular technologies at particular phases in their life cycles. This philosophy has strongly influenced economic growth policy in the United States for decades. Certainly, tax policy has an important role in stimulating R&D as a response to high levels of risk associated with this category of investment. However, as with other STID policy instruments, issues of effectiveness abound.

The realization that other economies, particularly Japan, had begun to increase R&D spending in the 1970s led to the application in 1981 of this policy tool in the form of the R&E tax credit. Since 1981, most industrialized nations have implemented some form of R&D-specific tax policy. However, tax incentives have some serious drawbacks, which must be understood and addressed to make this policy instrument effective.

The Nature of the R&E Tax Credit

The credit was designed to emphasize significant advances in technology, as opposed to incremental improvements, product engineering and so on (hence, the name R&E, rather than R&D, tax credit). As such, it was a response to a growing point of view in the late 1970s that the composition of industrial R&D was shifting toward shorter-term objectives at the expense of the longer-term, higher-risk research that is necessary to provide new technology platforms for future economic growth. This intended focus of the credit is evidenced by the many tax rules written by the Treasury to define 'qualified research expenditures' for which the credit applies (Sawyer, 2004). For example,

- The taxpayer must be attempting to obtain knowledge that exceeds, expands, or refines the common knowledge of skilled professionals in a particular field of engineering, and the (R&D) process must rely on principles of physical or biological sciences, engineering, or computer science (Treasury Regulations § 1.41–4(a)(3)).

- Substantially all of the research activities must be part of an experimentation process. Under Treasury Regulations § 1.41–4(a)(5) and (6), at least 80 percent of the research costs must be due to developing hypotheses, designing experiments to test and analyze those hypotheses, conducting experiments and refining or discarding the hypotheses.

- Before or during the early phases of the project, the taxpayer must document the principal questions to be answered and the information sought (Treasury Regulation § 1.41–4(d)).

The Impact of the Credit

NSF and Internal Revenue Service (IRS) data show that real dollar claims for the credit over the first two decades of its existence (1981–2001) totaled $58.6 billion. This amount is 47 percent of the $124.4 billion in total real increases in industry-funded R&D and some might therefore view it as representing the approximate share of the growth in industry R&D over this period that is attributable to the credit – assuming a unit price elasticity of demand for R&D (that is, a dollar-for-dollar impact from the credit).

However, uncertainty over the price elasticity of R&D makes any asserted impact of the credit on industry R&D spending suspect. Moreover, most readily available data are claims for the credit. Not all claims are allowed, and, in fact, it is estimated that approximately 20 percent of claims are denied. In addition, the deduction for qualified R&D expenses on corporate income tax returns must be reduced by the amount of the credit. If one assumes an average marginal tax rate of 30 percent, a rough 'adjusted' credit would account for 26 percent of the cumulative increase in industry-funded R&D spending over the two decades. While considerably smaller than 47 percent, neither number means much unless assessed in the context of a proper economic model.

With respect to price elasticity, economic studies are in disagreement over the level of responsiveness of corporate R&D to tax incentives. Several analyses estimated an impact as little as 15–35 cents in increased spending for every dollar of tax expenditure. Other studies estimated a short-term impact of one dollar of increased spending for each dollar of tax expenditure and two dollars or more of increased spending over time (General Accounting Office, 1996; Atkinson, 2007b).

Moreover, these studies do not take the strategic nature of R&D into account and hence other factors that affect R&D investment. The importance of R&D for long-term corporate success implies a relatively low price elasticity of demand for R&D, which in turn implies that the credit's impact on fluctuations in R&D spending is likely overestimated. In fact, the same emerging technological capabilities of other economies that motivated the establishment of the credit in 1981 were perceived by US industry and led to substantial increases in R&D spending before the credit was enacted.

Such trends do not mean that R&D tax incentives are ineffective, only that they must be large enough to significantly and permanently lower the user cost of R&D and thereby affect strategic resource allocations within the corporation. Assessing the magnitude and sustainability of such a tax incentive is increasingly critical not only because of the global increase in technology-based competition but because most economies now provide an equal or greater tax incentive.

International Comparisons

Getting the structure and magnitude of R&D tax policy correct is increasingly important as globalization has resulted in numerous and diverse tax incentives across economies. At least a general insight into the relative efficacy of these alternative incentive structures can be gained by comparing growth rates in industry-funded R&D with the existence and relative strength of the various tax incentives employed. Most countries allow tax benefits (a credit or immediate expensing) for the capital costs associated with R&D. However, capital costs account for only about 10–13 percent of total R&D costs, which means that the impact of such incentives is small (Hall and Van Reenen, 2000). All countries allow R&D operating costs to be expensed.

Thus, differential impacts of tax incentives across countries will be due to differences in either tax credits or in deductions greater than 100 percent of qualified R&D expenditures. Table 10.1 compares the growth in industry-funded R&D with the existence of such tax incentives (incremental credits, flat credits and 'super deductions' of more than 100 percent) for a number of relatively R&D-intensive economies over the first two decades since the enactment of the US R&E tax credit in 1981.

Based on a 'user cost of R&D' index developed by Bloom et al. (2002), Canada and Australia have the most generous tax treatment of R&D. As Table 10.1 indicates, these two countries rank first and fourth in terms of growth in industry-funded R&D in the two decades since the US R&E tax credit was implemented.

Table 10.1   Growth in Industry-Funded R&D Compared to R&D Tax Incentives, 1981–2001

Country	Change in R&D (%)	R&D Tax Incentive
Australia	733.9	125% super deduction + a 175% incremental deduction
Finland	510.8	None
Sweden	286.7	None
Canada	240.9	Flat 20% credit
United States	201.4	20% incremental credit
Japan	165.7	Flat 10% credit (15% for small firms)
France	138.8	Incremental credit of 50%
Germany	97.1	None
United Kingdom	53.6	None*

Note: *In 2002, the UK instituted a super deduction of 125% (150% for small and medium enterprises); this 'credit' is refundable for net-loss years.

Source: OECD.

However, the two economies with the second and third largest growth rates for industry-funded R&D over this time period, Finland and Sweden, provide no tax incentive beyond the common business expense deduction. Moreover, Canada does not use an incremental tax credit (it has a 20-percent flat credit) and Australia uses a 125-percent super deduction for R&D expenses (effectively a flat credit) plus a larger deduction for R&D increases. In fact, a survey of 25 industrialized economies by Hall and Van Reenen (2000) found that only six relied on an incremental tax credit.

The general proposition that tax preferences for R&D can affect the user cost of risk capital and hence decisions by companies with respect to location of R&D facilities and operations is supported in a study by Billings (2003). He estimated the effect of such incentives by relating the average rate of growth in R&D spending relative to the comparable rate of growth in the United States for seven industries across 11 other countries over a 10-year period (1991–2000). This approach provided 458 industry years of data after eliminating industries in countries with incomplete time series or outliers. Industry years with tax-based incentives had an average annual increase in industry R&D spending of 9.61 percent compared to 2.24 percent average annual growth for years without tax-based incentives. Thus, the average growth rate for industry years with a tax incentive is more than four times the average growth rate for industry rates without such an incentive.

However, because these averages do not reveal potentially significant differences in leveraging effects from alternative tax incentives across countries, Billings also estimated the average 'effective tax credit' (equivalent flat tax credit rate above normal business deductions for R&D) available to 20 US multinational companies in seven economies. As shown in Figure 10.2, the United States ranks near the bottom. Only France was estimated to have a lower effective R&D tax incentive.

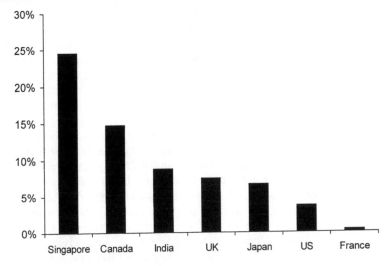

Source: Billings (2003, Table 3, Panel B).

Figure 10.2   Estimated Average Equivalent Flat R&D Tax Credit for 20 US Multinationals in Seven Countries

France's low estimated tax subsidy provides a good example of the need for thorough analysis of tax policies. Simply stating the apparently generous 50-percent incremental credit (along with a number of other incentives) conveys the impression that France is an attractive location for corporate R&D based on relative user costs. France even touts their tax incentives as a marketing strategy aimed at multinational companies. However, the total credit in any one year is limited to €6.1 million (approximately $7.7 million). Because the 20 companies used in Billings's simulated tax incentive calculations have large R&D budgets, this limitation greatly reduces the strategic influence of the calculated effective tax subsidy.

At the national economy level, a recent OECD study ranked the United States 17th among OECD nations with respect to average generosity of R&D tax incentives. Thus, in the 25 years since the United States initiated an R&D tax incentive, competing economies have more than caught up. A number of states have recently implemented additional R&D tax incentives in an attempt to close this gap, but the result is an incomplete response to the need to provide incentives for corporate R&D investment within the domestic economy.

Problems with the Structure of the R&E Tax Credit

The current US tax credit suffers from a number of problems. First, and perhaps most important, the potential for a significant and lasting effect on company R&D spending is muted by the R&E tax credit's incremental structure. Whereas, a flat credit affects total R&D spending year after year through a permanent price subsidy for all company R&D, the cost-reducing impact of an incremental credit is limited to a calculated increment of total R&D spending. Moreover, that subsidy is generally realized at a declining rate due to base creep, as discussed below. In effect, the price of the eligible incremental R&D will most likely go back up in the years after the credit is first taken.

Second, the extensive rule writing and constant audits of claims for the credit necessary to enforce compliance for such a targeted tax incentive have created a substantial time and cost burden on the Treasury. According to one source, a quarter of the audit resources of the IRS's small and midsize business division are allocated to examining claims for the R&E credit. Consequently, in 2001, the Treasury proposed changing the existing set of rules to broaden coverage of the tax credit and thereby reduce the administrative burden of ensuring compliance, as well as increase the credit's impact (Herman, 2001). In fact, compliance costs for the relatively straightforward Canadian flat tax credit are estimated to be only 0.7 percent of the amount of the credit claimed by Canadian industry (Gunz et al., 1995).

Such problems emphasize the difficulty in managing a targeted credit and imply that tax policy may not be effective in changing the composition of R&D. What should be included in R&D is enough of a challenge, but defining boundaries of particular types of R&D or distinguishing among the phases of the R&D cycle is difficult at best. Thus, in spite of the substantial resources expended by the Treasury for rule writing and audits, it would seem likely that unqualified expenditures are receiving the credit and qualified expenditures are being rejected.

Third, that the R&E tax credit has never been made a permanent part of the tax code (it has been renewed 11 times during its 25-year history) and has been modified several times indicate a lack of understanding and hence consensus on the part of policy makers with respect to the precise roles and expected impacts of different tax incentives on R&D. For example, the credit was originally 25 percent of the increase in R&D spending relative to a base level determined by a formula. The Tax Reform Act of 1986 reduced the credit to 20 percent. Further, the formula used to calculate the credit originally defined the base amount of R&D as a moving average of the previous three years of R&D spending. As R&D spending increases in most years for the typical firm, the resulting 'base creep' reduced the potential value of the credit for firms with expanding R&D investment.

In response, the Omnibus Budget Reconciliation Act of 1989 changed the method for calculating the base amount. The new method used a fixed R&D intensity (R&D/sales), calculated as the average for the 1984–88 period (0.03 for younger companies). This intensity ratio is multiplied by the average sales for the four years preceding the year when the claim for the credit is made to determine the base level. While this method eliminated an explicit R&D base creep, it substituted an indirect one through a sales-driven adjustment to the base level. Firms experiencing sales growth now pay a price in the form of the base creep that was the target of reform. This method can be especially severe for small, fast-growing R&D-intensive firms who are realizing rapidly increasing sales from previously successful innovations. Thus, at least to a degree, the base-creep problem was shifted from one subset of R&D-intensive firms to another. Only if sales do not grow can an incremental increase in R&D receive the maximum subsidy over that project's lifetime, but such a firm would likely not be in business very long and certainly would not produce the cash-flow growth needed to fund successive increases in R&D spending.

Fourth, small firms can be disadvantaged in several additional ways. In new industries like biotechnology, companies can operate at a loss for many years. Sustaining R&D expenditures through long development periods often forces financing options that require these firms to give up major shares of equity. Because the tax credit is not refundable, it provides no support for these firms, thereby contributing to the undesirable financing arrangements.

Moreover, by being less diversified, small firms can experience a substantial jump in R&D investment in a single year. Such instances are common when a major R&D project reaches the development stage, which requires much larger amounts of R&D spending than earlier phases of the R&D cycle. In such situations, a firm may not be able to take full advantage of the tax credit because qualified research expenditures are limited to 200 percent of the calculated base amount of R&D. That is, the increase from which the credit is calculated can never be more than the base amount, so that a 100 percent increase in qualified research expenditures above the calculated base in a particular year is the maximum amount (increment) to which the credit can be applied. A firm with a 200 percent increase above its base amount of R&D would therefore only realize a 10 percent tax credit on the total increase. Therefore, small firms, even when profitable, can be penalized by the current structure of the credit.

Fifth, the amount of the tax credit is partially offset by the requirement to reduce the business expense deduction for qualified research expenditures by the amount of the credit. In effect, this reduces the value of the credit by a company's marginal tax rate. Such an 'adjusted' credit is the true value of the tax incentive, which is considerably lower than the nominal rate.

The R&E Tax Credit's Role in Federal R&D Policy

The rationale for using a tax-based subsidy to stimulate R&D is the belief that this mechanism provides a market-oriented response by leaving the decision of the composition of a company's R&D portfolio up to corporate decision makers. However, if the intent of the credit has been to shift industry R&D portfolios toward longer-term, higher-risk research, any such effect, if it exists at all, has been quite weak. In fact, Figure 10.3 indicates that the opposite is occurring. Development expenditures, which focus on shorter-term objectives, have dominated the growth of industry R&D over

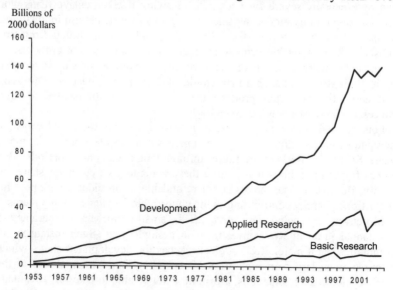

Source: NSF, *National Patterns of R&D Resources.*

Figure 10.3 Industry-Funded R&D by Major Phase, 1953–2004

the past three decades. Even though the R&E tax credit contains a provision for university-funded research, the increasing strategic focus on applied R&D has resulted in industry funding only a small fraction of academic research (approximately 5 percent). Thus, this academic research credit has had virtually no impact. IRS data for 2003 show that while industry claimed $92.9 billion as R&D expenditures qualifying for the regular credit, only $0.3 billion in basic research funded at academic institutions was claimed as qualifying under the special credit.[3]

One possibility is that the increase in development expenditures has been due, in part at least, to the existence of the credit. That is, instead of shifting the composition of R&D, the result may have been the stimulation of more of the type of R&D that industry was already doing. Sufficiently strong flat tax incentives can have such an effect, as previously indicated by data from other countries. However, interviews with industry R&D managers for an OTA study indicated little impact by the credit on any type of decision making. OTA concluded that the US R&E tax credit 'represents more of a financial tool than a technology [investment] tool' (Office of Technology Assessment, 1995). As a result, the credit is of primary interest to corporations' tax accountants and appears to have relatively little effect on R&D resource allocation. This finding was reinforced by an Industrial Research Institute's 1996 R&D spending survey, in which 55 percent of responding companies indicated that the credit was 'not at all' influential in establishing the even level of their companies' R&D investment.

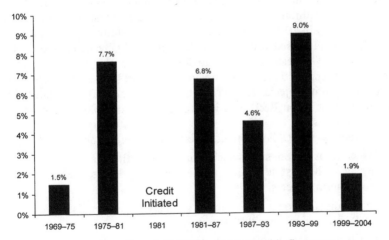

Source: National Science Board, 2006. The last interval is five years.

Figure 10.4 Average Annual Growth in Industry-Funded R&D Before and After Initiation of the R&E Tax Credit

That the R&E tax credit has had little measurable effect at the national economy level is also apparent when industry R&D spending is divided into six-year intervals, two intervals before and three after the implementation of the credit in 1981. Using such intervals, Figure 10.4 shows that not only did the credit apparently have no discernable leverage on industry R&D but the reverse trend seems to have occurred. The 1969–75 period had a relatively low average annual growth rate, while the next interval that immediately preceded the initiation of the tax credit had a much higher average annual rate of increase. Then, for the six-year period immediately following the credit's implementation, the average growth rate dropped slightly and then declined more substantially in the next interval before finally showing above-average growth in the information technology investment binge of the last half of the 1990s. In spite of the existence of the credit, the growth rate for industry-funded R&D then dropped precipitously in the first half of this decade.

In the context of the uncertainties with respect to the R&E tax credit's role and impact, an interesting trend is the growth in the credit relative to federal non-defense R&D funding, which is the major alternative method of supporting industry R&D. The estimated adjusted tax expenditure for the credit has increased relative to non-defense R&D spending from 1.4 percent of this spending in 1981 to 10.0 percent in 2001. If intramural R&D were removed from total non-defense spending, the percentages would be higher.

Given the strategic nature of R&D, company investment decisions are made largely on the perceived need for new products, processes and services to meet competition and achieve growth in market share. However, as implied in Figure 10.3, the increased foreign competition over the past three decades has increased investment risk, particularly by compressing R&D cycle times. The result has been to force US industry to focus more on shorter-term applied R&D. This compositional shift has resulted in less risky but lower-profit projects. The current tax credit is not large enough to have much effect at all on R&D, and it is certainly not capable of reversing this compositional shift.

In summary, the R&E tax credit suffers from several problems:

1. The credit is incremental, which limits the benefit for a new R&D project largely to its first few years and at declining levels, thereby favoring shorter-term projects.

2. The credit is targeted, which places uniquely large administrative costs on the Treasury to manage this tax expenditure.

3. The formula for calculating the credit is complex and, more important, reduces its value to many firms.

4. The credit's net effect is too small to achieve a policy goal of significantly increasing even the amount of industry R&D.

Reforming the Tax Credit

The previous assessment leads to the policy conclusion that the current tax credit is neither correctly structured nor large enough to measurably affect

R&D investment. To remedy the problem, the guiding principle should be that a tax incentive for R&D is best applied to broader market failures, that is, when (i) aggregate R&D of the type already being conducted is deemed inadequate, and (ii) boundary conditions can be easily defined and enforced so that leakages to non-targeted investments are minimized, thereby avoiding expensive government management efforts.

A preferred approach would be to substitute a flat tax credit or a super deduction, which would apply to all legitimate R&D. Such a mechanism would have a continuous and larger cost-reducing impact on R&D and would be much less burdensome to administer. Most important, such a tax incentive would efficiently increase all applied R&D while leaving targeted long-term, high-risk R&D to direct funding programs, which are better suited for supporting early-phase technology research.

The budgetary cost of a flat tax with significant impact would likely be greater than the current incremental credit. However, if analysis shows that the rate of return is higher from R&D than from alternative investments (as the discussion in Chapter 3 clearly indicates), then the policy conclusion is that not enough investment funds are flowing into R&D and incentives (in the most efficient form) are required.

The Bottom Line

To have a significant impact, a tax incentive should be focused on stimulating the amount of industry-funded R&D, as opposed to affecting the composition of spending. Thus, the policy target should be the vast majority of industrial R&D, which is efficiently conducted by individual firms. The main advantages of tax policy for this type of R&D are its neutrality with respect to project selection and the low policy management costs.

However, the advantages of tax policy quickly degrade when attempts are made to target it at early phases of the R&D cycle or at R&D aimed at technology elements with infrastructure character. Underinvestment problems that occur at specific phases of R&D or for infratechnologies should be handled with direct government funding.

Because, as currently structured, the R&E tax credit probably has had at most a minor and transitory effect on industry R&D spending, consideration should be given to a flat tax credit at a level sufficient to significantly lower the cost of all R&D year over year. Most countries realize that tax policy is most effective at stimulating more of the same type of investment that industry is already pursuing and structure their tax incentives accordingly.

DIRECT FUNDING

The policy rationales for direct funding vary over the R&D cycle. In the initial phase of this cycle, industry is not and will not be a significant source of funds for basic research because of the pure public-good character of scientific knowledge. Thus, government is the dominant supporter, conducting modest proportion of this research itself and funding universities to do the rest.

For generic technology research, the issue is more complicated. NSF data show that universities now conduct substantial applied research ($9.2 billion in 2004). While this amounts to a modest 14 percent of the national total, universities focus on the longer-term, higher-risk portion of applied research. Thus, they account for a larger share of new disruptive generic technologies. However, US industry funded only 5.0 percent of academic research in 2004, a quarter of which was for applied research (approximately $0.5 billion or 6.0 percent of university-performed applied research). Thus, most of this critical early-phase technology research at universities is also funded by the federal government (National Science Board, 2006a).

A frequently cited reason for small and declining industry-funded applied research at US universities is the inability to agree on acceptable IP arrangements. This problem has been blamed on Bayh–Dole, which conveys virtually all IP to universities from federally-funded research, thereby providing a standard with which industry cannot compete.

Some indications exist that this situation partially explains industry's rapidly growing investment in long-term, high-risk research in other countries. For example, a Booz Allen study states that companies are shifting disproportionate amounts of R&D to China and India. These two countries are projected to account for 77 percent of all newly established R&D sites by US firms between 2005 and 2008, which clearly reflects more than just a reaction to the rapid growth of Asian markets.

In Europe, where the interactions between universities and industry have been criticized in the past, industry funding of academic research has been increasing in recent years, reaching 6.8 percent of the total in 2001. In several European countries (for example, Germany and Belgium), industry funds over 12 percent of total academic research. In contrast, US industry's small share of such funding has declined from 7.4 percent in 1998 to the current 5.0 percent.

Theoretically, an attractive feature of direct funding is that government support for research with public-good characteristics in partnership with industry and universities allows the allocation of funds to different technologies at appropriate points in these technologies' life cycles, but only at those points. That is, cycle phasing of research incentives based on the evolutionary pattern of a particular emerging technology is a clear advantage of the direct funding mechanism – if managed correctly.

In contrast, a tax incentive targeted at a specific phase of the R&D cycle will require substantial government management expense to audit corporate tax returns for compliance with rules defining qualified expenditures. The alternative is to accept substantial leakage of tax expenditures to unintended types of R&D. Equally important, an accurately targeted tax incentive is difficult to turn on and off as the evolution of market failures requires over a technology's life cycle.

However, the nature of interactions between public and private funding of R&D has been researched for several decades without resolution (David et al., 2000). Some research shows a positive (complementary) relationship, while some studies find a negative (substitution or 'crowding-out') relationship for this interaction. Such contradictory findings are explained in part by the unit of analysis used (the firm, the industry or the national economy) or by the phase of the R&D cycle examined (basic, generic, applied or development). In general, the models are poorly worked out (Tassey, 2005b).

A Case Study in Policy Malfunction: The Advanced Technology Program

Into a policy void, incorrect decisions will rush. The history of the ATP is an example of the consequences of inadequate policy analysis – by both opponents and proponents of the program.

The ATP was created in 1988 to provide critical and systematic funding to emerging technologies in support of economic growth. This mission is identical to the one that DARPA has supplied for more than three decades in support of military technology needs.[4] Without the benefit of either adequate theoretical or empirical analysis, ATP's budget experienced a roller-coaster pattern. When first conceived, it was envisioned as eventually a $1-billion-per-year program. In fact, the program grew rapidly from initial funding in 1990 of $10 million to a 1995 budget of $431 million. However, because ATP was focused on supporting economic growth rather than a specific social mission, such as national defense or health care, the program has been the focus of intense, interminable debate. The year 1995 turned out to be the peak for its budget. From that time forward, funding was successively reduced until a decade later in 2005 it had shrunk to $142 million.[5] The FY 2006 budget of $80 million only allowed funding of commitments from previous years.

The rationalization for ATP, as is the case for most policy instruments, was based on only general perceptions of the existence of a market failure – in this case, systematic underinvestment in a specific phase of the R&D cycle. Opponents relentlessly invoked the black-box model and argued against the need for the program, labeling it as 'corporate welfare'. This term is used rather loosely, but basically it means providing financial incentives to private companies for expenditures that they would make anyway in their own interest. In effect, the adherents to the black-box model argued that the results of early-phase technology research are private goods and hence offer sufficient private rates of return to bring forth desirable levels of industry funding.

The contradiction between rationalizations for supporting mission-oriented research ('DARPA's only charter is radical innovation'[6]) and rejection of a similar mission for ATP based on the corporate welfare argument results from the black-box model's denial of the quasi-public-good nature of generic technology research. Proponents of research in support of a social mission might argue that the public-good target is a reason for underinvestment, whereas the objective of economic growth provides sufficient market-based incentives for the required investment. But, if this were the case, the biotechnology industry would never be expected to make a profit in delivering the public good, health care. In fact, all viable industries, whether final consumption at the end of the relevant supply chain is a public or private good, make a profit.

Government R&D funding policies for public and private goods diverge only at the applied R&D phase when the desired innovations in support of the public good cannot be delivered through the normal market mechanism or when adequate spin-off markets do not exist. Such cases (military-specific hardware, for example) require development support farther forward in the R&D cycle and often some kind of a procurement policy that basically guarantees a sufficiently large market.

Generic technologies, by virtue of their economies of scope seldom have this characteristic of limited market applications. Proof is provided by the many commercial applications resulting from DARPA-funded research. Generic biotechnologies, which were supported to increase the quality of health care, are finding important applications in many other areas (chemical processing, agriculture, computing and so on). And, of course, the target markets are quite lucrative for successful new drugs.

In the face of this misconception of the nature of technology-based economic growth, supporters of the ATP provided inadequate theoretical and empirical analyses to rationalize the alleged market failures that the program was created to help remove. Only a small number of ATP-sponsored studies can be said to have substantively addressed the underinvestment phenomena of early-phase, proof-of-concept research (Jaffe, 1998; Branscomb and Auerswald, 2002).

In spite of a number of allegations to the contrary, the ATP was not a threat to 'crowd out' private venture capital (VC) because the VC market has never been a major source of funds for proof-of-concept research and venture capitalists certainly have no incentive or ability to identify and manage such research (Branscomb and Auerswald, 2002; also Figure 5.8). Nor can the VC industry collectively allocate funds to provide a diversified portfolio of generic technologies that a large economy like the United States needs to have under development at all times. Only when proofs of concept are available (that is, the risk spike is largely overcome) does private venture capital begin to flow into a specific emerging technology. Consequently, at any point in time, venture capital tends to be skewed toward a few hot technologies for which at least some portion of the generic technology is already available.

The ATP did sponsor a variety of impact assessments of ongoing and completed projects. In fact, it was undoubtedly evaluated more intensively than any other R&D funding program. In spite of this effort, its detractors simply responded that the same rates of return would have been forthcoming from private-sector investment, in effect, arguing that an unneeded subsidy to corporate America was being offered; that is, the risk spike does not exist. For the most part, ATP never provided an adequate theoretical or empirical rejoinder to these proponents of the black-box model.

In this regard, it is notable that the total cost of ATP over its 16-year history was $2.5 billion. During that time, industry has spent $1.85 trillion on R&D. If this is corporate welfare, it has been a poor effort. In fact, with the exception of several years in the mid-1990s, the level of funding was way too small to have much effect, even on the lower-cost generic technology research phase.

Still, any amount of funding is not justified if it does not address a systematic market failure. The rationale for funding generic technology research in mission agencies is based on the argument that social goals other than economic growth, such as health care, do not respond sufficiently to the profit motive and, therefore, the entire R&D cycle plus eventual deployment will experience inadequate private-sector investment.

As indicated above, pharmaceutical companies make billions of dollars developing new drug therapies, which support a 'health-care' objective, so the black-box model would imply that no government funding for biotechnology research is needed. Nevertheless, the NIH funds not only basic research but also considerable early-phase technology research. In some instances, more than one market failure is a work (for example, AIDS vaccines where third-world societies cannot afford to pay). In these cases, all phases of the R&D cycle, including the final development phase (clinical trials), are supported.

Moreover, many generic technology research programs at mission-oriented agencies in effect treat this phase of the R&D cycle as a pure public good by funding all of the research costs. In contrast, ATP projects were cost shared to varying degrees in recognition of the quasi-public-good nature of generic technologies that provide platforms for innovation in most industrial technologies. Large companies or industry consortia were required to cost share (on average about one-half of the total cost of a project). This approach forces technical and market risk assessments to be made by industry and thereby invokes market discipline in proposing and managing projects targeted at overcoming the risk spike. The government's share subsidizes the high level of such risks as well as the large discounting associated with potential investments in radically new technologies that may pay off only relatively far into the future.

Still, opponents of the ATP have argued that, whatever the program rationale, large firms should not receive government funding because they have a lot of retained earnings and therefore do not need any external help to finance their R&D. Ignored in such a position is the fact that large firms need a large portfolio of applied R&D projects for diversification purposes, so the same short-term focus applies to them as to small firms.

A position against government-industry cost sharing of generic technology research requires invoking the black-box model, which assumes that technology is a homogeneous entity; that is, a single risk–reward factor exists that drives the investment decision. Under this point of view, no matter how large the black box (that is, how capital intensive is the R&D required to develop it), or how high the risk, or how different from a firm's current market focus is the potential scope of market applications, or how long in the future is the expected commercialization date, it is simply asserted that large companies somehow have the ability and the incentive to fund sufficient long-term, high-risk research to meet the future needs of a large, diversified economy.

Defensible arguments can be made for large firms funding at least some breakthrough technology research because (i) large firms can often capture some portion of the economies of scope that characterize many radically new technologies; that is, their production and marketing capabilities are sufficiently broad to pursue at least several of the potential markets for a new technology; (ii) by virtue of their size, large firms can spread risk across a larger number of cash flows; that is, they can 'afford' to allocate some funds to high-payoff, high-risk projects in a portfolio management sense; and (iii) funding generic technology research in a large company can be rationalized even if knowledge spillovers at this early phase of the R&D cycle are substantial. With respect to this last factor, some spillovers accrue to small firms that are suppliers to the large firm. These small firms absorb the portions of the generic technology needed for their niche markets, which enhances their ability to supply the large firm with components and subsystems.

Single large companies first *demonstrated* the transistor, the integrated circuit, the laser, the graphical user interface and so on, but all of these breakthroughs have subsequently been drawn upon in a large number of markets (both components and systems) by many firms of all sizes to the substantial advantage of the US economy. However, in addition to the fact that today large companies increasingly do not have the market dominance necessary to rationalize these investments, this pattern of single-firm generic technology research was slow and uneven. Today, speed and efficiency of both R&D and the subsequent technology transfer within an entire supply chain are essential, if a significant share of the supply chain's value added is to be retained within the domestic economy. Economies around the world are responding to this imperative by creating regional technology clusters of universities, government research institutes and high-tech firms, with research costs shared by government and private companies.

In arguing against government funding of long-term, high-risk research for large firms, opponents are implying that large firms have the same scope of interest and levels of resources as a national government and hence apply the same low discount rate to prospective technology research investments. Because large firms can capture portions of the rate of return (RoR) on many breakthrough technologies, cost sharing the generic technology research makes sense. This is the ATP approach.

The critical differences between a traditional industry-only funding model and a cost-shared government–industry model are embodied in the ability of the government role to: (i) remove information asymmetries and thereby coordinate roadmaps for emerging technologies; (ii) promote balanced funding across all elements of the generic technology; (iii) through a lower discount rate, have the capacity to provide sustained funding for many years, if necessary; and (iv) promote greater research efficiency and subsequent knowledge transfer to potential innovators through GUIR partnerships.

In an attempt to respond to the perceived difference between the ability of large and small firms to bear the risk of a single research project (assuming that one addresses the vagueness of where to draw the line between large and small), ATP financed all direct research costs for small firms (these firms paid only indirect costs). However, if such cost-sharing mechanisms for single firms are still unacceptable, the government program could be limited to funding only consortia, as does the European Framework Program (Europe's counterpart to ATP). Consortia, especially as part of the technology cluster growth model, have the advantages of both greater research efficiency and more-rapid diffusion of the technical knowledge produced to the participating companies and to other companies, as well.

The major policy point is that the conditions warranting single-firm funding and those requiring GUIR arrangements have not been fully analyzed. However, while single-firm funding might be rationalized for the reasons stated, the dominant approach is increasingly likely to be the funding of generic technology research within clusters of universities and firms. In retrospect, ATP should have been constrained to fund multiple-firm projects and especially consortia involving universities, if for no other reason than the policy arena is not sophisticated enough to distinguish between conditions justifying single- and multiple-firm funding rationales.[7]

One additional problem with some government funding proposals is the requirement for some form of recoupment – a requirement that the recipient of government research funds pay back to the government a share of profits from any successful commercialization resulting from the subsidized research. Recoupment provisions imply that commercialization is expected to result directly from removal of the barrier requiring the subsidy. The implication is that the problem is a failure in the VC market.

However, proofs of concept and spillovers to multiple firms resulting from early-phase technology research are not going to directly generate sales and profits. Only after additional private investment will commercialization and profits be realized. The excessive time discounting, technical risk, and spillovers associated with generic technology research rationalize government subsidies. Moreover, the frequent substantial spillovers benefit firms with no government assistance and hence recoupment obligation. Thus, although all firms absorbing the generic technology will have to make substantial applied R&D investment and assume equal commercialization risk, the subsidized firm will have to pay the recoupment royalty from successful innovation while imitators will not.

In policy terms, the objective of overcoming the risk spike and thereby facilitating large amounts of privately funded applied R&D would be inhibited by a recoupment policy. Why provide a subsidy to induce high-risk research by increasing the expected RoR and then turn around and lower that expected RoR by requiring a royalty on any eventual profits? For that matter, as a practical consideration, the fact that intermediate private investments are necessary to apply a generic technology in a commercial sense means that constructing an efficient mechanism for attributing eventual profits to the government subsidy would be difficult at best and lead to frequent confrontations and hence policy management costs.

The Policy Response to Inadequate Private Investment in Generic Technology Research

The cost of early-phase technology research is relatively small compared to what is invested in subsequent applied research and especially in development. However, such early-phase investment is increasingly shunned by industry in the face of the shorter technology life cycles and hence higher risk spikes caused by growing global competition. Nevertheless, limited theoretical work and almost no relevant time-series data have made this argument difficult to support.

Conceptually, the importance of overcoming the risk spike is demonstrated in Figure 10.5. Although emerging technologies have superior *potential* performance relative to cost, they initially suffer from lower performance/price ratios (point *B*) relative to the current mature technology (point *A*). As described in Chapter 5, this situation occurs because (i) new technologies often have multiple components that do not evolve at the same pace, (ii) functionally inadequate interfaces exist for these components; that is, system productivity is compromised, (iii) adequate technical infrastructure support is not available, and (iv) low initial market volume and suboptimal production processes keep prices high, thereby limiting realization of economies of scale and scope. All of these factors contribute to degraded initial performance.

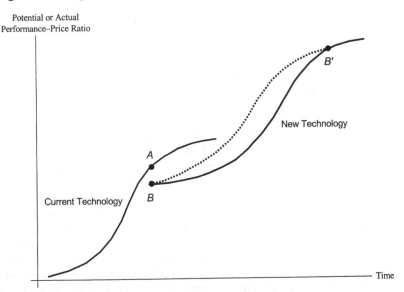

Figure 10.5 Life-Cycle Market Failure: Generic Technology

The expectation of such conditions occurring results in longer predicted times to significant market penetration for the new technology and hence lower net present value estimates for proposed R&D investments. Yet, competitive pressures frequently lead to attempts at innovation before the generic technology is mature. As the examples from biotechnology in Chapter 4 indicate, the less adequate the generic technology, the less efficient the subsequent applied R&D and, therefore, the lower the rates of innovation.

Increased funding for generic technology research accelerates the reduction of the risk spike by developing proofs of concept for emerging technologies faster and more completely. This risk reduction leads to a more rapid decline in the initial performance/price gap with the mature technology. The result is a more-efficient R&D cycle and a more-rapid market penetration enabled by higher performance/price ratios between points B and B', as indicated by the dashed line in Figure 10.5. Still, even with persistent government funding, reduction in the risk spike can take years.

The Policy Response to Inadequate Private Investment in Infratechnology Research

Economies have always needed a variety of techniques, methods, data and information to perform product creation, to control manufacturing processes and to execute market transactions in an efficient manner. The advent of the factory system in the 19th century required the standardization of parts so that they could be produced in mass production modes in different locations and then assembled by yet another entity into the final product. The higher-order product (the system) could then also be more easily repaired when one of its components malfunctioned.

Today, the increasing complexity of technology means that virtually all economic activity depends on the capability to measure, control and interconnect systems of individual technologies. As described in Chapter 8, varied systems technologies such as cell-phone networks, electric power grids, health-care information systems and stock markets dominate modern economies. Even a process such as R&D, once correctly characterized as a group of people working together in a single location without much external dependence, now requires sophisticated information network support. The term 'bioinformatics' has been coined because of the rapidly growing need by biotechnology research for access to technical infrastructure such as critically evaluated scientific and engineering databases and computer-based simulation models. Such tools enable the efficient conduct of research and then the seamless movement of experimental data to other locations in research networks. The need to produce, qualify and interpret data and then to communicate with research partners through interoperable networks demands sophisticated infratechnologies and associated standards.

The increasing complexity of individual devices that make up modern technology systems requires ever more sophisticated measurement, testing and calibration infrastructures. For example, NIST estimates that 3.5 million devices are calibrated annually in the US economy in order to maximize their accuracy and precision. Scientists are designing new products from the atom up, which requires incredibly sophisticated measurement and testing techniques.

As discussed in Chapter 4, the economic impact of infratechnologies across the R&D, production and commercialization stages of technology-based economic activity is substantial. While additional generic technology research makes the S-shaped growth curve steeper with the result that eventual commercialization is more rapid, the ubiquitous impacts of infratechnologies raise efficiency over the entire life cycle, as indicated by the shift upward of the entire 'New Technology' growth curve in Figure 10.6. Thus, the collective efficiency gain from multiple infratechnologies over a technology's life cycle, represented at any one point in time by an upward shift such as that from C to C', accelerates market penetration of a new technology and more quickly delivers its benefits to society.

For such gains to be realized the infratechnologies must be developed, embodied in standards and delivered to industry. Industry must then assimilate these non-product standards into operations and demonstrate compliance. However, the high rates of return found by the NIST economic

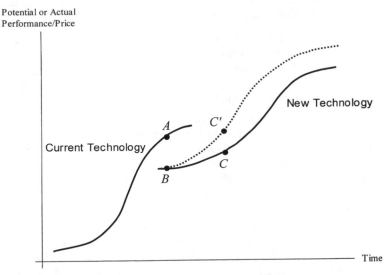

Figure 10.6 Life-Cycle Market Failure: Infratechnology

impact studies imply an underfunding of this element of industrial technology. In fact, the same general underinvestment problem arises for infratechnologies as occurs with generic technologies. In fact, the public-good content of infratechnologies at least equals that of generic technologies. Yet, because infratechnologies are also quasi-public goods, STID policy analysis will have a difficult time determining optimal levels of government support.

Spillovers of infratechnologies have good and bad aspects (good for the entire industry, bad for a company making an investment in them). In fact, spillovers of infratechnologies may be a more serious market failure than is the case for generic technologies. The reason is that many infratechnologies must be commonly used (that is, as standards) to have maximum economic impact. As a result, spillovers must be uniform and complete within an industry or group of industries. Further, even if individual firms invest in developing some portion of an infratechnology, it is typically not in those firms' interest to hold on to the intellectual property because their customers benefit from a resulting standard and demand its availability to all suppliers. For this reason, much infratechnology research is funded by government and, in many cases, government also conducts the research due to the existence of sizable economies of scope (Tassey, 2000, 2005a).

More broadly, technologically complex infrastructures are not receiving adequate levels of resources due to a poor understanding of their roles in long-term economic growth and the quasi-public-good character of the component infratechnologies. A number of factors have been discussed in previous chapters that contribute to this situation:

1. *Segmented and ubiquitous nature.* Any one infrastructure element frequently has modest economic impact, but a high-tech industry depends on hundreds of such elements, so the collective economic benefit is substantial. This fact is largely unrecognized and undocumented, except for the economic studies done by NIST.

2. *Invisibility.* The economic infrastructure (roads, bridges, canals, telephone networks) that enabled the Industrial Revolution was physical and large and hence highly visible, thereby facilitating creation of support for optimal investment levels. However, most technical infrastructure underlying today's high-tech industries is non-physical and therefore largely invisible. Measurement and test protocols, scientific and engineering databases, interface specifications, quality assurance techniques and so on, are often delivered through integrated systems of hardware and software and, as methods or procedures, are much more difficult to visualize and understand. Only when such technical infrastructure is aggregated into one of the few large and ubiquitous technology-based economic infrastructures, such as the Internet, is direct contact by consumers sufficient to provide the visibility needed to receive adequate policy attention.

3. *Reliance on private markets.* More than its competitors, the US economy relies on private institutions to provide both the technical infrastructure and the standards that facilitate its deployment. These institutions, such as standards development organizations, consortia and various associations, are typically funded at meager levels. They are also staffed by industry personnel who rotate to these organizations for brief periods of time from their home companies, causing continuity, institutional memory and other problems that reduce the effectiveness of such organizations.

4. *Management.* The number and variety of infratechnologies needed to support each stage of technology-based economic activity present a severe portfolio management problem. Thus, even if public- and private-sector role issues were resolved, setting priorities, conducting research in a timely manner, and deploying the resulting technical information through an efficient standards process and other dissemination mechanisms present extremely difficult challenges.

5. *Quasi-public-good character.* Although some of the needed infrastructure

is provided by industry, its public-good content results in free-riding problems and consequently leads to substantial underinvestment. This barrier is accentuated in the US economy because of persistent ideological disputes over public versus private roles.

In summary, the quasi-public-good content and the relative invisibility of the knowledge-based infrastructure that increasingly dominates modern economies combine to make the rationales for government support difficult to describe and convey to policy makers. ATP's economic rationale has been attacked consistently and its budget drastically reduced. NIST's budget for infratechnology research has been constrained over several decades, resulting in large part from the difficulties in convincing the policy arena that such infrastructure is essential to the advancement and utilization of industrial technology. Because infratechnologies leverage industry's investments in innovation and subsequent technology diffusion and market penetration, investment should grow at approximately the same rate as industry R&D spending, which has not been the case.

STRUCTURING STID POLICIES

Presidential Science Adviser, John Marburger, assesses the state of US policy by the following: 'What's being done to determine the effectiveness of science policy? Not very much. Is what is being done now inadequate? Yes, it is inadequate, and it's inadequate because it doesn't really exist' (Jacobson, 2005). This assessment resonates with the critique of current policy analysis capability in previous chapters. Much of the trend data and certainly the conceptual models presented are not incorporated in current policy analysis because the analytical capability 'doesn't really exist.'

The Emerging Technology Research Portfolio

The analysis in earlier chapters tells us that the indirect spin-off model for government R&D funding once worked well, but that in the converging global economy several factors make this approach increasingly inadequate. Further, while the DoD is still a major supporter of emerging technologies, it is increasingly constrained to fund a more focused set of applied R&D programs and is depending more on advancements in the private economy to supply major elements of new military technologies. As a result, policy makers should now understand that the economy needs a broader and growth-oriented portfolio of emerging technologies to support a large and diversified economy, as well as military and other social needs. Moreover, with greater dependency on technology for economic growth, it matters greatly how many and in what time frame new technologies emerge. Thus, the risk spikes associated with proofs of concept must be overcome in a timely manner relative to global competition, and diverse technical and innovation infrastructures must be upgraded and better integrated with private-sector investment.

More specifically, if the black-box model can be discarded once and for all, issues of government funding of early-phase generic technology research and infratechnology research can be resolved and updated policies implemented. Adoption of multi-element technology growth models will enable getting research done in a timely fashion and ensure that research results are diffused widely to the domestic firms that drive private-sector innovation. Doing so requires accepting the following five principles:

1. The 'corporate welfare' argument can be rejected because the risk spike lowers the private risk-adjusted RoR below the corporate hurdle rate, resulting in underinvestment in generic technologies.

2. The 'picking winners and losers' argument can be rejected because generic technologies are only proofs of concept, which means that many specific technologies can be developed by industry by drawing upon a single generic technology. Thus, the government role is to help industry acquire the fundamental technical knowledge that enables the applied R&D and the subsequent market decisions that ultimately determine the domestic industry's success or failure.

3. The fact that generic technology is a quasi-public good, rather than a pure public good as is scientific knowledge, means that a limited set of firms will ultimately benefit from any one generic technology. The reason is that these firms can capture a share of the resulting intellectual property and hence the ultimate economic benefits. Thus, maximization of economic growth potential within the domestic economy requires mechanisms that not only conduct the research efficiently but disseminate the research results quickly.

4. Modern R&D cycles are complex and lengthy, requiring varied technical methods, data and protocols. The underlying infratechnologies have a strong public-good character and therefore require both more government participation in joint planning and direct support of the required research.

5. The above principles collectively imply the need for more sophisticated and efficient research processes, in particular GUIR networks. Funding research consortia pools risk and complementary research assets. Assurance that all complementary research assets are available and efficiently integrated is increasingly critical, as emerging technologies are all multidisciplinary. The collaboration approach also provides a built-in technical knowledge diffusion mechanism by virtue of the fact that multiple companies participate directly in the research. Such consortia are increasingly embedded in broader clusters that drive regional economic growth through even broader technology-diffusion mechanisms. In this

growth model, multiple stakeholder management of the consortium's research portfolio also increases the potential breadth of dissemination, including to firms outside the consortium such as innovative startups.

These principles were reflected in an ATP project with the US disk-drive industry. This industry is a classic example of the hollowing out of value added occurring in many domestic industries due to a growing capacity by foreign governments to establish research networks in their own economies and then provide subsequent manufacturing incentives. In 1992, ATP contributed $5.5 million to the National Storage Industry Consortium (NSIC), a group of US disk-drive manufacturers, for research to create new generic technologies. ATP's cost sharing enabled the industry to collectively overcome the risk spike and undertake the early-phase research, funded largely at universities. The result was a new generic head technology called giant magnetoresistance (GMR), which subsequently led to a series of innovations by individual companies in small disk drives. These new drives have formed the basis for an explosion of small consumer electronic devices that can hold 20 gigabytes and more of music, TV shows, movies and photographs. Small disk drives also enabled the creation of other multibillion dollar consumer electronic products, such as iPod, Tivo and X-Box.[8]

However, no matter how successful individually, research such as the NSIC-ATP project must be assessed as part of a dynamic portfolio that supports the generic technology base of an industry over time. In the above example, the NSIC-ATP project enabled maintenance of a US leadership position in the disk-drive industry during the 1990s. Yet, global convergence continues to hollow out US market shares in computer components because control of high-tech manufacturing is often followed by control of design and increasing amounts of this manufacturing are offshore.

Currently, US firms still lead in supplying disk drives for enterprise computers and PCs because US computer firms still dominate these markets. However, US industry's presence in small disk drives for notebook computers and consumer electronics is almost non-existent as first production and then R&D became controlled largely by Asian companies. Furthermore, with respect to the elements of disk-drive technology itself, only one independent US company (Komag, with 29 percent of the market in 2005) still exists and no independent US head suppliers remain (McCormack, 2005b). Thus, over time, the decoupling point has moved backward in the supply chain and offshore.

A major policy point is that while individual breakthrough research strategies can increase the potential portion of value added accruing to a domestic industry, a broader supply-chain strategy is required to enable co-location synergies among tiers in a domestic supply chain and thereby to secure much larger shares of valued added for the domestic economy. Supply-chain synergies shorten lead times and increase general exchanges of knowledge, thereby conferring competitive advantage on domestic firms in several related industries.

Further, the above example of collaborative disk-drive research cannot be an isolated and limited-duration effort for the particular component technology in question. Future technology life cycles in the magnetic-disk-drive industry will be dependent on nanoscience, which will enable creation of higher-capacity and lower-cost storage technologies. To this end, ATP and the US disk-drive industry collaborated on a breakthrough recording technology called 'heat-assisted magnetic recording'. The same approach as in the first project was used to cost share the research with several universities and small firms with complementary technical skills.

In this last example, the research is actually aimed at two life cycles beyond the previous collaborative research project. In between is the current emerging technology, 'perpendicular recording', which arranges magnetic charges (the ones and zeros of the digital world) on end and which is about to replace the current technology's approach of placing them flat on the disk's surface. Perpendicular technology greatly increases storage density. However, when eventually developed, heat-assisted magnetic recording offers even greater densities by heating the precise spot on the memory medium where data bits are being recorded.

As described in Chapter 8, the process of new technology life cycles based on new generic technologies that drive innovation is relentless. Management of generic technology research and the transitions between cycles are critical to long-term competitive success. Unfortunately, the ATP is too small to support the portfolios of such programs within and certainly across the multiple high-tech industries required to provide the number and scope of generic technologies needed for future economic growth. Thus, the competitiveness of the US economy is constrained to depend on a skewed portfolio resulting from dominance of the federal R&D budget by a few large-mission S&T agencies.

The University Fix

The importance of university research is evidenced by NSF data, which show that academic R&D doubled between 1994 and 2004 from $21.6 billion to $42.4 billion. This growth rate is significantly above the growth rate for national R&D as a whole, which increased 84 percent over the same period. The university role is also broader than many realize. In particular, applied research accounted for approximately 22 percent of academic research in 2004, which indicates a significant role for universities in advancing the early phases of new technology development. The latter focus is even more significant because academic research tends to be more disruptive in character than is the case for similarly classified research performed by industry.

Inspired by Bayh–Dole, which allows universities to own the intellectual property resulting from government-sponsored research, the amount of research conducted beyond basic science is of increasing importance to university officials. An annual survey by the Association of University Technology Managers (AUTM) found that 15,573 invention disclosures were made in the fiscal year 2002 by 221 universities and 7,741 new US patent applications were filed. Some 3,673 patents were awarded, which brought the total number of university patents issued since 1993 to 28,093.[9]

Universities not only develop human S&E capital and conduct breakthrough research, but they also provide the increasingly important role of a conduit for diffusion of the resulting technical knowledge to industry. As new technology is increasingly science based, the efficiency of the link between science and technology provided by university professors' direct interactions with companies enhances the productivity of R&D. These person-to-person interactions are recognized as the most efficient means of transferring the tacit knowledge, which characterizes much of modern generic technology, to industry so that innovation can occur.

However, an important policy issue is the fact that, while universities have become an increasingly critical performer in a national *technology* research network, they cannot provide the necessary management for the advancement of new technology platforms. Individual universities receive research grants for specific areas of research that contribute to the evolution of a platform. Thus, no one university has the perspective or the incentive to design and manage the broader research portfolio as does a government program or a government-promoted management structure consisting of all stakeholders.

A second issue with respect to reliance on universities as a primary and uncoordinated source of breakthrough research is the efficiency of intellectual property transfer to the private sector. Codified technical knowledge is transferred to industry through licenses, which AUTM data show totaled 4,673 (including options) in 2002. Some 28,086 licenses were active in this year. Universities reported receiving royalties on product sales from 22.4 percent of these active licenses.

However, while the incentive of intellectual property rights has succeeded in focusing university officials on early-phase technology development, licensing of the resulting patents raises some concern with respect to desired wide and rapid diffusion of intellectual property. In particular, the issuance of an exclusive license can inhibit the diffusion of breakthrough technologies compared with alternative research mechanisms, such as GUIR research consortia where multiple participants all have access to the intellectual property produced. In this regard, AUTM data show that of 4,594 licenses and options issued in 2002 that were characterized by survey respondents as to type of exclusivity, 46.5 percent were exclusive and 53.5 percent were non-exclusive.

Exclusive licenses frequently lead to disputes. For example, a University of Wisconsin foundation holds a key patent on stem-cell research. An exclusive license was originally assigned to a biotech firm, Geron Corp., but the company subsequently relinquished a portion of the coverage of the patent with respect to certain applications under legal pressure. This pressure came largely from California, which has launched a $300 million, 10-year stem-cell research program (Regalado and Hamilton, 2006).

Even non-exclusive licenses from individual universities can be inhibiting to innovation. Several biotechnology firms have claimed that the licensing fees demanded by the University of Wisconsin are too high, given the risk, commitment of private R&D funds, and time required for achieving commercialized products. Although 12 companies have licensed the patent, at least one firm, Invitrogen Corp., decided to locate its stem-cell research in Asia to avoid the required royalties (the patent was only filed in the United States).

The policy implication is that entities must be established that manage emerging technology research portfolios across universities or technology clusters, typically consisting of a university and several companies, not only to attain research efficiency but also to ensure wide use of the resulting generic technologies. Such models need to be carefully constructed. The California research program should result in multiple companies developing stem-cell therapies. However, this program includes a form of recoupment (subsidized companies must pay a 25 percent royalty on realized income). Such an arrangement, as discussed above, creates a different set of problems for technology transfer policies.

In general, industry has shown increasing reluctance to fund breakthrough technology research at universities because of what are viewed as excessive IP ownership demands. This situation may at least partially explain why applied research conducted at universities grew more slowly during the period 1994 to 2004 (from $5.4 billion to $9.2 billion) than did the national total – a 71 percent increase versus 81 percent growth for all applied research.

At least prototype models of needed research portfolio management models exist. For example, the DARPA model uses the 'focus program' concept to fund new technology platforms. Collaboration is an increasingly critical mode for research that seeks to develop emerging technologies because of modern technology's complexity and hence the need for complementary research assets and subsequent tacit knowledge-based diffusion mechanisms. Such models can assume several forms, but some government funding and influence on the research portfolio is usually required.

In Europe, a number of alternative collaborative research mechanisms exist that involve universities. For example, the Interuniversity Microelectronics Centre (IMEC), based in Leuven, Belgium, consists of a number of universities that conduct generic technology research with multiple industry partners. IMEC was started by the government of Flanders to be a center of excellence in semiconductor technology and thereby drive regional economic growth. The center gets about 82 percent of its funding ($242 million) from industry participants. Eight of the world's leading semiconductor companies are participating. Intellectual property from 'pre-competitive' research programs is shared with all participants and is licensed to other firms, as is done by US universities. IMEC also engages in more applied research with individual companies. In this case, the resulting intellectual property is assigned to the participating company (Wolff, 2006).

The Bottom Line

Technology cluster models are evolving throughout the world economy to address growing technological complexity, stronger links between science and emerging technology platforms, and the need for R&D cycle efficiency. These institution-based innovation infrastructures combined with direct funding of the quasi-public elements of R&D and more general financial incentives through the tax system constitute an essential set of complementary policy responses to a complex set of underinvestment phenomena.

This complexity stands in stark contrast to a still-dominant philosophy that at best regards spillovers as the only market barrier to R&D investment and at worst regards technology as a proprietary black box that implies the only government role in support of economic growth is to fund basic science.

However, the reality of technology-based growth is becoming clearer to many national governments and, in the United States, to many state governments. This growing understanding of the appropriate policy models is evidenced by the evolving multiple government roles:

1. R&D funding programs;
2. tax expenditure programs;
3. government research at national research laboratories and institutes;
4. coordination and management of research portfolios;
5. intellectual property management;
6. technology transfer functions;
7. innovation incubators and science parks;
8. education and training programs in universities and vocational schools;
9. entrepreneurial training in university outreach programs; and
10. technical management information from government agencies (for example, the National Quality Award).

NOTES

1. The full text of the Summit's statement and its participants can be accessed at http://usinnovation.org.

2. See http://www.whitehouse.gov/news/releases/2006/01/20060131-5.html.
3. An alternative credit is available for firms with relatively modest average annual increases in R&D. $28.6 billion were claimed as qualified expenditures under this option in 2003, less than one-third the amount under the regular credit. Moreover, tax expenditures under this alternative credit amounted to only 12.6 percent of the amount of the regular credit claimed by industry.
4. The ATP was created by Congress in 1988 under the Omnibus Trade and Competitiveness Act, which formed NIST out of the almost century-old National Bureau of Standards (NBS). The laboratory research programs of the NBS (providing industry and other federal agencies with infratechnologies and standards) were combined with two new programs, the ATP and a technology transfer program, the Manufacturing Extension Partnership.
5. Due to rescissions/sequesters, the actual ATP budgets in 1995 and 2005 were $341 million and $140 million, respectively.
6. Anthony Tether, DARPA Director, quoted in Carey (2004).
7. However, over its 16-year history, only 8.9 percent of ATP single-firm awards went to large firms (greater than 500 employees), and the number of very large (Fortune 500) companies receiving such funding was only 4.3 percent of total awards. In contrast, 35.1 percent of total awards went to single small firms. Funding the last is more politically acceptable but possibly no more justified on a market-failure basis, except when creating a new industry or modifying an existing industry structure is an objective. If the lead firms in ATP-funded consortia are included, then over half (53.1 percent of awards) went to either individual small firms or research consortia led by a small firm. Another 14.2 percent went to 'medium' firms (larger than 500 employees but not in the Fortune 500) and 13.2 percent went to universities or non-profit organizations. Less than one-fifth (19.2 percent) went to either single Fortune 500 firms or consortia led by such firms.
8. Mark Kryder, Chief Technology Officer, Seagate Corp., testimony before the Congressional R&D Caucus, 2005.
9. See http://www.autm.net/surveys/dsp.Detail.cfm?pid=100.

11. To Compete or Not to Compete

It is impossible to open up new territory unless one is prepared to leave the safe anchorage of established doctrine and run the risk of a hazardous leap forward.

Werner Heisenberg

The previous 10 chapters have demonstrated the tremendous complexity of technology-based economic growth and, therefore, the equally complex policy analysis and management required to support attainment of competitive advantages for domestic industries. Industry leaders have warned repeatedly that the US position in the widening technology-based global economy is in decline. They make these warnings as American citizens, while at the same time allocating R&D and manufacturing resources globally to serve their companies' and stockholders' best interests.

Castigating these managers for globally distributing company resources is one of the ultimate examples of denial. One part of the denial is failure by society to recognize and admit to the changing reality of global competition and to respond by replacing obsolete economic assets and practices with updated investment strategies. Such behavior derives from a focus on what worked in the past, even though economic conditions were very different from current ones. Such denial is the hallmark of a leading economic power as it steadily loses its leadership position. This is the installed wisdom effect.

The other part of the denial is that, to the degree that the decline in competitiveness is recognized, refusal to act is rampant. Those with a stake in the status quo and their defenders in government argue for old models of competitive strategy and economic growth. Specifically, factions with vested interests in economic assets such as physical and intellectual capital, existing labor skills, or simply a fear of the trauma and the cost of change, resist adaptation. This is the installed-base effect and it is widespread.

In different ways and to different degrees across countries, both corporations and workers who have understood and admitted to the need for dramatic change look to government to catalyze and support adaptation. Today, adaptation means greater investment in technology and the skilled labor to productively use it. If the correct economic growth model is applied,

304   *Technology-Based Political Economy*

the ultimate measure of economic performance – the standard of living – will respond with above-average growth. While the US growth model has emphasized technology and a dynamic competitive environment, the European model for most of the post-World War II period emphasized combinations of state-owned businesses, overly protective labor laws and only modest investment in technology. The result has been a per capita income gap of about 30 percent (in purchasing power parity terms) in favor of the United States compared to the 15 original members of the European Union.

But, times are changing. The expanded and better-integrated EU is moving toward more competition-based industry structures, slowly removing restrictive labor practices, and has a goal of a 50 percent increase in its average R&D intensity. Developing economies have their own handicaps but are working desperately to copy and eventually improve upon the US growth model. Equally important, a number of emerging economies are amassing huge foreign exchange reserves that can be used to invest in technology-based assets.

Across the global economy, these strategies are centered on the development and use of technology. And, while no single economy is yet the equal of the United States in terms of absolute R&D capacity, the collective capability of an increasing number of economies with at least some technology-based sectors is steadily eroding US competitiveness in market after market and will continue to do so unless radical changes are made.

THE BOTTOM LINE

The two major trends confronting all national economic growth policies are (i) the evolution of corporate strategies from the traditional one in which most assets are located in the domestic economy to the international focus of recent decades characterized by offshoring manufacturing to the more recent truly global philosophy of distributing even R&D investment to wherever such investment can be most productive; and (ii) the globalization of financial markets whereby major amounts of capital are relocated on a regular basis to any national economy where the expected returns are greatest.

Moreover, the concept of the technology life cycle tells us that as technologies mature, decoupling and general diffusion of technical knowledge increase competition – which today is global in scope. This phenomenon improves economic efficiency for a time. However, excessive investment and shrinking profit margins eventually bring an end to the Schumpeterian cycle.

In this situation, the only viable strategy for high-income economies – at least ones that wish to remain so – is to stay ahead of the technology life cycle, which includes being first movers in succeeding life cycles. A technology-based growth strategy to accomplish this requires a broad and deep innovation infrastructure, which is composed of a set of specific infrastructures described in the preceding chapters: technical, educational, financial.

The macroeconomic trends described in Chapter 2 are a recipe for severe financial trouble for the US economy. Even more important for long-term growth are structural problems, in particular, inadequate investment in human and intellectual capital. These assets are the drivers of the high-income economy. Thus, the imperative is a dramatic shift to investment-driven growth. This investment must be technology-based.

More specifically, the following changes are mandatory:

1. *Policy Analysis Capability:* the S&T policy apparatus will require substantial upgrading and restructuring.

2. *Focus on Supply Chains:* increasingly irrelevant distinctions, such as those between manufacturing and services, must be de-emphasized with the focus shifting to developing strategies for comparative advantage in high-tech supply chains (manufacturing and derived services) and cross-linking of supply chains within broader technology sectors.

3. *Education Reform:* a massive restructuring of the education system is required, including higher pay for teachers, much greater use of technology, new curricula, lengthened school year and higher performance standards.

4. *The amount of R&D:* R&D investment must be increased; specifically, the R&D intensity of the US economy should be raised over a period of years to the 5 percent range.

5. *The composition of R&D:* the distribution of funds among types/phases of R&D must be improved through adjusted research portfolio strategies that achieve more breakthrough technologies for a wider range of industries and markets.

6. *Technical infrastructure:* effective support of technology-based growth requires expansion of investment in infratechnologies and associated standards.

7. *R&D efficiency:* R&D productivity must be increased through greater use of technology-based cluster models and other forms of research networks that emphasize GUIR collaborations; such technology clusters must proliferate and become more dispersed geographically to broadly leverage

entrepreneurial and skilled labor assets and hence the overall productivity of the innovation infrastructure.

Collectively, the implementation of these mandates will increase innovative capacity – the only strategy for maintaining a high-growth economy. The term 'innovative capacity' may have a buzz-word ring, but it is a real and complex core element of economic growth strategy. Simply put, innovative capacity is the availability of the integrated private and public economic assets needed to drive the technology life cycle and the transition between life cycles. These assets are allocated across a portfolio of technologies and, within each technology's life cycle, across the several phases of R&D, production and market development.

Morgan Stanley points out that the combined growth rate in 2005 for the two largest-population countries, India and China, was an astounding 14.5 percent, more than four times the European growth rate of 3.5 percent and 2.4 times the US growth rate of 6.1 percent. However, because of the much larger size of the US economy, every one percentage point of growth in the US economy on a dollar basis is worth seven times the increment generated by a one percentage point of nominal Chinese growth and 18 times the same growth increment generated in India. The ratios are similarly high when Europe is compared to these two countries. Nevertheless, such large output-growth differentials will disappear fairly rapidly given the current differences in growth rates. Morgan Stanley estimates that China's annual increase in GDP will exceed that of Japan's by 2015 and by 2025 exceed both Europe's and the US's output deltas.

The unprecedented number of countries acquiring technology-based innovative capacity and the lack of sufficient modification of domestic investment strategies strongly implies an increasingly rapid decline of former leadership positions for those economies that do not radically restructure themselves. As Intel's CEO, Craig Barrett, put it, 'US leadership is under assault [and] the initial step in responding to this challenge is that America must decide to compete. If the US does not compete and win, there will be very serious consequences for our standard of living and national security'.

However, the United States is increasingly not competing. Its small and geographically-concentrated high-tech sector, its under-skilled labor force relative to current and especially future requirements and its lack of a capable STID policy analysis capability are conspiring to allow global convergence to erode domestic economic growth and the potential to increase the standard of living for its citizens.

As the economies of multiple countries converge, significant value added is taken away from the established economies. Many existing companies and their consultants rationalize this evolutionary process as efficiency enhancing, realized through tactics such as 'outsourcing' and 'global partnering'. Such corporate strategies work for a while and can work indefinitely for appropriately agile and strategically focused companies. The result is, in fact, increased global economic efficiency. However, these resource reallocations coupled with indigenous investment also cause a loss of value added and hence jobs from technology-based industries in at least some established industrialized nations.

This result comes to pass because the converging economies gain equal footing in terms of global competitiveness and invest in the infrastructure to become innovation leaders in emerging technologies. The retreat to narrowly focused strategies for competing that characterizes an increasing number of American and European companies is a telling indicator of future decline. At the same time that value-added shares are being eroded, the established firms in the 'defender' industries are ignoring the emerging disruptive technologies that ultimately bring them down. The only difference today from past patterns of decline is that the new innovators are increasingly likely to emerge outside the established economies. Thus, domestic economic renewal is constrained.

A 2006 IBM survey of the CEOs of 750 leading companies across the global economy found that 76 percent ranked business partner and customer collaboration as top sources of innovative ideas. In stark contrast, only 14 percent of these same CEOs ranked internal R&D as a top source of new ideas. 'New ideas' was defined broadly to include new business models, as well as new products, processes, and services. However, the eighth place ranking for internal R&D begs the questions of what will be the sources of technological innovation in the future for these companies and how will they compete against true innovators elsewhere.

These trends are occurring in the face of the reality that technology is an increasingly pervasive force affecting all aspects of life. It now dominates the ways by which we design our work strategies, manage our society and conduct our daily lives. Every sector – industrial, economic, educational, financial, medical and political – is now driven at the core by technology. You cannot read this book without becoming impressed with the overwhelming complexity of the modern technology-based economy and hence the challenges facing nations everywhere in designing and managing flexible and adaptive economic growth policies. These complexities make change difficult, but the greatest threat to necessary adaptation is delay. The longer structural problems in the economic system go untreated, the more difficult it is to correct them.

Resistance to change is exemplified in today's global economy by a mindless adherence to the static version of the law of comparative advantage. The reality of the marketplace is its dynamic character, which increasingly includes government support for the establishment of new disruptive technologies. Failure to implement efficient combined public–private efforts to design and manage the right set of programs to achieve Schumpeter's creative destruction within the domestic economy will result in new comparative advantages being established outside this economy and thereby the loss of domestic economic growth potential.

In summary, during periods of rapid growth, the rising economic tide lifts all boats and the standard of living grows seemingly without end. But, as Warren Buffet put it, 'It's only when the tide goes out that you can see who is swimming naked'. The US economy is in the process of having its economic clothes ripped off by the rapid ebbing of its most important economic assets. Make no mistake about it, such assets, including technology and human capital, depreciate. The indicators cited throughout this book show this to be the case, but the needed policy responses have been lacking.

MANAGING LONG-TERM COMPETITIVENESS

The technology-based economy cannot be put together quickly, even under a crash program. R&D and technology acquisition capabilities take time to acquire and to integrate with manufacturing and marketing, which themselves must adapt to changing global market requirements. The infrastructures that support adaptive change take just as long to accumulate and integrate effectively with private investment. Venture capital markets only evolve in economies where sufficient technology-based investment makes such an infrastructure worthwhile. World-class research universities evolve equally slowly. Years of education and experience are required to produce enough researchers and instructors to staff these schools. Research programs in universities and government laboratories must have minimum-scale support and continuity of funding. In turn, research universities must be large enough to spin off trained scientists and engineers to staff the industrial supply chains that apply university-produced breakthrough technologies.

Expanding innovative capacity requires a policy process that defines and responds to a comprehensive set of indicators. Over the previous 10 chapters, the indicators that reflect on the condition of the technology-based economy have been identified and assessed. The scope of these indicators is broader than commonly presented in reports issuing sets of policy recommendations. The main reason is the absence in most policy exercises of an integrated analysis of technology life cycles, supporting infrastructures, other types of investment, and the ultimate economic growth objectives in both a static and a dynamic context.

America ascended to world economic leadership by (i) making mass production with interchangeable (standardized) parts the mainstream method of production, and (ii) for more than a century continuously developing new high-productivity technologies. These technologies, first textile and raw material processing in the last half of the 19th century, then machinery making and chemical and steel production before World War I, and consumer durables throughout the 20th century, produced the highest per capita incomes in the world (Harley, 2003). American technological leadership continued in the last part of the 20th century with digital electronics and most recently biotechnology. In concert with this succession of multiple technology life cycles, a number of critical infrastructures have evolved, such as electrical power, communication networks, transportation systems and information systems. Innovation infrastructures, such as intellectual property rules, government research, standardization and, more recently, regional technology development clusters have become increasingly essential.

In considering proposals to expand technology-based economic activity within the domestic economy, a critical factor is the relative mobility of various economic assets. Any investment creates value added (profits, wages and salaries), not only by virtue of its direct impact but also by indirect effects from demand for supporting services. Bill Gates points out that Microsoft conducts 85 percent of its research in the United States. When a company has made such a commitment that includes research facilities, establishment of a supplier network, integration with the supporting technical and educational infrastructures of the local and national economies, and adaptation to cultural and political environments, it has a vested interest in remaining in that economy. Co-location of these last activities contributes substantial additional value added to the domestic economy – and takes value added away from other economies that do not provide an attractive innovation infrastructure. This is the *dynamic* law of comparative advantage at work.

However, if a company can only find 50 percent of the needed skilled labor it needs domestically and it cannot import the other half, at least on a temporary basis, it has no choice but to begin to offshore R&D. Similarly, if the domestic innovation infrastructure cannot supply the research support through universities and government research institutes and if the provision of technical infrastructure (infratechnologies and standards) is poorly timed with respect to technology life cycles and if intellectual property and tax policies are too restrictive, the overall expected rate of return on domestic R&D diminishes to the point that companies become receptive to more attractive environments elsewhere. In fact, Microsoft now conducts significant portions of its breakthrough software research outside the United States.

In spite of increasing efforts by many national governments to adjust to the emerging global paradigm, corporations such as Microsoft, IBM, Intel, and others around the world have adapted to a greater degree. By participating in worldwide research networks, these companies are taking the final adaptive step in becoming truly global. As such, the challenge to domestic economic growth policies continues to rise, as private R&D resources move rapidly and willingly to more attractive locations. The complex innovation infrastructures that determine the relative competitiveness of alternative global locations for R&D and manufacturing cannot be assembled quickly or easily.

At various points in the preceding chapters, seemingly contradictory arguments have been made that on the one hand point to the shortening of technology life cycles and rapid shifting of competitive positions among nations, while on the other hand making the case that the accumulation of technology-based economic assets is a slow and complex process, which once in place are difficult to imitate. However, these two propositions are not at odds with each other if the dynamics of global competition are taken into account. Accumulation of these assets is a mandatory cost of entry into the technology-based global economy and, once achieved, provides a set of comparative advantages. Yet, the dynamics of resource allocation today mean that such advantages are constantly under attack by competing economies, so that static economic growth policies guarantee relentless, if slow, economic decline. Thus, the message for growth policy is to maintain constant adaptive strategies that both build and adjust domestic innovation infrastructures.

In the end, the competitiveness of an economy depends on four types of investment: (i) research and development; (ii) human capital; (iii) technologically advanced manufacturing plants and equipment; and (iv) technically sophisticated and easily accessible infrastructure.

These four investment categories are being pursued at a furious pace throughout the global economy. This dynamic investment-driven environment means that traditional adjustment mechanisms such as currency depreciation are less effective at redressing trade imbalances and restoring domestic growth, as the static law of comparative advantage implies. In other words, economies in decline are chasing moving targets due to dynamic comparative advantage strategies pursued by most nations. Reallocation of existing economic assets will therefore be increasingly unsatisfactory. In contrast, superior innovation infrastructures, once in place, constitute immobile assets and therefore resist global reallocation in spite of currency adjustments.

If the response is to cling to the installed base with investment dictated by the installed wisdom, adaptation will be prevented, resulting in declining returns on investment, lower real incomes, and, ultimately, a lower standard of living. Trying to legislate change out of existence only results in becoming its victim.

The policy lessons are:

1. The high-income economy must be the high-tech economy — *requires high R&D intensity.*
2. R&D funding strategies in large countries or blocks of smaller countries must diversify beyond IT and biotechnology — *requires portfolio management.*
3. Technologies evolve in cycles — *requires dynamic policy management.*
4. Technology-based competitiveness is a public–private problem — *requires cooperative public–private planning, research, infrastructure investment and market development.*
5. Technology-based growth policy must be improved — *requires resources and integration of STID with other economic policy areas.*

This book has attempted to illuminate these five lessons in a way that can lead to the creation of the needed policy models and subsequent actual policies. The potential salvation is that major portions of an economy's assets are relatively immobile. One of the two major categories of immobile technology-based assets is skilled labor. The other category consists of the institutions that produce the skilled labor and generic technology assets and also coordinate the innovation infrastructure. These largely public institutions take a long time to evolve and to become productive at a world-class level.

National policies have a lot to say about the scope and evolution of such institutions and the amount and type of the skilled labor pool. Because of the global reach of private-sector strategies and the domestic focus of government growth policies, success for any economy in the future will be determined to a greater degree by the competitive policies of that economy's government as a critical complement to the historical reliance on creative destruction through internal market dynamics. In sum, excellence in these public institutions is imperative, as the future efficiency of government will be as important as efficiency in corporate strategy. The concept of the 'public–private technology-based growth paradigm', first mentioned in the Preface and developed in the succeeding chapters, drives the general model. Successful implementation will require both adequate resources and creative and stable management.

Bibliography

Abernathy, W. and J. Utterback (1975), 'A Dynamic Model of Product and Process Innovation', *Omega: The International Journal of Management Science*, **3**: 639–56.

Acs, Z., D. Audretsch and M. Feldman (1994), 'R&D Spillovers and the Recipient Firm Size', *Review of Economics and Statistics* **76**(2): 336–40.

AeA (2005), *Losing the Competitive Advantage*, Washington, DC: American Electronics Association.

Armbrecht, F.M. Ross (2004), 'Foreign R&D Labs in China See Missions Expand, Practices Advance', *Research–Technology Management* **47** (January–February): 2–4.

Arthur, W. Brian (1988), 'Self-Reinforcing Mechanisms in Economics', in P. Anderson, K. Arrow and D. Pines (eds), *The Economy as an Evolving Complex System*, Reading, MA: Addison-Wesley, pp. 9–31.

Arthur, W. Brian (1989), 'Competing Technologies, Increasing Returns, and Lock-In by Historical Events', *Economic Journal* **99**: 116–31.

Arundel, A. and J. Hollanders (2005), *Innovation Strengths and Weaknesses*, Brussels: European Commission (December 5).

Atkeson, A. and P. Kehoe (2001), 'The Transition to a New Economy after the Second Industrial Revolution' (NBER Working Paper 8676), Cambridge, MA: National Bureau of Economic Research.

Atkinson, Robert (2005), *The Past and Future of America's Economy*, Cheltenham, UK and Northampton, MA, USA: Edward Elgar.

Atkinson, Robert (2006), 'Is the Next Economy Taking Shape?', *Issues in Science and Technology* (Winter): 62–8.

Atkinson, Robert (2007a), 'Deep Competitiveness', *Issues in Science and Technology* (Winter): 69–75.

Atkinson, Robert (2007b), 'Expanding the R&D Tax Credit to Drive Innovation, Competitiveness and Prosperity', Washington, DC: Information Technology and Innovation Foundation (April).

Audretsch, D. and M. Feldman (1996), 'R&D Spillovers and the Geography of Innovation and Production', *American Economic Review* **86** (3): 630–40.

Baily, M., D. Farrell and J. Remes (2006), *US Productivity Growth, 1995–2000*, Washington, DC: McKinsey Global Institute.

Baker, Pam (2005), 'The End of Transistors in Computers?', *NewsFactor Network* (March 2).

Basu, S., J. Fernald and M. Shapiro (2001), 'Productivity Growth in the 1990s: Technology, Utilization, or Adjustment' (NBER Working Paper 8359), Cambridge, MA: National Bureau of Economic Research.

Battelle (2006), '2006 R&D Funding Improves Amid Increasing Restraints', *R&D Magazine* (January).

Baumol, William (1967), 'Macroeconomics of Unbalanced Growth: The Anatomy of Urban Crisis', *American Economic Review* **57** (June): 418–20.

Besanko, D., D. Dranove and M. Shanely (1996), *Economics of Strategy*, New York: John Wiley.

Billings, B. Anthony (2003), 'Are US Tax Incentives for Corporate R&D Likely to Motivate American Firms to Perform Research Abroad?', *Tax Executive* (July-August): 291–315.

Bivens, Josh (2005), 'Shifting Blame for Manufacturing Job Loss: Effect of Rising Trade Deficit Shouldn't Be Ignored', Economic Policy Institute Briefing Paper, Washington, DC.

Blair, M. and T. Kochan (2000), 'Introduction' in M. Blair and T. Kochan (eds), *The New Relationship: Human Capital in the American Corporation*, Washington, DC: Brookings Institution.

Bleha, Thomas (2005), 'Down to the Wire', *Foreign Affairs* **84** (May/June).

Bloom, N., R. Griffith and J. Van Reenen (2002), 'Do R&D Tax Credits Work? Evidence from a Panel of Countries 1979–1997, *Journal of Public Economics* **85**: 1–31.

Boer, F.P. (2005), 'Valuation of Technology Using Real Options', *Research–Technology Management* **42** (July–August): 26–30.

Bonvillian, William (2006), 'Power Play', *The American Interest* **2** (November–December): 39–48.

Boskin, M. and L. Lau (2000), 'Generalized Solow-Neutral Technical Progress and Postwar Economic Growth' (NBER Working Paper W8023), Cambridge, MA: National Bureau of Economic Research.

Bowonder, B., J. Racherla, N. Mastakar and S. Krishman (2005), 'R&D Spending Patterns of Global Firms', *Research–Technology Management* **48** (September–October): 51–9.

Bozeman, B. and A. Link (1984), 'Tax Incentives for R&D: A Critical Evaluation', *Research Policy* **13**: 21–31.

Bozeman, B. and A. Link (1985), 'Public Support for Private R&D: The Case of the Research Tax Credit', *Journal of Policy Analysis and Management* **4** (Spring): 370–82.

Brady, Diane (2005), 'The Immelt Revolution', *BusinessWeek* (March 28).

Branscomb, L. and P. Auerswald (2002), *Between Invention and Innovation* (NIST GCR 02-841), Gaithersburg, MD: National Institute of Standards and Technology.

Brodd, Ralph (2005), *Factors Affecting US Production Decisions: Why Are There No Lithium-Ion Battery Manufacturers in the United States?*, Report prepared for NIST, Advanced Technology Program, Gaithersburg, MD: National Institute of Standards and Technology (June).

Brunnermeier, S. and S. Martin (1999), *Interoperability Cost Analysis of the US Automotive Supply Chain* (Planning Report 99–1), Gaithersburg, MD: National Institute of Standards and Technology (March).

Cameron, Gavin (1998), 'Innovation and Growth: A Survey of Empirical Evidence', Nuffield College, Oxford, UK.

Cameron, Gavin (1999), 'R&D and Growth at the Industry Level', Nuffield College, Oxford, UK.

Carey, John (2004), 'Can Uncle Sam's Cash Still Unlock the Future?', *BusinessWeek* (October 11).

Chandler, Alfred (1990), *Scale and Scope: The Dynamics of Industrial Capitalism*, Cambridge, MA: Harvard University Press/Belknap.

Chesbrough, Henry (2004), 'Managing Open Innovation', *Research–Technology Management* **47** (January–February): 23–6.

Christensen, Clayton (1997), *The Innovator's Dilemma*, Cambridge, MA: Harvard Business School Press.

Christensen, C., S. Anthony and E. Roth (2004a), *Seeing What's Next: Using the Theories of Innovation to Predict Industry Change*, Cambridge, MA: Harvard Business School Publishing Corp.

Christensen, C., C. Musso and S. Anthony (2004b), 'Maximizing the Returns from Research', *Research–Technology Management* **47** (July–August): 12–18.

Cohen, L. and D. Levinthal (1989), 'Innovation and Learning: The Two Faces of R&D', *Economic Journal* **99** (September): 569–96.

Comin, D. and T. Philippon (2005), 'The Rise in Firm-Level Volatility: Causes and Consequences' (NBER Working Paper W11388), Cambridge, MA: National Bureau of Economic Research (May).

Conway, Benjamin (2005), 'Biotech and Pharma in a Turbulent World', *Genetic Engineering News* **25** (September 1).

Corcoran, Elizabeth (1994), 'The Changing Role of US Corporate Research Labs', *Research–Technology Management* **37** (July–August): 14–20.

Council on Competitiveness (2004), *Innovate America*, Washington, DC.

Criscuolo, C., J. Haskel and M. Slaughter (2005), 'Global Engagement and the Innovation Activities of Firms' (NBER Working Paper 11479), Cambridge, MA: National Bureau of Economic Research (June).

CSTB (Computer Science and Telecommunications Board) (2000), *Making IT Better: Expanding Information Technology Research to Meet Society's Needs*, Washington, DC: National Academy of Sciences, National Research Council, Computer Science and Technology Board.

CSTB (Computer Science and Telecommunications Board) (2002), *Information Technology Research, Innovation and E-Government*, Washington, DC: National Academy of Sciences, National Research Council, Computer Science and Technology Board.

CSTB (Computer Science and Telecommunications Board) (2003), *Innovation in Information Technology*, Washington, DC: National Academy of Sciences, National Research Council, Computer Science and Technology Board.

Darby, M. and L. Zucker (2003), 'Grilichesian Breakthroughs: Inventions of Methods of Inventing and Firm Entry in Nanotechnology' (NBER Working Paper 9825), Cambridge, MA: National Bureau of Economic Research.

David, Paul (1990), 'The Dynamo and the Computer: An Historical Perspective on the Modern Productivity Paradox', *American Economic Review* **80** (May): 355–61.

David, P. and B. Hall (2000), 'Heart of Darkness: Modeling Public–Private Funding Interactions Inside the R&D Black Box', *Research Policy* **29**: 1165–83.

David, P., B. Hall and A. Toole (2000), 'Is Public R&D a Complement or Substitute for Private R&D? A Review of the Econometric Evidence', *Research Policy* **29** (April): 497–529.

Dean, J. and P. Tam (2005), 'The Laptop Trail', *Wall Street Journal* (June 9).

DePalma, Angelo (2005), 'Twenty-Five Years of Biotech Trends', *Genetic Engineering News* (August).

Dosi, Giovanni (1988), 'Sources, Procedures, and Microeconomic Effects of Innovation', *Journal of Economic Literature* **26**: 1120–71.

Dosi, G., P. Llerena and M. Labini (2005), 'Evaluating and Comparing the Innovation Performance of the United States and the European Union', report prepared for the *TrendChart* Policy Workshop.

Dosi, G., K. Pavitt and L. Soete (1990), *The Economics of Technical Change and International Trade*, New York: New York University Press.

Duga, Jules (1994), 'IRI Forecast Reflects Major Change in How US Industry Will Perform R&D', *Research–Technology Management* **37** (May–June): 9–11.

Dunne, Timothy (1994), 'Plant Age and Technology Use in US Manufacturing Industries', *The RAND Journal of Economics* **25** (Autumn): 488–99.

Dutton, Gail (2005), 'Navigating Stem Cell Fact and Fiction: Appraising the State of the Technology', *Genetic Engineering News* **25** (July).

Eisen, P., J. Jasinowski and R. Kleinert (2005), *2005 Skill Gaps Report: A Survey of the American Workforce*, Washington, DC: National Association of Manufacturers.

Engardio, P. and B. Einhorn (2005), 'Outsourcing Innovation', *BusinessWeek* (March 21).

Feldman, Maryann (1994), *The Geography of Innovation*, Dordrecht: Kluwer Academic Publishers.

Ferguson, Charles (2004), *The Broadband Problem: Anatomy of a Market Failure and a Policy Dilemma*, Washington, DC: Brookings Institution Press.

Finan, William (1998), *Metrology-Related Cost in the US Semiconductor Industry, 1990, 1996, and 2001* (NIST Planning Report 98-4), Gaithersburg, MD: National Institute of Standards and Technology.

Fingleton, Eamonn (1999), *In Praise of Hard Industries*, Haslett, MI: Buttonwood Press.

Flamm, Kenneth (1988), *Creating the Computer: Government, Industry, and High Technology*, Washington, DC: Brookings Institution.

Freeman, Christopher (1986), *The Economics of Industrial Innovation*, Cambridge, MA: MIT Press.

Freeman, Richard (2005), 'Does Globalization of the Scientific/Engineering Workforce Threaten US Economic Leadership?' NBER Working Paper 11457), Cambridge, MA: National Bureau of Economic Research.

Friedman, Thomas (2005), *The World is Flat: A Brief History of the Twenty-First Century,* New York: Farrar, Straus and Giroux.

Gallaher, M., A. Link and J. Petrusa (2006), *Innovation in the US Service Sector,* New York: Routledge.

Gallaher, M., L. R. Mobley, G. Klee and P. Schryver (2004a), *The Impact of Calibration Error in Medical Decision Making* (NIST Planning Report 04-1), Gaithersburg, MD: National Institute of Standards and Technology.

Gallaher, M., A. O'Conner, J. Dettbarn and L. Gilday (2004b), *Costs of Inadequate Interoperability in the US Capital Facilities Industry* (NIST GCR-867), Gaithersburg, MD: National Institute of Standards and Technology.

Gallaher, M., J. Petrusa, A. O'Conner and S. Houghton (2007), *Economic Analysis of the Technology Infrastructure Needs of the US Biopharmaceutical Industry* (NIST Planning Report 07-1), Gaithersburg, MD: National Institute of Standards and Technology.

Garrett, David (2006), 'Samsung Develops Marathon Fuel Cell', *NewsFactor Network* (December 28).

Garten, Jeffrey (2005), 'The High-Tech Threat from China', *BusinessWeek* (January 31).

General Accounting Office (1996), *Tax Policy and Administration* (GAO/GGD-96-43), Washington, DC.

Geppert, Linda (1994), 'Industrial R&D: The New Priorities', *IEEE Spectrum* (September): 30–41.

Gomory, R. and W. Baumol (2000), *Global Trade and Conflicting National Interests*, Cambridge, MA: MIT Press.

Griffith, Rachel (2002), 'How Important is Business R&D for Economic Growth and Should the Government Subsidize It?', Institute for Fiscal Studies (IFS Briefing Note BN12), London.

Griffith, R., S. Redding and J. Van Reenen (1998), 'Productivity Growth in OECD Industries: Identifying the Role of R&D, Skills, and Trade', Institute for Fiscal Studies, London.

Griliches, Zvi (1988), 'Productivity Puzzles and R&D: Another Non-explanation', *Journal of Economic Perspectives* **2**: 9–21.

Griliches, Zvi (1992), 'The Search for R&D Spillovers', *Scandinavian Journal of Economics* **94** (Supplement): 29–47.

Griliches, Zvi (1995), 'R&D and Productivity: Econometric Results and Measurement Issues', in Paul Stoneman (ed.), *Handbook of the Economics of Innovation and Technological Change*, Cambridge, MA: Blackwell, pp. 52–89.

Guerrera, F. and R. Waters (2006), 'IBM Calls for End to Colonial Companies', *Financial Times*, June 11.

Gunz, S., A. Macnaughton and K. Wensley (1995), 'Measuring the Compliance Cost of Tax Expenditures: The Case of Research and Development Incentives', *Canadian Tax Journal* **43** (working paper is available at: http://strategis.ic.gc.ca/pics/ra/wp6e.pdf).

Hagedoorn, J. and N. Roijakkers (2006), 'Inter-Firm R&D Partnering in Pharmaceutical Biotechnology Since 1975: Trends, Patterns, and Networks', *Research Policy* **35**: 431–46.

Hall, Bronwyn (1996), 'The Private and Social Returns to Research and Development', in B. Smith and C. Barfield (eds), *Technology, R&D, and the Economy*, Washington, DC: Brookings Institution and American Enterprise Institute, pp. 140–83.

Hall, B. and J. Van Reenen (2000), 'How Effective are Fiscal Incentives for R&D? A Review of the Evidence', *Research Policy* **29**: 449–69.

Hamm, Steve (2005), 'Linux, Inc.', *BusinessWeek* January 31, 60–68.

Harley, Knick (2003), 'Growth Theory and Industrial Revolutions in Britain and America', *Canadian Journal of Economics* **36** (4): 809–31.

Health Grades, Inc. (2004), *Patient Safety in American Hospitals* (July).

Hecker, D. (1999), 'High-Technology Employment: A Broader View', *Monthly Labor Review* (June).

Hecker, Daniel (2005), 'High-Technology Employment: A NAICS-based Update', *Monthly Labor Review* (July): 57–72.

Heim, Kristi (2004), 'US Chip Makers Face Risks in Boosting Manufacturing in China', *Seattle Times* (April 5).

Henderson, R., L. Orsenigo and G. Psiano (1999), 'The Pharmaceutical Industry and the Revolution in Molecular Biology: Interactions among Scientific, Institutional, and Organizational Change', in D. Mowery and R. Nelson (eds), *Sources of Industrial Leadership,* Cambridge, MA: Cambridge University Press.

Herman, Tom (2001), 'Treasury to Reverse Clinton-Era Rules on Research Credits', *Wall Street Journal* (December 2): A2.

Hicks, D., A. Breitzman, Sr, K. Hamilton and F. Narin (2000), 'Research Excellence and Patented Innovation', *Science and Public Policy* **27** (5): 310–20.

Hill, Susan (2006), 'S&E Doctorates Hit All-Time High in 2005', *InfoBrief* (NSF 07-301), Washington, DC: National Science Foundation, Division of Science Resources Statistics.

Jacobson, Ken (2005), 'White House to Create Metrics to Prioritize Federal R&D Spending', *Manufacturing and Technology News* **12** (September 20).

Jaffe, Adam (1998), 'The Importance of "Spillovers" in the Policy Mission of the Advanced Technology Program', *Journal of Technology Transfer* **23**, 11–19.

Jaffe, A., M. Trajtenberg and R. Henderson (1993), 'Geographic Localization of Knowledge Spillovers as Evidenced by Patent Citations', *Quarterly Journal of Economics* **108** (3): 577–98.

Jankowski, John (2005), 'Academic R&D Doubled During Past Decade, Reaching $40 Billion in FY 2003', *InfoBrief* (NSF 05-315), National Science Foundation, Division of Science Resources Statistics.

Jones, C. and J. Williams (1998), 'Measuring the Social Rate of Return to R&D', *Quarterly Journal of Economics* **112** (November): 119–35.

Jones, C. and J. Williams (2000), 'Too Much of a Good Thing?: The Economics of Investment in R&D', *Journal of Economic Growth* **5** (March): 65–85.

Johnson, Peter (2005), 'RTD, Innovation and Growth: Evaluation Requirements and Challenges in Europe', European Commission, Brussels (May).

Jorgenson, Dale (2001), 'US Economic Growth In the Information Age', *Issues in Science and Technology* (Fall): 42–50.

Jorgenson, Dale (2005), 'Moore's Law and the Emergence of the New Economy', *Semiconductor Industry Association 2005 Annual Report.*

Kash, D. and R. Rycroft (1998), 'Technology Policy in the 21th Century: How Will We Adapt to Complexity?', *Science and Public Policy* **25** (April).

Keller, Wolfgang (2000), *Geographic Localization of International Technology Diffusion* (NBER Working Paper 7509), Cambridge, MA: National Bureau of Economic Research.

Kim, W. Chan and Renée Mauborgne (1997), 'Value Innovation: The Strategic Logic of High Growth', *Harvard Business Review* **75** (1) (January–February): 102–12.

Kingscott, Kathleen (2001), 'Lowering Hurdle Rates for New Technologies', in Charles Wessner (ed.), *The Advanced Technology Program: Assessing Outcomes,* Washington, DC: National Academy Press, pp. 112–16.

Klevorick, A., R. Nelson and S. Winter (1995), 'On the Sources and Significance of Inter-Industry Differences in Technological Opportunities', *Research Policy* **24** (March): 185–205.

Kline, S. and N. Rosenberg (1986), 'An Overview of Innovation', in R. Landau and N. Rosenberg (eds), *The Positive Sum Strategy: Harnessing Technology for Economic Growth,* Washington, DC: National Academy Press, pp. 275–305.

Kodama, Fumio (1991), *Analyzing Japanese High Technologies: The Techno-Paradigm Shift*, London: Printer Press.

Kostov, R., J. Stump, D. Johnson, J. Murday, C. Lau and W. Tolles (2005), 'The Structure and Infrastructure of the Global Nanotechnology Literature', Arlington, VA: Defense Technical Information Center (DTIC Technical Report ADA435984).

Landes, David (1969), *The Unbound Prometheus: Technological Change and Industrial Development in Western Europe from 1750 to Present,* Cambridge: Cambridge University Press.

Lee, Hau (2004), 'The Triple-A Supply Chain', *Harvard Business Review* **82** (October): 102–12.

Lee, Sheena (2006), 'Innovation, Design Freshen "Made in Taiwan" Tech Label', Reuters, December 28.

Leech, D., A. Link, J. Scott and L. Reed (1998), *The Economics of a Technology-Based Service Sector* (NIST Planning Report 98-2), Gaithersburg, MD: National Institute of Standards and Technology.

Lerner, Josh (1996), 'The Government as Venture Capitalist: The Long-Run Impact of the SBIR Program' (NBER Working Paper 5753), Cambridge, MA: National Bureau of Economic Research.

Lerner, Josh (2005), 'The University and the Start-Up: Lessons from the Past Two Decades', *Journal of Technology Transfer* **30** (January, special issue in honor of Edwin Mansfield): 49–56.

Levy, F. and R. Murnane (2004), *The New Division of Labor: How Computers are Creating the Next Job Market*, Princeton, NJ: Princeton University Press and the Russell Sage Foundation.

Link, Albert (1999), 'Public/Private Partnerships in the United States', *Industry and Innovation* **6**: 191–217.

Link, Albert (2001), 'Enhanced R&D Efficiency in an ATP-Funded Joint Venture', in Charles Wessner (ed.), *The Advanced Technology Program: Assessing Outcomes*, Washington, DC: National Academy Press.

Link, Albert (2005), *Economic Factors Related to the Development and Commercialization of Biotechnologies,* report prepared for the Center for Applied Economics, University of Kansas.

Link, A.N. and J.T. Scott (1998), *Public Accountability: Evaluating Technology-Based Institutions*, Norwell, MA: Kluwer.

Lum, T. and D. Nanto (2006), *China's Trade with the United States and the Rest of the World*, Congressional Research Service Report to Congress, Washington, DC (January 23).

Mairesse, J. and P. Mohnen (2004), 'The Importance of R&D for Innovation: A Reassessment using French Survey Data' (NBER Working Paper 10897), Cambridge, MA: National Bureau of Economic Research.

Mansfield, Edwin (1985), 'How Rapidly Does Industrial Technology Leak Out?', *Journal of Industrial Economics* **34** (December): 217–23.

Mansfield, Edwin (1986), 'The R&D Tax Credit and Other Technology Policy Issues', *American Economic Review* **76**: 190–94.

Mansfield, Edwin (1990), 'Academic Research and Industrial Innovation', *Research Policy* **20**: 1–12.

Mansfield, E., J. Rapoport, J. Schnee, S. Wagner and M. Hamburger (1971), *Research and Development in the Modern Corporation*. New York: W. W. Norton.

Mansfield, E., J. Rapoport, A. Romeo, S. Wagner and G. Beardsley (1977), 'Social and Private Rates of Return from Industrial Innovations', *Quarterly Journal of Economics* **91** (May): 221–40.

McAfee, Andrew (2000), 'Economic Impacts of the Internet Revolution: Manufacturing', paper presented at the Brookings Institution/Department of Commerce conference on 'The E-Business Transformation: Sector Developments and Policy Implications' (September 26).

McChesney, R. and J. Podesta (2006), 'Let There Be Wi-Fi', *Washington Monthly* (January/February).

McCormack, Richard (2005a), 'Defense Analyst Says US Has No Ability to Assess China's Breakthroughs in Science and Tech', *Manufacturing & Technology News* **12** (June 1).

McCormack, Richard (2005b), 'A Relatively Small Investment by Government Generates Billions of Dollars in Return', *Manufacturing & Technology News* **12** (June 1).

McCormack, Richard (2007), 'China Creates a Massive Foreign Investment Fund', *Manufacturing & Technology News* **14** (June 29).

McGuckin, R. and B. van Ark (2002), *Productivity, Employment, and Income in the World's Economies*, New York: The Conference Board.

McMillan, G., F. Narin and D.L. Deeds (2000), 'An Analysis of the Critical Role of Public Science in Innovation: The Case of Biotechnology', *Research Policy* **29** (January): 1–8.

Messler, Jr, Robert (2004), 'Growth of a New Discipline', *Materials Today* (March): 44–7.

Mishel, L. and J. Bernstein (2006), 'Earnings Premium for Skilled Workers Down Sharply in Recent Years', Washington, DC: Economic Policy Institute (February 22).

Mishell, L., J. Bernstein and S. Allegretto (2005), *The State of Working America 2004/2005*, Ithaca, NY: Cornell University Press.

Morell, J.A. and T.A. Phelps (2001), 'A Review of Interoperability Issues in the Automotive Industry', paper prepared for the National Coalition of Advanced Manufacturing (NACFAM) (http://www.erim.org/whatsnew.html).

Moris, Franciso (2004), 'Industrial R&D Employment in the United States and in US Multinational Corporations', *InfoBrief* (NSF 05-302), Washington, DC: National Science Foundation, Division of Science Resources Statistics.

Moris, Francisco (2005), 'The Research and Experimentation Tax Credit in the 1990s', *InfoBrief* (NSF 05-316), Washington, DC: National Science Foundation, Division of Science Resources Statistics.

Morrow, Jr, K. John (2005), 'Antibody Therapeutics Dominate Meeting', *Genetic Engineering News* (February 1).

Narin, F., K. Hamilton and D. Olivastro (1997), 'The Increasing Linkage Between US Technology and Public Science', *Research Policy* **26** (December): 317–30.

National Academies of Science (2005), *Rising Above the Gathering Storm: Energizing and Employing America for a Brighter Economic Future*, Washington, DC: National Academy Press.

National Research Council (1999), *Funding a Revolution: Government Support for Computing Research*, Washington, DC: National Academy Press.

National Research Council (2005a), *Measuring Research and Development Expenditures in the US Economy*, Washington, DC: National Academy Press.

National Research Council (2005b), *Manufacturing Trends in Electronics Interconnection Technology*, Washington, DC: National Academy Press.

National Science Board (2000), *Science and Engineering Indicators 2000* (NSB 00–1), Washington, DC: National Science Foundation.

National Science Board (2004), *Science and Engineering Indicators 2004* (NSB 04–1), Washington, DC: National Science Foundation.

National Science Board (2006a), *Science and Engineering Indicators 2004* (NSB 06–1), Washington, DC: National Science Foundation.

National Science Board (2006b), *America's Pressing Challenge – Building a Stronger Foundation*, Washington, DC: National Science Foundation.

National Science Foundation (2003), *National Patterns of Research and Development Resources: 2003*, Washington, DC: National Science Foundation.

Nelson, R. and S. Winter (1977), 'In Search of a Useful Theory of Innovation', *Research Policy* 6: 36–76.

Nelson, R. and S. Winter (1982), *An Evolutionary Theory of Economic Change*, Cambridge, MA: Harvard University Press.

Nelson, R. and G. Wright (1992), 'The Rise and Fall of American Technological Leadership: The Postwar Era in Historical Perspective', *Journal of Economic Literature* 30 (December), 1931-64.

Nevins, A. and F. Hill (1957), *Ford: Expansion and Challenge, 1915–1933*, New York: Charles Scribner's Sons.

Nordhaus, William (2006), 'Baumol's Disease: A Macroeconomic Perspective' (NBER Working Paper 12218), Cambridge, MA: National Bureau of Economic Research.

OECD (2000), *A New Economy? The Changing Role of Innovation and Information Technology in Growth*, Paris: OECD, Directorate for Science, Technology and Innovation.

OECD (2004), *Science, Technology and Industry Outlook*, Paris: OECD, Directorate for Science, Technology and Innovation.

OECD (2005), *Science, Technology, and Industry Scoreboard 2005*, Paris: OECD, Directorate for Science, Technology and Innovation.

Office of Technology Assessment (1995), *Innovation and Commercialization of Emerging Technology*, Washington, DC: US Government Printing Office (September).

Oliner, S. and D. Sichel (2000), *The Resurgence of Growth in the Late 1990s: Is Information Technology the Story?*, Washington, DC: Federal Reserve Board.

Palley, Thomas (2006a), 'The Economics of Outsourcing: How Should Policy Respond?', report by Foreign Policy in Focus, Washington, DC (March 2).

Palley, Thomas (2006b), 'Rethinking Trade and Trade Policy: Gomory, Baumol, and Samuelson on Comparative Advantage', paper presented at the Woodrow Wilson Policy Center forum on Global Competition and Comparative Advantage, New Thinking in International Trade, Washington, DC (June 13).

Pillsbury, Michael (2005), *China's Progress in Technology Competitiveness: The Need for a New Assessment*, report for the US–China Economic and Security Review Commission, Washington, DC.

Pollard, Sydney (1981), *Peaceful Conquest: The Industrialization of Europe, 1760–1870*, Oxford: Oxford University Press.

Popper, S., V. Greenfield, K. Crane and R. Malik (2004), *Measuring Economic Effects of Technical Barriers to Trade on US Exporters* (NIST Planning Report 04-3). Gaithersburg, MD: National Institute of Standards and Technology.

Porter, Michael (2000), 'Location, Competition, and Economic Development: Local Clusters in a Global Economy', *Economic Development Journal* 14: 15–34.

Porter, M. and S. Stern (2005), 'Ranking National Innovative Capacity: Findings from the National Innovative Capacity Index', in *The Global Competitiveness Report*, 2005–2006, Geneva: World Economic Forum.

Porter, M. and D. van Opstal (2001), *US Competitiveness 2001: Strengths, Vulnerabilities and Innovation Priorities*, Washington, DC: Council on Competitiveness.

Ralston, William (2005), 'Services Innovation: Challenge for Manufacturers', *SCAN* (D05-2500), Menlo Park, CA: SRI Business Intelligence.

Rajagopalan, R., M. Francis and W. Suárez (2004), 'Developing Novel Catalysts with Six Sigma', *Research–Technology Management* 47 (January–February): 13–16.

Rapport, Alan (2006), 'Where has the Money Gone? Declining Industrial Support of Academic R&D', *InfoBrief* (NSF 06-328), Washington, DC: National Science Foundation, Division of Science Resources Statistics.

Regalado, A. and D. Hamilton (2006), 'How a University's Patents May Limit Stem-Cell Research', *Wall Street Journal* (July 18).

Rhoads, Christopher (2005), 'AT&T Inventions Fueled Tech Boom, and Its Own Fall', *Wall Street Journal* (February 2).

Rice, M., G. O'Conner, L. Peters and J. Morone (1998), 'Managing Discontinuous Innovation', *Research–Technology Management* 41 (May–June): 52–8.

Roach, Stephen (2005), 'The Big Squeeze', *Global: Economic Comment*, Morgan Stanley Research (April 4).

Roach, Stephen (2006a), 'The Global Delta', *Global: Economic Comment*, Morgan Stanley Research (January 13 & 17).

Roach, Stephen (2006b), 'China's Rebalancing Challenge', *Global: Economic Comment*, Morgan Stanley Research (April 24).

Roach, Stephen (2007), 'India on the Move', *Global: Economic Comment*, Morgan Stanley Research (February 7).

Romer, Paul (1990), 'Endogenous Models of Technological Change', *Journal of Political Economy* 98: S71–S102.

Rosenberg, Nathan (1976), 'On Technological Expectations', *Economic Journal* 86 (September): 523–35.

Rosenberg, Nathan (1982), *Inside the Black Box: Technology and Economics*, Cambridge and New York: Cambridge University Press.

RTI International (2002), *The Economic Impacts of Inadequate Infrastructure for Software Testing* (NIST Planning Report 02-3), Gaithersburg, MD: National Institute of Standards and Technology.

RTI International (2005), *IPv6 Economic Impact Assessment* (NIST Planning Report 05-2), Gaithersburg, MD: National Institute of Standards and Technology.

Salter, A. and B. Martin (2001), 'The Economic Benefits of Publicly Funded Basic Research: A Critical Review', *Research Policy* 30: 509–32.

Saminather, Nichola (2006), 'Biotech's Beef', *BusinessWeek* (November 6).

Samuelson, Paul (2004), 'Where Ricardo and Mill Rebut and Confirm Arguments of Mainstream Economists Concerning Globalization', *Journal of Economic Perspectives* **18** (Summer): 135–46.

Sawyer, Adrian (2004), 'Potential Implications of Providing Tax Incentives for Research and Development in NZ', report for the Royal Society of New Zealand, Canterbury, New Zealand (February).

Scalise, George (2005a), Testimony before the US China Economic and Security Review Commission, Washington, DC (April 21).

Scalise, George (2005b), 'Choosing to Compete: If Manufacturing Goes, What Happens to the Ecosystem?', *SIA Summer Newsletter*: 6–7.

Schumpeter, Joseph (1950), *Capitalism, Socialism, and Democracy* (3rd edition), New York: Harper & Row.

Scott, Robert (2006), 'Trade Picture', Economic Policy Institute, Washington, DC (February 10).

Service, Robert (2005), 'Intel's Breakthrough', *Technology Review* (July): 62–5.

Shackelford, Brandon (2006), 'US R&D Continues to Rebound in 2004', *InfoBrief* (NSF 06-306), Washington, DC, National Science Foundation, Science Resource Statistics.

Silverthorne, Sean (2005), 'The Rise of Innovation in Asia', *Working Knowledge*, Harvard Business School (March).

Stern, S., M. Porter and J. Furman (2000), 'The Determinants of National Innovative Capacity' (NBER Working Paper 7876), Cambridge, MA: National Bureau of Economic Research (September).

Stigler, Joseph (1957), 'Perfect Competition, Historically Contemplated', *Journal of Political Economy* **65**: 1–16.

Stokes, Donald (1997), *Pasteur's Quadrant: Basic Science and Technological Innovation*, Washington, DC: Brookings Institution.

Stolper, W. and P. Samuelson (1941), 'Protection and Real Wages', *Review of Economic Studies* **9** (November): 58–73.

Studt, T. and J. Duga (2000), 'Industry Spends Big on Development while Feds Focus on Research', *R&D Magazine Online*.

Svensson, Peter (2007), 'IBM's Chip Techniques a "Tremendous Breakthrough"', *NewsFactor Network* (May).

Tan, P., T. Downey, E. Spitznagel, Jr, P. Xu, D. Fu, D. Dimitrov, R. Lempicki, B. Raaka and M. Cam (2003), 'Evaluation of Gene Expression Measurements from Commercial Microarray Platforms', *Nucleic Acids Research* **31**, 5676–84.

Task Force on the Future of American Innovation (2005), 'The Knowledge Economy: Is the United States Losing Its Competitive Edge?' (http://www.futureofinnovation.org).

Tassey, Gregory (1992), *Technology Infrastructure and Competitive Position*, Norwell, MA: Kluwer.

Tassey, Gregory (1996), 'Choosing Government R&D Policies: Tax Incentives vs. Direct Funding', *Review of Industrial Organization* **11**: 579–600.

Tassey, Gregory (1997), *The Economics of R&D Policy*, Westport, CT: Quorum Books (Greenwood Publishing Group).

Tassey, Gregory (2000), 'Standardization in Technology-Based Markets', in A. Link and D. Roessner (eds), *The Economics of Technology Policy*, special issue of *Research Policy* **20**: 587–602.

Tassey, Gregory (2003), *Methods for Assessing the Economic Impacts of Government R&D* (NIST Planning Report 03-1), Gaithersburg, MD, National Institute of Standards and Technology (September).

Tassey, Gregory (2004), 'Policy Issues for R&D Investment in a Knowledge-Based Economy', *Journal of Technology Transfer* **29**: 153–85.

Tassey, Gregory (2005a), 'Underinvestment in Public Good Technologies' in F.M. Scherer and A.N. Link (eds), *Essays in Honor of Edwin Mansfield*, special issue of *Journal of Technology Transfer* **30**: 89–113.

Tassey, Gregory (2005b), 'The Disaggregated Technology Production Function: A New Model of University and Corporate Research', in A. Link and D. Siegel (eds), *University-Based Technology Initiatives*, special issue of *Research Policy* **34**: 287–303.

Tennenhouse, David (2004), 'Intel's Open Collaborative Model of Industry–University Research', *Research–Technology Management* **47** (July–August): 19–26.

Tewksbury, J., M. Crandall and W. Crane (1980), 'Measuring the Societal Benefits of Innovation', *Science* **209** (August): 658–62.

Thursby, M. and J. Thursby (2006), *Here or There? A Survey on the Factors in Multinational R&D Location and IP Protection*, Kansas City: Kauffman Foundation.

Triplett, J. and B. Bosworth (2003), '"Baumol's Disease" Has Been Cured', *Federal Reserve Bank of New York Economic Policy Review* (September): 23–33.

van Ark, B., C. Guillemineau and R. McGuckin (2006), *As US Productivity Slows, Emerging Economies Grow Rapidly, but Europe Falls Further Behind*, New York: Conference Board.

van Grinsven, Lucas (2005), 'TV Tube Makers Fight LCDs with Thinner Tubes', *Reuters* (February).

Veverka, Mark (2005), 'Razor's Edge', *Barron's* (July 25).

VLSI Research Inc. (2005), 'Chip Making Markets' (Company report, October 10).

von Hippel, Eric (1990), 'The Impact of "Sticky Data" on Innovation and Problem-Solving', Working Paper 3147-90-BPS, MIT Sloan School of Management.

Warda, Jacek (2006), 'Tax Treatment of Business Investments in Intellectual Assets: An International Comparison', OECD Science, Technology and Industry Working Papers, Paris: OECD.

White, W., A. O'Connor and B. Rowe (2004), *Economic Impact of Inadequate Infrastructure for Supply Chain Integration* (NIST Planning Report 04-1), Gaithersburg, MD: National Institute of Standards and Technology.

Williams, Brendan (2005), 'Reducing Risk with "No Research, Development Only" Approach', *Genetic Engineering News* (April 1).

Wolff, Michael (2006), 'Netherlands "Technopole" Takes Open Innovation to Next Stage', *Research–Technology Management* **49** (March–April): 2.

Yoshida, Phyllis Genther (2004), 'Japan's "New" Industrial Policy Revives Old Successful Ways', *Research–Technology Management* **47** (November–December): 2–4.

Index